THE CLASSICS
OF **WESTERN**
SPIRITUALITY

THE CLASSICS OF WESTERN SPIRITUALITY
A Library of the Great Spiritual Masters

President and Publisher
Lawrence Boadt, C.S.P.

EDITORIAL BOARD

ANGELIC SPIRITUALITY

MEDIEVAL PERSPECTIVES ON THE WAYS OF ANGELS

TRANSLATED AND INTRODUCED BY
STEVEN CHASE

PREFACE BY
EWERT H. COUSINS

PAULIST PRESS
NEW YORK • MAHWAH, N.J.

Unless otherwise noted, all scripture quotations are translated from *Biblia Sacra Vulgata* (Latin Vulgate) or from Latin references embedded in texts.

Book design by Theresa M. Sparacio

Cover and caseside design by A. Michael Velthaus

Library of Congress Cataloging-in-Publication Data

    Angelic spirituality : medieval perspectives on the ways of angels / translated and introduced by Steven Chase.
       p. cm.—(The Classics of Western spirituality)
    Includes bibliographical references and index.
    ISBN 0-8091-3948-0 (paper); ISBN 0-8091-0513-6 (cloth)
    1. Angels. 2. Spirituality—Catholic Church. 3. Catholic Church—Doctrines. 4. Angels—History of doctrines—Middle Ages, 600–1500. 5. Spirituality—Catholic Church—History of doctrines—Middle Ages, 600–1500. 6. Catholic Church—Doctrines—History— To 1500. I. Chase, Steven. II. Series.
BT966.3 .A54 2002
235′.3—dc21

                                 2002006340

Published by Paulist Press
997 Macarthur Boulevard
Mahwah, New Jersey 07430

www.paulistpress.com

Printed and bound in the
United States of America

Contents

CONTENTS

Translator of This Volume

STEVEN CHASE is resident associate professor of spirituality at Western Theological Seminary in Holland, Michigan. He holds a Ph.D. degree in historical theology from Fordham University and a M.Div. from Princeton Theological Seminary. He served as assistant professor of historical theology and Christian spirituality at the Graduate Theological Union in Berkeley California, 1994–1998. He has also taught at numerous Roman Catholic and Protestant seminaries in the United States, Canada, and Korea. He is the author of *Angelic Wisdom: The Cherubim and the Grace of Contemplation in Richard of St. Victor* (University of Notre Dame Press, 1995) and the editor of *Doors of Understanding: Conversations in Global Spirituality in Honor of Ewert Cousins* (Franciscan Press, 1997). He is founder and current cochair of the Christian Spirituality Group of the American Academy of Religion and is currently working on a book on models of prayer in Christian faith and practice. Research and translation for this book was done partially during resident sabbaticals at the Center for Theological Inquiry in Princeton, New Jersey (1996, 1998).

Author of the Preface

EWERT COUSINS is professor emeritus of theology at Fordham University, editorial consultant for the Paulist Press series the Classics of Western Spirituality, and the editor and translator of its Bonaventure volume. He is also general editor of the twenty-five-volume *World Spirituality: An Encyclopedic History of the Religious Quest*, author of *Bonaventure and the Coincidence of Opposites* and *Christ of the 21st Century*, and director of both the spirituality program at Fordham University (1975–80) and the Center for Contemporary Spirituality (1981–2000). In addition, Dr. Cousins has been a consultant to the Vatican Council for Interreligious Dialogue (1974–85) and a member of the advisory board of the Monastic Interreligious Dialogue, Christian and Buddhist. He has served as a visiting professor at Columbia University, New York University, and Hebrew University in Jerusalem and held the Paluch Chair of Theology at Mundelein Seminary in Chicago (1996–97, 1999–2000).

For Rachel

Every good and perfect gift
is from above
coming down
from the Father of Lights.
—James 1:17

Acknowledgments

It is an honor to have Dr. Ewert Cousins write the preface to this book, the genesis of which has its roots in his wisdom, guidance, and friendship. I am deeply grateful to Dr. Bernard McGinn who, as editor-in-chief, was willing to take on this "thematic" volume for the Classics series and who never wavered in support, encouragement, or in providing valuable counsel. I would like to thank Dr. Richard Wevers for reading and commenting on portions of the manuscript. I would also like to acknowledge the work and friendship of Dr. Grover Zinn, whose writings on medieval spirituality have always inspired me. Dr. Paul Rorem's masterful work on Pseudo-Dionysius has been of immense aid. Dr. Mary A. Suydam, through her papers and through subsequent conversations, has added substantially to my understanding of medieval angelic devotion.

I was fortunate, during residences in 1996 and 1998 at the Center of Theological Inquiry in Princeton, New Jersey, to find needed quiet as well as collegial conversation, both of which motivated me to complete substantial portions of the book.

I have had the pleasure of working with a number of editors at Paulist Press, but would like to thank especially Dr. Christopher Bellitto, whose guidance played an essential part in giving birth to this book.

Penultimate recognition must go to Richard of St. Victor, who, as a fellow watcher of birds, lured me into an interest in angels. Richard begins his greatest work on contemplation by comparing patterns of birds in flight to various ways of thinking, meditating, and contemplating. From there, he deftly moves to angelic flight and angelic contemplation. But by then, of course, I was hooked.

Finally, and as always, I offer my deepest appreciation and affection to my wife, Dr. Leanne Van Dyk. Without her constant encouragement and love this book would never have been completed. The book is dedicated to our daughter Rachel, who truly is a gift of light.

Abbreviations

Alan, *Hier. Alani*	Alan of Lille. *Hierarchia Alani*, ed. Marie Thérèse d'Alverny (Paris, 1965).
Augustine, Migne, ed., *De civ. Dei*	J. P. Migne, ed. *Patrologia cursus completus.* Series Latina. Vol. 41 (Paris, 1841).
Augustine, *De civ. Dei*	Augustine, St., Bishop of Hippo. *De civitate Dei: Corpus Christianorum.* Series Latina. Vols. 47–48 (Turnolt, 1955).
Bernard, *In Psalmum*	Bernard of Clairvaux. *S. Bernardi Opera, Vol. IV, Sermones.* In *Psalmum "Qui habitat,"* ed. Jean Leclercq and Henri-Marie Rochais (Rome, 1966).
Chase, *Angelic Wisdom*	Steven Chase. *Angelic Wisdom: The Cherubim and the Grace of Contemplation in Richard of St. Victor* (Notre Dame, Ind. and London, 1995).
DS	*Dictionnaire de spiritualité: ascétique et mystique, doctrine et histoire*, ed. M. Viller and C. Baumgartner (Paris, 1932–95).

Dionysius, *CH*

Dionysius the Areopagite. *On the Celestial Hierarchy*. In *Pseudo-Dionysius: The Complete Works*, trans. Colm Luibheid (New York, 1987).

Dionysius, *Hiér. cél.*

Denys the Areopagite. *La hiérarchie céleste*, ed. Gunter Heil, trans. Maurice de Gandillac (Paris, 1958).

De sex alis cherub.

[Anonymous]. *De sex alis cherubim*. In *PL* 210:269–80.

Dionysiaca

Philippe Chevalier. *Dionysiaca: Recueil donnant l'ensemble des traditions latines des ouvrages attribué au Denys de l'Aréopage*. 2 vols. (Paris, 1937–50).

Eriugena, *Exp. coel.*

Johannes Scotus Eriugena. *Expositiones in ierarchiam coelestem S. Dionysii* (Turnholt, 1975).

Gallus, *Com. Cant.*

Thomas Gallus. *Commentaires du Cantiques des Cantiques*, ed. by Jeanne Barbet (Paris, 1967).

Gallus, *Extractio*

Thomas Gallus. *Paraphrase de l'abbé de Verceil Thomas Gallus sur la Hiérarchie dans cieux*. In *Dionysiaca* 2:1041–66.

Gregory, *Hom. XXXIV*

Gregory the Great. *XL homiliarum in Evangelia*. In *PL* 76:1188–96.

Hugh, *Com. hier. coel.*

Hugh of St. Victor. *Commentariorum hierarchiam coelestem S. Dionysii Areopagite*. In *PL* 175:923–1154.

PL

J. P. Migne, ed. *Patrologia cursus completus*. Series Latina. 221 vols. (Paris, 1844–1904).

ABBREVIATIONS

Rorem, *P-D*

Paul Rorem, *Pseudo-Dionysius: A Commentary on the Texts and an Introduction to Their Influence* (New York, 1993).

Umiltà, *Sermoni*

Umiltà of Faenza. *I sermoni di Umiltà da Faenza*, ed. Adele Simonetti (Spoleto, 1995).

Preface

Throughout the history of Christianity, angels have played a major role. The roots of this tradition go back to early Judaism, where angels performed a variety of functions, as is clear from the following texts from scripture. After Adam and Eve were banished from paradise, "at the east of the garden of Eden he placed the cherubim, and a sword flaming and turning to guard the way to the tree of life" (Gen 3:24).

In the time of the patriarchs, when God directed Abraham to sacrifice his son:

> Abraham built an altar there and laid the wood in order. He bound his son Isaac, and laid him on the altar, on top of the wood. Then Abraham reached out his hand and took the knife to kill his son. But the angel of the Lord called to him from heaven and said, "Abraham, Abraham!" And he said, "Here I am." He said, "Do not lay your hand on the boy or do anything to him; for now I know that you fear God." (Gen 22:9–12)

As is told in a later account, when Jacob set out for Haram, he lay down with a stone as a pillow and had a dream that there was "a ladder set up on the earth, the top of it reaching to heaven; and the angels of God were ascending and descending on it" (Gen 28: 12).

In the era of the prophets Isaiah had this vision:

> I saw the Lord sitting on a throne, high and lofty; and the hem of his robe filled the temple. Seraphs were in attendance above him; each had six wings: and with two they covered their faces, and with two they covered their feet, and with two they flew.

And one called to another and said: "Holy, holy, holy is the Lord of hosts; the whole earth is full of his glory" (Isa 6:1–3)

This vision featured prominently in the history of Christian mysticism, especially among Franciscans in the high Middle Ages.

In the New Testament, angels are prominent in the major events of the life of Christ: his birth, passion, and resurrection. These angels not only announce the good news, they also reassure and give strength. The angel Gabriel announced the coming of the Christ child to Mary:

And he came to her and said, "Greetings, favored one! The Lord is with you." But she was much perplexed by his words and pondered what sort of greeting this might be. The angel said to her, "Do not be afraid, Mary, for you have found favor with God. And now, you will conceive in your womb and bear a son, and you will name him Jesus. He will be great, and will be called the Son of the Most High." (Luke 1:28–32)

Upon his birth, nearby shepherds are startled by an angelic visitation.

Then an angel of the Lord stood before them, and the glory of the Lord shone around them, and they were terrified. But the angel said to them, "Do not be afraid; for see—I am bringing you good news of great joy for all the people: to you is born this day in the city of David a Savior, who is the Messiah." (Luke 2:9-12)

At the beginning of his passion, Jesus knows that death is approaching and prays earnestly to the Father, on the Mount of Olives. "Then an angel from heaven appeared to him and gave him strength" (Luke 22:43). When the mourning women come to the tomb of Jesus, they find it empty and the stone rolled away. "While they were perplexed about this, suddenly two men in dazzling clothes stood beside them. The women were terrified and bowed their faces to the ground, but the men said to them, 'Why do you look for the living among the dead? He is not here, but has risen'" (Luke 24:4–6)

References to guardian angels are made in the temptation of Christ where Satan quotes the Psalmist: "'He will command his angels....'On their hands they will bear you up, so that you will not dash your foot against a stone'" (Matt 4:6). When the disciples ask Jesus "Who is the greatest in the kingdom of heaven?" he calls a child to him and tells them: "Take care that you do not despise one of these little ones; for, I tell you, in heaven their angels continually see the face of my Father in heaven" (Matt 18:1, 10).

In the Book of the Apocalypse or Revelation, angels both protect and destroy. Four angels at the four corners of the earth stand poised for destruction while another calls in a loud voice: "Do not damage the earth or the sea or the trees, until we have marked the servants of our God with a seal on their foreheads" (Rev 7:1–3).

In contrast to the banishment of humankind from paradise and from intimate communion with God, found in the beginning of Genesis, near the end of the Apocalypse, the angel gives to John a final vision of God and "his servants" face to face. The culminating revelation is God himself: "Then the angel showed me the river of the water of life, bright as crystal, flowing from the throne of God and of the Lamb through the middle of the street of the city" (Rev 22:1–2). In the heavenly paradise, redeemed humanity is so close to God that his name is on their foreheads, so elevated, that they reign with him in his light forever. "His servants will worship him; they will see his face, and his name will be on their foreheads. And there will be no more night; they need no light of lamp or sun, for the Lord God will be their light, and they will reign forever and ever" (Rev 22:4–5). Thus, the angels in scripture are both avengers and protectors, messengers of both damnation and salvation; but in the Apocalypse, the angel is also the revealer of the beatific vision.

HIERARCHY OF THE PSEUDO-DIONYSIUS

In the early patristic period, angels were treated in the context of scripture, for example, by Origen, who situated them within the larger framework of his exegetical project. During the unfolding of the patristic period, Augustine and Gregory the Great, whose selections appear in this volume, incorporated the angels into their theological and spiritual teaching. But it was with the writings of the

Pseudo-Dionysius, especially the *Celestial Hierarchy*, in the late fifth or early sixth century, that a major shift occurred, expanding the treatment of angels, both theologically and spiritually. This shift provided a trajectory that set the dominant pattern for the treatment of angels throughout the high Middle Ages. These writings took the form of commentaries on the *Celestial Hierarchy*, a number of which are included in part in the present volume. Almost two-thirds of the primary texts in this volume are commentaries on the *Celestial Hierarchy* of the Pseudo-Dionysius. Steven Chase has focused chiefly on this commentary tradition, providing, in many cases, English translations for the first time.

The influence of the Pseudo-Dionysius was much enhanced by the fact that his texts were received into the patristic period as if they were the authentic works of Dionysius the Areopagite, the disciple of Paul and first Christian bishop of Athens. It was only many centuries later that the work was judged to be that of a fifth- or sixth-century Neo-Platonist whose identity has not been adequately determined. The erroneous association with Paul the apostle gave the work an aura of apostolic authenticity.

The *Celestial Hierarchy* ushered into Christian spirituality a notion that had a transforming effect, namely that of angelic hierarchy. The term means a holy principle, but in reference to the angels, it meant an organizational pattern in which groups of angels were arranged in a descending or ascending order in accordance to one's perspective, for example, seraphim (love), cherubim (knowledge), thrones (forever in the divine presence), dominions (benevolent rule), powers (courage), authorities (lift up inferior angels), principalities (manifest transcendent principles), archangels (interpreters of divine enlightenment), and angels (revelation to the world). These nine levels provide the framework of the human spiritual journey. Angelic spirituality, then, consists largely in the awakening of these levels in the human person and in the movement of the soul to greater union with God. This is accomplished through the direct ministry of angels and through the correspondences latent in the soul that can be awakened in the spiritual journey.

With the appearance of the *Celestial Hierarchy*, one can observe a trajectory moving from the Pseudo-Dionysius through those who wrote commentaries on the text. In the thirteenth century, with the founding of the universities, there emerged a new genre, not a commentary, but a summa. Did a new genre emerge that could be called a summa of angelic spirituality? Not a fully developed genre, but there is reason to claim that a shortened version appeared in Bonaventure's *Soul's Journey into God*. For in this remarkably compressed text, the Franciscan master condenses into a short treatise the very core of the deep connection of angelic spirituality with the human spiritual journey.[1]

BONAVENTURE'S ANGELIC SPIRITUALITY

I would like to summarize the major themes of angelic spirituality with the example of Bonaventure's *Soul's Journey into God*. This extremely compact treatise contains a synthesis of the twelfth-century monastic commentaries on the *Celestial Hierarchy* of the Pseudo-Dionysius along with the Platonic and Aristotelian philosophies that were current at the University of Paris, where Bonaventure and Thomas Aquinas taught. In this perspective the content and method reflect that of thirteenth-century philosophy, but the overarching structure and method are those of symbolic theology, specifically rooted in the contemplative method of angelic spirituality. The focus here is precisely on the correlation among the angelic hierarchies, especially the seraphim and cherubim, and the human spiritual journey. In making the correlation, Bonaventure brings to light the metaphysical and epistemological ground of the interaction between angels and humans in the spiritual journey, which is at the very heart of angelic spirituality.

In the prologue of the *Soul's Journey*, Bonaventure describes the insight that led him to write the *Soul's Journey into God*. Two years after being elected minister general of the Friars Minor in 1257, he made a pilgrimage to Mount La Verna in Tuscany to the site where Francis had received the stigmata some thirty years before. "While I was there," he writes, "reflecting on various ways by which the soul ascends into God, there came to mind, among other things, the miracle which had occurred to Blessed Francis in this very place: the vision of a winged Seraph in the form of Christ crucified."[2] Bonaventure continues, "While reflecting on this, I saw at once that this vision represented our father's rapture in contemplation and the road by which this rapture is reached."[3]

Note that the vision is of the seraph, coming from the highest level of the celestial hierarchy. At the same time, Bonaventure saw that the six wings of the seraph symbolized the stages of the spiritual journey. This reveals the very nature of angelic spirituality described above, namely, the intimate correlation between the angelic choirs and the human spiritual journey. As Bonaventure says, "The six wings of the Seraph can rightly be taken to symbolize the six levels of illumination by which, as if by steps or stages, the soul can pass over to peace through ecstatic elevations of Christian wisdom."[4]

With the seraphic vision as an organizing principle, Bonaventure in the next six chapters takes the reader on a spiritual journey by contemplating God first through and in the mirror of the sense world, and next in our internal perception of beauty, then in the faculties of our soul, then in the same faculties restored by grace. The guiding source in these stages is Augustine, especially in his Christian Neo-platonic ascent to God that he describes in the vision he shared with his mother at Ostia.

When Bonaventure reaches the fourth level, he meditates on the reflection of God through the mirror of the soul reformed by grace. There he speaks of the soul as being transformed by the angelic hierarchies and being itself hierarchized.

In the *Soul's Journey into God*, Bonaventure tells us that "The soul, by entering into itself, enters the heavenly Jerusalem, where beholding the choirs of angels, it sees in them God, who dwells in them and performs all their operations."[5] He then quotes Bernard of Clairvaux, who says that "God loves in the Seraphim as charity, knows in the Cherubim as truth, is seated in the Thrones as equity, reigns in the Dominations as majesty, rules in the Principalities as principle, guards in the Powers as salvation, acts in the Virtues as strength, reveals in the Archangels as light, assists in the Angels as piety."[6]

PREFACE

In the next two stages, Bonaventure focuses on the cherubim by entering symbolically into the Temple in Jerusalem and mediating on the two angelic figures over the ark. The first cherub symbolizes the contemplation of God in the divine unity. The other cherub symbolizes the contemplation of God as Trinity. Between the two facing cherubs is the mercy seat, which symbolizes Christ. These angelic figures draw Bonaventure into the contemplation of Christ, which leads to the final step of mystical ecstasy as described in a text from the *Mystical Theology* of the Pseudo-Dionysius. With this Bonaventure's *Soul's Journey* comes to an end. The journey that was begun with the vision of the six-winged seraph in the form of Christ crucified has proceeded through the choirs of angels and reached its climax with Christ between the two cherubs as the soul enters into the divine darkness and mystical ecstasy.

I believe that the present volume throws much light on Bonaventure's *Soul's Journey*, which in turn illumines the nature of angelic spirituality. In reading the selections in this volume, one becomes aware that we humans are surrounded by a community of heavenly beings who illumine, inspire, guide, and elevate us on our spiritual journey. Through them the warmth of God's love and the clarity of his light encompass and lift us up into the inner life of God.

Notes

1. Although references are made to Bonaventure's *Soul's Journey* in the introduction to this volume, the text of the *Soul's Journey into God* is not included because it appears in its entirety in the Bonaventure volume of the Classics of Western Spirituality.

2. Bonaventure, *The Soul's Journey into God*, Prologue, no. 2 in *The Soul's Journey into God, The Tree of Life, The Life of St. Francis*, translated by Ewert Cousins, Classics of Western Spirituality (New York, Mahwah, N.J.: Paulist Press, 1978), p. 54.

3. Ibid.

4. Ibid., Prologue, 3.

5. Ibid, c. 4. no. 4; p. 90.

6. Ibid.; Bernard of Clairvauxs, *On Consideration*, V, c. 5, no. 12.

General Introduction

THE WAYS OF ANGELS

And what are the ways of the holy angels?
—Bernard of Clairvaux,
Sermons on Psalm 90, 12.6

The Lord said to Moses and Aaron, "I am the Lord your God; consecrate yourselves and be holy, because I am holy" (Lev 11:44). Within the Christian tradition, the angels are a means of exploring the nature of holiness.

Men and women of faith, imagination, heart, and intellect have, from the church's beginning and in unison with Saint Bernard of Clairvaux, asked questions about the nature, the ministry, the pathways, and the reality of angels. Answers have ranged from the bizarre to the contemptuous, from the seemingly psychotic to the frankly incredulous, from claims of frequent citings or absolute identity between the human and angelic to claims that angels are "nothing but idle and useless human ideas...[and] hodge-podge."[1] Yet between these uncritical claims on the one hand, and supra-critical denials on the other, there exists a range of answers that is truly startling, answers that, as the following collection will demonstrate, cross and intersect the full spectrum of Christian spiritual thought, devotion, and practice. The translations in this volume, and the introductions and notes that accompany them, provide just a few of the most compelling answers to Saint Bernard's question concerning the "ways of the holy angels."

As the selections from this volume make clear, the question of the angels is always posed in the context and service of two larger

1

questions: How is God present in the world? and What is our response to that presence? In the same sermon in which he asks the question concerning the angels, Bernard goes on to say, "I think it is also good to hear something about the manifold pathways to the face of the Lord."[2] Elsewhere, a near contemporary of Bernard, Alan of Lille, similarly teaches that "many are the ways or forms of seeing God."[3] In both cases Bernard and Alan of Lille are responding to the question of the nature of God's presence in the world and our response. According to these writers God's presence in the world is varied and manifold, the ways of responding to God are many. For both writers as well, this fulcrum point of presence and response is the point where questions concerning angels begin to make sense and to find their application. Thus an imaginative, theologically precise, and experientially honest account of angels is one valuable way of assisting us to walk the manifold pathways and envision the many forms of seeing the One God.

Angelic spirituality as a way of experiencing God's presence and responding in love is a form of mystical consciousness. It is a process of spiritual formation in that it teaches the human soul to imagine how we might respond in love to God's presence. It calls us to self-transformation, awakening the soul to God's presence at the center of every created reality. As doors to the invisible, the angels open the heart to transcendence, to mystery, and to hope.

As the writers in this volume will demonstrate, the various angelic orders are like glass cathedral windows, each illuminating different hues, shapes, and colors of holiness. The angels, in a sense, are co-workers with Christ and the Spirit in the work of sanctification. The angelic hues and colors represent the spectrum of light by which the Spirit unites us to Christ. As the theological formulation of our response to God's presence, the doctrine of sanctification helps us to find a language for that complex and lifelong process of spiritual formation and transformation. Angelic spirituality thus belongs, with regard to theology, in the doctrine of sanctification.

The texts in this volume represent a sample of writings within the broader tradition of angelic spirituality. Differences in cultures, politics, theology, experience, and much more ensure that the tradition is not unbroken or monolithic. But it is coherent. It is held together by that One God active in the world and by the response of men and women to that God through the centuries. Angelic spirituality thus focuses on the invisible creations of God who assist men and women to see God's actions and to respond with obedience and love.

ORGANIZATION AND EMPHASIS

And all this shall be done graciously, without business or
travail of thyself,
only by the ministration of angels,
through the virtue of their lovely, blind work.
—Anonymous, *Book of Privy Counsel*, 4

This book is divided into three sections. The first is the present General Introduction. The following two sections contain texts on angelic spirituality in translation along with introductions and notes on each text and author. Section One of the translated texts consists of representative writings from a variety of time periods and genre. Selections in this section explore issues in angelic spirituality ranging from metaphysical issues to practical, formative, devotional, and contemplative themes. Section Two, related thematically to the first, consists of selections from medieval commentaries on Dionysius the Areopagite's *Celestial Hierarchy*. These commentaries explore angelic spirituality in the light of symbolic theology, the moral life, contemplation, esthetics, and mystical consciousness as it developed and evolved throughout the medieval period and beyond. A brief comment on Dionysius and his *Celestial Hierarchy* is given at the beginning of Section Two. Additional information on the Dionysian influence is given in the individual introduction before each selection and in the notes.

Throughout this book emphasis is placed not on traditional metaphysical questions concerning angels per se (though such questions will be of interest), but rather on angelic spirituality as it is illuminated and developed by the various authors in this book. In addition, the discussion that follows on themes in angelic spirituality

3

will also leave aside certain traditional approaches already investigated by others. These include approaches focusing primarily on angels in literature, myth, and legend,[4] as well as in cross-cultural perspective.[5] It will also leave aside approaches primarily concerned with psychology[6] and social history.[7] Instead, this volume will explore the history, theology, and philosophy of angels[8] but most particularly the "spirituality of angels." The material, tools, and procedure for this approach surface primarily from two sources: first, from the methodology currently employed in the contemporary study of Christian spirituality in the academy; and second, from the themes in angelic spirituality that surface naturally from the selections contained in this volume. The two sources are, of course, related and mutually informing. The first source represents a new academic discipline, currently in flux, but vibrant and growing. This volume will not explore this source explicitly but will assume it.[9] The second source is the explicit ground of this book. The texts contained here in translation represent something of the range of medieval angelic spirituality.[10] At the same time they also serve as a basis for deeper understandings of contemporary spirituality and as a source for the reader's own spiritual formation as he or she encounters the manifold varieties of angelic spirituality.

The remainder of this Introduction will explore the variety of themes found in angelic spirituality as it is represented in the Latin Christian tradition.[11] Information on authors, periods, genres, and themes specific to individual works will be found in the shorter introductions preceding each selection. Information on the editions used for translation of each selection and in some cases on translation of particular words or phrases will be found at the end of each of these shorter introductions under "Notes on Translation."

Though the translated works in this volume are focused on the period from roughly the fourth to the thirteenth century in the Latin West, many of the themes and issues raised and addressed are found throughout the Christian tradition from its birth to contemporary times. In fact, renewed interest in angels today in Christian as well as quasi-religious and secular contexts is one of the more important reasons for retrieving something of the wisdom of angelic spirituality from the Christian past. Such retrieved wisdom sometimes requires re-translation for application to present-day questions; sometimes it does not. But the wisdom *is* there, ready to guide, inspire, and even transform us, ready, today, to expand and deepen our visions of and response to the holy countenance of God.

THEMES IN ANGELIC SPIRITUALITY

His face was like the face of an angel.
—Acts 6:15

As with precritical exegesis in general, an exploration into the nature of angels and their impact upon Christian spirituality can be divided roughly into a "literal" investigation and a "spiritual" inquiry. A literal investigation would ask questions about the reality of angels. Do angels really exist? What do they look like? What is the evidence for their existence? In general, this book will leave such questions aside, though its underlying assumption is that the literal and spiritual questions regarding angels are intimately related. Thus this book explores angelic "reality" from a historical, theological, and spiritual point of view, but it does not ask questions directly concerning the ontological reality of angelic presences.[12]

Because this book, its introductions and its translated text, pursues what might be called the spiritual inquiry, the inquiry is not limited to a single modality but is multivalent and hermeneutical. Thus the book is, following the model of the medieval spiritual exegesis, concerned first of all with the allegorical power of angels. How do angels symbolize something deeper about the core of the divine nature, about the human person, or about a particular path of devotion? And following a spiritual inquiry, the book is also concerned with the anagogic power of angels. How do angels represent, assist, and teach ascent to God from immanent realities, or how do angels lead us to the very heart and center of the transcendent? And likewise on the basis of a spiritual inquiry, the book examines the tropological essence of angels. That is, how do angels teach and evoke spiritual formation, the process of *paideia*, the moral life? In what way do they function as models of a life *lived* at the center with God? How do they exemplify a life of virtue? How do they escort us on the path of compassion and charity?

This spiritual aspect of the inquiry is also hermeneutical in that it involves readers or "practitioners" of angelic spirituality in the very angelic illuminations they encounter. That is, as readers/practitioners encounter the message of the angels, they become transformed by that message. The etymology of *angel* is, of course, "messenger." The angelic message encountered, wrestled with, interpreted, and applied becomes one's own personal "message" in and to the world. It becomes a message founded in God and lived out in response to God's presence.

The modernist attempt to cordon off the spiritual inquiry from the literal investigation has left men and women with a strong sense of alienation and loss, one might even say dismemberment.[13] The writers represented in this volume, on the other hand, were formed in a wisdom or sapiential tradition that knew the dangers of such a split. Exegetes from the period, for example, cautioned over and over not to separate the literal interpretation of reality from the spiritual application. Spiritual writers of the period combined intuitive and creative imaginations with precise critical reflection on the nature of visible reality. Yet the intent of this focus was to use these visible forms of loveliness as guiding hands into invisible reality. Theologians of the period combined acute and incisive rational inquiry with wordless contemplation, liturgical worship, and other projects of the heart that explored divine realities seemingly beyond reason.

It is no wonder, then, that angelic spirituality was alive and well during the roughly ten centuries represented in this book. For teachers of this period, angels *are* the integration of the literal and the spiritual, they *are* the exemplars of an integrated formulation uniting doctrine with the practice of devotion, and they *are* those divine beings at home in both the visible "sacred veils" of the created world and in the invisible court of God. The angels as revealed in scripture and attested by men and women of faith *are* the literally rational and the spiritually mysterious. Thus, for the spiritual masters represented in this volume, in order to "fly" with the angels

6

into the light of the Father, the soul must be intimate with the material world as well as the spiritual.

As the themes in angelic spirituality are described below, it will become obvious that, though we are dealing with material from centuries ago, from a foreign culture, from a religious world view different from our own, the themes nevertheless strike cords that are hauntingly familiar, even modern. The power of angels depicted in these writings is not the power of right thinking or orthodoxy, not the power of logic or reason only, not the power of the merely visible (though these things they certainly are). Rather, the power of angelic spirituality from this distant culture is the power to inspire us, to renew us, to reform and lead us into the boundlessness of God and at the same time into the God who is closer to us than our own heartbeat, who, as the apostle Paul says, "Is near to you, in your mouth and in your heart" (Rom 10:8). Angelic spirituality in the Christian tradition is sapiential formation into the small and particular as well as into the large and unifying.

Clearly, the encounter with the invisible and transcendent must be personalized and therein validated and actualized on a human level. In her book on Satan, for instance, Elaine Pagels tells us:

> In 1988, when my husband of twenty years died in a hiking accident, I became aware that, like many people who grieve, I was living in the presence of an invisible being—living, that is, with a vivid sense of someone who had died. During the following years I began to reflect on the ways that various religious traditions give shape to the invisible world, and how our imaginative perceptions of what is invisible relate to the ways we respond to the people around us, to events, and to the natural world....As I proceeded to investigate Jewish and Christian accounts of angels and fallen angels, I discovered, however, that they were less concerned with the natural world as a whole than with the particular world of human relationships.[14]

Pagels's personal and concrete experience and later research lead her into the presence of the invisible. Though the lens through which she interprets her experience is initially grief and her focus theodicy, her experience and research draw her into that "invisible world" that in turn heightens her awareness of the visible "natural world," the events of her life, and the people around her. But this invisible reality, as she says, comes alive most clearly in "human relationships." These texts, and their subjects, invite us to personalize the invisible things of creation, to formulate and encounter them with imagination and intuition, and to enter the natural world and that most important web of human relationships with angelic wisdom, discernment, joy, love, and praise.

Angels in Scripture

We also understand by the two angels [the two cherubim on the ark of the covenant]
the two Testaments, first the one and then the one that follows.
These angels, by their placing, have been united with the body of the Lord himself,
since both testaments equally announce the message of the incarnation, death, and resurrection of the Lord.
—Gregory the Great, *Homilies on the Gospel, Homily 25*

Angelic spirituality in the Christian tradition is grounded in scripture. This ground does not, therefore, belong primarily within the domain of history, science, or philosophy but in the realm of faith. Thus, for instance, the Nicene Creed, drawing upon the biblical witness, posits a statement of belief in angels for recitation by believers when in the beginning it states:

I believe in the Father almighty, maker of heaven and earth, and of all things visible and invisible.

As a matter of religious belief, the angels, as inhabitants of heaven and as created, invisible beings, are revealed in innumerable places in both the Old Testament and the New Testament. Through this biblical witness the angels are *in* revelation, and their existence is a content *of* revelation.[15]

Medieval exegesis understood angelic beings to be fluid and subtle. The angelic essence, their names, their ministries, and their functions were varied and complex. For example, the "angel of Yahweh" was often seen as a circumlocution for God's own presence as much as a being in its own right (Judg 6:11–24); at other times the angel appeared as a distinct figure "like a man of God" (Judg 13:2–23). At still other times the "angel of the Lord" was seen as an angel like any other bringing a message of hope (Gen 16:7–16), serving as covenant maker between God and the people of Israel (Gen 22:9–19). As the following themes in angelic spirituality will show, the angels, whether distinct and clearly defined beings or rather puzzling and oddly shaped, fluid concoctions (see the winged figures of cherubim of Ezekiel's vision, Ezek 1:28) represented the wide and ever-changing texture of God's relation to the world. In scripture as well they range in identity from the divine to the human pole, not neglecting the fullest range of possible identities in between.

This is not the place to detail fully the complete and frankly daunting range of biblical references to angels.[16] But several references of particular importance to the subject of angelic spirituality are in order. As scripture is the basis of angelic spirituality, an examination of angels in the Bible delineates their functions and their ministries.

The word *angel* (in Greek, *angelos;* in Hebrew, *mal'ak*) means "messenger"; in scripture the angels are often depicted as messengers moving between God and humanity (for example, the ladder in Jacob's dream upon which the angels ascended and descended, Gen 28:12). These angels carry messages and the law from God, and prayers from men and women to God (Dan 3:25). In the Hebrew scriptures no single term corresponds to the English word for angel. Instead, the Hebrew Bible contains a rich vocabulary and range of expressions, ranging from "sons of God" (Gen 6:2) to "divine beings" (Ps 29:1) to "holy ones" (Ps 29:1) and more. The expression "angel of Yahweh" is ubiquitous. And as terms denoting functions, both *angelos* and *mal'ak*, meaning "messenger," can refer equally to human or angelic beings. Consequently, there are occasionally passages in which it remains disputed whether the reference is to a heavenly being or a human one (cf. Judg 2:1; Mal 3:1).[17]

As with their designation and name, angels in the Hebrew Bible exhibit a variety of functions. They are depicted, for instance, as comprising a heavenly court that God consults and that surrounds God, singing God's praises (1 Kgs 29:19–23; Job 1:6–12; Isa 6; Ps 148:2). They serve as a heavenly army comprising thousands of "holy ones" (Deut 33:2), and in one instance Joshua encounters a "commander of the army of Yahweh" (Josh 5:14). As messengers in the Hebrew Bible, angels announce births (Gen 16:11–12; Gen 18:9–15), give reassurances (Gen 31:11–13), commission persons to tasks (Exod 3:2), and communicate God's word to prophets (2 Kgs 1:3, 15; Isa 6; Jer 23:18). An angel may also intervene at crucial moments to guide a person's actions (Gen 16:19; Gen 22:11–12; Num 22:31–35). Angels serve as an invisible company who are close to God and who support and aid those who trust God (2 Kgs 6:15–17). Prophetic messages are also articulated largely in terms of angelic visions, giving added authority to the prophetic claim (see the visions of Zechariah). The angel as teacher and mediator of revelations is a common Old Testament motif. Such an angelic revealer serves as a heavenly guide and interpreter of mysteries and visions (see Dan 7–12). Frequently the angel's appearance is described in terms of light, fire, shining metals, or precious stones (Dan 10:5–6; 2 Macc 3:25–26), and their garments are white linen or white with golden sashes (Dan 10:5, 12:6; 2 Macc 3:26). Just as there are angels watching over the natural workings of the cosmos, so there are in the Hebrew Bible angelic leaders of nations whose actions are sometimes directed by God but who also act to oppose the angels God has assigned to help Israel (Dan 10:13; 12:1). The notion that Israel was aided in times of crises by angels was also widely shared (2 Macc 3:24–26; 11:8).

Already included among the angels in the Old Testament, and of paramount importance for the development of angelic spirituality, are the seraphim of Isaiah 6 and the cherubim. The cherubim appear guarding paradise (Gen 3:24), standing atop the ark of the covenant, there sheltering and guarding the place of God's presence (Exod 25, 37; 1 Kgs 6; 2 Chr 3, 5), standing on either side of God, the "Shepherd of Israel," as God leads and judges Israel from heaven's angelic throne (Ps 80:1; 99:1) and in Ezekiel's vision (Ezek 10:5). In addition, the heavenly realm called the Thrones upon which God sits over Israel appears in Psalms 11:4, 99:1, and 122:5.[18] Angels named in Hebrew scripture include Michael (Dan 10:13),

Gabriel (Dan 8:16), and Raphael (Tob 7:8). In the tradition of angelic spirituality these, along with the named angels in the New Testament, are considered to be archangels.

In the New Testament, angels who live in the presence of God, sing God's praises, combat evil powers, comfort the distressed, look upon the face of God, bring messages, and mediate between humanity and God were taken for granted. As echoed in the Nicene Creed, they were created by God (Col 1:16). They are described as spirits (Heb 1:7), as holy (Mark 8:38; Luke 9:26), as robed in white garments (Matt 28:3; John 20:12; Rev 19:14), as radiating great light (Matt 28:3; Luke 24:4; Acts 10:30; Rev 10:1), thus radiating the glory of God (Luke 9:26; Acts 12:7; 2 Pet 2:10; Jude 8) and praising God (Luke 2:13–14; Rev 7:11–12). In form, angels are akin to humankind and often referred to as men (Mark 16:5; Heb 13:2) but are different enough to evoke fear (Matt 28:1–8; Luke 1:11–12; Acts 10:4) and worship (Rev 19:10) from human beings. Angelic knowledge is more comprehensive than humankind's but not unlimited (Mark 13:32; Eph 3:10; 1 Pet 1:12). Angels possess their own languages (1 Cor 13:1), are intently concerned with the salvation of humankind (Luke 15:10; Eph 3:10; 1 Tim 5:21; 1 Cor 4:9), offering prayers of the saints on the golden altar (Rev 5:8; 8:3–4) and ministering to the Christian (Heb 1:14). They can represent and comfort the stranger, the outcast, and the unexpected, as in the call to love one another constantly in the knowledge that the stranger or outcast is an angel of God in disguise (Heb 13:1–2). Since the angels in heaven always see the face of the Father in heaven (Matt 18:10), they can likewise guard the humble and the childlike, who are the true inheritors of heaven.

The angel Gabriel, the messenger, announces to Mary her vocation as mother of Christ (Luke 1:26–38), and the angel Michael, a warrior, fights for God against powers of darkness (Jude 9; Rev 12:7). An unnamed angel tells the shepherds of the birth of Jesus (Luke 2:8–20). In their role as servants, angels minister to Jesus in the desert (Matt 4:11) and in the Garden of Gethsemane (Luke 22:43). Twelve legions of them are readied for his defense at his arrest (Matt 26:53), and they roll the stone from the entrance of the tomb at the resurrection (Matt 28:2). In short, Jesus speaks of them as "ascending and descending upon him" (John 1:51). As well as through their direct presence, the angels also deliver their messages in a dream (Matt 1:20–21; 2:13, 19–20) or in a vision (Acts 10:3–6). New Testament writers also assumed that the angels served as intermediaries through whom the law was given by God to Israel (Acts 7:53; Gal 3:19; Heb 2:2). Angels were also witnesses to the incarnation (1 Tim 3:16). Paul assumes the angels can preach the gospel (Gal 1:8), and the Pharisees assume that an angel could have spoken with Paul (Acts 23:9). They are harbingers of the births of John the Baptist (Luke 1:11–20) and Jesus (Luke 1:26–38); they advise Joseph about the nature of Mary's child (Matt 1:20–21), proclaim the birth of Jesus to the shepherds (Luke 2:8–14), give instructions to the women at the tomb and announce to the women the resurrection of Jesus (Matt 28:2–7; John 20:12f.). Two angels speak to the disciples at Christ's ascension (Acts 1:10). Angels, as guides, advisers, and comforters, figure in the early life of the church as depicted in Acts (7:30; 8:26; 10:3–6, 30–32; 11:13–14; 12:6–11). They play a prominent role as citizens of heaven (as depicted in Revelation), are integrally involved in judgment, both in an ongoing capacity (Acts 12:20–23) and at the final consummation (1 Thess 4:16; Rev 5:1–2, 8–9, 10:1–7, 15–16), will accompany Christ at his *parousia* (Matt 16:27; 25:31; Mark 8:38; 2 Thess 1:7; Jude 14–15), will gather the elect (Matt 24:31), and will separate the evildoers from the elect for destruction in fire (Matt 13; 25:31–46; Jude 14–15). As guardians, the angels watch over children (Matt 18:10), guard the seven churches in Revelation (2—3), and release Peter from prison (Acts 5:19–20).

Pauline angelology expands the notion of the angels in the New Testament. Paul mentions angels often, and the archangels once (1 Thess 4:16), as heavenly beings who normally receive a call and message from God, who "sends" them to earth on their appointed mission. Paul recalls the Old Testament in commenting that the angels serve as intermediaries in the giving of the law (Gal 1:8; 4:14; 2 Cor 11:14). Paul also associates the angels with the *parousia* and with the final resurrection (1 Thess 4:16; 2 Thess 1:7), and he calls the "chosen angels" to witness in 1 Timothy 5:21. But Paul is cautious about the possibility of angels taking over the work of the sole mediator, which is Christ. He respects the reality and work of the angels, but not to the detriment of the work of Christ (see Heb 2:2–3).

Of critical importance for angelic spirituality as it is formulated in the medieval period is Paul's use and description of the celestial "powers."[19] As will be seen from the writings in this volume, these angelic designations became essential to the full and proper functioning of the various angelic missions. In addition to Seraphim, Cherubim, Archangels, and Angels, Paul mentions five separate powers that came to be interpreted as separate orders or classes of angels: the Rulers *(archai)*, cited eight times; the Authorities *(exousiai)*, seven times; the Powers *(dynameis)*, three times; the Lordships *(kyriotêtes)*, two times; and the Thrones *(thronoi)*, cited once. These heavenly beings are mentioned particularly in the epistles of captivity (Col 1:16; 2:10; 2:15; Eph 1:21; 3:10; 6:12), but they are also already present in 1 Corinthians 15:24, Romans 8:38, and 2 Thessalonians 1:7. In addition, the Authorities and Powers are mentioned alongside the Angels in 1 Peter 3:22. Paul's interpretation of these five spiritual powers as angels would have lasting impact within the Christian tradition from the earliest times to the present. With the four classes of angels mentioned above, these five together form the nine angelic orders, which constitute the biblical backdrop at the core of angelic spirituality.

In summary, much is said in the Hebrew scriptures and in the New Testament concerning angels. It is clear that biblical revelation is the source of angelic wisdom and spirituality. On the other hand, much is omitted. We do not know from scripture, for instance, where angels came from, how they were created, or why. We do know they were created by God, in that God created all things (Col 1:16). But we do not know for certain how many there are (though there are "myriads upon myriads"), nor do we know if they have organization or ranks. The Bible gives no history of the angels, and apart from a very few archangels, it provides no names. In short, scripture gives no specific doctrine of angels, nor does it give the exact relation of angels to humanity or to God. Yet, other important Christian doctrines are also not given specific and immediately recognizable shape in scripture. The doctrine of the Trinity, for instance, or of the two natures of Christ, or even of the Holy Spirit must, like the doctrine of the angels, be fleshed out, as it were, from the reliable biblical witness. Spirituality, likewise, as it evolved in the context of angels, was also fleshed out and lived. Such, of course, is the nature of a living tradition. In that sense angelic spirituality is one of many traditions within a larger tradition. It is experienced, reflected upon, practiced, visualized, and validated in community, by faith, in accordance with scripture.

Thus from the ground of God's self-revelation in scripture, the ministry of angels began to be understood and practiced within the ongoing witness of the community of the faithful. We turn now to those angelic functions, natures, and names that the medieval mystical writers taught would deepen our participation in God, our understanding of self, and our compassion for the world.

Angelic Functions, Ministries, and Names

Are not all angels ministering spirits sent to serve those who will
inherit salvation?
—Hebrews 1:14

Every visible thing in this world is put under the charge of an angel.
—Augustine, *De diversis questionibus*

The functions, ministries, and names of angels are the ground upon which devotional and ethical practices in angelic spirituality developed. These spiritual practices evolved and found expression on the basis of four interrelated processes. These included (1) *lectio*, exegesis, and theological reflection on the biblical narratives; (2) the maturation, in the context of pagan angelologies, of an explicitly Christian doctrine of angels; (3) the struggle to find a language and practice for expressing the invisible, incomprehensible, and transcendent world and the influence of that world on the visible world; and (4) the personal experience with angels on the part of the Christian community of faith. These various processes worked in tandem, together shaping spiritual practice, formation, and devotion. In the survey of ministries that follows, these four elements were constantly woven and rewoven into the fabric of angelic spirituality.

As this tradition developed in the Latin West, the angels came to be seen as messengers from God who illuminated something about God even as they served as a kind of code for the interpretation of that same God. As messengers of God the angels proclaimed the divine will. In illuminating God the angels imitated, looked upon, modeled, and had uninterrupted participation in the very God they then revealed. As codes or ciphers for interpreting this divine light, angelic ministries served as a kind of lens that allowed the soul to "see" the angels, to "see" the manner in which they participated in God, and thus to "see" something of the divine mystery itself. As messengers, illuminators, and ciphers, the angelic ministries guided the development of the soul and the community in holiness.

Traditional interpretations of the functions of angels are vast. In one way or another they encompass every conceivable aspect and nuance of the relationship between God and humanity. As such, though their functions are not limited to these, they echo many of the angelic themes encountered in the biblical narrative. Angels in angelic spirituality have traditionally served the functions of messenger, protector, mediator between God and humanity, participants in songs of praise, helpers and savers, ministers to humanity and world, heralds of peace, avengers, guardians, guides, escorts, agents of centering in God, symbols of flight and ascent, paths to divine union, and many more.[20] Angels are often associated with visions, prophecies, and discernment. At times the angels serve as guides or spirits that "awaken" the visionary to the vision; at other times they serve as interpreters of the vision itself, thus assisting the visionary or prophet in discernment.[21] As was apparent in the biblical witness, angels sometimes signify the presence of God; sometimes they even seem to *be* God.[22] At other times they shelter and define the space of God's presence with their wings, becoming, as it were, a womb for the birth of God in the soul.[23] Not only do they observe and assist with what happens here on earth, they also serve as collaborators in God's providence, assisting

Christ in the economy of salvation. Often, as well, they are akin to Greek psychopomps, guides of souls after death. In this case they guide souls not through hell or in a "neutral" afterlife, but in heaven.

The angels also serve as symbols. As such, the angels are *polysemic*. That is, they have the capacity of possessing many levels of meaning at once, they point beyond themselves giving added meaning to ordinary experience, they become agents of transformation guiding the soul along the path of the spiritual quest, and they express certain patterns of ultimate reality that can be expressed in no other way.[24]

In the tradition of angelic spirituality all of these functions serve to call men and women to various lives of service and paths of faith. Thus, as noted above, angelic spirituality is less concerned with the natural world, or even the celestial world as a whole, than it is with the particular world of human relationships. Denys Turner, summarizing the medieval understanding of the role of angels in human relationships, points out three ways in which angels and humanity are related: (1) the human person contains in microcosm the whole or "macro" cosmic reality, thus containing something of angelic reality; (2) the human soul can, through grace, "interiorize" the angelic hierarchy itself; and (3) the embodied character of human beings reflects, through the very *relation* of the spirit to the body, the relation of God to creation and hence the relation of angels to God.[25]

The means by which angelic ministries reveal their existence in the realm of human relationships varies from writer to writer. For Gregory the Great, for instance, it is the names of angels *(angelorum nomina)* and the description of their duties *(ipsa officiorum vocabula)* by which the angels become "visible" to us. Their service or duty is the outward sign by which we recognize them, and in turn their ministry is the mode through which they are named.[26] Gregory says:

> But why do we touch upon these choirs of steadfast angels by listing them, if not to describe their ministries in a plain manner? We ought to know that whatever angels are called, their name signifies a service....Archangels are distinguished by personal names in order to point out by words what their action signifies....Those spirits that are sent take on their name-word according to the service they perform.[27]

16

In a similar way Umiltà of Faenza teaches that it is the very ministry of angels that, as it is carried out in the human realm, makes their presence known to us. In this case, however, in a beautiful passage, Umiltà does not so much "see" the invisible angels but rather "hears" their sweet song as they carry out their ministry from God:

> God dignified them [the angels] with every adornment, placing them above the firmament. God gave them knowledge of every science with which they might be servants and ministers of divine greatness. God gave wings to each so that those messengers who carry extraordinary news of the most noble magnitude might fly quickly, crossing over every barrier, reaching every height. For it is on account of their sublime beauty that they are ministers of the Trinity. Whenever they unfurl their wings in flight and then gather them gracefully together again, they make their ministry a sweet song. Since they are spirits endowed with the power of the most high, they make a song that no other creature is able to sing.[28]

For John Scotus Eriugena, on the other hand, the link between angelic ministry and visibility is light. The angels, in Eriugena's teaching, *are* light. They are invisible light, to be sure, when contemplating God. But through the action of their ministries reflected in their names, they become visible light, or theophanies, in the sphere of human affairs:

> Clearly, these things teach nothing other than the Seraphim's name and the nature of their manifestation—indeed, these things stand for the very essence of "Seraphim." And the name and the manifestation signify the nature of "Seraphim," so that this relation of signification always remains changeless. What, above all, the name and manifestation signify is light. The Seraphim are light.[29]

In these writers, as in others, the tradition of angelic spirituality recognizes that the primary means by which the angels become "visible" to us is through their ministry. The various names of the angels reflect their ministry and help to make the "outlines" of a given angelic theophany visible. This will be made clearer in the section below entitled "Angels and Spiritual Paths," but as an example, it can be noted that the name of the archangel Gabriel, for instance, means "strength of God." Gabriel's ministry is as a warrior of God. The name thus clarifies something of both the celestial nature of Gabriel and of the earthly function of his ministry. As another example, the name Cherubim in Hebrew means "fullness of knowledge." The ministry of understanding, of intellectual pursuit, of knowledge, of wisdom, is the ministry of and the identifying mark of the Cherubim. The Cherubim become "visible," for instance, as we ourselves pursue and apply knowledge as a spiritual practice. This in turn draws our attention toward God.

It is perhaps appropriate that angels are most clearly revealed through their ministry as it is pursued in the order of human relations. Angelic ministry, whatever its form, is *from* God and *to* humanity. As our own ministry renders God visible to others and others visible to us, so the angelic ministries, in illuminating and serving God and neighbor, illuminate their own existence and nature to us. As Umiltà of Faenza so nicely phrased it, if the ministry of angels is their song, then we hear their music as they fly to do God's will.

Angelic Orders and Hierarchy

These orders all gaze upward and prevail downward,
so that toward God all are drawn, and all do draw.
—Dante, *Paradiso*, XVIII

As angelic spirituality developed through the early Patristic period and into the medieval period and beyond, the angels were grouped in hierarchical orders. Scripture itself is not without hints that some angels were higher or closer to God than others.[30] But it was certainly the influence of Neo-Platonist metaphysical notions of emanation from and return to "the One" *(hen)* and of the mediating quality of intelligences between humanity and the gods that influenced Christian thinking and practice concerning the angels.[31] In that Christianity has always been syncretic in its formulation of theology, spirituality, and liturgy, the fact that Neo-Platonic cosmological views influenced its angelology does not detract from the

18

"purity" or "apostolic warrant" of angelic spirituality. It simply explains something of its history and philosophy.

However, the fact is that writers from Ambrose to Jerome, from Dionysius the Areopagite to Gregory the Great, and from Hugh of St. Victor to Umiltà of Faenza all used the biblical narrative, the available philosophy of the time, the doctrine of the tradition, and current spirituality to group the angels according to orders and classes. The exact location of each angelic type within the angelic orders varied from writer to writer, yet all of the orders were found in scripture. The *usual* number of orders was nine: the Seraphim, Cherubim, Thrones, Dominions, Principalities, Powers, Authorities or Virtues, Archangels,[32] and Angels. Each order represented a particular angelic function or ministry as well as, in most cases, a corresponding human ministry or process of formation. Explained in more detail below, the Seraphim, for example, meaning "fire-makers; carriers of warmth" in Hebrew, came to represent the ministry or path of love. Cherubim, meaning "fullness of knowledge" in Hebrew, came to represent the ministry or path of knowledge or scholarship. All of the celestial orders, though the place of each order and its exact function often varied from writer to writer, had corresponding ministries and spiritual paths.

A few examples of the arrangement of the angelic orders proposed by various Latin writers, along with Dionysius the Areopagite, are given below. The Seraphim is always the highest order or the order closest to God, while the Angels are usually the lowest. Note that, significantly, the orders are not always listed from lowest to highest.

Ambrose[33]	Jerome[34]	Gregory the Great[35]	Dionysius the Areopagite[36]
Angels	Archangels	Angels	Seraphim
Archangels	Angels	Archangels	Cherubim
Dominions	Thrones	Thrones	Thrones
Powers	Dominions	Dominions	Dominions
	Powers	Virtues	Powers
	Cherubim	Principalities	Authorities
	Seraphim	Powers	Principalities
		Cherubim	Archangels
		Seraphim	Angels

By the time of Gregory the Great the overwhelming preference was for nine angelic orders. The exact order, however, often varied from those of Gregory and Dionysius presented here.[37] The preference for starting with Angels or with Seraphim generally depended on the emphasis of the writer. If the writer's emphasis was on the angels as an anagogic tool that lead the soul ever higher or deeper into God, the orders generally started with the Angels and led "up" to the Seraphim. If the emphasis was on the procession of angelic lights "down" from God as a means of describing and symbolizing the fullness of God's ongoing revelation in the world, the orders generally started with the Seraphim and proceeded "down" to the Angels. But these preferences were merely for emphasis, since all of these writers, regardless of emphasis, recognized the importance of the opposite position as well. Thus the "ascent" and "descent" of the angels were seen to be parts of a larger whole.

This larger whole was most often described by means of the concept of hierarchy. Today many people distrust this concept. Hierarchy is thought to be stiff and rigid, not to mention oppressive. It is true that hierarchy as a social or political structure has been used to subjugate, control, and oppress. But the metaphysical and cosmological world view that developed the concept of hierarchy understood it in a different, even life-affirming way. Grounded in Neo-Platonic speculation on the metaphysical path of mediation between the human person and the pure realm of ideas (or, put another way, on the ontological relation between the human person and the gods), hierarchy originally was simply the sacred or holy (*hier*) source or first principle (*archia*).[38] As such, it was a structure or process grounded in divine reality.

One of the first uses of this word in Christian writings is by Dionysius the Areopagite (Pseudo-Dionysius) in the late fifth or early sixth century.[39] Dionysius, the anonymous but supposedly apostolic Dionysius the Areopagite of Acts (17:34), uses hierarchy to mean more than just rank or order. For Dionysius, in both the angelic and the human realms, hierarchy is a sacred order that makes knowledge and activity possible:

> In my opinion a hierarchy is a sacred order, a state of under-
> standing and an activity approximating as closely as possible to
> the divine. And it is uplifted to the imitation of God in propor-
> tion to the enlightenments divinely given to it....The goal of a
> hierarchy, then, is to enable beings to be as like as possible to
> God and to be at one with God.[40]

Hierarchy is, first, that divine ordering making possible knowledge
and activity that lead to union with God in the sense that we become
"fellow workers with God" (1 Cor 3:9). And it is, second, that
process whereby one then shows forth that divine energy which has
been manifested within. Hierarchy in this sense is thus a vehicle for
divine manifestation or theophany. Hierarchy *is*, in fact, a theophany
of God. Thus the angelic hierarchy represents divine light as it is
shown forth in the angels, which are each in themselves a theophany
of God, each in themselves drawing other beings into God.

Still, because of its historical misuse, it might be helpful to
reconceptualize hierarchy in order to get closer to the original
meaning of Dionysius and the other writers in this volume. Probably most helpful in this regard is to envision hierarchy not in terms
of a ladder or steps in which those on a "higher" rung are somehow
closer to God or in a position to oppress those on a "lower" rung
but rather as a circle. Thought of in this way, the celestial hierarchy
is a circle containing within it concentric circles at the very center
of which is God. The "hierarchy of the soul" is likewise a series of
concentric circles at the center of which is the core or ground of the
soul. Thus the inner journey, rather than a ladder, is a metaphor
closer to the original conception of hierarchy. Visual depictions of
the angelic hierarchy in the medieval period often showed such
concentric circles around a central sphere symbolizing God.

In this sense the manner in which hierarchy was conceived and
depicted in the medieval period and the manner in which it functioned in spiritual practice was like a mandala.[41] As a mandala, the
various angelic orders combined to move whoever participated in
them inward toward the center, where one would encounter God at
the center of one's true self. The center would radiate out toward the
circumference of the various orders and so illuminate them with

something of the reality of the center. This hierarchy/mandala thus functions according to the principle of the relation between the microcosm and macrocosm or the alpha and omega.[42] That is, the variety of orders, or individuals, or stages of spiritual development within a hierarchy maintain the unique attributes of their particular nature while at the same time illuminating or showing forth something of the whole of the hierarchy symbolized in its essence by the center. Thus in the angelic hierarchy, for instance, each angel is a particular manifestation, illumination, or theophany of an attribute or name of God, yet at the same time it participates, in a very real sense, in the fullness of God. The angelic Seraphim, for instance, manifest the particular divine attribute of love, and they assist the man or woman of faith in the path of *agape*. And since "God is love" (1 John 4:16), to "touch" the love of the Seraphim is thus to "touch" God. But God is knowledge, goodness, power, wisdom, and discernment as well. And so other angels of the angelic hierarchy are theophanies of these attributes. The Cherubim manifest knowledge and direct the soul on the path of knowledge; to "touch" the knowledge of the Cherubim is to "touch" divine wisdom. Likewise, the angelic Thrones are generally spoken of as teaching and being ministers of discernment. They lead the soul in the path of discernment, wherein the soul "touches" God at the point of God's discerning judgement. In each case, because of the manner in which hierarchy functions to order human knowledge and activity, to "touch" love is in some sense to "touch" the knowledge and discernment of God, to "touch" knowledge is likewise to be grounded in the holiness of the love and discernment of God, and so on.

A few examples may help to clarify this aspect of hierarchy. Teresa of Avila, in *The Interior Castle*,[43] compares the human soul and the spiritual journey to the soul's center to a castle or mansion with many rooms. Teresa speaks of seven "orders" of mansions, in each of which there are many rooms. Teresa teaches that the soul progresses through the first order of mansions to the seventh, bringing with it the experiences and wisdom of having crossed all seven mansions to the center. Once at the center, the soul wanders freely from room to room, carrying with her the wisdom of all rooms. Yet each room has its own particular wisdom to teach about the center, its own particular lesson for the soul. The castle, as Teresa of Avila has envisioned it, is thus a mandala that functions as a hierarchy. It is a holy first principle, a hierarchy that can in a sense be interiorized and accessed in moments of recollection, prayer, or even, as she says, in the labor of charity.

Another example of the way in which the relation between the whole and the parts functions in hierarchy is illustrated by the hologram.[44] Normal vision shows the parts of a photograph to be independent of each other; in the portrait of a woman holding a bouquet, for instance, the flowers could be cut out of the picture without altering the woman's face. But when the photograph is analyzed holographically by passing a laser light through a half-silvered mirror, interference patterns reveal that each part of the photographic record contains information about the entire image; the image can in principle be derived from its parts. Thus, "the form and structure of the entire object may be said to be *enfolded* within each particular region of the photographic record."[45] Finding a parallel to the hologram in the angelic hierarchy, we could say that each angel "enfolds" the form and structure of entire hierarchy. The hierarchy itself being the sacred ground of God, each angel thus contains information about the entire "map" or "image" of God.

As a final example, hierarchy might be compared with the game of baseball. The baseball field can be likened to the structural ground of hierarchy. The game is played on the diamond, a kind of mandala, especially if viewed from a point above the stadium. In this case, Dionysius's hierarchical order, knowledge, and activity correspond to the rules of the game (order), the skill and experience of each of the players (knowledge), and the actual play of the game itself (activity). Especially apt in this analogy is the idea of play as a kind of reality that incorporates the rules and skills of the players while at the same time transcending them, becoming a kind of heightened reality of its own.[46] In this example the dialectic of the whole and the parts, or the alpha and omega, works as well. Each player in each position—the pitcher, the catcher, and so forth—displays a particular set of skills and activity, yet at the same time each participates in the "heightened reality" of the play of the game. The game itself, then, as many commentators have noted, incorporates rules, skills, and play in such a way that both participant and spectator enter a kind of transcendent world of time and space. They enter, as it were, into a liturgical sense of time enfolded in the sacred ground of time.

None of these analogies is sufficient in itself to evoke the full sense of the angelic hierarchy as it was conceived by writers in this volume.[47] For finally, as a mandala, as a manifestation of the coincidental relation in opposition between the whole and the parts, hierarchy leads ever deeper into paradox and mystery. As the sacred ground, as the divine source itself, hierarchy is finally not captured in drawings or analogies or visions. It is to be participated in; it is an activity. It is a comprehensive manifestation of God, a comprehensive spiritual path.

Angelic or celestial hierarchy is not, however, for the writers in this volume, the "highest" or most sublime hierarchy. Dionysius the Areopagite, for instance, reveals that it is Jesus himself who is the source and perfection of all hierarchies:

> Indeed the Word of God teaches those of us who are its disciples that in this fashion—though more clearly and more intellectu-ally—Jesus enlightens our blessed superiors [angels], Jesus who is transcendent mind, utterly divine mind, who is the source and the being underlying all hierarchy, all sanctification, all the workings of God, who is the ultimate in divine power.[48]

Alan of Lille likewise points out that the Trinity itself is a hierarchy upon whom the angelic hierarchy is secondary and dependent:

> The celestial hierarchy is the dominion of the celestial spirits who, balanced in equilibrium, are secondary in likeness only to the most sublime hierarchy. This hierarchy has grade, sustains differentiation, and admits of comparison. Members of this celestial hierarchy are distinguished from, yet related to the highest Trinity in three ways: (1) by adoption, (2) by participation, and (3) by the supreme worthiness by which they are fit to their tasks. This second hierarchy proceeds from the first supercelestial hier-archy, it never recedes from the first, it is under obedience to the first, and it looks back[49] constantly upon the first.[50]

Yet humanity, through the perfecting work of Christ and the Spirit, can participate in and imitate the missions of the angels. And within the angelic hierarchy there are many activities, many modes of contemplating the divine truth, many missions, many ways of seeing, and many paths into God.

Angels and Spiritual Paths[51]

> But then with the help of angels, yet the soul seeth more.
> —Walter Hilton, *Scale of Perfection*, ii. 46

Alan of Lille defines theophany as a path to the divine or a vision of God. He adds that "many, however, are the paths or forms of seeing God." For the writers of this volume, the angels as divine theophanies help illuminate these many ways and paths of seeing. As such, the angelic hierarchy represents a comprehensive developmental map of spiritual consciousness. Individual orders within the angelic hierarchy represent varied and unique paths into God, modes of being, one might say, in that each in its unique way illuminates something of God's divine nature. Each order represents a mode of divine proximity. At the same time, each manifests a particular teaching, a particular form of guidance or spiritual assistance, a particular beauty and power that serve to purify one's individual path while drawing one ever nearer to God. The angels in this sense are accommodations to our human nature flowing out from the abundance of divine love. All have eyes to see, yet all "see" differently.

Still, in the Christian tradition of angelic spirituality, Christ is the primary guide, the way, and the goal. As the writers in this volume make clear, the mission/function of the angels is one of assistance and accommodation in the work of Christ and the Holy Spirit. For the salvation of creation, Christ became human, not angelic.[52] Theologically, the role of the angels is most apparent in the process of sanctification. It is in this process of sanctification that the ministries of the angels represent pluralistic variety enfolded in the unifying work of Christ. And perhaps most important, it is in this process that the angels perform their manifold

25

missions, not so that humanity might worship them, but so that all creation might worship God—Father, Son, and Holy Spirit.

With innumerable examples of the use of angels as models of mystical consciousness and spiritual paths, a natural place to begin is with the seminal work of Dionysius the Areopagite. Dionysius described the distinctive attributes of each of the nine angelic orders. His focus was thus primarily on the angels as theophanies or illuminations of divine attributes, not explicitly on the ministry of each angel or on the corresponding human spiritual path the angel personified. Later practitioners would make this more explicit connection between the angels as divine theophanies and angels as exemplars of human ministries. The following chart outlines Dionysius's depiction of angelic attributes:

Dionysius the Areopagite, *Celestial Hierarchy*

Angelic Order	Attribute[53]
Seraphim	perennial circling around divinity; penetrating warmth
Cherubim	power to know and see divinity
Thrones	forever in divine presence
Dominions	disinclined to tyrannical dissimilarities; benevolent rule; free lifting up
Powers	courage in divine activity
Authorities	lift up lower ranks into divinity
Principalities	manifest transcendent principles to all orders, angelic and human
Archangels	interpreters of divine enlightenments
Angels	revelation to the world

In the sixth century Gregory the Great used the angelic orders, their names, and their attributes to describe various types of ministry, both angelic and human. Using the angels as a referent, he outlined the wide variety of gifts, tasks, calls, and responses according to which a ministry might take shape. A given ministry was sketched both with regard to its spiritual path or active component and with regard to its mode of contemplation. Thus, a given angelic order represented a particular ministerial vocation mapped out in the context of an integrated active and contemplative life. The angels, for Gregory, represent the perfection of this integration. They contemplate God unceasingly, yet they are "active" in their ministry to humanity. But as Gregory makes clear, the spiritual paths of a given angelic order are also the modes of awareness by which a particular portion of humanity responds to God's call. Thus some men and women will reflect the contemplative and active gifts of, say, the order of the Thrones, while others will be called to respond and reflect the ministry of, say, the order of the Archangels. Though our modes of contemplation and active spiritual paths might shift from time to time during our lives, at any given time we can identify the charism of one angelic group or another reflected upon and acting within us.

As can be seen from the following chart, Gregory the Great starts from the "lowest" angelic order working his way "upward" to the angels "closest" to God. This indicates that he is primarily concerned not with the descent of divine attributes through the angelic hierarchies (as was Dionysius, for instance), but with the effect the angels have on the ascent of the human soul. Of particular interest also are the angelic Thrones, who, sitting in the divine presence, have a twofold mode of contemplation: first, to contemplate and dwell in that presence itself; and second, out of that dwelling in God's presence to contemplate discernment. The Cherubim teach the contemplation of knowledge. In doing so they dwell in "immediate proximity to God." The spiritual path of the Cherubim is centered in the mind, pursuing wisdom and understanding. The ninth and final angelic level, that of those "united to God," according to Gregory, are the Seraphim, whose mode of contemplation is pure love and whose spiritual path is the contemplative desire for God alone. Of these Seraphim Gregory says, "They love, they burn, they rest in love."[54]

Gregory the Great, *Homilies on the Gospels* 34

Order	Ministry/Mode of Contemplation	Ministry/Spiritual Path
Angels	comfort to humanity; announce messages	give the little they have to others
Archangels[55]	comfort; announce important messages	announce secrets of heaven (prophets/visionaries)
Virtues	signs and wonders	do miracles and work signs

Powers	power, courage, perseverance	cast out evil spirits by prayers and power
Principalities	preside over good spirits	virtuous rulers
Dominions	bring all ministries to completion	purity; ordered desires without vice
Thrones	discernment; sit in divine presence	contemplative discernment of good and evil
Cherubim	knowledge (immediate proximity)	filled with love of God and neighbor (full knowledge of law=charity)
Seraphim	love (united to God)	contemplative desire for God alone

One work that is not represented in this volume but which added its own nuance and insight into spiritual paths in angelic mysticism is *The Soul's Journey into God* by thirteenth-century Franciscan saint, Bonaventure.[56] In this work the angelic hierarchy is interiorized and becomes the template or model for what Bonaventure calls the "hierarchic soul." The overall effect is of a developmental process of spiritual growth within the human person that parallels the ascent within the angelic hierarchy to God. Though in Bonaventure, Christ is the "supreme hierarch," the angels as a whole provide a comprehensive map or method that reflects Christ and categorizes the spiritual paths by which we contemplate divinity "in our minds, where God dwells through the gifts of the most abundant charity."[57] The "maps" provided by Bonaventure can be outlined as follows:

Bonaventure, *The Soul's Journey into God*, 4.4

Angelic Order[58]	Soul Marked by:	Spiritual Path
Angels	announcing	assisting in the Angels as piety
Archangels	declaring	revealing in the Archangels as light
Virtues	leading	acting in the Virtues as strength
Powers	ordering	guarding in the Powers as salvation
Principalities	strengthening	ruling in the Principalities as principle
Dominions	commanding	reigning in the Dominions as majesty

Thrones	receiving	seated in the Thrones as equity
Cherubim	revealing	knowing in the Cherubim as truth
Seraphim	anointing	loving in the Seraphim as charity

Another example of the angels used as a developmental map of spiritual consciousness is drawn from Alan of Lille's twelfth-century *Treatise on the Angelic Hierarchy*. The following chart, distilled from the *Treatise*, shows the orders of angels, their gifts, attributes, spiritual paths, and correlative human orders.

**Alan of Lille, *Treatise on the Celestial Hierarchy*
On the Angelic Theophanies**[59]

Epiphany[60]	Gifts[61]	Attributes
Seraphim	love	fiery, mobile, keen sighted delicate, illuminated/ing
Cherubim	knowledge	most full of knowledge of divinity
Thrones	discernment	examine celestial/earthly justice

Uperphany		
Dominions	reverence, awe	govern lesser spirits
Principalities	teachings of spiritual practices	rule lower orders spiritual practice of justice
Powers	guarding against evil forces	deter demons from practicing evil guard against temptations

Upophany		
Virtues	knowledge of and participation in God	bring miracles into being
Archangels	knowledge of and participation in God	receive, reveal, display highest celestial secrets, messengers of mystery
Angels	knowledge of and participation in God	announce lesser things

Order	Spiritual Path	Correlative Human Order
Seraphim	allure humanity into burning, divine love	contemplatives; give themselves in all things to God
Cherubim	lead humanity into understanding of divinity	*magistri in sacra pagine*; teachers, masters of holy scripture

29

Thrones	seats of discernment; bring justice	those summoned to the task of discerning good and evil; discretion of spirits; just judges
Dominions	show humanity the nature of humility	rational rulers and citizens
Principalities	summon humanity to leadership as a spiritual practice	those who govern with justice; spiritual teachers
Powers	teach the practice and forms of spirituality	those who defend the good against evil and instruct others in resisting evil
Virtues	bring miracles into world for humanity	healers; miracle workers; those with spiritual gifts
Archangels	reveal celestial and divine mysteries	prophets with pure intentions
Angels	assist humanity in diverse hardships; revelation	those with welfare of humanity foremost in their hearts

Also of importance is what Alan of Lille calls the *exordo*, which comprises those orders or groups of spiritual beings working against the angelic beings to darken the way of humans. These are the fallen angels. The *exordo* represents Lille's awareness of the real power in the world of negative or evil spiritual forces and their radical conflict with positive spiritual beings waged on the battle ground of the human soul. Psychologically, the *exordo* also signifies the shadow or dark side of human nature and its internal conflicts. Alan of Lille describes the *exordo* and their attributes as follows:

Exordo	Attributes of *Exordo*
Antiseraphim	shut humanity off from love of God and neighbor; love of world
Anticherubim	shut humanity off from knowledge of God; seek the judgment of a given age over the Wisdom of God
Antithrones	seduce humanity to fall away from balanced judgment; cause some to prefer tyrants
Antidominions	lure humanity into irrational governance
Antiprincipalities	suggest tyranny as the proper exercise of power
Antipowers	offer evil to humanity; resist the Powers
Antivirtues	tricks and illusions to ridicule humanity
Antiarchangels	shape false doctrines of God; false prophecy
Antiangels	oppose the welfare of others; suggest false things concerning God

Another powerful example of this tradition is from the thirteenth-century Victorine, Thomas Gallus. In his *Prologue* to the *Commentary on the Song of Songs*, Gallus assimilated and modified the Latin tradition that interprets the celestial hierarchy as representative of various divine theophanies and devotional paths. Gallus's modifications use the celestial hierarchy as an analogue to the human soul.[62] Thus, for example, the first hierarchy of the human soul corresponds to the first angelic hierarchy, that of the order of Angels. In this first angelic order, according to Gallus, knowledge and love are held together in a kind of reciprocal balance. This simple balance is the angel; the angels speak to this balance; their simple speech simply announces.

According to Gallus's teaching, other interiorized angelic hierarchies assist the soul in apprehending those divine illuminations that aid the soul in fleeing from evil and establishing a hunger for the good. These are the principalities of the soul. The powers of the soul assist growth in holiness by not only teaching discernment of good and evil, but by acting as agents in helping men and women actually choose good over evil. Having determined the correct course of action and having chosen the good, the angelic virtues of the soul assist in carrying that action through to its end with a resolute will. Gallus continues to draw a complete map of the human soul based on the various interiorized qualities of power, beauty, wisdom, and goodness drawn from the nine angelic orders. Gallus also uses the nine angelic orders to illustrate the relation of divine grace and human response. The powers of human nature and responses are represented by the first three angelic hierarchies. The power for ministry unleashed by the integration of nature and grace is represented by the second three angelic hierarchies. Lastly, the soul represented by the Thrones, Cherubim, and Seraphim is made totally receptive to every mode and manner of the divine visitations of grace and thereby absorbed in a longing wholly devoted to God.

As a final example of a map of spiritual consciousness based on the angelic orders, the anonymous twelfth-century text entitled *On the Six Wings of the Cherubim*[63] describes the soul's "flight" into the illumination of love. Using the structure of the wings and feathers of the Seraphim as a metaphor for the path of the life of faith and the soul's journey into God, this author describes a path through the heart, body, and mind into love of neighbor and love of God. Such flight is supported on the strong wings and delicate feathers of the angelic Seraphim, whereby the soul hovers in both the active and contemplative life. In the following outline of *On the Six Wings of the Cherubim*, the human soul flies by means of the first two wings, which together form compunction or affective devotion, then by means of the two wings representing purification of body and mind, and finally by means of two wings representing love of neighbor and love of God. Thus the teaching in this treatise is grounded in an anthropology of body, mind, and heart, an ethic of forgiveness, perseverance, courtesy, and charity, and a contemplative practice insisting upon the integration of the natural and material world, one's neighbor, one's soul, the celestial spirits, and God.

On the Six Wings of the Cherubim (Anonymous)

First Wing: Self-Knowledge Through Confession

First Feather:	Truth
Second Feather:	Integrity
	place, time, mode, number, persons, aspects of sin revealed
Third Feather:	Endurance
	drives out shame, fear, contempt, despair, presumption, perversity, ignorance, forgetfulness, negligence, compulsion
Fourth Feather:	Humility
	a mind, tongue, face of humility
Fifth Feather:	Simplicity

Second Wing:	Satisfaction[64]
First Feather:	Turning from evil
	from vanity (love of self), injustice (love of world), malice (hatred), irreverence (loss of love of God)
Second Feather:	An effusion of tears
Third Feather:	Bathing and drying the wounds of sin
Fourth Feather:	Bestowing of alms
Fifth Feather:	Prayerful devotion

GENERAL INTRODUCTION

Third Wing: Purification of Body

First Feather:	A virtuous eye
Second Feather:	Purity of hearing
Third Feather:	A scent of modesty
Fourth Feather:	Temperate taste
Fifth Feather:	A holy touch

Fourth Wing: Purity of Mind

First Feather: Sincere and upright disposition of mind
                right and sincere desire

Second Feather: Delight of the mind in the Lord
                creates and forms contemplation

Third Feather: Thinking that is ordered and elegant
                pure conception of place; discerning
                conception of time

Fourth Feather: A holy will
                pure mind and good will; a contemplation of peace
                through angelic guidance

Fifth Feather: Simple and pure intention
                contemplative reflection through which the soul acts;
                through the eye of charity all acts become good

Fifth Wing: Love of Neighbor

First Feather: Do no injury by word or deed (this is the first
                motion of love)
                forms the virtue of innocence

Second Feather: Do good in every word and deed (this is to
                breathe the living flame of love)
                elevates and perfects compassion

Third Feather: By courtesy, not to be used up in good works
                (this is a friend of love)
                develops the virtue of charity

Fourth Feather: Laying aside the soul for another (this boils
                up the fever of love)
                illuminates the virtue of self-abandonment

Fifth Feather: To persevere in the love of neighbor (this is
                the virtue of love)
                perfects the virtue of perseverance

Sixth Wing: Love of God

First Feather:	Longing and striving after nothing but God
	this is the motion of this love
Second Feather:	Fecund distribution of the love of God
	this is the charity of this love
Third Feather:	To relinquish all things to God
	this is the act of this love
Fourth Feather:	Complete abandonment to the will of God
	this is the boiling passion of this love
Fifth Feather:	Perseverance in all these things
	this is the unceasing nature of this love

Clearly, that shared participation between the visible and material beings of creation and the invisible and immaterial beings of creation is a mutually enhancing one. Sharing in the process of sanctification, humanity and the angels join together in the evolution of growth in spiritual consciousness. For, on the one hand, as Gregory the Great so clearly states, humans are called to share in angelic ministries:

> Clearly, there are ways of human life that coincide with single orders of angelic bands. By means of a correspondence in virtue, these people are counted worthy of the heavenly city by sharing in the angelic nature....Lead yourself home into your inner most self, that is, into the core of your being. Examine the merits of your inner secrets and inmost understanding. Look inside yourself and see if what you are doing now is good,...see if you are among the number of those bands of spirits [angels]; see if you find your vocation among them.[65]

Yet, on the other hand, as Hugh of St. Victor teaches, the angels are themselves able to "stand" in the presence of God only to the extent that they fulfill their mission to guide and assist humanity: "Thus the seraphim themselves rise when they set us upright, they walk when they help us to make progress, and they stand when they transfix us in holy understanding."[66]

The manifold paths of the angels call us to ever-expanding modalities of divine encounter in self, world, and neighbor, and to an ever-expanding appreciation of the holiness of God. As we listen, witness, and participate in the angelic illuminations and ministries, we begin to realize the full range of God's manifestations, God's ways of being, and the theophanies of God's presence.

Angels as Light

It is not in our power to see, but in God's to appear.
—Augustine, *On Seeing God*

In the tradition of angelic spirituality, the angels *are* light. They participate in the light of the Father, enlightening the world, and through our participation in the angels as light we are, as Thomas Gallus describes it, "taken up to unity by contemplating the simple ray of the Father Himself."[67]

Much of the medieval association of angels with light is based on the work of Dionysius the Areopagite and his interpreters, especially Eriugena.[68] Light, for these writers, in addition to being a name of God,[69] illuminates the perceptible symbols (sometimes called "sacred veils") by which we may be drawn to God. Such perceptible symbols, according to Dionysius, are divinely appointed appearances of beauty that serve as signs of divine, invisible loveliness.[70] Light for these writers is also an image of the archetype of the good, and thus, strictly speaking in the Christian tradition, an image of God. Light plays a role in the capacity of both beauty and the good to draw us toward God; as an image of the good, light illuminates symbols or images that become, to our eyes, images of beauty. In turn, this essentially cataphatic stream of angelic spirituality draws humanity into God by means of the beauty of the images that light illumines. The angels, as light, are thus both the good and perfect gifts from the Father of Lights (Jas 1:17) and the lights that draw humanity back into the Father of Lights.

Gregory the Great expresses the relation between God, the angels as light, and beauty in this way:

> That angel which was first established is spoken of by the prophet, *You were the seal of likeness, full of wisdom and perfected in beauty; you were among the delights of God's paradise....* The prophet

quickly adds: *Every secret stone was your secret covering: carnelian, topaz, and jasper, chrysolite, onyx and beryl, sapphire, carbuncle, and emerald.* Behold, he mentioned the names of nine stones, since there are nine perfect orders of angels. This same first angel was made visible, adorned and covered with the nine kinds of stones.[71]

The angel, as light, is an image of God, expressed "in greater likeness in this first angel than in humanity," as Gregory adds. As such, angels serve as both a symbol of God and as an object of contemplation that, through the beauty of their various forms (represented in this case by the nine stones), draw us back into God, the Father of Lights. In Gregory, the beauty of the nine precious stones is what makes the angel *visible*.

Of course there is also within the Christian apophatic tradition the acknowledgment that a vision of the face of God, a vision of incomprehensible light, is so brilliant that it ends in overwhelming blindness, in darkness. The angels in this sense reflect or veil the divine ray, effectively concealing the face of God. Yet at the same time they also serve to accommodate the overwhelming brilliance of the divine light to our human natures. Jesus, the light of the Father, is, in a similar sense, accommodated to our nature in the incarnation. Likewise, the angels are "incarnated" in their various forms of beauty, thereby "toning down" the blast of divine, immaterial light. God as light is thus beheld in the protective accommodation of the beauty of the angel.[72]

Though there are many strong apophatic features of angelic spirituality as represented in the writings in this volume, the tradition of the angels as light is clearly intended to address the perceptible, cataphatic, and anagogic quality of heavenly beings. In depicting this quality of angels, Dionysius notes:

God modeled [our hierarchy] on the hierarchies of heaven, and clothed these immaterial hierarchies in numerous material figures and forms so that, in a way appropriate to our nature, we might be uplifted from these most venerable images to interpretations and assimilation which are simple and inexpressible...any thinking person realizes that the appearances of beauty are signs of an invisible loveliness. The beautiful odors which strike the senses are representations of a conceptual diffusion. Material lights are images of the outpouring of an immaterial gift of light.[73]

Here the material lights and the immaterial gift of lights are akin to the energy and essence distinction in Gregory Palamas and the Eastern Church. Though the angels themselves continually see the face of the Father (cf. Matt 18:10), for men and women the uncreated light blinds created vision. Not only would uncreated light blind, as scripture says, but also no one who looks full into the light from God will live.[74] But the angels, in a sense, ensure against this kind of blindness; the angels are veils, accommodated to our nature. They are the immaterial *gift*, the good and perfect *gift* of creaturely accommodation and divine vision.

All commentaries on Dionysius's *Celestial Hierarchy* begin with the verse from James, "every good and perfect gift coming down from the Father of Lights" (Jas 1:17). To understand how angels were thought to function both as gifts of the Father and as deifying objects of contemplation, it is helpful to look again at Dionysius on the subject of the angels as light. First of all, it is clear that Jesus alone is the true light of the Father:

> Let us, then, call upon Jesus, the Light of the Father, the "true light enlightening every man coming into the world," "through whom we have obtained access" to the Father, the light which is the source of all light.[75]

This very light, by means of perceptible symbols, "makes known to us the most blessed hierarchies among the angels."[76] As Thomas Gallus says, commenting on this passage:

> And the universal light proceeding from the Father himself admits not only celestial minds to communicate knowledge and participation of itself, but also advances to us through the distribution of goodness. Again, [this is] as if the unifying virtue so fills us with itself that it arouses those who are separated from the depths to a knowledge and desire for the light itself.[77]

The eternal light is also made visible to us through the mediating gift of scripture, which itself "illuminates." Hugh of St. Victor, for instance, teaches that "[scripture] is the light, by way of the various figures of symbols, through which that most blessed and immaterial hierarchy of angels is manifested to us."[78]

Reflecting his reworking of Neo-Platonic sources, which taught the procession *(exitus)* and return *(reditus)* of all being from the "One," Dionysius also teaches that angels and angelic souls proceed from the source of the good (a primary name of God), manifest the good, and reflect the light from the good back to the good. Of the angels themselves, Dionysius says:

> Their longing for the Good makes them what they are and confers on them their well-being. Shaped by what they yearn for, they exemplify goodness and, as the Law of God requires of them, they share with those below them good gifts which have come their way.[79]

"Shaped" by what they yearn for, the angels yearn for the Father of Lights, in turn sharing this gift of light with humanity. Dionysius adds, "The angelic messengers of the divine source reflect the light glowing in the inner sanctuary." Likewise, those human souls who "strive toward angelic life"[80] are shaped by what they yearn for, and in turn illuminate those around them while reflecting that light back to the Father.

Receiving every good and perfect gift from the Father of Lights, the angels are conformed to and participate fully in light. The angels in contemplation, and by implication our own contemplation of the angels, are, as Eriugena says, "filled with the abundance of the...most divine light." Eriugena goes so far as to say that the three "Persons" of the Trinity itself are a "three-fold luminosity," or,

> three heavenly lights illuminating in three ways: this light shines in the Father by whom all things are, this light shines through the Word through whom all things are made, this light shines in the Gift by whom all things are blessed.[81]

Shaped by what they yearn for, in immediate proximity to the One God in three lights, the angels are themselves light. Clothed by scripture in symbols accommodated to our nature, the angels radiate the "divine ray" in a visible form of beauty that we can "see" and live. The various manifestations of that light, the manifold forms of seeing God, are the angelic theophanies themselves.

Angels as Theophanies

> Every visible and invisible creature can be called a theophany,
> that is, a divine apparition or a self-manifestation of God.
> —Eriugena, *Periphyseon*

The theme of angels as theophanies of God assisting in the spiritual formation of the soul is closely related to the theme of the angels as light. But whereas the theme of the angels as light focuses on the goal of the spiritual journey, that is, the uncreated light of the Father of Lights and Jesus as the Light of the Father, the theme of angelic theophanies focuses on the many possible maps of the journey itself. That is, as with the theme of the angels as spiritual paths, each angel is a revelation or theophany of a particular "voice" of God. By listening to and discerning the true voice of God, one begins to follow one's own God-given path to holiness.

Of course, a theophany is not technically a voice but rather a vision of God. The word is derived from *theo*, which means "God," and *phania* or *phany*, which can be variously translated as "light," "vision," "apparition," or "manifestation." The word applied to angels is based on the fact that the angels themselves are "light" and represent various ways of "seeing" God. Thus angels as theophanies represent an appearance of God, a "God-light," a way of seeing divinity, a divine revelation. Humans require revelation in the form of theophanies accommodated to our vision. The angels, however, as Alan of Lille says:

> Look upon God not according to these theophanies but according to the simple, unmixed theophany, because the all-encompassing light of God is simple. The angels themselves contemplate God through themselves without mediation, without image.[82]

39

Unlike the angels, revelation to men and women requires the image provided by a theophany. Alan of Lille goes on to define theophany, by which we might see something of the nature of God, as "a sequence of signs…received by a mind cleansed of images…[leading to] an appearance of God."[83] Thus, for Alan of Lille, a theophany is a series of symbols descending from God, the uncreated symbol, much as the good and perfect gifts descend from the Father of uncreated light. But, for Alan, the mind that receives the theophany or revelation must itself be cleansed of images or symbols. Alan implies here that something of a purifying nature must take place in the mind before the heart is prepared for a vision of God. The angels first cleanse the mind; second, they illuminate the mind by becoming themselves the "sequence of signs"; and third, they draw the soul into a "vision" of God. The angels as theophanies are therefore a model of the classic three-stage progression of the mystical life: purgation, illumination, and union. Union, in this case, is described in terms of vision. Dionysius the Areopagite, in fact, first introduced this classic formulation of purgation, illumination, and union in the context of his discussion of the function of angels and hierarchies in the *Celestial Hierarchy*.[84]

The angels then, each in its particular way and through its particular charism, serve to wash the soul in light, illuminate the soul with the messages of heaven, and draw the soul into a unifying vision of God. As mentioned in the section on the angels and spiritual paths, the angelic theophanies illuminate a variety of ways of seeing God. These range from love, knowledge, discernment, compassionate governance, formation in virtue, to examination of conscience, meditation, and charity. Umiltà of Faenza, for instance, provides an example of angelic theophany that illuminates, in particular, the *wisdom* of God:

> One [of Umiltà's personal angels] comes from that order of angels who are given to Christians as guardians in this life. I know this for certain, I learned it through having heard their [angelic] speech. Her appearance is of overwhelming beauty, like a precious stone or a pearl of great value. And I love her before all others that remain as her companions. She is called

the angel Sapiel, a name that reason reveals as meaning divine wisdom.[85]

Most of the themes in angelic spirituality are related in some way to this theme of the angels as theophanies of God. Several themes in particular should be mentioned in conjunction with theophany.

i. Apophatic and Cataphatic Method

Apophatic (or negative method) and cataphatic (or positive method) are both at the core of angelic spirituality, providing two separate but interdependent models of how the angels are related to the world. Simply defined, the apophatic way stresses the dissimilarity between God and creature. As a theological position, the apophatic way emphasizes that the all-transcendent God is ineffable, incomprehensible, and wholly other. As a mode of speaking about God, the apophatic way denies to God every imperfection found in created things; thus there is no speaking of divinity, no name that fully identifies it, no complete knowledge of it. As a mode of contemplative ascent to God, the apophatic way tells the seeker to "Leave behind...everything perceived and understood, everything perceptible and understandable...and strive upward as much as you can toward union with him who is beyond all being and knowledge."[86] The cataphatic way stresses the continuity between God and creature and the possibility of divine revelation in the word of scripture and the Word of Christ. As a theological position, the cataphatic way recognizes that God can be known (if not *what* God is, at least *that* God is) by the light of natural reason, by means of created things, and that God does reveal the divine self in accommodation to our nature. As a mode of speaking about God, the cataphatic way states that God must possess every true perfection found in creatures, yet creatures do not possess the perfection of God. Dionysius's primary treatise on cataphatic method is *The Divine Names*, in which he insists that God is manifest in the world and is "therefore known in all things."[87] As a mode of contemplative ascent, cataphatic theology contends that the triune God can be found in all created things as

41

shadows, echoes, pictures, vestiges, representations, or footprints. It cannot be overemphasized that the apophatic way is inextricably linked to the cataphatic way. The ineffable God *has* spoken God's word and Word.[88] That is, the transcendent God is also radically immanent; the invisible God was seen "face to face" by Moses and Jacob (Gen 32:30; Exod 33:11).

The angels, as no other created beings, represent this inextricable link between the transcendent and the immanent nature of God. Insofar as they are light, as we have mentioned, they are the cataphatic path. Thomas Gallus says of the Seraphim:

> From this order a flood of divine light, cascading through the correct sequencing of orders, flows in succession through all the angelic orders.[89]

The Seraphim, and all the angels receiving the flood of divine light, represent cataphatic ways of knowing by which God illuminates the human soul. They are modes of revelation and ways of speaking positively about the triune nature of God, whose footprints cover the created world. In contemplation, the angels assist humanity to "uncover" the face of God in the mundane. That is, they teach and lead the human soul into the light of divine presence that reaches from the smallest stone to the chance encounter, from the birds of the sky to the fish of the sea, from the innocent child to the daily routine, from an act of charity to an imaginative act of creation. As cataphatic light they help illuminate the "good" of God's creation; they are revelations, showings of divine immanence.

Yet at the same time, angelic spirituality is a spirituality of God's transcendence. The angels represent paths into divine darkness. This is an encounter with God not in the sense of darkness as evil but in the sense of dark knowledge of God as unknowing, as the cloud in which God is hid in ineffability and incomprehensibility. For Richard of St. Victor, for instance, it is the Cherubim that lead the soul into the "secret places of divine incomprehensibility."[90] Often orders of angels represent "ecstasy of mind" or "alienation of mind," indicating that path into God that is beyond reason, beyond speech, beyond any means of human understanding. Thus Thomas Gallus writes:

> But the knowing that is beyond intellect, this wisdom of the heart is the servant of the throne of God. This is the secret and hidden wisdom of which the Apostle spoke to the mature at Corinth.[91]

Gallus goes on to describe the angelic Thrones as that order "receptive to the highest divine visitations by ecstasy of mind." He also teaches that the Cherubim represent that point at which divine transcendence is "understood" as beyond the grasp of human reason. "In this order," he says, "the intellect, although it has been thus drawn upward into its completion, does not pass beyond its capacities. Rather, understanding here reaches the consummation of its knowledge and light."[92] Thus the Cherubim, and beyond them the Seraphim, represent forms of mystical consciousness that reach beyond the borders of reason and language, beyond the revelations of light, beyond the aid of symbol and metaphor. These forms of mystical consciousness lead, in some instances, through the Seraphim into love, and, in other instances, beyond the Cherubim into incomprehensible emptiness. Within both traditions of angelic spirituality, however, the path of the angels leads into the Trinity: the Trinity as love in the case of the Seraphim, the Trinity as incomprehensibility in the case of the Cherubim.[93] Finally, each of the angelic orders, in fact, does "speak" in its own way of the attributes and names of God, yet at the same time each reveals the "silence" of the unspeakable nature of God.

The angels are indeed light, but they are just as clearly gates into the darkness of God, into that God beyond mind, understanding, and reason. In this sense the wisdom of angelic spirituality is that the angels as divine theophanies reveal at the same time that they conceal. This revealing/concealing power of light is expressed clearly in the Jewish Kabbalah:

> When powerful light is concealed and clothed in a garment, it is revealed. Though concealed, the light is actually revealed, for were it not concealed, it could not be revealed. This is like

wishing to gaze at the dazzling sun. Its dazzle conceals it, for you cannot look at its overwhelming brilliance. Yet when you conceal it—looking at it through screens—you can see and not be harmed. So it is with emanation: by concealing and clothing itself, it reveals itself.[94]

In the clothing of the angels we are made simultaneously aware of all that is concealed in their revealing.

ii. Like and Unlike Symbols

One of the primary contributions of Dionysius the Areopagite's *Celestial Hierarchy* is his use of angels and angelic contemplation to discuss symbols and how symbols lead the soul anagogically into God. For Dionysius, some symbols have similarity to what they symbolize. For example, some symbols from scripture depicting God are similar to what God truly is: God as love, being, or goodness, for example. Other symbols for God in scripture, drawn from the material world, seem ridiculous. Dionysius gives examples, including God as a man of war, a passionate lover, jealous, deceitful, or arrayed in tasteless jewelry.[95] Perhaps surprisingly, Dionysius insists that unlike symbols are more appropriate to God initially because they make concrete a fundamental principle about God's transcendence: God infinitely transcends anything we can say about God. In a tangle of apparent opposites, Dionysius describes his method, correlating symbols of similar and dissimilar quality to God as follows: one begins through a process of affirmations descending through similar symbols of increasing incongruity; one then one moves into the process of negations ascending through dissimilar symbols of decreasing incongruity.[96] This complex web is in fact a simple method for affirming what is like God and denying what is unlike God. The place of the angels in this web is as symbols of beings who are at once like God (spiritual, blessed, invisible, transcendent beings) and also unlike God (created, derivative, contingent beings).

Within this relation between similar and dissimilar, there is an obvious correlation between similar symbols, affirmations, and the cataphatic way, on the one hand, and between dissimilar symbols, denials, and the apophatic way, on the other. In fact, similar symbols are the way in which contemplation through the cataphatic way is activated; dissimilar symbols activate the apophatic way. Dionysius discusses symbolic theology in the context of angels, precisely because of the dissimilarity between the descriptive symbols in scripture of angels and what is in fact their true nature. For instance, the angels are described in scripture as "wheels," "chariots," "thrones," and so on. This is obviously not an adequate symbol for any angel. This dissimilarity of symbol, according to Dionysius, "goads" us into moving even beyond angels in our attempt to appropriate a "true" symbolic representation of God.

Dissimilar images thus have their primary value in uplifting the contemplative beyond the material and mundane world and into the invisible things of the world of the spirit. As one writer has pointed out, the anagogic value of dissimilar symbols becomes apparent precisely as they trouble, stir, shock, and goad:

> The dissimilar images [of angels]...their failure is a stimulant for the spirit which prevents it from becoming sluggish or hypnotized by figures through which the natural enchantment might perhaps otherwise jeopardize one's motion toward God.[97]

In angelic spirituality of the medieval period, angels are thus symbols of contemplation conformed to our understanding and at the same time are themselves beings who contemplate the hidden divine nature. On the basis of the symbolic theology of the period, intellectual and sensible symbols were the starting points of this contemplative ascent, leading by means of the contemplation of divine theophanies or angels, into the contemplative vision of God. John Scotus Eriugena explains:

> Both kinds of symbols, intellectual and sensible, are contemplated by this hidden, yet discerning understanding. Sensible symbols are contemplated in the understanding of the celestial beings. These symbols of the senses would include the sacraments of the old law, for example, the tabernacle and all those

things which the Lord commands to be done in it. Also the visions of the prophets...and ecclesiastical mysteries of the new testament. The holy angels clearly discern the innermost light of all these things.

And then, there are intellectual symbols. These do not come naturally to mind for us unless we speak of intellectual symbols as theophanies, in which one encounters an appearance of truth invisible in itself *(per se)*, now, however, in a manner unknown to us as intellectual symbols. They lack the likeness of any material thing.[98]

Thus, through the "spiritual senses," humans can contemplate sensible symbols and thereby come to a spiritual consciousness of divine things conformed to our understanding. Intellectual symbols lead into mystical consciousness of truth itself. They allow comprehension of "every invisible thing" and are in fact both the angelic theophanies *and* the symbols by which the angels contemplate the "incomprehensible." Eriugena continues:

> And so, in theophanies themselves, that is, in the divine manifestations they contemplate with the eye of understanding, the angels gaze upon the most intimate recesses of divine understanding, just as many things are given to us to know by means of sensible symbols, so that we too are invited to comprehend certain hidden mysteries of God.[99]

The best sustained discussion of symbols in this volume can be found in Hugh of St. Victor's *Commentary on the Celestial Hierarchy*.[100] In Hugh's work the symbolic nature of angels plays a role in spiritual formation and functions in the discipline of anagogic contemplation. Discussing the wisdom of the Christian, Hugh makes a distinction between symbols of nature (roughly equivalent to similar symbols) and the symbols of grace (roughly equivalent to dissimilar symbols). By doing so, as the introduction to Hugh's work points out, the Victorine is able to link the work of Christ to the angels. The angels, through the symbols of grace in the "humility" of their various missions on earth, reflect and imitate the humility of Christ. As symbols of various anagogical paths into God, they also parallel and reflect the victory of Christ's humility.

iii. The Visible and the Invisible

The theme of the invisible *vs.* the visible nature of angels has been discussed at some length above. It is, however, inextricably bound with the theme of angelic theophanies as well. Theophany, after all, is fundamentally a "visible" manifestation of God. Yet angels are just as fundamentally "invisible," as is God in God's transcendent nature. We are thus again confronted with the paradox inherent in angelic theophany: the invisible God is visibly manifested by means of invisible angelic natures. The paradox is implicit in all dialectical mysticism that attempts to approach the heart of the mystery of God. The paradox of this mystery is expressed in various ways. These include the mysteries of God's unity (oneness) and diversity (threeness), Christ's incarnation as God in human form, God's immanence and transcendence, God's initiative in grace and our response in faith, our knowledge of God as both light and dark, contemplative wisdom as both full and empty, God's presence as being at both the center and the circumference of our consciousness. There are many more such expressions of divine mystery and the paradox of our understanding. The angels participate in these "coincidences of opposites," through which they reveal (or conceal) something of the nature of God as well. They represent the apophatic and cataphatic ways, like and unlike symbols, the visible and the invisible worlds. Angels are thus symbols of revelation in concealment. As such, they are in the perfect "position" to mediate the visible and the invisible without collapsing their very real difference. Gregory the Great, for instance, teaches that angelic beauty, name, and ministry render the invisible angel visible (they are made visible from the "top down," as it were). Hugh of St. Victor, on the other hand, teaches that the angels demonstrate the invisible mysteries of God clothed in the visible symbols they manifest (from the "bottom up," as it were).[101] In either case, the angels as theophanic symbols serve as a kind of crossroads between humanity and God, mediating divine mystery to human nature.

Angelic wisdom and formation understand that the "impossible possibility" of visibility in invisibility, for instance, is grounded

47

in the mystery of God. As it is precisely in God's unific simplicity that the trinitarian diversity of Persons springs and has its root,[102] so it is likewise precisely in the visible through which the invisible is first encountered. Richard of St. Victor uses the image of "hovering" to describe this paradoxical aspect of angelic ministry and contemplation. As do birds, he notes, angels, and by their example humans, can "hover," still in their motion, contemplating the various manifestations of God's incomprehensible wisdom.[103] Still in their motion, the invisible angels become visible by means of the ministry of their message.

It is not surprising then, that within the theme of angelic theophany, this dialectic of opposites, coinciding as they do even in the very inner trinitarian life of God, should arise again and again. The angels as a symbol of the coincidence of divine opposites hover in each paradox and provide a particularly useful method of approach into the divine mystery.

Angelic Knowledge, Angelic Love

Those who have merited the abundance of knowledge
and the abundance of riches of the understanding of God
can be taken for the Cherubim,
because the Cherubim themselves are translated as "fullness
of knowledge."
—Origen, *Homilies on Numbers*

The Seraphim burn with incomparable love.
—Gregory the Great, *Homily 34*

One of the primary themes within Christian spirituality, mysticism, and spiritual formation in general is that of the relation of knowledge and love.[104] This theme, also expressed in terms of the relation between mind and heart, or between intellect and affect, is at the core of Christian angelic spirituality. Almost from its inception, the spiritual tradition of devotion to angels has used the Cherubim and Seraphim to illuminate this relation: the Cherubim, whose name in Hebrew means "fullness of knowledge," have represented the path of knowledge, mind, or intellect, while the Seraphim, whose name means "burning" or "fiery," have been interpreted as representing the path of love, heart, or affect.[105]

Nearly all of the writers in this volume assume this distinction between the Seraphim as love and the Cherubim as mind. It is such a strong assumption, in fact, that from at least the twelfth century any discussion describing love as fiery, burning, penetrating, or warm ought to be considered in the light of the tradition of the Seraphim, even if no explicit mention is made of angels. Likewise, debates on the primacy of mind in the ascent to God can be understood most fully in the context of the Cherubim as a symbol of the fullest powers of the mind.

Just a few of the many possible examples of the use of Seraphim and Cherubim will help to situate this discussion. In Gregory the Great we find:

> Cherubim means "fullness of knowledge." These most sublime bands of spirits are rightfully called Cherubim because they are so full of the most perfect knowledge that they contemplate the glory of God from the vantage point of immediate proximity. According to the ways of created beings, the Cherubim know all things fully as they draw near, through the merit of their worthiness, to the vision of their Creator. Those bands of holy spirits called Seraphim who, because of a singular attraction to their Creator, burn with an incomparable love. Thus Seraphim are called "burning or incandescent." The Seraphim, since they have been so united to God that no other spirit may intervene between them and God, burn all the more fiercely as they see God more intimately. Their love is truly a flame, since the more acutely they look upon the glory of God's divinity, the more savagely they burst into flame with God's love.[106]

Similarly, Alan of Lille describes Seraphim and Cherubim as follows:

> Seraphim are the supereminent ones of the society of celestial spirits. They are fiery, mobile, keen sighted, discriminating, delicate, illuminated by an unmediated fountain of lights....Thus this order is most elegantly called Seraphim, which means burning, because they glow with great love for the divine....The

49

> Cherubim is that angelic order, along with the first seraphic order, most in accord with fullness of knowledge....Therefore those angels which, after the first order, are filled most with knowledge and have been allotted an office of ministry which leads men and women into knowledge of God are those spirits comprising the order of Cherubim.[107]

Though it is not mentioned explicitly, this same distinction between the Cherubim as knowledge and the Seraphim as love is apparent in Section Two of *On the Six Wings of the Cherubim*.[108] This work is structured on the basis of the six wings of the seraphim of Isaiah 6, and it is a penitential manual explicitly on the supremacy of love. Wings five and six are respectively "love of neighbor" and "love of God."

In other visionaries, mystics, and spiritual writers throughout the medieval period and beyond, the Cherubim and Seraphim are symbols or guides into the mind and heart. Thus Hildegard of Bingen, the twelfth-century Benedictine, wrote:

> Therefore, those in the first of those other armies seem to be full of eyes and wings, and in each eye appears a mirror and in each mirror a human form, and they raise their wings to the celestial height. These are the Cherubim, who signify knowledge of God, by which they see the mysteries of the celestial secrets and fulfil their desires according to God's will....And those in the second army burn like fire, and have many wings, in which they show as if in a mirror all the church ranks arrayed in order. Those are the Seraphim, and this means that they burn for love of God and have the greatest desire to contemplate Him.[109]

For Hadewijch, a thirteenth-century Flemish Beguine, the face of the Seraphim, put simply, reveals love:

> And that Countenance [of the Six-Winged Seraphim] disclosed itself wholly with everything that was; and Love sat there adorned.[110]

Richard of St. Victor, a twelfth-century Victorine, on the other hand, uses the Cherubim as a means to speak of the uses of reason or mind in the context of contemplation. For Richard, the angelic Cherubim are useful in exploring the relation of contemplation according to reason and contemplation "beyond" reason. The Cherubim can "fly" into the latter form of contemplation, but only with the aid of grace:

> The last two kinds of contemplation are expressed by an angelic figure....And perhaps not without cause did this last angelic figure receive the name "cherubim"; perhaps for the reason that without the addition of this highest grace no one would be able to attain to fullness of knowledge. But one of the two cherubim was said to stand on one side and the other on the other side....Consider, I ask you, how aptly they are set over against each other and are placed in opposition, the former of which seem to agree with reason, the latter to go against reason.[111]

As a final example Bonaventure, a thirteenth-century Franciscan, used the Seraphim as a structuring symbol to organize his seminal treatise, *The Soul's Journey into God.* Drawing on Francis of Assisi's earlier mandelic vision of the Seraphim as love with six fiery wings at the center of which hung the crucified Christ,[112] Bonaventure organized his first six chapters by means of the six wings of the Seraphim. Bonaventure writes that the first two wings symbolize contemplation of God's vestiges in the natural world, the second two wings the contemplation of God's image in the human soul, and the third two wings represent respectively, contemplation of divine unity as being and contemplation of the blessed Trinity as the good. As a function of intellect, these final two modes of contemplation for Bonaventure are in fact represented by Cherubim:

> By this Cherubim we understand the two modes or stages of contemplating the invisible and eternal things of God: one is concerned with the essential attributes of God and the other with those proper to the Persons.[113]

But finally, just as it was for Francis, Bonaventure's journey leads the soul ultimately into a seventh stage, where rest is given to the

51

intellect (the way of the Cherubim), and where, through ecstasy of mind, our affection (the way of the Seraphim), passes over entirely into God. Thus Bonaventure's path of the soul is a journey through intellect into love centered in God.

The relative value or significance of the heart and the mind has been debated throughout Christian history. For some writers in certain periods, the mind is the highest and best route into God; for others, love is the form of consciousness that brings one closest to God. Yet others balance the relation of mind and heart, seeing both as equally important in the soul's ascent into God. Every conceivable permutation of relation between the intellect and the heart has also been explored. The writers in this volume show a wide range of preferences and relations. Bonaventure's seventh chapter, in which the soul passes through intellect into affect, illustrates the importance that Cherubim and Seraphim play in Christian spirituality, yet it also illustrates the *tendency* within the angelic tradition to assign priority to the path of the heart. Put simply, based on their relative position within the celestial hierarchy, the Seraphim are "closer" to God than the Cherubim. Love is therefore often assigned a position closer to the heart of God than is knowledge. Both are important and necessary paths to God, but as Alan of Lille says, the Seraphim are preeminent:

> This description suggests a threefold aspect to the ministry of Seraphim, Cherubim, and Thrones: a triple gift, a triple power, and from these conditions a triple clothing—love, knowledge, and discernment. Among these orders of angels, the Seraphim have preeminence....Now, because after love the most worthy and fruitful thing is knowledge, it is necessary to take up that order which, after the Seraphim, has the fullest comprehension of divinity [i.e., the Cherubim].[114]

The preeminence of the Seraphim is expressed in many ways. From Gregory the Great we hear, concerning the Seraphim, that "no other spirit may intervene between them and God." Though the order of the angels, as depicted by writers on angelic hierarchy, is varied, the position of the Seraphim is fixed: as love, they are the highest order, the order closest to God. Scripture also supports the preeminence of the way of love. Paul says in Romans, "Charity (love) is the fullness of the law" (13:10), and in 1 Corinthians, "If I have the gift of prophecy and can fathom all mysteries and all knowledge, and if I have a faith that can move mountains, but have not love, I am nothing" (13:2) and "Now these three remain: faith, hope, and love. But the greatest of these is love" (13:13).

Surely, without love, "I am nothing," and just as surely, in angelic spirituality, the Seraphim exemplify formation in the path of burning love for God and neighbor. However, the complexities of the relation between love and knowledge are intricate and difficult to sort out. Indeed, the greatest is love, but the three-legged foundation of faith, hope, and love, without the legs of either faith or hope, collapses just as quickly as it does without the leg of love. This sacred first principle of faith, hope, and love resembles the angelic hierarchy, which requires each of the angelic forms of consciousness in order to function as a whole. For love to be full it must contain knowledge, discernment, power, discretion, justice, humility and so on through the hierarchies. The angelic hierarchy functions in a way similar to that of the sacred principle of faith, hope, and love. It lifts up the Seraphim into the very center of God's presence, there to see without image and in light. But such vision is only possible in the simultaneous presence of all the other angels and their various gifts to love.

Just how the gifts of love and knowledge intermingle is explored in intricate detail by Thomas Gallus in his *Prologue* to the *Commentary on the Song of Songs*. In the *Prologue* Gallus interiorizes the angelic hierarchy in the human person. Such an interiorization forms what might be called an "angelic anthropology" within the hierarchized soul. This angelic anthropology is developmental in that the human soul moves through the various "Angels of the soul," arriving finally to the "Cherubim of the soul," and the "Seraphim of the soul." Each developmental or spiritual stage contains all of the previous even as it moves into the next "higher" stage. As in Gallus's *Extract*, in the *Prologue* love is the driving force of the soul's journey into God; love is thus the way, the guide, and the goal.[115] Yet the goal in this journey is obtained only by first incorporating, then surpassing mind. This is accomplished by means of "wisdom of the Christian descending from the Father of Lights" (Jas 1:17). It is the wisdom of the heart, the wisdom of divine love distributed by God.[116] Gallus utilizes the angelic orders, as the various "lights" from the "Father of Lights" to teach the subtle movement of the soul from intellect to knowledge and finally to the full wisdom of the Christian, which is love. For Gallus, the soul begins to move "beyond" mind when it reaches the seventh order of the Thrones, which are "through ecstasy of mind, totally receptive to the highest divine visitations." That is, the Thrones receive divine illuminations from "the hidden places of the mind."[117] With the eighth order of the Cherubim, the intellect is drawn up by God to the apex of its abilities; it can go no further than a simple surface contact with God, where it has been drawn "all the way to the final point at which the weakened intellect passes away."[118] But the ninth order of the Seraphim contains the source of all longing for God. Only at the level of the Seraphim does the soul reach "the burnings of brilliant radiance and shining of fiery ardor…only the highest love can unite the soul to God."[119]

Thomas Gallus's fascinating explanation of the relation between love and knowledge, though complex, is typical of explanations throughout angelic spirituality. Love, represented by the Seraphim in closest and most immediate proximity to God, is "higher" than knowledge, represented by the Cherubim. But love must pass through the insight of knowledge and intellect, as it must through all the developmental stages represented by the angels of the soul. The mystical consciousness of the Seraphim as love carries with it all the previous levels of spiritual insight as it moves in love to God.

Imitation of Angels

But clearly thus far our Cherubim do not have wings,
or if they have, they have not yet stretched them out.
Perhaps we have not yet completed that angelic form
in its full integrity according to the meaning of the Lord.
—Richard of St. Victor, *The Mystical Ark*

Can we imitate the angels? How and to what degree does our imitation draw us into God? To what degree does our imitation of angels affect our spiritual formation in this life? Ought we to speak of deification through angelic imitation? These and other critical issues cluster around the general theme of the imitation of angels. It is quite clear that writers in angelic spirituality believe that there is an important link between human and angelic existence and ministry. Gregory the Great's unequivocal statement, for instance, that "clearly there are ways of human life that coincide with single orders of angelic bands" is one example of this link. Bernard of Clairvaux points out that our imitation of angels as guides and teachers is established by God as an implication and promise of creation and of eschatological hope:

> And so then it is in God that we can love his angels affectionately, as our future fellow heirs, in the meantime established by the Father and set before us as guides and teachers.[120]

The link between human and angelic ministry as it is accomplished in the providence and will of God is elaborated even more explicitly in Alan of Lille. For Alan, the "imitation of angels" can mean either our imitation of angels or the angels' imitation of God. Alan of Lille plays on this ambiguity when he teaches that angelic instruction leads men and women not only into imitation of angels but into imitation of God:

> Also all angels are spirits of divine administration and in all of their duties they dwell contemplatively in God.[121]…Humanity, meditating upon the goodness of divine governance, is instructed by angelic nature so that God might be imitated in God's self and so that humanity might receive the highest image and superexcellent likeness. That is, humanity becomes the image and likeness of the highest superexcellent God.[122]

Angelic spirituality establishes a core relation between all of the angelic functions and ministries and our imitation of them. Angelic guardianship, for instance, and our own spiritual formation based on the guidance of angels, are both bonded closely to the imitation of angels. This core relationship is, according to writers in this volume, established by God for the fulfillment of the divine will and promises. It is directed ultimately toward a life of virtue and happiness in this world and an eschatological life of fulfillment and goodness in the heavenly court of the world to come.

Angels themselves are able to be "made like God" (that is, deified) through their communication and cooperation with the good reflected in God's habits and acts. The consensus of writers on angelic spirituality is that, in imitating the angels, men and women, to the degree that they are able, become themselves "like God." The family of issues related to the imitation of angels thus explore the degree, manner, and process of this human "God-likeness" or deification.

i. Angels and Divine Presence

The angels provide a means of exploring the agency and nature of divine presence. Related to the issue of divine presence is the important question of mediation in mystical consciousness. One of the best, current definitions of mysticism defines mysticism partially in terms of this quality of mediation:

> The mystical element in Christianity is that part of its belief and practices that concerns the preparation for, the consciousness of, and reaction to what can be described as the immediate or direct presence of God.[123]

The question of mediation is based upon the distinction between created beings and their Creator. That is, in mystical consciousness of the presence of God, what is the relation between the human creature and God? Do creatures experience God mediated *through*, for instance, language, culture, bodies, minds, communities, symbols, imagination, or expectations? Or is there an unmediated consciousness of God unfiltered by any of these categories? The first set of questions reflects contemporary contextualist positions, which emphasize cultural particularity. The second reflects contemporary models of "pure consciousness." Together with those aspects of the angelic tradition that tend to emphasize synthetic, symbolic, imagistic, and participatory forms of knowing, these questions reflect potential ways of experiencing and expressing mystical consciousness. The questions are as much at the forefront of spirituality, philosophy, and theology today as they were during the time of the writers represented in this volume.[124] In fact, one of the primary issues addressed within the theme of angelic imitation is this question of mediation. Different orders of angels within the angelic hierarchy, their different "ways" of seeing and dwelling in the divine light, typify the range of mediated and unmediated encounters with the presence of God.

Though a full expression of mystical consciousness is expressed in the nine orders of angels, the Seraphim and Cherubim are especially helpful in distilling the nature of divine presence to its essential terms. The Seraphim, as the path or mystical experience of love, generally exemplify the possibility of direct, pure, simultaneous, and immediate relation with God. The "relation" could be spoken of metaphorically as a touch, or vision, or absorption, or contact with God, but with the Seraphim the divine presence is somehow simultaneous with their burning love.[125] The Cherubim, as the path or mystical experience of intellect, generally exemplify one form (though probably the most pure form) of mediated consciousness. The path of intellect or mind usually represents a form of symbolic representation that requires categories of mediation such as language, culture, or images. Thus with the Cherubim or intellect, language or symbolic images generally "mediate" the experience of God's presence.

The writers in angelic spirituality thus found a ready means for teaching the agency and nature of divine participation. On the unmediated relation of the Seraphim with God, Alan of Lille says, for instance:

> The Seraphim are illuminated in an unmediated way because God illuminates nothing of God's own essence by mediation. The Seraphim are irradiated by God's brilliance, receiving God's radiance with immediate understanding. On the other hand, the Seraphim are said to illuminate the center orders by mediation because they in turn illuminate God by means of mediated revelation.[126]

57

For Alan, the direct essence of God warrants no mediation. In the literature of angelic spirituality, the seraphic attributes of burning, fire, and light are particularly useful for depicting this immediate participation in divine essence. Gregory the Great notes:

> Those bands of holy spirits are called Seraphim who, because of a singular attraction to their Creator, burn with an incomparable love. Thus Seraphim are called "burning or incandescent." The Seraphim, since they have been so united to God that no other spirit may intervene between them and God, burn all the more fiercely as they see God more intimately. Their love is truly a flame, since the more they look upon the glory of God's divinity, the more savagely they burst into flame with God's love.[127]

The Seraphim actually burn brighter as they glow with the more brilliant flame that is God. Gregory teaches that the Cherubim, on the other hand, are "so full of the most perfect knowledge that they contemplate the glory of God from the vantage point of immediate proximity." The difference here between being "united…so that no other spirit may intervene" and "immediate proximity" is a difference defined by the metaphor of space. Spatially, no creature intervenes between the Seraphim and God. The Cherubim are in immediate proximity, but they are only near, in what we might call a "proximate" relation with God.[128]

The relation between unmediated and mediated consciousness and between love and knowledge and how these two themes are exemplified in the love of the Seraphim and the knowledge of the Cherubim is of great importance. If the angel's ministry is our ministry, as the writers in this volume firmly believed, then the nature of our love and knowledge affects the way we experience God. Thus for instance, the explication by Thomas Gallus on the relation of knowledge and love as exemplified by the "angels of the soul" is also a discussion on the nature, medium, and manner of God's presence to us. For Gallus, each angelic path into mystical consciousness is also a path that reflects relative proximity to God, a theophany within which God's essence is clothed for our "perception." Gallus's Cherubim of the soul balance intellect and affect

58

perfectly, and intellect is perfected in this balance and comes into contact with God. Still, the Cherubim can go no higher than "touch"; that is, a contact with God mediated by the metaphor of perception, which is itself a metaphor implying that the body "mediates" the divine contact. As Gallus says, at the level of the Cherubim, the "intellect does not have the natural strength to ascend on its own....The weakened intellect passes away," and not having the capacity to reach beyond touch, "understanding here reaches the consummation of its knowledge and light."[129] Only with the Seraphim, the path of burning love, is the soul able both to experience the fullest encounter with God and "live." Only with the Seraphim is the soul able simultaneously to be drawn into an unmediated presence of God, where it "lovingly embraces God and is wrapped in the loving embrace of the Bridegroom."[130]

Whether a given writer expresses the angelic contemplation of God in terms of mediated or unmediated union, the implication in all of angelic spirituality is that, through imitation of the angels, human beings can share in that same divine union. A salutary word, however, comes from Augustine. We may imitate the angels, but we do not worship them. We may imitate the angels, but they themselves do not mediate between God and humanity. That is a work solely of the man Jesus Christ, and so our worship is of Christ and our imitation of angels is in the larger context of the imitation of Jesus:

> It thus became necessary that the Mediator between ourselves and God have both a transient mortality and a permanent blessedness....This is why it is not possible for even good angels to mediate between the misery of this mortal life and the blessedness of immortality.[131]

ii. Deification and Mystical Union

The nature and language of mystical union continue the preceding discussion on mediation. Both are presented in the context of angelic imitation. Whether the angelic nature (or the human person in imitation of angels) enjoys a "pure consciousness" of the presence of God is also a question of deification. Deification, or *theosis* as it is called in the Eastern Church, concerns the "God-likeness" of men and women and means literally "to be made a God." Cognate concepts in these writings on angelic spirituality include words that imply being "formed" or "conformed" to God. The idea of these latter concepts is that spiritual formation conforms the human person ultimately to the "form" of God, making the person finally *deiform*. Threads within the Christian tradition variously place the emphasis in deification on God, the community, or the human person. Thus in some strands the dominant note is placed squarely on the divine nature, so that conformity to God is truly to be made "Godlike." In others the primary element is found within the relations making up the community of God, wherein deiformity is to be found in love and participation with the neighbor. In still others human anthropology is the dominant thread, so that divinization is to a large extent "humanization" or the actualization of the human spirit. How these various threads are emphasized, how they are interrelated, and how they interact with various images from the natural world, from communities, from scripture, and from liturgy help to determine the particular language by which union with God is described. Angels, again, assist spiritual writers in clarifying and in sorting out the many threads and delicate relationships that influence how one "sees" or is "formed" to God.

Umiltà of Faenza names one of her personal guardian angels Emmanuel, which means "God with us," to indicate an immediate and intimate relationship with God. The angel has a "clear spark" that "divine love inflamed," by which Umiltà describes a union of identity between the angel and God based on images of light and fire. As near as is possible to God, Emmanuel likewise brings Umiltà into God, where together they "remain in the imperial courts of the highest heaven, contemplating the nobility of divine beauty."[132] Bernard of Clairvaux uses images of intimacy, spatial continuity, and familial closeness to describe deifying union with God when he says of the angels that they are

> those blessed spirits, those most intimately bound together with God, those most closely continuous and united to God, those true members of the household of God.[133]

Thomas Gallus finds a direct link between imitation of angels and union or deification when he teaches that all hierarchies are "conformed to God" and that "by manifesting the celestial hierarchy to us," we "are made co-workers with God by being made Godlike."[134] Eriugena also connects imitation of the angels to deification to a life of virtue and the formation of divine habits *(habitus)*. The Thrones, Cherubim, and Seraphim, for Eriugena, all share in "God's work." They cooperate with God in the "administration and foundational support" of all beings beneath them. And it is precisely through formation in the divine will, through "communion and cooperation with the Good reflected in God's habits and acts," that they are deified or "made like God." Eriugena says finally that "in imitation of the habits of God, [as exemplified by the angels], virtue becomes the habit of the rational, discerning soul."[135] Such habits of virtue are made available to men and women in imitation of angels. The careful reader of these texts on angelic spirituality will find imaginative and abundant examples of the deiforming qualities of angels and how their ministries speak in compelling and diverse terms of union with God.

iii. Angelization

One helpful way of speaking of imitation of angels and the many expressions of mystical union they exemplify is *angelization*.[136] The term does not imply dissociation from what is human, but rather it is meant to imply an integrative relation between the free gift of divine grace and human agency. *Angelization* is thus a word that expresses that median point between humanity and divinity that, requiring them both to dwell as they are, is nonetheless a new creature of their joint creation. Richard of St. Victor describes what is meant by angelization as that process by which "the human soul transforms itself into the symbolic expression of heavenly and winged beings and transfigures itself into their image."[137] Though potentially a misunderstood term, *angelization* is nonetheless appropriate for describing the ongoing process of purification, reformation, and restoration of the human soul through angelic imitation. It is, in short, a form of sanctification. Angelization includes both human actualization and deification; it includes both the created world and the soul as well as more glorious flights into the manifestations of God's wisdom. As a process, it is a journey, a transformation of consciousness, a path through a life of virtue and ongoing spiritual formation. And finally, angelization as contemplative and active imitation of angels represents the "immediate consciousness of the presence of God." It is, as Bernard of Clairvaux implied, an embrace of the Bridegroom, fellowship in the house of God, dwelling at the center of life in joy with God.

Angelic Contemplation, Angelic Action

Their angels always see the face of my father.
—Matthew 18:10

There is perhaps no greater lesson to be learned from angelic spirituality than that the contemplation of God benefits others. Writing on contemplation, Raimundo Panikkar has pointed out the universal nature of this link between contemplation and worldly well-being:

> To look at the birds of the sky is to see them flying. One is reminded of those verses of Acarya Atisa, the great Buddhist sage of the Mahayana tradition, saying that a bird with folded wings cannot fly up into the sky just as a man who has not unfolded primordial wisdom cannot contribute to the well-being of the world. To look at the birds is to fly with them. To contemplate is this undivided holistic activity.[138]

In this "undivided holistic activity" of contemplation, the angels see the face of the Father. Modern thinking tends to separate contemplation and action, pure theory from applied practice, the peace of the heart from the activity of the intellect. But that is not the ancient wisdom of contemplation as undivided and holistic. We moderns, as Panikkar continues, "have divided contemplation into theory and practice." The ancient wisdom is alive in the writers of this volume; for them the active ministry of the angels is an expression of angelic contemplation.

The tradition that insisted on this interdependence of moral action and theoretical consideration is an old one.[139] In this ancient conception *theoria* (contemplation) is not purely theoretical in the modern sense of the word. Formerly, those who dedicated themselves to *theoria* chose a *bios*, a way of life that is the best realization of those capacities that are essential to being human. This *bios theoretikos*, the life of contemplation, was not only a process of gazing upon God, but was a way of life dedicated to the well-being of the world. The guiding hand in the life of *theoria* involved a practical or active component, referred to as the *praktikos*. *Praktikos*, in turn, characterized the life lived according to the precepts of *theoria*. For the medieval writers on angelic spirituality, the life of contemplation was indeed a life formed in spiritual practices and the ethics of charity. The ideal of integration between contemplation and action, in which the practice of contemplation includes *praktikos* and the exercise of action includes *theoria*—this ideal is always difficult to achieve. But the angels provide exemplars and guides into the possibility of its realization. They represent a variety of contemplative forms, objects of meditation, spiritual exercises, and modes of *praxis* or action.

Gregory the Great, perhaps our most consistent and imaginative writer on the imperative dialectic of action and contemplation, is explicit in connecting the ministry of the angels with their contemplation of God. He says of the angels, that "when they come among us to implement their exterior ministry, they are nonetheless never absent interiorly through contemplation." Although the angelic spirits are limited, as Gregory says, the highest spirit, God, is not circumscribed. Thus, "the angels God has sent are still before God since they operate in God's presence."[140] Bernard of Clairvaux links the relation of contemplation and action to angelic ascent and descent. The angels ascend through the influence of the Son of Man, they descend (or more properly condescend) on our account:

> In this way those blessed spirits ascend by means of the contemplation of God. And so they ascend through compassion for you, so that they may preserve you in all their ways. They

ascend to God's face, they descend at God's pleasure, *For he has given his angels charge over you.* However, in descending they are not cheated of God's glorious vision, because *They always behold the face of the Father.*[141]

Alan of Lille links angelic contemplation and action when he says that "all angels are spirits of divine administration and in all of their duties they dwell contemplatively in God." At the same time he links angelic activity to human ministry and contemplation: "Humanity, meditating upon the goodness of divine governance, is instructed by angelic nature so that God might be imitated in God's self."[142]

The link established by these writers between contemplation and active ministry is strong and unbreakable. It should come as no surprise, then, that in the context of a devotion to the ministry or *praxis* of angels, one can find instruction on the nature and methods of contemplation on almost every page of these writings as well. The "spiritual paths" represented by the nine angelic orders within the celestial hierarchy are not only "paths" of ministry, they are "paths" or "modes" of contemplation. The angels and men and women in imitation of angels, as Bernard taught, "ascend and descend" along both of these paths. Thus the path of love is a way of ethical compassion as much as it is a way of contemplation of God as love. The path of the intellect is a therapeutic way of healing and discovery as much as it is a way of contemplating the mind of God. And the path of discernment is as much a way of assessing, judging, and choosing the good as it is a way of contemplating the justice and mercy of God.

There are many other possible descriptions of the formative and unitive quality of life of contemplation one could draw on from this volume. Augustine, for instance, focuses on the quality of silence in contemplation and on the angelic use of dogma or doctrine as an object of contemplation:

> Now certainly, those angels learn about God not through noisy, spoken words, but by being themselves in the presence of unchangeable truth. That is, in the presence of the only-begotten Word. And they know this Word himself, and the Father and the Holy Spirit. And they contemplate and know

64

this to be the indivisible Trinity, and that within it the three persons are of a singular, unified substance without, however, being three gods but one God. They know those things better than we understand ourselves.[143]

John Scotus Eriugena gives an almost ecstatic description of angelic contemplation, grounded in light as the primary angelic and trinitarian essence. He tells us that angelic contemplation is "filled with the abundance of the highest of all immaterial knowledge, one could say the most divine light." Eriugena goes on to say:

> By means of contemplation these celestial beings have full, supermundane knowledge of the light which surpasses every light; by contemplation they have knowledge of the source of beauty which forms all things....By the fullness of its contemplation, this hierarchy of celestial essences is said to be superemanating beyond all others.[144]

Alan of Lille's discussion of contemplation echoes the theme of the levels of mediation in one's experience of God. Of the angels he says, "They themselves contemplate God through themselves without mediation, without image." Drawing on Romans 1:20, on the other hand, he teaches that in contemplation men and women "comprehend the invisible things of God by a likeness through those things which have been made."[145] These teachings represent the application of angelic wisdom to contemplation of God. If they are not always explicit in linking a practical application to each contemplative encounter, the underlying assumption concerning the nature of *theoria* would insist that they are indeed linked.

And many writers, in fact, are explicit about that connection. Richard of St. Victor's twelfth-century treatise, *The Mystical Ark*, for instance, teaches mystical prayer through six levels of contemplation. The final two levels of contemplation focus on the Cherubim, leading through the intellect to an ecstatic encounter with the Trinity. But since, as Richard says, his treatise is a tropological interpretation of the Cherubim, it is clear that he is concerned with the ethical and active components of contemplation as well.[146] Thomas Gallus, as we have seen, uses the full angelic hierarchy to demonstrate nine levels within the human soul that activate both an active ministerial and a contemplative aspect. For instance, Gallus's first level of the soul, the Angels, practices the ministry of bringing good news to the poor, which flows from a contemplative exercise of balancing knowledge and love for neighbor without judging either with regard to propriety or impropriety. Gallus moves through the nine orders to the Seraphim, which on both the active and contemplative levels "contain the source of all longing sighs for God."[147]

And finally, Umiltà of Faenza manages, in a beautiful image, to unite contemplation and motherly action in the person of Christ. Through meditation and contemplation she seeks to behold Jesus, and in doing so implies that she, as Mary, will give birth to compassion through action modeled in Jesus. She says:

> O holy angels of God and all Archangels, O Emmanuel and Sapiel, who are my angels, I pray to you, most sweet ones, that from all your powers you might assist me to picture the Virgin's chamber before my eyes so that I might be able to contemplate our holy Mother and her glorious Son and from her lap receive her child into my arms.[148]

Umiltà's sermon leads us into two final themes in angelic spirituality: the relation between the angels and Christ and, as symbolized here by mother and infant, the issue of the primacy of community in the life of a Christian.

Angels and Christ

I tell you the truth,
you shall see heaven open,
and the angels of God ascending and descending
on the Son of Man.
—John 1:51

The history of the relation of Christ and the angels in Christian theology and spirituality has been a fluid one. Some early angel-Christologies celebrated Christ's angelic qualities, and in fact clearly claimed that Christ himself *was* an angel. Later angelic spiritualities equated imitation of angelic qualities and ministries with imitation of Christ. All of these forms of angelic devotion explored the variety of ways in which angels shared in Christ's life and ministry. Expressions of angelic mysticism arose in the context of the *imitatio Christi*, establishing at times a profound link between Christ and the angels. The link, for instance, between Christ's work in his passion and the Seraphim was particularly strong, while at other times an equally clear link was maintained between the resurrected Christ and the full wisdom of the Cherubim. These manifestations of the relation between Christ and the angels were woven in innumerable patterns and variations throughout the period represented in this volume and beyond. However, what is consistent throughout the history of Christian angelic spirituality is that while the angels may in some sense point or redirect our attention to Christ, it is Christ alone who is the fulfillment and summation of angelic reality. Whether in the work of justification, salvation, sanctification, or consummation, whether in the practice of charity or the life of contemplation, whether in scripture or in liturgy, whether in physics, music, mathematics, or rhetoric, whether in earth, water, fire, or heaven, Christ alone is the center of angelic knowledge. Augustine highlights this imperative in the context of life in both the heavenly and earthly city:

> Therefore, when he chose to be in the form of a servant, and lower than the angels, so that he might be our mediator, Christ nonetheless remained higher than the angels in the form of God. He was at one and the same time the way of life on earth and life itself in heaven.[149]

Still, drawing once more from Alan of Lille, there are many forms and ways of seeing God. Thus angelic spirituality has continued to imagine the angels as participants with Christ in accommodating us to the truth that is God. The following comments will explore some of the various expressions of the relation between Christ and the angels outlined above. As with all of the themes in angelic spirituality, these expressions are not continuous or uninterrupted within the tradition, but they do represent a coherent pattern of devotion and spirituality.

Early in the history of christological formulations, Jesus Christ was considered to be an angel, if not by nature, at least by function.[150] In fact he was often called the Angel of Great Counsel or envisioned as one of the Seraphim or one of the wings of the seraphim in the vision of Isaiah 6.[151] In this tradition the angel of Isaiah 6 was considered to be a messianic title. Christ was therefore equated with the angels, and as an "angel" his ministry was associated with the titles of messenger and teacher. Thus, by extension, the Old Testament theophanies were, almost without exception, "seen to be 'Christophanies' because they were all appearances of the Angel of the Lord who was known from Isaiah 6 to be Christ."[152] Though many of the early church fathers referred to Christ as an angel, the old angel-Christology later died away as it was absorbed into new formulations of Nicene orthodoxy.

Still later expressions of angelic spirituality embrace formulations of an intimate relation between the angels and Christ without claiming complete identity. Eriugena, for instance, finds a correspondence between the etymology of the word *cherubim* (fullness of knowledge) and Christ: "By the word *cherubim* is signified not inappropriately the very Word of God Itself." He then generalizes from this correspondence, seeing all the angelic ranks as symbols for the second Person of the Trinity:

> By a kind of wonderful metaphor the Wisdom of God (Christ) is intimated in Holy Scripture by the names of all the heavenly essences.[153]

Richard of St. Victor, in his *Mystical Ark*, also uses the Cherubim to point the contemplative reader in the direction of the wisdom of the Word. In this case, in a tropological exegesis of Exodus 25, Richard describes the Cherubim as sitting atop the ark of the covenant, their wings sheltering the ark, their gaze transfixed on the mercy seat. In an obvious example of an Old Testament theophany reinterpreted as a Christophany, Richard teaches that God's Old Testament presence on the mercy seat, between the two Cherubim, is now a promise of Christ's presence in the heart of the believer. In both cases—upon the ark and within the heart—the Cherubim "shelter" the divine presence.[154]

Elsewhere, the writer/redactor of *On the Six Wings of the Cherubim*, having brought together materials that focus on the love of the Seraphim and their ability to reach from the most mundane into the most secret things of God, instructs the reader that the seraphim of Isaiah 6 is "an exemplar of the total person of Christ." As such, they represent an outline, tracing the person and work of Christ, of the soul's journey into God:

> These Seraphim, beginning from the face then through to the center and all the way to the feet, are like the outline of a path into God according to the visions of the prophets Isaiah and Ezekiel.[155]

In Hugh of St. Victor's *Commentary on the Celestial Hierarchy*, the angels participate with Christ as the light of the Father, while in Eriugena the highest angelic hierarchy is deified by Christ's light, having direct participation in Jesus through that light. Eriugena says:

> The Seraphim, Cherubim, and Thrones are drawing near to Jesus himself in primary participation of the knowledge of His deifying light; they are being fully deified in the illuminations of Jesus Himself. Clearly, no image, no sacrament, no formal likeness of any kind comes between them and Jesus Christ Himself with whom they dwell in divine proximity.[156]

Related to these expressions of angels as partakers in Christ's glorified being is the work of Christian visionaries and mystical writers who reestablished an ontological identity between angels and the earthly ministry of Jesus. This genre of angelic spirituality centered especially on Christ's passion and grew largely out of the new medieval devotion to the humanity of Christ.[157] Perhaps the clearest expression of this spirituality of intense identification with Christ can be found in Saint Francis of Assisi. Through his vision of the six-winged Seraph at Mt. Alverna and Francis's subsequent stigmata, a nearly complete identity was established between Francis the man, the Seraphim as love, and the burning love of Christ crucified.

Drawing on other Victorines such as Richard and Hugh, and on the new mysticism of love exemplified by Bernard of Clairvaux, Thomas Gallus had laid the groundwork for this intense and intimate identification in his *Prologue* to the *Commentary on the Song of Songs*. In the *Prologue*, Gallus, in the context of his teaching on contemplation, internalizes the angelic hierarchy within the human soul. As noted above, each angelic hierarchy thus becomes a developmental stage in contemplation and in humanity's growth in divine consciousness. Christ's own humanity as the practical, not to mention salvific, pattern of this growth in human understanding runs implicitly as a thread throughout Gallus's *Prologue*.

Bonaventure, especially in his *Soul's Journey into God*, utilizes this teaching of Gallus on the internalized angelic hierarchy and combines it with the vision, life, and stigmata of Francis. Bonaventure speaks of Christ as the "supreme Hierarch," who encompassed, integrated, and would finally consummate both the celestial hierarchy and the human person.[158] Thus in this vision of angelic spirituality, the angels of the human soul functioned in the formation of the person, while the love of Jesus Christ crucified functioned as the door and path into God. Francis of Assisi was Bonaventure's primary model for uniting this angelic/Christic path into God with the way of compassion, humility, and poverty. Retracing Francis's steps to the very mountain where he had his vision of "a six-winged Seraph in the form of the Crucified," Bonaventure writes of the relation between Christ and the Seraphim:

> The six wings of the Seraph can rightly be taken to symbolize the six levels of illumination by which, as if by steps or stages, the soul can pass over to peace through ecstatic elevations of Christian wisdom. There is no other path but through the burning love of the Crucified, a love which so transformed Paul into Christ when he *was carried up to the third heaven* (2 Cor 12:2) that he could say: *With Christ I am nailed to the cross. I live, now not I, but Christ lives in me* (Gal 2:20).[159]

For Bonaventure, the cross of Christ is the mirror of salvation. The angels, reflected with Christ in that mirror, offer ever new refractions of our brokenness as well as glimpses of the many paths to peace, which peace is "proclaimed and given to us by our Lord Jesus Christ."[160]

Christ is the summit and final expression of every aspect of the celestial hierarchy. Still, the angels *participate* and are *co-workers* in union with Christ in the economy of salvation and the process of sanctification. They dwell with all the heavenly hosts in the court of heaven, ministering to humanity in different and manifold ways. Every cooperative way, each of the manifold ministries of the angels returns new light to Christ, the light of the Father.

The Angelic Choir

And at the midpoint, with outstretched wings,
I saw more than a thousand Angels jointly making festival,
each one distinct in radiance and in ministry.
—Dante, *Paradise* XXXI

The individual angelic orders also participate in the communal wisdom of angels. Together, the angels comprise a community of diverse participation living always and in all things with God as their center. This God-centered community is the consummation and summation, though not the conclusion, of all the angelic ministries. It is a consummation in that it brings every angelic work, every active and contemplative form, into the fullness of its power. It is a summation in that through the *community* of angels every aspect of angelic spirituality is brought to fruition and actualized. Yet it is not a conclusion. The nature of the angelic community is such that to participate with the choir of angels is to enter an ever-deepening process that forms people and transforms souls. Certainly, there are unique, specific, and personalized journeys into God. But these individual paths of faith are undertaken in the community of faith; they are mutually confirming and mutually celebratory. In this walk of the community of faith, the angelic choirs lead but they do not exhaust, they authenticate but they do not terminate, they consummate but they do not conclude.

71

CONCLUSION: WHY ANGELS NOW?

The visible world is a part of a more spiritual universe
from which it draws its chief significance.
—William James, *The Varieties of Religious Experience*

The angels, as Karl Barth has said, are heaven itself coming to earth with God, invading the world. He adds, "Heaven dawns on earth, and in the beauty, work and witness of angels there lies the basis of the fact that the mystery of God can have a place in the earthly realm."[161] Yet modern men and women have hesitated to speculate on the unseen or even on the mystery of life on earth under God. The bright light of Enlightenment Rationalism, combining with earlier Humanist and Reformation movements, has had a profound effect on contemporary religious awareness.[162] The modern period has tended to emphasize the disjunction between faith and reason, thereby precipitating a process of the devaluation and "resolution" of mystery. There has been a turn to the self; general skepticism concerning the intuitive imagination, the numinous, or the invisible; the victory of positivist optimism in the redemptive possibilities of empiricism, science, and technology; and secular "faith" in mechanistic materialism. The effect of these trends in the lives of modern men and women has been to shut them off not simply from angels but from transcendence in any form, from mystery, and often from their very souls as well.

Yet today, into this modern world that seems no longer habitable in the ordinary way, the wing-beat, the in-breaking mystery, and the provocation of angelic visitation flutter across our vision.[163] Angels today are crossing the great gulfs of doubt and self, hovering on the borders of the seen and the unseen, escorting souls into the secret places of divine incomprehensibility, and announcing the arrival of Easter in ordinary things. Shaped by what we long for, as Dionysius the Areopagite teaches, those who long for and hunger after the face of God are being shaped by the light of angels.

This book seeks to respond both to current spiritual longing and to postmodernist skepticism by retrieving a spiritual tradition whose roots tap deep into the religious consciousness of the Christian

Latin West. In one sense, alluding to David C. Steinmetz, the angels as retrieved from this tradition are a premodern response to a postmodern set of concerns.[164] Angelic spirituality, a mystical consciousness of spiritual formation and transformation, responds to the renewed interest in and need for the transcendent, the unsayable, and the "unseen" world. It responds to our search for fresh languages of virtue, to our thirst for a renaissance of spiritual practice and devotion, and to our intuition that intellect, affect, memory, and imagination are somehow related and mutually enhancing. It responds to laments for the loss of "humanness" and to pleas for new approaches to holiness. To put it simply, angelic spirituality responds to our desires for a more profound and immediate encounter with God. Thus, an examination of angelic spirituality, as grounded in the texts of the Latin West, gives fresh insight into the widespread longing for spiritual sustenance. These texts, however, remind present-day pilgrims that angelic flight is "grounded flight"—it is flight grounded in God's gracious activity. But these texts also remind the modern pilgrim that God and God's ways in the world are marvelously inventive, surprising, and transforming.

Angels help us to experience holiness, transcendence, and power beyond ourselves. They help us to be formed by an ethics of reception, to experience the subtle shifts of light between the seen and the unseen. As a form of mystical consciousness, angelic spirituality is a way of experiencing and describing "consciousness of…the immediate and direct presence of God." The angels are messengers; they are translators of mystical consciousness. They "translate" between God and humanity, between soul and neighbor, between our world and our hopes and dreams and expectations. George Steiner, in his book *Real Presences*, has wisely noted that "the master translator can be defined as a perfect host."[165] As master translators, the angels witness to the concept of courtesy; theirs is the mastery of a message that informs even as it comforts, that forms even as it casts out darkness. Theirs is the perfection of compassion in accommodation of our circumstances. Theirs is a translation of consciousness that brings peace even as it enlightens.

The writers on angelic spirituality in this volume have shown, however, that a concept of courtesy cannot be divorced from concepts of love, concepts of knowledge, or even concepts of materialism, secularism, or empiricism. These writings on contemplation of angels emphasize that the angels function as mediating doorways to the unseen world who have, at the same time, an effect in the real world. As master translators, the angels have one "wing" in the seen and one "wing" in the unseen, one "wing" in science as well as one "wing" in the metaphysical, one "wing" in the mystical and one "wing" in the mundane. As perfect hosts, the angels, in witness to Christ, play servant to men and women who are guests in the entirety of God's good creation.

The message of the angels is a breath of God, an inspiration. The ethic of angels is an axle on the wheel of courtesy, the spokes their many acts, the rim their pageant of prayers. The flight of the angels restores mystery. The song of the angels is the incense of the cosmos, tuned by light and burning with love. The community of the angels is the perfume of friendship. The vision of the angels is of the hem of the gown of God. The ministry of the angels is the work of the Spirit. The fellowship of angels is like a simple meal with Jesus.

Note on Translation: Detailed notes on editions used for translations in this volume are given at the end of the introduction section for each writer. Following the example of many critical editions used for this volume, the names of the various orders within the angelic hierarchy will be capitalized (e.g., Seraphim, Cherubim, Angels). Reference to angels and archangels in a more generic sense will be lower case throughout.

Section One

Augustine of Hippo

De civitate Dei

Selections
from
City of God

Introduction

In *City of God*, Saint Augustine of Hippo (354–430) addresses several issues that would be of repeated interest to later medieval writers on angels.[1] The questions, as Augustine formulated them, and the manner in which they were addressed, came to define the nature of medieval angelic spirituality. These questions included: (1) What is the legitimate role of angels in salvation history, given the mediatory and healing roles of Jesus Christ? (2) How are men and women like and unlike the angels? (3) Are the angels to be imitated rather than invoked, and if imitated, whom and in what manner do the angels wish us to worship? (4) What are the ministries of angels and how do they fulfill God's providence? (5) What does scripture teach us concerning the creation of angels? (6) What is the nature of the angels' vision of God, and, related to this issue, what is the nature of the angels' knowledge and contemplative love of God?

In its entirety, *City of God* is a masterly theological reflection on the history of the world. It is also an inspired analysis of the destiny of humankind according to the objects of one's love. As Augustine explains, "Two loves have built two cities, self-love in contempt of God has built the earthly city; love of God in contempt of oneself has built the heavenly city."[2] The first five books of *City of God* argue against the pagan claim that polytheism accounted for the prosperity of Rome. The next five books argue against the pagan and Neo-Platonic idea that polytheism leads to happiness. The final twelve books shift the perspective to the history of salvation, describing creation, the rise of the two cities and finally eschatology, including death, judgment, heaven and hell.

The following overviews set the stage for selections translated from Augustine's *City of God*. Focusing on the issues raised by Augustine on angelic spirituality, the translated sections present the angels as true citizens of the Heavenly City, who, as exemplars of God-directed love, also participate as companions to the good citizens of the Earthly City.

Book VIII, Chapter 25. In Book VIII Augustine turns to a discussion of natural theology and asks whether worship of the gods is of any aid in securing blessedness in the life to come. After answering that question firmly in the negative, Augustine turns to the similarities and differences between angels and humans and emphasizes, once again, that the angels are not sufficient as mediators between God and humanity. Only Christ, both divine and human, is able to serve as mediator. Though the angels serve in many ways as models of the Christian life, humans are radically dissimilar to them. Still, even though men and women remain on earth and they in heaven, Augustine identifies one important feature all share: faith.

Book IX, Chapter 15. In this chapter Augustine, in conversation with Peripatetic and Stoic philosophers and Platonists including Apuleius and Plotinus, again argues that Christ alone can mediate between God and humanity. Some Greek philosophers had suggested that demons could assist or complete the mediation. Augustine disagrees. He focuses on the *necessity* of the transitory act of humility on the part of the Word that brought Jesus Christ to the "lowly" position of humanity. He acknowledges a debt to the philosophers in their predications concerning God, namely, God's exaltation, eternity, and blessedness. And he likewise concedes their predications about humanity, namely, humanity's lowliness of habitation, mortality, anxiety, and misery. But against the philosophers he argues that in order for lowly, mortal, and anxiety-ridden humanity to be raised to exaltation, eternity, and blessedness, the mediator must partake of lowliness *and* exaltation, mortality *and* immortality, misery *and* blessedness. This Christ alone has done. The good angels, he declares, are not able to mediate humanity's condition; they are themselves exalted, eternal, and blessed, not lowly or miserable. The bad angels are a tantalizingly deceptive alternative. They are so tempting precisely because they have more in common with humanity than do the good angels. The fallen angels, in common with humanity, are miserable, and they are immortal, the latter predicate being, as Augustine notes, potentially very attractive, even enticing. There is a warning here. As the "pagan" philosophers believed, so Augustine believes: the bad angels are dangerous and compelling. But only Christ offers the full road of mediation to God. Augustine is also careful to point out that this mediation leads not to the angels but to the Trinity. The chapter also emphasizes the metaphor of "participation" as the concrete mode of our awareness of God.

Book X, Chapter 7. In this chapter Augustine discusses the Greek concept of *latreia (λατρεία)*, meaning worship, service, religion, piety, and cultus, for which parenthesis can find no Latin equivalent (see *City of God*, X.1). His primary point is that true *latreia* is due to the one true God alone. It cannot be given to the pagan gods or to intermediary gods, including demons or good or bad angels. For Augustine, the Platonists misunderstand the worship of God, veering away from true worship by giving divine honor to the good or bad angels. He is particularly intent on eliminating the practice of theurgy. Theurgy was thought to cleanse the soul, make the gods respond, and finally deify the soul thus uniting it to god through a variety of devotional, cultic, and worship practices (see *City of God*, X.9–11; 26–32). For Augustine, the essence of Christian *latreia* is mercy, and mercy is best reflected in love of God and love of neighbor. "Our good is nothing else than to be united to God," he says, which means to love God with all one's heart, soul, and mind, and our neighbor as ourself (Matt 22:37–40). "This is worship of God, true religion, right piety, and the service due to God" (*City of God*, X.3). It is in this context that the good angels, through the very fact of love, direct one's love towards God, and not toward themselves.

Book X, Chapter 15. Augustine here continues the discussion of the true nature of worship in the context of the angelic ministries. He also points out the similarities and dissimilarities between how we enjoy God and how the angels enjoy God.

Book X, Chapter 25. In this chapter Augustine notes that before the Law it was by faith that the saints of old cleaved to God, but that even the ungodly enjoyed God's carnal and earthly promises. He then looks in detail at Psalm 73 as an example of the temporal rewards of the ungodly and the future rewards and present blessings of the saints. It is by an inward cleansing of the flesh by the heart that one enters the sanctuary of God. But for now, as Psalm 73 continues, the godly are to place their hope in God, so that "they may announce" God's praises. To "announce" is, as we know, what angels do. Thus, as the godly do in fact announce God's praises, they indicate that their attention is captured by the song of the angels themselves. Having captured humanity's attention, the angels wish only that men and women dwell with them, attentive finally not to them, but to their God.

Book XI, Chapter 9. Book XI begins Part Two of the *City of God*. In his first ten books Augustine was concerned to refute the enemies of the city of God. In Part Two he turns to the origin and destiny of the two cities and the separation of the good and bad angels. After laying out his purpose, he treats of the knowledge of God that no one can attain except through the mediator, Jesus Christ. He then speaks of the authority of scripture, the creation, and then in Chapter 9, of the scriptural warrant for the creation of angels. Augustine develops his full doctrine of the creation of angels by assuming that the words *heaven* and *light* in scripture are references to angelic beings.

Book XI, Chapter 29. This final chapter is a meditation on the knowledge the angels have of the uncreated Trinity, God the Father, Son, and Holy Spirit, as well as on the nature of angelic contemplation of the created world. Their knowledge and contemplation revolve solely around the love of God. In this life the two cities are defined by the direction of love. Love directed toward things of this world defines the earthly city; love directed toward

God defines the heavenly city. For Augustine, men and women who compose the City of God will eventually be lifted free and brought to their goal. For the present, those men and women can imitate the knowledge and love of the angels. Then, in the life to come, like the angels, they will find eternal blessedness in the contemplation of God their creator.

Note on Translation: The following selections were translated on the basis of a comparison of two editions of *De civitate Dei:* the first, the Benedictine Edition of the Complete Works of Augustine (Paris, 1679; Venice, 1729; Paris [Migne, ed.], 1841) found in *PL* 41; the second, *Corpus Christianorum*, Series Latina, vols. 47–48 (Turnholt: Brepols, 1955). There are several English translations. Two of the most reliable are *Augustine: The City of God Against the Pagans*, trans. Henry Bettenson, intro. David Knowles (New York: Penguin Books, 1972) and *Saint Augustine: The City of God*, trans. Marcus Dods, intro. Thomas Merton (New York: The Modern Library, 1950).

 Selections
City of God

Book VIII, Chapter 25: *Concerning those things that may be held in common by the Holy Angels and by good men and women.*

Therefore, we have absolutely no need to solicit the beneficence of the gods, or rather the good angels, through the mediation of demons.[3] Rather, we ought to seek God through our similarity to the good angels, specifically through our joint possession of a good will, through which we are united with them, sharing with them our life, our being, and our presence in the worship of the one God, even if we are not able to see the holy angels with the eyes of the flesh. We remain as distant from them in terms of relative physical location, and in merit of life, as we are miserable through our inconstant will, and through frailty and weakness of our character. Indeed, it is not because we dwell on the earth under the condition of life in the flesh that we are not able to join them. Rather, we are prevented from their fellowship because in the impurity of our hearts, we have a mind inclined only toward earthly things.[4] When we become restored to health we become as the angels are. We are brought near them even in the present time by faith, if we believe, by their assistance, that we will be made blessed by the same God through whom they have become blessed.

Book IX, Chapter 15: *Concerning the Mediator between God and humanity, the man Jesus Christ.*

1. But if, as is much more probable and believable, it is argued that all men, however long they are mortal must of necessity be miserable, we ought to seek a Mediator who is not only man but also truly God. In this way, by the intervention of the blessed mortality of this Mediator, men and women can be led out from the deep misery of mortality into blessed immortality. Two things were necessary in mediation: that he become mortal, and that he not remain mortal. Indeed, he did become mortal, not by relinquishing the divinity of the Word to infirmity, but by assuming the infirmity of the flesh. He did not remain mortal in the flesh, but he raised it from the dead; the flesh is the very fruit of his mediation, so that those for whom the Mediator effected redemption might not dwell eternally in the death of the flesh. It thus became necessary that the Mediator between ourselves and God have both a transient mortality and a permanent blessedness so that through what was transient he might be united to mortal humanity and through what is permanent he might transfer humanity from death to what is permanent. This is why it is not possible for even good angels to mediate between the misery of this mortal life and the blessedness of immortality. The good angels are both blessed and immortal; the evil angels, however, have the potential to mediate[5] because they are immortal along with the good angels yet steeped in misery along with us. Opposed to these evil angels is the good Mediator who, in opposition to their immortality and misery, even though he has chosen to become mortal for a time, remains blessed throughout eternity. It is thus, by the humility of his death and the benevolence

82

of his blessedness, that he has destroyed those proud immortals and poisonous wretches, preventing them from seducing[6] mortals to immortal misery by their boasting of perverted immortality. This is ignored by those whose hearts God has cleansed by faith, having freed them from impure domination by these most unclean spirits.

2. What medium can humanity, mortal and pitiful, distant from immortality and blessedness, choose through which it might be coupled with the immortal and the blessed? The immortality of the demons, which might be enticing, is in fact misery; the mortality of Christ, which might offend, exists no more. On that side we should fear eternal misery; on the other, death, which is certainly not something eternal, is no longer to be feared, and blessedness, which is eternal, is to be loved. The immortal and miserable mediators, that is, the evil angels, interpose themselves in the midst of this situation in order to prevent us from crossing over to a happy and blessed immortality, because misery, which impedes such a crossing over, continues to exist in them. But the mortal and blessed Mediator interposed himself in order that, having passed through mortality, he might from mortals make immortals (showing us his power to do so in his own resurrection). We mortals then are raised from misery to that blessed company from whom he had never departed. There is then a wicked mediator who separates friends, and the good Mediator who reconciles enemies. And the wicked mediators who separate friends are numerous, legion. The multitude who are blessed become so only by participation in the unity of God. The miserable multitude of evil angels are deprived of this unity of participation; they separate in order to hinder rather than unite in order to aid in the process of blessedness. And by their very multitude they try in whatever way they can to protest and oppose and prevent us from arriving at that one, blessed good to which we are being led. We are being led not by the efforts of many, but by the work of the one, true Mediator. This mediator, whose participation makes us blessed, is himself the uncreated Word of God through whom all things are made.[7]

He is not Mediator because he is the Word, that most blessed and most immortal Word dwelling the greatest possible distance from the misery of mortals. Rather, he is Mediator because he is human. This humanity of Jesus Christ shows men and women not only true blessedness, but also that, in order to obtain the only good, the true and beatific good, it is not necessary to seek other mediators[8] through whom we believe ourselves to be setting off on the ascent that penetrates into divinity. No, the blessed and beatific God, having become a participant in our humanity, has offered a shorter route[9] to participation in his divinity. For he does not lead us through[10] on a journey to liberation from mortality and misery to the immortal and blessed angels so that we can become immortal and blessed through participation in their nature, but rather he leads us directly to that Trinity, by whose participation the angels themselves are blessed.[11] Therefore, when he chose to be in the form of a servant,[12] and lower than the angels, so that he might be our Mediator, Christ nonetheless remained higher than the angels in the form of God. He was at one and the same time the way of life on earth and life itself in heaven.

Book X, Chapter 7: *How the Holy Angels, on account of love for us, wish to direct our worship[13] toward the one true God and not themselves.*

It is fitting that these immortal and blessed spirits, having been seated on celestial thrones, and who joyfully together praise their Creator by direct participation in him, firm in his eternity, certain of his truth, holy by his grace in order that we miserable mortals should become joyful and immortal, should love us with compassion, but not wish us to sacrifice[14] to them, but rather to him, in whose sacrifice they know themselves to participate along with us. Indeed, with the angels, we are the one city of God, of which is said in the Psalms, *Most glorious things are spoken of you, O City of God.*[15] Part of that city is in us even as we are wandering[16] here below; part in them is aiding from above. From that eternal city where the will of God is the intelligible and incommutable law, from that heavenly meeting place where there is a concern for us, holy scripture descended to us through the ministry of the Angels.[17] In that scripture it is written, *He who sacrifices to any God, except to the Lord only, he will be torn out by the roots* (Exod 22:20). This scripture, this law, these precepts have been confirmed by miracles.[18] The law and the miracles make it sufficiently evident to whom these immortal and blessed angels, who desire us to be immortal and blessed as they are, wish us to sacrifice.

Book X, Chapter 15: *On the ministry of the Holy Angels, by which they serve*[19] *the providence of God.*

And so it has pleased divine providence to ordain the course of time, as I have said and as we can read in the Acts of the Apostles,[20] so that the law concerning the one worship[21] of the true God should be given in the proclamation[22] of angels. The person of God himself visibly appeared in the angels by means of sure signs through the creature subject to him. (But this is certainly not the person of God as God is through his substance. That substance always remains invisible to corruptible eyes.) And syllable by syllable through the transitory words of human speech, the Creator speaks. But according to God's own nature God speaks not in a bodily but a spiritual voice, not to sense but to understanding, not in words dwelling in time, but, if I may say so, eternally, neither beginning to speak nor coming to the end of speech.[23] And the angels, who have been eternally blessed in enjoying God's incommunicable truth to the full, hear God in a more complete way. They hear the message of their ministry not with the body but with the mental ears. And in whatever ineffable way they are made to hear, they perform their external ministry immediately and effortlessly in the sensible and visible world. However, their ministry, in this case the law, is given to us within the providential distribution of time so that the law might have, as I have said, an earthly aspect, a temporal promise that nevertheless symbolizes eternal ones. And it is these eternal promises that few understood, though many celebrated them through outward and visible rites. Nevertheless, the most open witness of all the words and rites of that law anticipated the worship[24] of the one God, not the one God of a crowd of many gods, but the God who made heaven and earth, and every soul and every spirit that is other than himself. God created. All else has been created. In order that they might exist, and that they might participate in well-being, all things stand in need of the one who created them.

Book X, Chapter 25: *That all saints, both under the earthly law and before the law of eternity, were justified by faith in the mysteries of Christ.*

[Augustine opens this chapter with illustrations of the fact that, before the law, saints of old held close to God by faith.]

Therefore, says the Lord, *Cleanse those things that are within, and the outward things will thus be cleansed also.*[25] The psalmist then says[26] that God himself, not anything coming from God, but God himself is his possession: *God of my heart, and God of my possession forever.*[27] Of the many things that might be chosen by men and women, the psalmist was satisfied only by choosing God alone. *"For behold,"* he says, *"those who are distant from you will perish; you destroy those who desert you by becoming harlots."*[28] That is, those who choose to be the prostitutes of many gods. Then follows the verse for which the rest of the psalm prepares us: *But for me, it is good to cleave to the presence of God*[29]—not to go far off from God, not to indulge in promiscuity with a multitude of gods. Then will this adhering union to God be perfected, when all that is to be set free has gained its freedom.

But for now, as the psalmist says, we must *place our hope in God.*[30] *"For that which is seen,"* as the apostle says, *"is not hope. For why would a man continue to hope for what he sees? However, if we hope for what we do not see, then we wait expectantly for it with patient endurance."*[31] Now since we are, for the present time, firmly established in this hope, let us do what the psalmist indicates in the words that end his psalm, that is, become his angels and messengers, announcing God's will and praising God's glory and grace. For when he said, *"To place my hope in God,"* he continues, *"so that I might announce*[32] *all your praises in the gates of the daughters of Zion."*[33] This is the most glorious city of God, this city knows and pays constant attention to the one true God. The message of this city is proclaimed by the holy angels, who have invited our attention to their society and who desire us to be with them in this city. For these angels do not in any way aspire to our worship of them as our gods, but that we dwell with them, attentive only to their God and ours. Nor do they desire us to sacrifice to them, but that with them we should be a sacrifice to God.

Without doubt, whoever abandons prejudice and malignant obstinacy and truly considers these things will be assured that all these blessed and immortal spirits do not envy us (for if they did in fact envy us they would not be blessed), but rather they love us, desiring us to become blessed with them. They look upon us with more pleasure and give us more assistance when, joining with them, we worship the one, true God. Their greatest pleasure and assistance comes when, rather than turning our attention to them through various sacrifices, we praise and worship the one God, Father, Son, and Holy Spirit.

Book XI, Chapter 9: *Concerning what scripture's divine testimony teaches concerning the creation of Angels.*

Now, I have undertaken to speak of the origin of the holy city.[34] I decided, therefore, first, to take on the task of speaking on the holy angels, who make up the greater part of this city, and of that city the more blessed part, since they have never wandered from there as though they were in a strange land.[35] As much as it is possible, with God's help, I will try to explain the angels as they are given witness in scripture. When sacred scripture speaks of the creation of the world, it is not clearly stated whether the angels were created, or in what order they were created. But mention is made of them implicitly under the name of *"heaven,"* when it is said, *In the beginning God made the heaven and the earth,*[36] or they are signified under the name of *"light,"* about which I will speak presently.

I do not believe the angels were passed over in Scripture, for several reasons. Scripture says that on the seventh day God rested from all the works that God had made. And scripture itself begins, *In the beginning God made heaven and earth* so that, before heaven and earth were made, God seems to have made nothing. Therefore, God began with heaven and earth. And the earth itself, was, according to what scripture says next, first *invisible and without form,*[37] light not yet having been made and darkness dwelling upon the abyss (that is, dwelling upon some indistinct confusion of earth and water, for where there is no light there is, of necessity darkness). Therefore, all things were given place and order by God's creating act; all these things were narrated by scripture as having been completed in six days. How then could the angels have been passed over as if they were not among these works of God, from which God rested on the seventh day?

Though the fact that the angels are the work of God is not passed over, it is not explicitly mentioned here. In other places scripture testifies to this fact with the clearest voice. For the hymn of the three youths in the furnace starts with the words: *Bless the Lord, all you works of the Lord,*[38] and after, among these works, the angels are named. And in the Psalms it is said: *Praise the Lord from the heavens, praise the Lord in the heights. Praise the Lord all his angels, praise the Lord all his powers. Praise the Lord sun and moon. Praise the Lord all stars and light. Praise the Lord heaven of heavens and praise the Lord waters above the heavens. Let them praise the name of the Lord. For the Lord God spoke and they were made; the Lord commanded and they were created.*[39] Here it is expressly indicated that the angels were made by God, for scripture says that God "spoke and they were made." Who then would be audacious enough to put forth the opinion that the angels were created after those other things enumerated in the narration of the six days? If any are bold enough to suggest such folly, they are refuted by scripture of equal authority where God says, *When the stars were made, my angels praised me with a loud voice.*[40] Therefore, the angels were created before the stars, and the stars were made on the fourth day. Shall we therefore claim that the angels were created on the third day? Certainly not! We know what was created on that day: the land was separated from the waters, and each of these two elements took on its own distinct substance and appearance, and the earth produced all that was to take root in it. On the second day then? No, not even on this day. For the firmament was created between the higher and the lower waters, and it was called *"heaven";* and the stars were placed in that firmament on the fourth day. Therefore, the conclusion is clear: if the angels are among the works of God of those days, they are that light which was called *"day."* The unity of this day is commemorated in scripture by its being referred to, not as "the first day," but *"one day."*[41] The second day and the third and the rest are not other days, but the same "one day" was repeated to bring the number of six or seven to fullness. This fullness represents the fullness of knowledge contained and represented in the seven stages of knowledge: the six stages encompassing the created work of God, the seventh stage representing God's rest.

For when God said, *"Let light be, and there was light."* If we are correct in understanding this light as the creation of the angels, they are truly made participants of the eternal light, which is itself the unchangeable Wisdom of God, which we call the unbegotten Son of God, through whom all things were created. Thus the angels, having been illuminated by the light that created them, have themselves become light and are called "day" through participation in that unchangeable light and day that is the Word of God, through whom the angels and all other things were made. This *is the true Light that illuminates every man and woman coming into this world.*[42] This Light also illuminates every pure angel, so that the angel may be light, not light in itself, but in God. But if an angel turns away from God, it becomes impure, as are all those who are called "impure spirits." They are no longer *light in the Lord*[43] but have become darkness in themselves, deprived of participation in the eternal Light. For evil has no nature in and of itself, but the loss of good has been given the name "evil."[44]

Book XI, Chapter 29: *Concerning the knowledge of the Holy Angels, by which they know the Trinity itself in its divinity, and by which they contemplate first the causes of God's works in the art of the worker, then God in the works of the artist.*

Now certainly, those angels learn about God not through noisy, spoken words, but by being themselves in the presence of unchangeable truth, that is, in the presence of the only begotten Word. And they know this Word himself, and the Father and the Holy Spirit. And they contemplate and know this to be the indivisible Trinity, and that within it the three Persons are one substance without, however, being three gods but one God. They know these things better than we understand ourselves. And there they know the created world better, also because they know created things in and through the Wisdom of God. They know them in the very art by which they were made, rather than in the created world itself. Consequently, they know themselves better in God than they do in themselves, though they also know themselves. Indeed, they were created, and they know themselves to be other than the Creator. In the Wisdom of God they know who they are in God by a daylight knowledge, as we have explained above,[45] and they know themselves in a kind of evening or twilight knowledge. For there is a great difference between understanding by means of reason the art by which a thing was made, and in understanding by means of dwelling in Wisdom the thing in its very self. For instance, the straightness of lines or the truth of symbolic representations is known in one way in the inner vision of the mind and in quite another way if they are drawn in the dust; likewise justice is known in one way as unchangeable truth, in another in the soul of a just person. So it is with all other things of creation: the firmament, which is called heaven, between the higher and the lower waters; the congregation of the waters on earth below; the exposure of the dry land, and the establishing of plants and trees; the foundation of the sun and moon and stars; the creation of the animals from the sea, the birds of the sky, and the fish and monsters of the deep; the calling into being of whatever walks and creeps on the earth and of humanity itself, which excels all things in the earth. All these things are known by the angels in one way as they are in the Word of God, in which they contemplate the eternally unchangeable causes and reasons according to which they were made. They are known in another as they are in themselves. In the Word of God they are contemplated with a clearer understanding; in themselves these things are contemplated with an understanding that is more obscure, an understanding that sees the work but to which the art of the Creator is hidden. However, when these works are referred to their Creator in praise and worship, it is just as if the dawn of morning sunshine lights the minds of those who contemplate them.

Gregory the Great

XL homiliarum in Evangelia
Forty Homilies on the Gospels, Book II
Homily 34

Introduction

What is the relationship between angels and the human person? For Gregory the Great, a partial answer to that question rests on the relationship between the active and the contemplative life. Pope, saint, and doctor of the church, Gregory the Great (Gregory I), is widely known for integrating the active and contemplative life. In the following homily he also teaches the integration of the two realms: humanity and angels. Humanity, he preaches, can participate more fully in God through a deepening understanding of God's knowledge and love. Devotion to and imitation of the angels show us a variety of pathways into that deeper understanding. In *Homily 34* from his *Forty Homilies on the Gospels*, Gregory the Great uses the angels as exemplars of the intimate union of contemplation and active ministry. By imitating the angels in these things, he suggests, we draw ever nearer to our Creator.

Born to a wealthy patrician family in Rome in 540, Gregory was given an excellent education and became a member of the civil service. After a short time as prefect of Rome, his father died and he sold his patrimony, established a monastery dedicated to Saint Andrew, and became a monk. In 579 he was established as deacon of the Christian community in Rome and was also sent as the pope's secretary to Constantinople. He was made pope in 590, during a turbulent time when Rome was under threat from the Lombards.

For the last decade of his life he attended to papal affairs, writing indefatigably to the end, though ill for much of the period.[1] He was, in fact, confined to his bed for much of the last five years of his life. He died in 604.

Gregory's longest work, a kind of *summa* of dogma, moral asceticism, and mysticism, is the *Book of Morals*, an exposition of the Book of Job. The *Pastoral Care*, written in the first months of his pontificate, sets forth his ideas on the office of the bishop and the care of souls. While the *Pastoral Care* was written for bishops and priests, Gregory's *Dialogues* were intended for the monks of his community. Written in 593–94 in the form of a conversation, the *Dialogues* deal with the life of holiness, the immortality of the soul, and the doctrine of heaven. The fourteen books of Gregory's *Letters* are a rich source of information on the history, administration, and theology of his pontificate. For all his writings, Gregory's primary textbook was the Bible, and many of his works are explicit scriptural homilies. Surviving from notes taken by monks are the two homilies on *Kings* and on the *Song of Songs*. Also available are *Homilies on Ezechiel* and *Forty Homilies on the Gospels*, the latter delivered in 590–91 and containing *Homily 34* on the angels.

Long accepted by the tradition as a master of spiritual teaching, Gregory the Great also has a reputation as a dogmatic theologian. His doctrine of angels is an example of that originality, combining saintly spiritual wisdom with original doctrinal contributions.[2] An intriguing question, with regard both to spirituality and to doctrine, is the reference Gregory makes to Dionysius the Areopagite. Toward the end of *Homily 34* Gregory says, "It is said that the Areopagite, an ancient and venerated Father, says...." There has been much discussion as to what, if anything, Gregory had read of Dionysius. Joan M. Petersen, who surveys the material extensively, breaks into two categories the evidence for the assumption that Gregory was referring in his sermon to Dionysius's *Celestial Hierarchy:* verbal similarities and renderings of Greek phrases into Latin, and similarities between his lists of the orders of angels and that of Dionysius.[3] With regard to the first category, Petersen concludes that all of Gregory's renderings of Greek expressions used by Dionysius are not translations from him but derived from other Latin writers, chiefly Jerome and Eucherius. With regard to the lists, she concludes that though the angelic lists do not match exactly, it is "probable that Gregory...derived one of his lists from him [Dionysius]."[4] Whatever the direct influence of Dionysius on Gregory the Great, by the time of Dante Alighieri (1265–1321), the tradition seems to have made its own decision.[5] In a famous passage from the *Divine Comedy*, Dante gives final authority to Dionysius, while letting Gregory find humor in his ordering of the angels:

> Dionysius gave himself to contemplation
>> of these same orders with such holy zeal
>> that he named and ranked them just as I have done.
> Gregory, later, differed with his conclusions.
>> But hardly had he wakened in this heaven
>> than he was moved to laugh at his own delusions.[6]

But regardless of whether Gregory got the orders "right," *Homily 34* as it stands is a masterpiece of integration. First, Gregory is explicit about what we might call a doctrine of relation between humanity and angels. "Certainly," he says, "there are ways of human life that coincide with the orders of angelic bands." He enumerates those human personalities and spiritualities, those vocations and gifts, that seem to correspond to the various angelic ministries.[7] Second, Gregory also integrates heart and mind. As with other medieval figures, Gregory is not so intent on distinguishing and separating the categories of heart and mind as he is in advocating and illuminating their relation. The Cherubim, which represent intellect, and the Seraphim, which represent love, cohabitate. They dwell together in the highest realms closest to God.[8] Human persons, already established in a bond with the angels, can thus themselves pursue the "cohabitation" of Cherubim and Seraphim, knowledge and love, in their own lives. A third integration can be cast most accurately not in the light of correspondence, but in the glow of fruitful intimacy. This is the integration of action and contemplation. Gregory says:

> Concerning those same angelic orders who are sent, we hold it to be certain that when they come among us to implement their exterior ministry, they are nonetheless never absent interiorly through contemplation. And therefore, they are both sent and at the same time they stand before God, since, although angelic spirits are limited, God the highest spirit is not circumscribed. Thus angels God has sent are still before God since they operate in God's presence.[9]

The angels exemplify the perfection of the integration of action and contemplation, the highest goal of human spiritual growth as well.

A final integration, one that reflects an issue at the core of all the medieval works on angels, is based on the relation of the visible and the invisible. How do essentially invisible beings become visible? The answer for Gregory is threefold: the invisible angels are made visible through their beauty,[10] their names,[11] and their ministries. Angelic ministries claim the majority of Gregory's attention. In addition to being the primary means to angelic visibility, their ministries are linked to all the other areas of integration as well: the highest form of ministry is done in knowledge and love of God; the angels serve as exemplars, parallel ministers, and intimate partners to men and women in every earthly ministry; and as the angels stand with God even as they are sent to the world, their visible ministry is a form of their invisible contemplation.

As action and ministry differ in each human person and angelic spirit according to gift and call, so too does the kind and quality of contemplation. This issue will be defined and drawn out with more detail and clarity later in the medieval period, especially in the commentaries on Dionysius's *Celestial Hierarchy*. But here in Gregory's work, as well, the highest orders of angels are in "immediate" proximity to God. Their contemplation is unobscured by any intermediary; in human terms neither language nor culture nor expectation nor any construct or de-construct mediates angelic contemplation. The quality of their contemplation is "face to face." Still, the quality varies. The Seraphim contemplate God with burning love, the Cherubim with full knowledge,[12] the Thrones through God's dwelling in the core of their intellect. These qualities, in turn, represent spiritual paths for people today, ways of dwelling in the love and knowledge of God while at the same time undertaking ministries that have the effect of making God's love and knowledge visible in the world.

Note on Translation: The following homily is translated from *PL* 76:1246B; 1249C–1256A. An English translation of this homily is also available in *Gregory the Great: Forty Gospel Homilies,* trans. Dom David Hurst (Kalamazoo, Mich.: Cistercian Publications, 1990).

Forty Homilies on the Gospels
Homily 34

Given in the Basilica of blessed John and Paul,
Friday after the octave day of Pentecost.

A reading from the holy gospel according to Luke 15:1–10:

At that time the publicans and sinners drew near to Jesus in order to hear him. And the Pharisees and scribes muttered saying, "This man accepts sinners and eats with them." And he spoke this parable to them saying, "Which of you who has a hundred sheep, if he has lost one of them does not leave the ninety-nine in the desert and go after the one which is lost until he finds it? And when he has found the sheep he lays it on his shoulders rejoicing. And coming home, he calls his friends and neighbors together saying, 'Rejoice with me, because I have found my sheep that was lost.' I tell you, so also will there be more joy in heaven over one sinner who repents, than over ninety-nine righteous persons who do not require repentance. Or, what woman, having ten silver coins, if she loses one silver coin, does not light a lamp, overturn the house, and seek diligently until she finds the coin? And when she has found it, she calls her friends and neighbors together, saying, 'Rejoice with me for I have found the silver coin which I have lost.' In the same way I say to you, there will be joy in the presence of the angels of God over one sinner who repents."

1. Summer, a period that has been very trying for me physically, has caused a long interruption in my speaking on the exposition of

the gospels. But because the tongue is silent, does that mean that charity then ceases to burn?[13] What I am saying is something that each of you recognizes within yourself. Very often charity is entangled in preoccupations, yet it blazes ever fresh in the heart, even though it may not be shown in our work. In the same way the sun may be covered by a cloud and is not seen from the earth, yet it still burns in heaven.[14] So too with the work of charity: interiorly, charity's burning produces heat within us yet may not be revealed in the flames of our labor in a visible way. But since the time for speaking has indeed returned,[15] your very zeal inflames[16] me so that its full outpouring releases me to speak at length as your minds eagerly absorb my words.

[Gregory proceeds with the portion of his homily on the parable of the ninety-nine lost sheep.]

6. *Or what woman, having ten silver coins, if she loses one silver coin, does not light a lamp, overturn the house, and seek diligently until she finds the coin?*[17] What is signified by the shepherd[18] is the same as what is signified by the woman: God and the Wisdom of God. And as an image is imprinted on a coin, the woman lost a silver coin when humanity, who was created in the image of God, recoiled from the likeness of its Creator by sinning. But the woman set the lamp alight just as the Wisdom of God appeared in humanity.[19] A lamp is a light in a clay vessel: truly the light in a clay vessel is divinity in the flesh. Wisdom herself says of the clay of his [Christ's] body, *My strength is dried up like an earthen vessel.*[20] Indeed, an earthen vessel is hardened in a fire. In the same way Christ's strength was dried up and hardened like clay when, in the tribulation of his passion, he made the body he had assumed strong for the glory of the resurrection.

[Gregory continues with the allegory of the lamp by explaining that the light of the lamp of Christ upsets our conscience. Like the woman, we "turn over" or clean our "house" and the coin is found.]

And when she finds it, she calls her friends and neighbors, saying, "Rejoice with me, for I found the coin which I had lost." Who are her friends and neighbors, unless they are those heavenly powers spoken of above?[21] They are close to the highest Wisdom when they draw near to him through the grace of their continuous vision.

But while we are on this subject, we ought not carelessly to let go of the issue of why this woman, in whom the Wisdom of God is symbolized,[22] is said to have ten coins, one of which is lost but then is found when she sets about searching for it. Without a doubt the Lord established the nature of the angels and humans so that they might become acquainted with their Creator through knowledge and love. The Lord wished this essential nature to stand firm throughout eternity, thus it was created in angels and humans in God's own likeness.[23] The woman had ten silver coins. There are nine orders of angels, and humanity was created as the tenth; thus the number of the elect has been made perfect.[24] After sin, humanity was not lost to its Creator; rather, eternal Wisdom, shimmering with his physical miracles like the light from the earthen vessel, restored it.

7. We spoke of the nine orders of angels because we know that sacred scripture clearly bears witness to Angels, Archangels, Virtues, Powers, Principalities, Dominations, Thrones, Cherubim, and Seraphim.[25] Nearly every page of sacred scripture bears witness to the existence[26] of angels and archangels. The books of the prophets, as is known, often speak of the Cherubim and Seraphim. And the apostle Paul enumerated the names of four orders when he said to the Ephesians: *Above every principality and power and virtue and domination.*[27] Again, writing to the Colossians he said, *Whether thrones or powers of principalities or dominations.*[28] Paul had already described the Dominations and Principalities and Powers to the Ephesians, having mentioned nothing concerning the Thrones. But when he dictated a list to the Colossians, he put the Thrones first. Thus, when the Thrones are joined to those four orders he had spoken of in Ephesians, that is, the Principalities, Powers, Virtues, and Dominations, there are five orders that are mentioned. When Angels, Archangels, Cherubim, and Seraphim are added, nine orders of angels are found to exist.[29]

The angel that was first established is spoken of by the prophet, *You were the seal of likeness, full of wisdom and perfected in beauty; you were among the delights of God's paradise.*[30] We should notice that it is not said that this first angel has been made according to the likeness of God *(similitudinem Dei)* but according to the *seal of likeness (signaculum similitudinis)*, since the angel is more subtle in its essential nature. It is thereby insinuated that the image of God has been expressed with greater likeness in this first angel than it has in humanity. The prophet quickly adds: *Every stone was your secret covering: carnelian, topaz, and jasper, chrysolite, onyx and beryl, sapphire, carbuncle, and emerald.*[31] Behold, he mentioned the names of nine stones, since there are nine perfect orders of angels. This same first angel was made visible, adorned and covered with the nine kinds of stones. When the first angel was brought forward before all the other angels, it was, in comparison to them, more illustrious.[32]

8. But why do we touch upon these choirs of steadfast angels by listing them, if not to describe their ministries[33] in a plain manner? Indeed, in the Greek language angels are called "messengers" and archangels are the most important messengers. We ought to know that whatever the angels are called, their name signifies a service, not their essential nature.[34] For the holy spirits of the heavenly homeland are indeed always spirits, but they are by no means always able to be called angels, since they are only "angels" when some message is announced through them. Thus the psalmist says, *He makes his spirits angels,*[35] as if to say plainly, he who always has them as spirits makes them angels when he wishes.

Those who announce less important messages are called "angels," those who announce the most important things are called "archangels." Thus it is not just any angel that is sent to the virgin Mary, but rather the archangel Gabriel.[36] For it was appropriate for an important angel to come on this ministry, a great angel who announced the greatest message of all. Archangels are distinguished by personal names in order to point out by words what their action signifies. Even in the holy city, where the fullness of knowledge[37] concerning the vision of the omnipotent God is perfected, the inhabitants are not given their own personal names because their individual spirits are able to be known without a name. But when they come to minister to us, they assume a name among us appropriate to their ministry.[38]

9. Michael means "who is like God." Gabriel means "the strength of God." Raphael means "the healing of God."[39] Whenever something of wondrous goodness is to be done, Michael is brought forward to be sent. By Michael's being sent we understand through his very act and name that no one is able to do what God is capable of doing. The ancient enemy, who through pride desired to be like God, said, *I will ascend into heaven, I will exalt my throne above the stars of God. I will sit in the mountain of the assembly, in the hiding places of the north. I will ascend above the height of the clouds, I will be like the most high.*[40] At the end of the world, when he is left to his own strength, the ancient enemy is to be destroyed by dreadful punishment when the archangel Michael is brought forward to do battle with him. So John said, *War was made with the archangel Michael,*[41] so that those who exalt themselves to the likeness of God through pride might learn, after having been destroyed by Michael, that no one is lifted up to a likeness of God by pride.

Gabriel, who is named the strength of God, was sent to Mary. Gabriel came to announce the one who was worthy to appear with humility to conquer the powers of the lower air.[42] The psalmist says of him: *Lift up your gates, you rulers, and be raised up you eternal gates, and the King of glory will enter. Who is this King of glory? The Lord strong and powerful, the Lord powerful in battle.*[43] And again: *The Lord of goodness, he is the King of glory.*[44] Therefore, through the "strength of God" the Lord of goodness was announced, coming powerful in battle against the powers of the lower air.

As I said above, Raphael is interpreted as "the healing of God," since, when he touched the eyes of Tobias as if performing a service for healing,[45] he wiped away the darkness of his blindness. The one sent to cure Tobias was therefore certainly worthy to be called "the healing of God." But since we touched upon interpreting the names of angels above, now we must briefly describe the words we use to indicate their duties.[46]

10. Virtues are those spirits through whom signs and wonders are most frequently accomplished. Those called Powers are those spirits who, more readily than the other ranks of angels, have comprehended the nature of potency, so that the opposing Virtues[47] are subject to their power. These opposing Powers are held back from tempting the human heart, no matter how much they might try to get the upper hand. Principalities are those who preside over the spirits of the good angels. When they arrange whatever it is that those good angels under them must do, they rule them in that they bring to completion their divine ministries. Dominations, by their dissimilarity to them, affirm the fact that they greatly transcend the power of the Principalities. For the Principalities exist between the Dominations and the rest of the spirits,[48] while the Dominations arrange whatever must be accomplished by those orders under their authority. Therefore, those masses of angels who are preeminent because of their wonderful power and who have subjected the other angels to obedience, those angels are called Dominations. Thrones are those bands of angels over which God omnipotent always presides to exercise divine judgment. Since in Latin we speak of seats as thrones, those called the "throne of God" are those so filled with the grace of divinity that the Lord sits in them and discerns his justice through them.[49] Thus in the Psalms it is said, *You who judge with righteousness, sit upon a throne.*[50]

Cherubim means "fullness of knowledge."[51] These most sublime bands of spirits are rightfully called Cherubim because they are so full of the most perfect knowledge that they contemplate the glory of God from the vantage point of immediate proximity.[52] According to the way of created beings, the Cherubim know all things fully as they draw near, through the merit of their worthiness, to the vision of their Creator.

Those bands of holy spirits are called Seraphim who, because of a singular attraction to their Creator, burn with an incomparable love.[53] Thus Seraphim are called "burning or incandescent." The Seraphim, since they have been so united[54] to God that no other spirit may intervene between them and God, burn all the more fiercely as they see God more intimately. Their love is truly a flame, since the more acutely they look upon the glory of God's divinity, the more savagely they burst into flame with God's love.

11. But what does it profit us to touch upon these angelic spirits, if we are not zealous to derive some profit by our contemplation of them? Indeed, it is agreed that the heavenly city is composed of angels and of humans. We believe that as many of humankind ascend there as there were elected angels who happen to remain. So scripture says, *He established the final number of people according to the number of angels of God.*[55] We ought to draw something from these distinctions among our fellow citizens of heaven[56] to use for our own dealings with people and thereby to inflame ourselves with enthusiasm for an increase in virtue and of good things. Since we believe that the multitude of humanity that ascends there is equal to the multitude of angels who never left, it remains for those humans returning to their heavenly home that they imitate something of these bands of angelic spirits in the process of their return.

Clearly, there are ways of human life that coincide with single orders of angelic bands. By means of a correspondence in virtue, these people are counted worthy of the heavenly city by sharing in the angelic nature.[57]

For instance, there are many people who comprehend little but who do not desist from making the little they do know piously available to their brothers and sisters. These people dwell among the Angels. And there are other brothers and sisters who have been revived by the gifts of divine bounty and who succeed in receiving and announcing the highest secrets of heaven. Where can we include these men and women except among the Archangels? And there are others who do miracles and who work powerful signs. With which angelic spirits do they coincide unless they come together among the portion and number of the supernal Virtues? There are yet other human spirits who chase evil spirits from the bodies of the obsessed, throwing the evil spirits out by the strength of their prayers and the power they have received. Where do these men and women deserve to be placed except among the celestial Powers? And there are some people who receive virtues transcending even the general merit of the elect, and since these are superior even to those blessed elect, they rule over these elect brothers and sisters. With whom do these souls share honor unless it be among the Principalities?

There are still others who have so dominated all vices and every desire in themselves that by virtue of their purity, they are called gods among human beings. Thus Moses was told, *Behold, I make you a god to Pharaoh.*[58] How are these souls to be counted then, unless among the number of the Dominations? And there are some who have domination over themselves by constant vigilance, scattering their vices and misplaced desire by constant watchfulness and by remaining always in holy fear; they receive this gift, among other virtues, so that they might correctly judge others. When divine contemplation is present in their minds, it is as if the Lord rules from a throne in these very men and women. The Lord examines the deeds of others from this seat and miraculously judges and disposes all things. What are these human spirits if not the Thrones of their Creator, and where are they to be listed if not among the number of the most glorious seats? When the holy church is guided by these Thrones, they often judge and guide even the elect concerning their imperfect actions.

And there are others still who are so filled with love of God and their neighbor that they are correctly called Cherubim.[59] Indeed, we said above that the Cherubim are called "fullness of knowledge," and Paul teaches us by saying, *Charity is the fullness of the law.*[60] All who are filled beyond all other things with charity toward God and neighbor gather among the Cherubim in a destiny that they merit.

And there are other brothers and sisters who, having been set on fire by contemplation, pant with eager desire for their Creator alone. For they long for nothing in this world, they delight only in love for eternity, they abandon every earthly thing, they transcend all temporal things with their minds; they love, they burn, and they rest in this love by their burning; they burn by loving and they set others on fire by their speaking. And those spirits whom they touch with their words burn continuously with the love of God. And what but Seraphim ought we to call these very spirits whose hearts, alight and burning, have been turned into fire? They illuminate the eye of the mind concerning celestial things, and they purge themselves of the rust of vices by tearful compunction.[61] How do those who have been so clearly illuminated by the love of their Creator receive their vocation, except among the number of the Seraphim?

But while I am speaking of these things, dear friends, lead yourself home into your innermost self, that is, into the core of your being. Examine the merits of your inner secrets and inmost understanding. Look inside yourself and see if what you are doing now is good; see if you are among the number of those bands of spirits whom we have briefly touched upon; see if you find your vocation among them. Woe to those souls who recognize within themselves something less than those good things we have enumerated. And more sorrow still to the soul who diminishes itself by understanding that it lacks these gifts and yet fails to bemoan that lack. Whoever these souls might be, my brothers and sisters, we ought to weep intensely for them, since they do not weep for themselves.

Therefore, let us meditate upon the gifts the elect have received, let us desire the virtue by which we might be able to love such gifts. Let those who recognize that the grace of these gifts is lacking within them weep. Those who truly understand this lack within themselves do not envy the greater grace of gifts in others. Likewise, even those blessed among the highest orders of spirits have been created so that some are placed before others.

It is said that Dionysius the Areopagite, an ancient and venerated father, says that those sent forth for explaining a ministry or function, either visibly or invisibly, are from the lower orders of angels, because only angels or archangels come to give comfort to humanity.[62] Since the most preeminent spirits are never used for exterior ministry, the highest orders of angels never retire from their profound intimacy with the other spirits and with God,[63] since those who are preeminent spirits are never used for exterior ministry. However, this seems to be contrary to what Isaiah says, *And one of the Seraphim flew toward me and in his hand was a charcoal, which he had taken with tongs from the altar, and he touched my mouth.*[64] But in this passage the prophet wishes us to understand that those spirits that are sent take on their name-word according to the service they perform.[65] Indeed, the angel who carried away a coal from the altar so that the sins of speech might be burned away is called Seraphim, which means burning. I feel that what Daniel says is similar and might help: *A thousand times a hundred thousand stood before him.*[66] For it is one thing to minister to someone, and another thing to stand before God. Those spirits are ministers of God's work who go out for the purpose of proclaiming something to us; those spirits stand before God who, by means of the most profound inner contemplation, enjoy intimacy with God to the full. These later spirits are not sent out to complete works.[67]

13. We have learned that in certain places of scripture some things are set in motion through the Cherubim and some are done through the Seraphim. We are unwilling to affirm, because there is no clear proof, whether those things that are set in motion are in fact done by the Seraphim or the Cherubim themselves or are done by other bands subjected to them, their names, which are greater, being selected because the things are done on their authority. However, we know this most certainly: for explaining the nature of ministry from on high, some spirits send others. Zechariah, testifying to this, said, *Behold, the angel who spoke with me came forward, and behold, another angel came forward to meet him, and said to him: Run, and speak to this boy saying: Jerusalem will be inhabited without a wall.*[68] Since one angel said to the other angel: *Run and speak*, it is without doubt that one sent the other. The lesser ones are sent; it is the greater ones who send.

But we also, concerning those same angelic orders who are sent, hold it to be certain that when they come among us to implement their exterior ministry, they are nonetheless never absent interiorly through contemplation.[69] And therefore, they are both sent and at the same time they stand before God, since, although angelic spirits are limited, God, the highest spirit, is not circumscribed. Thus the angels God has sent are still before God because they operate in God's presence.

14. We ought to know also that sometimes the orders of blessed spirits obtain the names of the orders neighboring them. The Thrones, who are the very seats of God,[70] are a special order of blessed spirits, as we have said, and yet the psalmist says, *You* *who are enthroned upon the Cherubim, shine forth.*[71] This is so because, though the orders are distinguished, the Cherubim are united to the Thrones by their proximity. Thus the Lord is described as *sitting upon the Cherubim* because of the fact that the Cherubim are equal to their neighbor, the Thrones, through the unity of their proximity. Thus in the heavenly city there are certain special attributes of a singular order that nonetheless are the common property of every order. And the part one order has within it, this part is possessed totally by other orders. But they are not included communally under one and the same name because that order which receives the total portion most fully on account of its ministry ought to be called by its private name, which is uniquely related to its ministry.

Thus we have said that the Seraphim are called *burning ones*, yet all the orders burn in the same way with love for their Creator. And truly, the Cherubim are *fullness of knowledge*, and yet who are ignorant in any of the celestial orders of anything when they themselves also see God, the Fountain of Knowledge. We have also called Thrones those orders upon which the Creator sits to watch over all creation, yet who are able to be blessed unless the Creator truly dwells within their mind.[72] A name has been given privately to each order, which it receives on account of the fullness of its particular service; yet all participate to some degree in each particular duty. For even if some have certain qualities that others are never able to possess, for instance, Dominations and Principalities are called by their special name, all celestial gifts are the unique possession of all. This is accomplished by means of the charity of the Spirit, through whom each quality or gift is possessed by each order in the name and person of others.

15. But behold, while we have been probing the secrets of the celestial citizens, we have digressed far from the orderly exposition of our theme. Therefore, let us breathe deep with longing for those celestial spirits of whom we have been speaking, but let us return to ourselves. We ought to remember that we are embodied beings. For the interim, let us keep silence concerning the secrets of heaven and, with the hand of repentance, cleanse those blemishes that have

appeared before the eyes of our Creator even from our creation from dust. Behold, divine mercy itself gives us this promise saying, *There will be joy in heaven over one sinner who repents.* Yet through the prophet the Lord says, *On whatever day a righteous person sins, I will forget all his righteous deeds.*[73]

Bernard of Clairvaux

In Psalmum "Qui Habitat"

Sermons on Psalm 90, "He Who Dwells"
[in the Shelter of the Most High]

From Sermons
Eleven and Twelve

Introduction

For Saint Bernard of Clairvaux (1090–1153), the towering twelfth-century monastic reformer, theologian, crusader, and mystic, the pathway leading back to God begins in humility. Its destination, as well as its driving dynamic, is love. The core of Bernard of Clairvaux's spirituality was based on love as the symbol of the soul's longing for Christ, and he charted a journey through the first stirrings of that love in humility to union in love with God.[1] Yet for Bernard the pathways of the Christian journey are many. The primary pathways follow the course of love, certainly. But the detours are frequent, the dead ends are dark and void, finally, of any form of love at all. Fortunately, along the routes of these spiritual pathways there are also many guides and protectors, including the angels. And as Bernard points out in another of his writings, the angels guide men and women along the many pathways of Christian faith in ways that not only circumvent the dead-end voids but serve to reveal God as *all in all* (cf. 1 Cor 15:28). Thus Bernard says:

> God loves in the Seraphim as charity, knows in the Cherubim as truth, is seated in the Thrones as equity, reigns in the Dominations as majesty, rules in the Principalities as principle, guards in the Powers as salvation, acts in the Virtues as strength, reveals in the Archangels as light, assists in the Angels as piety.[2]

Probably finding their completed form in the year 1139, Bernard's *Sermons on Psalm 90* is a sort of treatise written in the literary style of sermons, but probably never delivered by him *viva voce* to any audience.[3] The overall theme of the *Sermons* is the Christian pilgrimage from conversion to consummation of the divinized soul in love. The general "shape" of the pathway, as well as its goal, is Christ. There are detours, snares, and hardships along the way, to be sure. Still, as Bernard points out, we do have sources of refuge provided by God: the sacraments, penance, the Eucharist, the imitation of the life of Christ, the "bread of angels,"[4] and the ministry of angels themselves. In the following *Sermons* Bernard looks closely at the pathways, guidance, and ministry of these angels. What he teaches is that:

> the angels ignite reverence because of their presence, bring forth devotion because of their benevolence, and bestow confidence because of their guardianship.[5]

Thus the angels assist in directing us along the paths of compassion and truth, which are the ways of the Lord and which, when they come together, result in the kiss of justice and peace.[6] As with Augustine, however, Bernard insists that angels do not covet our worship or our adoration; they are not the goal of the Christian journey. "All our love and honor," he says, "is returned finally to God."[7]

But until such time as our love is fully returned (and even when it is, in this life, it is returned only for the briefest of moments), we can never forget that we are still pilgrims and therefore able to lose our way. To continue on our proper path we need humility and self-knowledge; we need discernment. To assist us in this, as Bernard points out, we may imitate the ways of the angels, which follow their own pathways of ascent and descent. They pursue ascending ways to contemplation of God and descending ways to bring compassion to us. The angels can also guide us into the ways of the Lord, which are the ways of compassion and truth. For the Christian life of faith, compassion is in part the return to the heart, the path of salvation. Truth is also the way of the heart; compassionate truth is to become, through humility, like a little child.

For the angels the path of truth is contemplation of God face to face; the way of compassion is to keep us in all our ways. Returning to the heart, we, like the angels, can "descend" to our neighbor through the active charity of compassion, thereby keeping "others" in all their ways. Likewise, we can, in humility, "ascend" to eternal truth through loving contemplation and union with God.

Bernard of Clairvaux was the recognized spiritual master of the contemplative way of love in the Christian tradition. In his *Divine Comedy* Dante chose Bernard as his spiritual guide into the climactic vision of heaven. The love of Beatrice had drawn Dante into the penultimate realms, where Bernard took over the task of guide, leading Dante first to the vision of heaven as a rose of light resplendent in saintly and angelic petals, then to Mary, and finally to his ultimate vision of God that united him to "the Love that moves the sun and the other stars."[8]

Note on Translation: The following sermons of Bernard are translated from *S. Bernardi Opera, Vol. IV, Sermones, In Psalmum "Qui habitat,"* ed. Jean Leclercq and Henri-Marie Rochais (Rome: Editiones Cistercienses, 1966). Another English translation is available in *Bernard of Clairvaux: Sermons on Conversion, On Conversion, a Sermon to Clerics and Lenten Sermons on the Psalm "He Who Dwells,"* translated with an introduction by Marie-Bernard Saïd (Kalamazoo, Mich.: Cistercian Publications, 1981). A partial translation of Sermon Eleven is available in French in *Saint Bernard: Oeuvres,* trans. M.-M. Davy, Des Maitres de la spiritualité Chrétienne (Aubier: Éditions Montaigne, 1950), 238–43.

 ### Sermons on Psalm 90, "He Who Dwells" *[in the Shelter of the Most High]*[9]

Sermon Eleven, on Verse Eleven

*For God has given the angels charge of you
to guard you in all your ways.*

2. Blessed are our brothers who have already been set free from the snare of the hunter, who have crossed over from the tabernacles of the militant to the courts of peace. Once the fear of evil has been put aside they are singularly lifted up to hope. To one and all is said, *No evil will befall you, no scourge come near your tent.*[10] This is a great promise, but what gives me the right to hope for it? How do I evade both evil and the scourge, how do I fly away, how might I go so far away[11] that they will not draw near to me? What merit, what wisdom, what virtue will carry me to this? *For he has given his angels charge of you, to keep you in all your ways.* In all ways? What ways? Those by means of which you depart from evil,[12] those by which you fly away from the wrath to come.[13] There are many ways and many kinds of ways;[14] indeed, there is great danger for the wayfarer.[15] When there are so many hostile ways, how easy it is for us to wander in our own path[16] if we lack the ability to discern ways. But God has not given the angels their commission to preserve us in all possible ways, but in all our own ways. Yet there are some journeys from which, rather than in which, we need to be protected.

3. Let us search our ways then, brothers. Let us also track the ways the demons, the ways of the blessed spirits, and the ways of the Lord...[17]

6. And what are the ways of the holy angels? Clearly, those which the Only Begotten[18] explained when he said, *"You will see the angels ascending and descending upon the Son of Man."*[19] Thus their ways consist in ascent and in descent. They ascend through the influence of the Son of Man; they descend, or more properly they condescend, on our account. In this way those blessed spirits ascend by means of the contemplation of God. And so they descend through compassion for you, so that they may preserve you in all your ways. They ascend to God's face, they descend at God's pleasure, *for he has given his angels charge over you.* However, in descending they are not cheated of God's glorious vision, because *they always behold the face of the Father.*[20]

7. I think it is also good to hear something about the manifold pathways to the face of the Lord. I would presume too much if I were to promise to reveal them all to you. However, we read concerning this that God will teach us the ways of the Lord.[21] Indeed, who else ought to be believed? And so God taught us God's ways when the Lord opened the mouth of the prophet, revealing that *all the ways of the Lord are compassion and truth*.[22] And so the Lord comes, to the individual and to the community alike, in compassion and in truth. When we become presumptuous concerning God's compassion and oblivious of God's truth, thereupon God is immediately absent. But neither is God present where great terror follows the recollection of truth, nor is there consolation from the memory of God's mercy.[23] Nor does anyone hold truth who does not know where compassion truly dwells; likewise compassion is unable to truly exist without truth. Therefore, where the paths of compassion and truth come together, there also one finds that justice and peace have kissed.[24] And the one who has established his dwelling in peace[25] must also be present. We have heard and known[26] all these things concerning the intimate connection between sweet compassion and truth because our fathers have announced them to us.[27] *Your compassion and your truth have supported me*,[28] says the prophet. And in another place the prophet says, *Your compassion is before my eyes, and I am well pleased with your truth*.[29] And the Lord himself has said concerning this, *My truth and my compassion shall be with him*.[30]

8. But consider also the manifest visitations of the Lord, how in him who is now eagerly anticipated we have a compassionate Savior, and how for the future we are sustained in him who is promised for the end of time as our truthful judge. This seems clearly expressed in the saying, *For God loves compassion and truth, the Lord gives grace and glory*.[31] However recollected Christ might have been in the prior visitation of his compassion and truth to the house of Israel,[32] in his final visitation, although he will judge the destitute of the world with balance and the people in his truth,[33] he will not judge without compassion, except those who were themselves clearly not compassionate.[34] These are the pathways[35] of eternity, concerning which you have from the prophet, *The hills of the world are scattered by the pathways of his eternity*.[36] Here, from scripture, I am easily able to prove this: *The mercy of the Lord is from everlasting to everlasting*,[37] and *The truth of the Lord endures forever*.[38] The hills of this world have been made low by these journeys of the soul. These hills are the proud demons, the rulers of this world[39] and of its darkness[40] who do not know the way of truth and compassion or remember their side alleyways.[41] Who can intervene between those hills and truth? Only *a liar and the father of lies.*[42] And further, concerning these things you have it clearly written that *there is not truth in him.*[43] Truly, how far the father of lies was from mercy is given witness by our own misery that is inflicted upon us by him. When could he ever have been compassionate when he was a killer of humanity from the beginning? And finally, *If a person is worthless to himself, to whom will he be good?*[44] A person is most cruel to himself who never is saddened by his own sinfulness, whose conscience is never pricked by his own damnation. Their false presumption has thrust them [such persons] off the path of truth,[45] their cruel obstinacy has shut off the path of mercy. They will never be able to attain this compassion on their own, nor receive it from the Lord.[46] It is in this way, then, that those swollen hills have been scattered by the pathways of eternity as they have turned away from the straight ways of the Lord[47] and have been bowed low through their winding and digressive steps that are not so much spiritual journeys of the soul as precipitous descents. But how prudently and profitably the other hills were scattered and brought low, to their salvation, by these eternal pathways. For they were not scattered as though they were opposing their own righteousness, but because they were bowed down by the spiritual pathways of God's eternity. Moreover, do not the hills of the world resolve to bow down when the high and powerful are inclined to the Lord[48] as devout subjects and when they adore the vestigial footsteps of God?[49] Are they not bowed down when they are converted from the pernicious haughtiness of vanity and cruelty to the humble side alleyways of mercy and truth?

9. It is not only the paths of the good spirits but also the elect among men and women who are guided in these ways of the Lord. And the first step[50] in the journey for pitiable humanity emerging from the depths of corruption is mercy.[51] This divine mercy makes a person extricating himself from corruption compassionate toward the son of his mother,[52] merciful to his soul,[53] and thereby pleasing to God. In this way a soul of mercy imitates the great work of the highest divine compassion, being pierced by compunction and moved to tears with him who was pierced for us, in a certain way dying for his own salvation, sparing himself no longer. This first compassion rescues the person returning to his heart,[54] and this first mercy enables the soul to activate the innermost secrets of the heart. It then remains to travel toward the royal road[55] and advance toward truth, and, as we so often commend you to do, to accompany confession of the lips with contrition of heart. *For humanity believes with the heart and so is justified, and confesses with the lips and so is saved.*[56] Turned to him in their heart,[57] it is necessary that one become small in one's own eyes, just as Truth himself has said, *"Unless you turn back and become as little children, you will never enter the kingdom of heaven."*[58] May we not wish to keep secret what we know only too well—that we are reduced to nothing.[59] May we not be ashamed to bring forth into the light of truth what we cannot see in secret without having been grasped by compassion. In this way humanity is brought along into the ways of mercy and truth, the ways of the Lord, the paths of life.[60] And the fruit of these ways is the salvation of the wayfarer.

10. That the angels direct their course along these same ways ought to be clear. For when they ascend to contemplation, they search out truth, in desiring which they are filled, and in being filled they long again. But when they descend, they bring compassion to us, that they may guide us in all our ways. These spirits are ministers sent to attend to us.[61] Clearly, they are our servants, not our masters. And in this ministry they imitate the example[62] of the Only Begotten, who did not come to be served, but to serve,[63] and who sat among the disciples as one who serves.[64] For the angels in contemplation the fruit of their angelic ways is their own happiness and obedience in love. This fruit pertains to us in that through them we grow toward divine grace and are guided in our ways here below. So then, it is said, *He has given his angels charge of you to guide you in all your ways*, in all your needs, in all your longings. Otherwise, you would run headlong into the ways of death.[65] That is to say, out of necessity you would rush immediately into obstinacy, or out of greedy ambition you would rush into stubborn presumption. Neither are the intended ways of humanity; they are the ways of demons. For when are men or women found to be most obstinate, if not in what they think or pretend to be necessary. "If you warn such a person," someone has said, "that person will answer, 'I am able to do what I am able to do, more than that I cannot do. If I could, perhaps I would feel different.'"[66] Why do we leap into obstinacy, if not from an impulse of powerful desire?

11. Meanwhile, God has charged the angels not to move you from your ways but to direct you in them, and through their own ways to guide your ways into God's. "How do they do this?" you ask. Clearly, just as the angels act from the purest charity alone, so you also, admonished at the very least by your own necessity, descend and condescend. That is, descending, seek to display compassion to your neighbor,[67] and in return, lifting up your desires with those same angels, strive to ascend with all the passionate longing of your soul to sublime and perpetual truth. Thus, in one place we are admonished to lift up our hearts with our hands,[68] while at the same time we hear every day, "lift up your hearts."[69] Elsewhere we are convicted by our negligence and told, *Sons of man, how long will you be dull of heart? Why do you love vanity and seek falsehood?*[70] An unburdened and lightened heart is a heart more easily lifted up to seek and love truth.[71] Do not be amazed that those who deign to guide us do not scorn to ingraft us into God by admitting us with them into the ways of the Lord. But how much more happily do they walk in those ways than we, how much more securely! And yet, though they too are far inferior to him, who is Truth itself and Mercy itself, they hover in the midst of mercy and truth.

12. How suitably God has separately graded these orders of angels to come together each at its own level! Yet God himself is the loftiest principle, supreme over all the orders; beyond God there is nothing, above God nothing. God placed the angels, not of the summit, but in safety near the summit without risk of harm, so that adhering in likeness to God, who does stand at the summit, they may be confirmed by power from on high.[72] Humanity, on the other

hand, is neither at the summit nor in safety but on guard, wary, alert. Further, they are on something solid, that is, the earth, having a bottom but not the lowest place, and thus it is both possible and necessary that they be on their guard. The demons, however, wander[73] in suspension randomly and without principle in the empty, windy air. They are unworthy to climb to heaven and they disdain to come down to earth.

This is sufficient for today. May God, from whom comes our sufficiency, give us grace enough to return to him! As it is, we are not sufficient in ourselves[74] to think anything by ourselves or for ourselves, unless God himself, who gives to all generously,[75] delivers it to us. Above all, God be blessed for ever and ever.[76]

Sermon Twelve, on Verse Twelve

On their hands they will bear you up
lest you strike your foot
against a stone.

2.[77] …However, if evil spirits descend to encompass us,[78] we still have every reason to be thankful to God, by whose command the blessed angels also descend to guide us and to guard us in all our ways. And not only this, but *"on their hands,"* the Lord said *"they will bear you up lest you strike your foot against a stone."*

3. What great teaching, admonition, and consolation are revealed for us, brothers, in these words of scripture. By which other of all the psalms are the downhearted so magnificently consoled, which of all the psalms so wondrously admonishes the negligent or teaches the ignorant? This is why divine providence wishes the faithful to preserve the verses of this psalm upon their lips, turning them over constantly in their mind, especially during the lenten season. From their usurpation by the devil himself an opportunity is found to make that most worthless and unwilling servant serve the sons.[79] Indeed, what could be more annoying to him, what more delightful for us, than that even his evil should work in us for good?[80] *He has given his angels charge of you to guard you in all your ways. Let them thank the Lord for his* *compassion, for his wondrous works for the sons of men.*[81] Let them give thanks and say, *Among the nations, the Lord has done magnificent things for them.*[82] *Lord, what is humanity that you should look upon us,*[83] *and that you should set your heart upon men and women?*[84] You have set your heart upon us, you attend to our needs,[85] you take care of us.[86] And so you sent your Only Begotten,[87] you sent your Spirit,[88] you even show forth your own face.[89] And so that heaven might not be empty of works of solicitude on our behalf, you sent us those blessed spirits in service for our ministry,[90] you assigned them to guide us, and you charge them to become our teachers. And this is not all. You not only made your spirits angels,[91] you made angels for the little ones, whose *angels always behold the face of the Father.*[92] And thus you make those blessed spirits not only your angels to us, but also ours to you.

4. *He has given his angels charge of you.* What wondrous esteem and truly great love of charity! But who gives charge, to whom, of whom, and for what purpose? We must consider these things zealously, brothers, we must diligently engrave this great charge in our memory. For who gives this charge? Whose angels are they? With whose charge do they comply? To whose will are they obedient? Surely, *he has given his angels charge over you to guard you in all your ways,* nor do they delay in doing so for they carry you in their very hands. Therefore the Lord, the highest majesty, *has charged his angels.* These angels are those sublime, those blessed spirits, those most intimately bound together with God, those most closely continuous and united to God, those true members of the household of God.[93] God has charged them to you. Who are you?[94]...

5. And so *he has given his angels charge over you to guard you in all your ways.* O wheat among the weeds! O grain among the chaff![95] O lily among the thorns![96] Give thanks to God, brothers, give thanks to the Lord. God has entrusted something precious to us for our safekeeping, the fruit of his cross, the price of his blood. God is not content with guardianship alone, which is of itself such little protection, so useless, fragile, so insufficient. *Upon your walls Jerusalem, he has set guardians.*[97] Even those who seem to be walls, even those reputed to be pillars,[98] need these guardians, and they most of all.

6. *He has given his angels charge over you to guard you in all your ways.* How this word ought to ignite reverence within you, bring forth devotion, bestow confidence. Reverence because of the presence of angels, devotion because of their benevolence, and confidence because of their guardianship. Walk cautiously;[99] the angels are everywhere near at hand, as God has charged them, in all your ways. In whatever small corner you will, in whatever quiet spot, have reverence for your angel. Would you have the audacity to do in an angel's presence what you would not in my sight? Do you doubt the presence of the angel you do not see? What if you heard? What if you touched? What if you smelled? Note that presence of something is established not only on the basis of sight. Not even all corporeal things are subject to sight. So how far removed from any corporeal sense are spiritual things, which need to be tracked down by spiritual senses? If you reflect upon faith, you find positive assent of the presence of angels, proof that they are never absent. It causes me no regret to say that faith regards the existence of angels with approval, since the apostle defines faith as being *"the conviction of things not seen."*[100] Thus they are present, and present to you, not only with you, but also for you. They are present that they might cover you with protection; they are present that they might do good for you. What will you render to the Lord for all his bounty?[101] Honor and glory to him alone,[102] if anything at all. Why to him alone? Because it is God who has given the charge, and because every perfect gift[103] is not a gift and is not perfect unless it is from God.

7. Yet as true as it is that God alone has given the angels this charge, it is nevertheless necessary to be thankful to them who obey God with such great charity and who come to our aid in our great need. Therefore, we are devoted to them, we are thankful for such grand guardians. Let us return love to them, let us honor them as much as we are able and as much as we ought. Yet all our love and our honor is returned finally to God, from whom, both for them and for us, all love and honor are poured out and by which we are able in turn to honor and to love. Surely, when the apostle said, *To God alone be honor and glory,*[104] it ought not be believed that he is contradicting the words of the prophet who gave witness that the friends of God ought also to be greatly honored.[105] I think this word of the apostle is like another where he said, *Owe no one anything, except to love one another.*[106] He did not wish to make this a defense for ignoring other responsibilities, especially as he himself said, *Honor to whom honor is due,*[107] and other things of this sort. But in order that you might understand more fully what he thought and admonished in both these verses, note that the light of lesser luminaries cannot be seen amid the rays of the sun. Do we, for all that, think that the stars have been removed? Or that they have been extinguished? Not in the slightest—they have been hidden for the time being by a fuller brightness and are not able to appear. In the same way, love prevails over all other obligations. Love alone should so reign in us that love appropriates for itself whatever we owe to others, outshining all other things. Thus we do everything on the basis of love. In the same way divine honor prevails and in a way prejudges everything, so that God alone is glorified not only before all things but in all things.[108] You can reasonably say the same thing concerning love. For what, beyond love, can individuals possibly hand over to others once they have given their whole heart, their whole soul, their whole strength[109] to their Lord God in love? And so then it is in God, brothers, that we can love his angels affectionately, as our future fellow heirs,[110] in the meantime established by the Father and set before us as guides and teachers. For now we are the children of God, even though it does not as yet appear so;[111] until that final day we are small children under guides and teachers, no different meanwhile from servants.[112]

8. Still, although we are children having a difficult, a very difficult and dangerous way remaining, what have we to fear under such guardians? Those who guard us in all our ways cannot be overcome or led astray, much less lead us astray. They are faithful, they are prudent, they are powerful. What should we fear? Let us, then, follow them, let us adhere to them, and we will dwell in the protection of the God of heaven. See how necessary their protection is, their guardianship in all your ways. *In their hands,* it says, *they will bear you up lest you strike your foot against a stone.* Does it seem a small thing to you that there is a stone of offense set along your way?[113] Consider what follows, *You will walk on the asp and the basilisk; you will trample the lion and the dragon underfoot.*[114] How necessary is a teacher, or even a porter, especially for a child traveling along these stages of the journey! *In their hands they will bear you up.* They will guide you in your ways, and they will lead the child where a child can walk. Moreover, they will not allow you to be tempted beyond what you can bear,[115] but they will support you in their hands that you may cross over every stumbling block. How easily one who is carried in their hands crosses over! As the common proverb goes, how buoyantly someone swims when another is holding up his chin.

9. Thus, whenever you encounter some great urge to temptation, or a furious tribulation threatening you, call on your guardian, your guide, your helper and consolation in tribulation and in opportunity. Shout out to God and say, *Lord, save us, for we are perishing.*[116] God does not sleep, nor does God slumber.[117] The Lord may, however, appear to hide in uncaring sleep for a time, for fear you might plunge headlong from these hands into a more dangerous way, simply because you were ignorant of that fact that you were being sustained by them. These hands are spiritual hands, and their assistance surely spiritual. Such spiritual aid is given to each of the elect for handling each difficulty, that is, the manner in which you discriminate among the various obstacles thrown your way, like so many walls of stones. This assistance is rendered spiritually in many ways by those angels set over you. I mention those obstacles that I believe are most common, and there are few among us who will not have experienced them. Is anyone in the midst of a violent storm, tossed about either by some physical infirmity, or by some worldly tribulation, or by some depression of the spirit, or by a certain apathy of soul? Already, such persons begin to be tempted beyond what they are able to bear.[118] They would be stumbling, striking their foot against a stone, if someone did not come quickly to their aid. But what is this stone? I understand it to be the stone of offense and the rock of scandal,[119] which shatters anyone who falls upon it, but which crushes anyone upon whom it falls.[120] I understand this stone to be the cornerstone, chosen and precious. I understand this stone to be the Lord Christ.[121] To murmur against Christ is to dash our

119

foot against this stone, being scandalized by a weak spirit in the midst of this storm.[122] And so there is need of angelic aid, of angelic comfort, of angelic hands when someone is already losing heart, already about to strike a foot against the stone. And truly, those who murmur and blaspheme do stumble against the stone, shattering and bruising not the stone they so furiously run up against but rather themselves.

10. I believe that sometimes men and women are supported by the angels as if by two hands, so that almost without consciously perceiving it they are carried over those very things that terrify them the most. And afterward they are not a little in awe at the ease with which they overcame something that at first had seemed so difficult. Do you wish to know what I understand these two hands to be? They reveal a double demonstration of the brevity of our present affliction compared to the eternity of our future reward. Or to put it another way, they reveal that painting or imprinting by which the heart feels, by some intimate affective knowledge, that this *slight momentary affliction is preparing for us an eternal weight of glory beyond all comparison, because we look not to the things that are seen but to the things that are unseen; for the things that are seen are transient, but the things that are unseen are eternal.*[123] Who could not believe that such good imprints upon the heart come from good angels, when it is certain, on the contrary, that the evil feelings flow into the heart through evil angels?[124] Have the angels as your familiars, my brothers, visit them with attentive consideration and devout prayer, for they are always present to guard and comfort you.

De sex alis cherubim

On the Six Wings of the Cherubim

Section One:
Hugh of St. Victor/Anonymous

Section Two:
Anonymous

Introduction

On the Six Wings of the Cherubim is a multifaceted treatise on the Seraphim (not, as one might think from the title, on the Cherubim!). The author uses the Seraphim as an outline or map of the spiritual journey. With the Seraphim as guides, the map developed in this treatise serves at once as an exemplar of divine incomprehensibility, an image or icon suitable for meditation upon God's mystery, and a model of the integration of time and eternity, body and spirit, and the created world with the "body" of God. The image of the Seraphim serves as well as a representation of the burning love of Christ and the active life of Christ's church in this age.

The treatise is, however, a redactive hybrid. *De sex alis cherubim*, or *On the Six Wings of the Cherubim*, has a long manuscript history of attribution to Alan of Lille (d. 1203).[1] In fact, it is found in its entirety only in Migne's volume devoted to Alan of Lille, *PL* 210:267A–280C. However, thanks to the work of Professor Grover Zinn, we know that much of Section One of the treatise is borrowed almost entirely and verbatim from a portion of Hugh of St. Victor's (c. 1096–1141) *De arca Noe morali*, or *On the Moral Ark of Noah*, found in *PL* 176:622C–626B. The portion of Section One not from Hugh's *Moral Ark* consists mostly of editorial insertions that hold the borrowed pieces together and that connect and bridge the material in Section One to Section Two. Marie-Thérèse d'Alverny, a noted authority on Alan of Lille, believed, wrongly as it turns out, that Alan did in fact write Section One. She speculated that Section Two was perhaps composed by Clement of Llanthony, an English Augustinian canon writing in the third quarter of the twelfth century. D'Alverny concluded that, overall, "the problem of authenticity of this text appears rather difficult to resolve."[2] This is certainly true of Section Two. Its author must remain anonymous. To sum up this issue of authorship: Section One was written by Hugh of St. Victor and an anonymous writer/redactor who may or may not have been the anonymous author of Section Two. In any case, it is probable that Alan of Lille did not contribute to the text at all.

Nevertheless, this delightful work on the Seraphim is a richly thoughtful and imaginative journey into God. Neglecting neither the created world nor the celestial heights, the human body nor the love of neighbor, the absence nor the presence of God, the work reflects the fiery outlines of the burning love of the Seraphim. Its writer/redactor, in bringing together Hugh of St. Victor's metaphysical work with what is essentially a penitential manual, has managed to bring together mind and heart and action, joining them around a central image of seraphic spirituality. It is, first, a philosophical and theological reflection on divine nature and attributes, and second, a manual for guiding the soul to love of neighbor and God. In both cases the shape of the logic, the shape of the journey is that of the Seraphim. And as we know from other writing on the subject, the shape of the Seraphim is the shape of love. It is with seraphic wings that we fly in the hot clear air of charity.

As Hugh says in Section One, the "contemplation of God's works fills our hearts." Using the seraphim of Isaiah 6 as a point of departure, this first section imagines a pictorial representation of the six wings of the Seraphim and God. Hugh uses the six wings and the various degrees of their flight to discuss the divine mystery including, among other attributes, the hidden and revealed natures of God, the "body" of God, creation and death, and redemption. He then invites us into contemplation of the Seraphim. This leads in turn to contemplation of all divine mysteries, leading in turn again to contemplation of the mystery of Christ, and finally to the contemplation of love itself and charity. The intent is that, as with the seraphim of Isaiah 6, the contemplation of love will guide us into ever deepening, divine understanding, which will result in our own "flight" into God and our own singing of God's praises, "Holy, holy, holy."

But the writer/redactor of *On the Six Wings of the Cherubim* was apparently not satisfied with Hugh's method of seraphic flight alone. For this writer, the very wings and feathers of the Seraphim needed careful grooming, preening, and care, or flight would not be possible. An awareness of the possibility of progress in holiness, an understanding that every aspect of angelic flight was a dependent reality and that that realty was God, a willingness to cleanse the body and focus the mind, and a growing wisdom concerning the various degrees of love of God and neighbor were all aids, for this anonymous writer, to successful "flight." And so, while Section One presents the seraphim as an exemplar of divine mystery and the "body" of God as equivalent to the created world and time, Section Two depicts the Seraphim as an exemplar of Jesus Christ himself in the fullness of his love and wisdom. This flight of love and wisdom is in part a flight back into the world, back into moral integrity and ministry to neighbor, and is itself "Christic flight," the humble flight of self-emptying, the flight of the servant.

Section Two, then, is a manual for imitation of what we could call a tropological Seraph, an angel whose flight and song of praise teach the recognition and growth of the moral or ethical self. Section One, on the other hand, is an anagogical Seraph, an angel of ascent, an angel whose flight leads into the mysteries of Christ, into the secret places of divine incomprehensibility, into peace. These two seraphic flight patterns are echoed in some of the last verses from scripture quoted in *On the Six Wings of the Cherubim*. Echoing the truth of the tropological Seraph, the treatise notes, *Greater love has no one than this, that they will lay aside their soul for the sake of a friend.*[3] And echoing the longing for peace of the anagogical Seraph, the author quotes, *Who will give me wings like the dove, that I might fly away and be at rest.*[4]

Finally, though the title of the treatise is *On the Six Wings of the Cherubim*, it is quite obvious that the writer/redactor intended not Cherubim but Seraphim. Section One explicitly names "seraphim" throughout, and being in part an exegesis of Isaiah 6, is focused on Isaiah's vision of the seraphim. In addition, the angels referred to are described as "burning," "fiery," "illuminating," attributes and characteristics associated with the Seraphim in the Christian tradition of angelic spirituality. Persons imitating these angels are also described with the same metaphors of fire and light. Angelic spirituality also, almost unanimously, describes the Seraphim, not the Cherubim, as having six wings. And finally, Section Two progresses through the first four wings to the final two, which again describe the seraphic attribute of love, in this case love of neighbor and love of God.

However, throughout the tradition of angelic spirituality, the Cherubim and Seraphim are often misconstrued and confused. In the Christian tradition, at the highest and deepest levels of self-understanding and divine union the categories of the Cherubim representing mind and the Seraphim representing love become fluid. At psychological, metaphysical, theological, and practical levels, the categories of knowledge and love, of Cherubim and Seraphim, of the mind and heart in God, intermingle.

Note on Translation: The full text, Sections One and Two, of *On the Six Wings of the Cherubim* is translated from *De sex alis cherubim* in *PL* 210:267A–280C. The text, as mentioned above, is attributed falsely to Alan of Lille. The portion of Section One that is from Hugh of St. Victor's *De arca Noe morali* can also be found in *PL* 176:622D–626B; 629D–630A. This portion from Hugh of St. Victor is available in English in *Hugh of Saint-Victor: Selected Spiritual Writings*, translated by a religious of the Community of St. Mary the Virgin (London: Faber and Faber, 1962), 52–58. In Section Two especially, I have translated *malum* as not only "evil," but also "harm," "affliction," "trouble," and by a family of words that reflect the metaphor of disease, that is, "sickness," "injury," "hurt," and "illness." Likewise with *peccatum*, I have used not only "sin" but also "iniquity," "transgression," "error," "lapse," and "fault."

On the Six Wings of the Cherubim
Section One

For an explanation of this drawing,[5] a discussion of the following authority seems to be in order.[6] Isaiah says, *I saw the Lord sitting upon a throne, high (excelsum) and exalted (elevatum).*[7] "High" indicates that it is in the most eminent, sublime place; "exalted" indicates that it has been transferred from the abyss to the higher places. Thus the "high thrones" are the angelic spirits, and the "exalted thrones" are the souls of the holy, having been translated across the abyss of this world to the joys of supernal peace.[8] And since God sits guarding both the angelic spirits and the holy souls, the Lord is said to sit upon both a high and an exalted throne.

Isaiah says following this that *the whole earth is full of God's majesty.*[9] By the "earth" the prophet signified every embodied creature who is filled with the majesty of God. Just as the divine essence, by reflective knowledge, guides the breath and spirit of created beings, so God brings the earth to completion by ordering and regenerating embodied creatures. Therefore, what is said elsewhere, *I fill heaven and earth,*[10] and again, *Heaven is my throne, and the earth is the footstool for my feet,*[11] is here described as, *I saw the Lord sitting,* etc., and then, *The whole earth is full of God's glory* and, *That which was under God filled the temple.*[12]

"The temple" is the spiritual understanding and capacity, whether of angels or of humanity, which is filled by those things that are under God. These things are "under God" because the immensity of divine labor is so great that nothing of the human or angelic capacity for understanding is sufficient for comprehending God's perfection. Our hearts are filled by the contemplation of these things, yet our hearts are not able to comprehend their immensity.[13] How then will we comprehend the Maker of the work when we are unable to grasp fully the works of the Maker?

Still, we are able to say that this *high and exalted throne* in which the Lord sits represents the eternity of God's divinity, since

concerning God alone is it said, *Who is dwelling in eternity.*[14] God is not one thing, God's eternity another, but as the throne is the seat of a ruler, so it is said that God alone sits in eternity.[15] And just as it is with God's essence, so it is also with God's omnipotence, neither beginning nor end can be found in either. God has always been, God has always been omnipotent, God has always been in and through God's own self, perfect and full, yet without excess. Therefore, it is said, *I saw the Lord sitting upon a throne, high and exalted,* for through God's eternity and by virtue of God's divinity God excels all creatures, transcending them in excellence, and ordering them through divine power.

Next the prophet says, *Those things below God filled the temple.* This can be understood as a kind of revolution of the seasons and as a circuit through the ages,[16] for while the seasons, in their journey, return back into themselves, they will also circumscribe a kind of circuit around the temple, thereby begetting life.[17] Thus when it is said, *Those things that were under God,* it ought to be understood that every "season" of the ages has been filled by the works of God so that every living thing trembles at the wonders of God. Thus you read, *Those things under him filled the temple.* That is, those things that filled the temple were under God since whatever revolves in the bounds of time is found between and beneath eternity. Indeed, the immensity of eternity surpasses the shallowness of temporal things far below it. Whatever is prior to time never begins, whatever lasts beyond time is indifferent toward the end, whatever is above time undergoes no change.

Upon it stood the seraphim.[18] The two seraphim are the two testaments.[19] And the seraphim (which means "burning"),[20] so beautifully represented in divine scripture, symbolize those men and women who are first illuminated by understanding and afterward are made to burn brightly with love. For surely, God reveals what our mind ought to desire. First God illuminates the mind as to its desires, then God restores the mind by setting it aflame. Thus our mind burns as the Seraphim bring burning into being, just as it is said elsewhere that whatever illuminates enlightens. Concerning this the apostle Peter said, *We have more certain words from the Prophets, which you will do well to attend to, as to a light shining in a dark place until the day dawns and the morning star rises in your hearts.*[21] Perhaps it is said, *The Seraphim stand upon it,* according to the similitude that Peter here utilizes allegorically to symbolize an effect that in turn produces the result of obedience in the heart. Thus the Seraphim themselves rise when they set us upright, they walk when they help us to make progress, and they stand when they transfix us in a holy undertaking.

But it ought to be inquired why God is said to sit upon the throne and why the Seraphim do not sit upon the throne but are said to stand upon it. And because in what was said above we have interpreted the throne in two ways, we ought to adapt the mode of our interpretation to the explanation of both. *I saw the Lord sitting upon a throne, high and exalted.* Therefore, if we take the throne of God to mean spiritual creatures, then God is correctly described as sitting upon a throne since the divinity of deity[22] is above all things. The divinity of deity neither advances in virtue nor gives birth to wisdom, since it is possible neither to augment what is already full nor to alter eternity.[23] But as often as the human mind is illuminated through an understanding of scripture, it is raised up to celestial contemplation and does indeed mount the throne. And if the mind transcends even the choirs of angels themselves, it advances into the very presence of the Creator. Such a mind in heavenly contemplation can ascend even upon the throne. But it stands; it does not sit as the Creator does. This is because the human mind advances to the place of the throne through labor, yet it is not able to remain in this place through its own nature. The labor of the soul is to stand; the quiescence or peace of the soul is to sit, a peace we have, as yet, not attained.

Moreover, unless God is sitting, nothing is above the throne of eternity. We ourselves stand when we begin to be through grace what God is in God's self through nature. Through our own nature, we are not able ourselves to arrive completely at that throne except through the labor of death. And while from the beginning of creation we are obliged to serve, we are nonetheless, through adoption, created to be inheritors of eternity.[24]

The prophet continues, *One [Seraphim] had six wings, and the other had six wings.*[25] That is, each had six wings joined two by two to make three pairs. The first pair represents the fact that both Seraphim conceal their own bodies with two wings; they do not conceal the Lord. In the same way both Seraphim extended two wings; this corresponds to the second pair of wings. In this second pair one wing is extended to conceal the head, not their own head in this case, but the "head" of the Lord. The other wing is extended to conceal the feet, again, not the feet of the Seraphim, but the "feet" of the Lord.[26] And finally, the third pair of wings represents the fact that both Seraphim, with two wings, flew, the one to the other.[27]

Therefore, if the Seraphim signify sacred scripture,[28] the three pairs of wings are the three senses of scripture: history, allegory, tropology. These in turn can be doubled,[29] since by a single reading souls can ascend to love of both God and neighbor. The two wings with which the Seraphim cover their bodies are the historical reading, which covers the mystical understanding with the garment of the letter. The two wings that are extended to the head and the feet of the Lord are allegory, since, when we learn the mystery of divine scripture, we penetrate, by an illumination of the mind, all the way to an understanding of divinity itself, which is before all things.

But it ought to be clearly understood that the wings that extend all the way to the head and also reach to the feet, by thus touching on both ends, also conceal divinity. This is so because, as often as we are torn away from ourselves by an inebriation of mind[30] to an understanding of this eternity, we find in the vision neither God's beginning nor end. We stretch out wings to the body when we understand God to have been before all things. These same wings cover God's "head" insofar as we discover no end in God. We also touch God's "head" when we consider God to be beyond all things, not only beyond time but also beyond even to eternity. But we touch God's "feet" when the more the human mind is polished to be made brilliant as it searches out and reflects the magnificence of God's eternity, the more we are made to wonder at the greatness of God's incomprehensible being.[31]

The incense burners that the angel has hanging down about it[32] signify the prayers of the contemplatives and the prayers of some actives and represent the duty of the holy angels to gaze upon the face of divine blessedness.[33] What was written in Isaiah, *They cover his face,*[34] and not God's head, ought to be understood in the same way as what has been written by Moses, *You will not be able to see my face, indeed, men and women will not see me and live.*[35] This is because such vision is the full understanding of divinity that is promised to the holy only in the eternal life, concerning which the apostle says, *We will see him face to face,*[36] and again, *Then I will understand just as I am understood.*[37] But throughout this degenerating mortal life, that face of God has been veiled and hidden. However, in the eternal life God will be revealed and manifested, not veiled.[38] So in the gospel the Lord bears witness to this when he says, concerning the good angel, *Their angels always see the face of my Father who is in heaven.*[39] Therefore it is important for the present treatment that in the sight of the angels the Lord's face remain uncovered. The words of the prophet are never changing,[40] still, it is said with truth that nothing concerning the beginning of God is understood, and so the head remains veiled from above. Thus what is said, *Their angels always see the face of my Father,* is surely able to stand, and as for ourselves, we must relinquish the unconcealed face of God to the angels. Other things we speak of now refer not directly to the words of the prophet, but to the picture.[41]

With two wings they flew.[42] These two wings, by which the Seraphim flew, signify tropology, since when we are instructed into good works by reading divine scripture, we are raised from one plane to another, and through such good works we even fly as *one to another.* We do this when we exhort ourselves and each other in zeal for good works. And in this "flight" of good works, flying we shout *holy, holy, holy*[43] when, through the good work of our Father who is in heaven, we seek not to increase our own glory, but God's alone. For what does it mean to shout *"holy, holy?"* unless to proclaim in an open way[44] that we have understood within ourselves the glory of our creation.

Having uncovered what God conceals, that the head and feet of the Lord are gathered together and hidden from us, it now remains to examine what ought to be considered concerning the rest of the body. If we designate the head of God to be that which was before the creation of the world, and God's feet to be what the future may hold after the consummation of this age, then we can truly understand the length of God's body between head and feet as that middle period between the beginning and the end of time. Therefore, the head and the feet are concealed because it is clear that we are not able to investigate the first and last things of God's body or of time. We are, however, able to see the things of the body, that is, the intermediate things of time; these things are "born" into the midst of the present age. This body is[45] the church, which began at the beginning of the world and will endure continuously to the end of the age. This is the ark, which extends all the way from the head to the feet, because the holy church itself extends all the way from the beginning to the end of time through the succession of generations. In this way the body of the Lord gives birth to no diminution; in this way the body of the Lord is brought to perfection. Indeed, if the holy church had already been perfected, as the apostle said, the end of the world would have already come about.[46]

But it ought to be understood that, just as in the drawing, where the wings encircle the feet and yet are neither in nor of the body, so also with the body of Christ. The body of Christ is the church, which dwells in the midst of evil nations. And when the church receives the assaults of the unfaithful, it is bruised by tempestuous storms as from outside the ark. At the same time, inside the ark, the church sustains the tribulations of the true brothers and sisters administered by the false brothers and sisters. Thus are the faithful tormented both inwardly and outwardly by death blows to the body. The unfaithful, whether inside or out, are not of the body of the church; they are opposed to any kind of holy body.

Still, all things are embraced in the arms of the body of the Lord. This means that all things of the universe are under his power, since no one is able to flee from his hands, whether to the right to their reward or to the left to their damnation. This is why members of the body who have recognized the power of the head are roused to salvation.

Christ, who on account of his compassion experienced trials and who by means of whose power prepares a remedy against all dangers, this Christ knows what it is that he sets free through the sacrifice of his body. The ark knows how to navigate the storm. The church, in a similar way, is cast upon the sea of life.[47] But this body, this church, is Christ, who is our navigator in the midst of the storm of life. Indeed, Christ is the very doorway to his church. The church is Christ's body, the medium through which Christ leads through himself into himself, providing shelter from the storm.

So that this Seraphim, an exemplar of the total person of Christ, might be made more clear to you, I depicted it in a visible form, with a head and bodily members.[48] This should more easily enable you, when you do see the whole Christ, to understand what we now refer to as Christ's invisible nature. Now I desire to represent the true person of this Seraphim to you, the Seraphim Isaiah himself testified to have seen. May the Seraphim I place before your eye be in concord with the exposition of Isaiah. And so that we do not pass beyond the intended goal of so great a matter, that is, the issue of the feet sitting upon the high throne, it is sufficient for me now (and for the listener) to recollect and bring to mind the Seraphim flying with their two wings. These Seraphim, beginning from the face, then through to the center and all the way to the feet, are like the outline of a path into God according the visions of the prophets Isaiah and Ezekiel.

On the Six Wings of the Cherubim
Section Two

The First Wing:
The First Feather of the First Wing

The first wing is not praise but confession. As the psalmist says, *Confess to the Lord for the Lord is good, His mercy endures forever,*[49] and of the guilty the apostle James says, *Confess your sins to each other.*[50] By means of confession we stand accused, the nature of errors is clearly brought to light. By means of confession the conscience is encouraged to narrate, with sorrow, one's infirmity, ignorance, and malice.

Thus the first feather of this wing is truth, a truth that denies every mere pretext of truth. For truth is not fiction; no mere imitation of truth ought to be a part of confession.[51]

HUGH OF ST. VICTOR/ANONYMOUS

The Second Feather of the First Wing

The second feather is integrity, which prevents the disfigurement or division of truth. Confession ought to be integrated, not mutilated or divided. The disfigurement of truth hides something. Confession of such disfigured truth allows repentance of some portion of sin, but not of everything; it reserves something harmful for itself. In fact, it retains certain hidden things in which it secretly delights. Such is the impiety of faithlessness, the flight from the righteous and from justice. The faithlessness of partial, disfigured truth contains within it a diminishing hope of forgiveness. It is the one wound sufficient for death.

Every division of truth fails to reveal the unity of integrity. Blessed Augustine, who, having been led to do so by modesty, repented every fault, has said that there are certain people who divide confession into parts within themselves and then, thus divided, wish to confess to diverse priests.[52] In this way, rather than reveal an integrated truth regarding sin, they seek to conceal its unity by confessing partial truths to different priests. In this way, through a series of partial confessions, they find a way to praise parts of themselves and to hold onto their hypocrisy. But they are, in fact, always deprived of the mercy that they think they will find through deception.

All things, especially the defects that keep us from the unity of truth, ought to be revealed in confession. Not only ought improper actions to be revealed, but their circumstances ought also to be brought forth. That is, the circumstances of place, time, mode, number, persons, and all aspects of the action relating to these things ought to be made clear. These things ought not to be negligently kept quiet but ought rather to be explicated diligently and detailed in confession. For there can be great diversity in detail between this place and that place, between one time and another, between this mode of behavior and that, between one person and another.

Perseverance in the habitual practice of confession, which looks time and again to the patience of God (who calls out to the penitent), calls forth that divine patience, nullifying divine wrath. In confession the whole person—sex, age, knowledge, conditions, necessities and order of life—ought to be given zealous consideration and expressly and habitually brought to light. Those who confess to each of these things will be, in a sense, dead to them.

The Third Feather of the First Wing

The third feather is endurance, since confession ought to be steadfast and morally strong. This feather of endurance drives out ten things that hinder confession. What are these? They are shame, fear, contempt of priests, despair, obstinacy, perversity, ignorance, forgetfulness, negligence, and necessity, which alone is excusable.

Unless we endure and our sins are uncovered and revealed in confession, later, during periods of trial, shame will diminish our strongest virtues. Shame resists even the most ordinary virtues with great strength. Fear thrusts anxiety into the heart of patience, driving out every fruit of patience. Contempt of the priesthood empties the heart of its deepest well of reverence, veneration, and love for the atoning work of Christ. Despair darkens the goodness of divine compassion. And obstinacy eviscerates the severe gravity of divine justice.

The reasonableness of faith exterminates perversion, and divine providence leads away from ignorance. The manner and labor of zealous confessional examination, recollected later in the memory, illuminate the darkness of forgetfulness. A fervent spirit plucks out and destroys laziness and the weakness of negligence. Negligence however, is not the cause of every mistake; often because of fate, necessity leads us to blunder.

The Fourth Feather of the First Wing

The fourth feather is humility, which excludes the character of pride. In confession one ought to maintain a mind of humility, a tongue of humility, and a face of humility. *The Lord opposes pride, but gives grace to the humble.*[53]

The Fifth Feather of the First Wing

The fifth feather is simplicity. Simplicity calls one to account for lack of endurance, ignorance, and evil while defending nothing, excusing nothing, and degrading nothing.

Therefore, confession ought to be based on truth, integrity, endurance, humility, and simplicity. It ought to be truth without disfigurement or division, without similitude; it ought to include integrity without diminution; it ought to accommodate endurance without wavering, hesitation, or despair; it must be done in humility without boasting or presumption; it ought to be undertaken with simplicity—a virtue without rival—making no excuses and finding no defenses for our wrong actions.

This is the first wing with its five feathers.

The Second Wing

Confession is followed by satisfaction.[54] These first two wings together create and form compunction. Indeed, in every action of repentance, it is necessary that compunction, confession, and satisfaction be established together. Compunction pricks the conscience, confession accuses, and satisfaction comforts. Compunction investigates the occasion of death, confession manifests it, and satisfaction cures it. Compunction enumerates evils, confession condemns them, and satisfaction corrects them. Compunction lances a sore, confession articulates a path into health, satisfaction applies the poultice. Compunction finds the wound, confession opens the wound, and satisfaction restores the wound to health.

Compunction is contrition of the heart, yet if compunction obstructs heartfelt repentance, it results in a sadness of soul. Such division of the heart calls forth bitterness of soul. But true, unified compunction gives birth to a sweet wonder appealing to the senses. As scripture says, *Tear your heart and not your garments,*[55] and elsewhere, *In your bed, search your heart.*[56]

Two situations create compunction: fear of God,[57] of course, and hope. Fear is the condition that begins compunction; hope is the motive of its consummation. Fear of God allows us to search our hearts, to acknowledge that humanity was indeed wondrously established by our Creator, to enumerate how we have been sustained by God without payment or profit, to accept how we have been made upright in essence and how we have been enriched in our human condition by reason. Compunction caused by fear also brings to mind other good things that the Creator will gather together and the evil that is redeemed by the Good itself.

On the other hand, fear reveals the distribution of justice and the threats of punishment, it can bring horror to the soul of the penitent, it confounds the mind, it darkens our path with forbidden things, and it stirs up a storm of mischief within the quiet of our security. Fear thus lays open the manner and number of our sins, the rigor of divine justice, and the intention of future judgment. Fear thus vexes the soul but by pricking the soul expels sin. The power of fear stands before hope and invigorates it; hope is thus greatly strengthened.

Fear Is Empty When It Is Not Made Firm by Hope

Without the fear of God, nothing exists; but if hope is absent, nothing good is present. Scripture says, *How exceedingly great is your sweetness, Lord, which you have hidden for those who fear you.*[58] However, nothing whatsoever will be present or sweet unless it is brought forth by hope. Therefore, from fear comes contrition of heart, while hope brings the fruit of contrition's labor. But how is virtue, the fruit of our contrition, strengthened by hope? From divine promise. Listen to scripture: *Hope in the Lord, and you will pasture in the Lord's richness,*[59] and also, *Hope in the Lord and the Lord will do this,*[60] and also, *The Lord does not abandon those who hope,*[61] and also, *Blessed are all who hope in the Lord.*[62] If, therefore, you fear the Lord to the point of experiencing compunction, you hope in the Lord in such a way that you will be reconciled to the Lord. If you fear God because God is able to destroy you in hell, hope in God *because God does not wish death by sins, but that you be converted and live.*[63] If you fear because Wisdom *knows the hidden things of the heart,*[64] hope in God because God *will illuminate the hidden things of*

136

darkness.[65] If you fear God because God leaves nothing unpunished, hope because God *will redeem Israel from all its iniquities.*[66] Therefore, as fear comes before and is followed by the virtue of compunction, so hope promotes and leads toward the fruit of reconciliation; through fear compunction is aroused, while through hope the grace of reconciliation is acquired. *At whatever hour he laments, he will be saved.*[67] Fear leads to tears; hope merits salvation.

We have briefly declared what compunction of heart is, where and to what it leads. We will now discuss satisfaction, which is the second wing.

Concerning Satisfaction. The Second Wing

Satisfaction is the fulfilled execution of an effective repentance, or, if you will, the worthy reproach and correction of sins.

Now we ought to ponder our iniquity in our heart according to the quality or kind of the transgression, with an eye toward correction and improvement. It is said, *Go, produce fruit worthy of repentance.*[68] Indeed, just as there is the tree and there is also the fruit, so there is one thing we may call repentance and another we may call the fruit of repentance, which is satisfaction. Repentance represents the sad recognition of having been lost, when you grieve because of the harm you have done.

Therefore, when you reject and condemn the malevolence you have caused, you participate in repentance. Subsequently, when by means of satisfaction you correct and set straight the harm you have done, you have the fruit of repentance. You do penitence if what you do displeases you, while you participate in the fruits of repentance if you no longer continue to chase after evil and thereby begin to purify the harm that you do. Repentance is acknowledging personal complicity; the fruit of repentance is choosing to accept correction. A person's choosing freely to repent reflects the degree of correction; for that reason it is necessary to perform the fruits of repentance with dignity. However, if in even a very small correction the affliction itself becomes in any way an object of desire, then the worthy fruit of your repentance does not accrue to you.

But you say to me, "How am I to know when my repentance might be worthy and complete?" And I must say that since this is something that you are never able to know, it becomes unavoidable that you must always repent. You are never able to do too much to satisfy the harm you have done, so it is better that you do more than enough rather than too little. For this reason satisfaction is restless, it is full of anxiety concerning works and zealous in prayer. But this is not all bad, for in this way a balanced sense of personal complicity is established whereby guilt ends but devotion goes on without end. However, in the interest of consoling the sinner's conscience during critical times of anxiety, the manner and degree of external repentance have been ordered in such a way that you begin to have full and perfect faith in the perfecting work of God. Through such faith one begins to have confidence, and under the assured expectation of healing, one resides in the hope of divine compassion concerning the indulgence and remission of sins. And thus with such a truth as the perfecting work of God, and with such great hope of divine compassion, you will be filled to the full with the blessed duties of repentance.

The First Feather of the Second Wing

The first feather of this wing is the complete renunciation of sin, which has the effect of shutting the devil's door. To renounce sin completely is to turn away from sickness. *Turn from sickness,*[69] scripture says. From what sickness? From the sickness of vanity, from the illness of injustice, from the injury of malice, from the evil of irreverence. *I do not sit,* said the psalmist, *with the assembly of the vain, nor do I consort with the unjust; I hate the congregation of the malicious, and I will not sit with the impious.*[70] These four paths give birth to four affections or negative states of mind. These are love of self, love of the world, hatred toward brothers and sisters, and the loss of the love of God. The first affection generates vanity, the second injustice, the third malice, the fourth gives birth to irreverence. Vanity moves back and forth into and out of the self; injustice is reflected in the face of the neighbor; malice is turned back upon a brother or sister; irreverence is extended into God. Those who seek to find out who they are on their own are vain and empty and foolish. They are enemies of the people. Full of greed for the purse of their own neighbors and seeking to acquire it for themselves with a sword, they aspire thereby to be glorified by the magnificence of their own misbegotten wealth. Those who wish to do harm to a brother or sister are of a malicious nature. Irreverent are those who do not give credit to God, or if they do give credit, do so with disdain or contempt.

The second feather of this wing is the streaming forth of tears. This washes and cleanses the wound of sins.

The third feather is the mortification[71] of the flesh. This feather bathes, wipes, and dries the wound of sin.

The fourth feather is the bestowing of alms. This feather binds the contrite, consoles the downhearted, and heals all things.

The fifth feather is prayerful devotion. This last feather maintains all healthy things in existence.

The Third Wing

The third wing represents purification of the flesh. The flesh of the body has been cleansed when no extravagance contaminates it. Extravagance rips away the seed of every virtue.

The first feather of this wing is the eye of virtue. This feather drives out wantonness. The feather circles the eye; it does not long for another; it does not see another's wife or husband, for instance, as an object of desire. Indeed, though luxuriant and even provocative forms hover before the eyes, the eyes and the mind of this feather seek out a modest appearance.

The second feather is purity of hearing. The pure of hearing are those who are not distracted by the voice of envy, who do not listen to words of slander or blasphemy, who do not assist false accusations, lies, irrationality, immodest song, or theatricality. They are enclosed, as it were, by virtue. They do not hear the opinions of the violent nor do they listen to the obscene; rather, they turn away from the mire of every corruption.

The third feather is the scent of modesty. If anyone receives this good and pleasant scent and seeks after the odor of sweet compassion by means of merciful works, the fragrance is modest. But, whoever marches along anointed with even the most distinguished perfumes and yet does not possess the scent of virtue, this person breathes the very filth of a putrid stench. The odor of this seemingly sweet perfume is, in fact, the most horrible stench of life.

The fourth feather is temperate taste. This feather undermines the immoderation of gluttony and drunkenness. *As for them [the enemies of the cross of Christ], their god is their stomach, and they glory in confusion, their wisdom is of the world.*[72] Concerning this, Gregory the Great said, "Any virtue is destroyed by carnal desire when the stomach is not satisfied to be simply full."[73] Thus the virtues of the soul are put to trial when the stomach is overindulged. Concerning drunkenness, anxiety, and debauchery the Lord has said, *See that your heart is not weighed down in dissipation and the anxieties of life, for that day will come upon you suddenly.*[74] Drunkenness is the parent of strife, the mother of anger, and the mistress of wantonness and disgrace. Those possessed by drunkenness are not in possession of themselves; those possessed by drunkenness are less than fully human; those possessed by drunkenness do not sin, rather they are themselves sin. Drunkenness is an alluring demon, a sweet venom, a voluntary madness, a seductive respectability, an injury to modesty. The Christian knows of but is not possessed by these.

The fifth feather is holy touch. The hand of a Christian does not come in contact with the sordid nature of sin; nothing unclean touches the flesh; if an unclean thing is touched it creates impurity. If members in the mandated offices of God serve devotedly, they ought to be called clean; and if any abound in excesses beyond the written or divine law, they ought to be called unclean and repudiated. Such actions are shameful. And this I believe to be what the apostle said, *Just as you used to deliver parts of your body in service to iniquity, so now deliver the members of your body to serve righteousness in the road of sanctification.*[75]

Thus the third wing is composed of a virtuous eye, purity of hearing, the scent of modesty, temperate taste, and holy touch.

The Fourth Wing

The fourth wing is purity of mind. The first feather of this wing is a sincere and upright disposition of mind. This disposition of mind ought to incorporate right and sincere desire. It will be right desire if the mind eagerly pursues what it ought to desire; it will be sincere desire if the mind exhorts one into the path of integrity. Amnon delighted in his sister.[76] The affective disposition of his delight was perhaps right desire, but since he delighted in his sister in a way that he ought not to have done, this same affective disposition was a wanton and completely insincere desire.

The second feather is the delight of the mind in the Lord. Scripture says, *Delight in the Lord, and the Lord will give you the requests of your heart.*[77] This feather creates and forms the virtue of contemplation. Concerning this the Lord has said, *Mary has chosen the better part, which will not be taken from her.*[78]

The third feather is well-ordered and elegant thinking. Such thinking receives nothing that is inelegant and brings one to a pure conception of place and a discerning conception of time.

The fourth feather is a holy will. Here, the peace of the angels from heaven is brought down to men and women of good will. *There is no peace for the wicked, says the Lord.*[79] Oh, how desirable is the name of peace! How it firms up the stable foundation of the Christian religion; how sweet are the words, *Glory to God in the highest,* and what is added, *And on earth peace to men of good will.*[80] Angels from heaven hasten to be in the society of men and women they consider to be of pure mind and good will. After perfection of the flesh, the angels delight in conveying these men and women up into the contemplation of true peace. Then dying together in the flesh, they gaze upon everything that the angels do or say concerning peace and the revealed radiance of good will. For men and women such as these, even if an infirmity or ignorance must be kept at bay by the performance of a good work, before the eyes of the highest judge and by the integrity with which they cling to a pure heart of good will, the judge excuses them.

The fifth feather is simple and pure intention. Concerning this the Lord has said, *If your eyes are simple, your body will be filled with light.*[81] In this, an intention is symbolized by the eyes, action is signified by the body. Therefore, we ought to understand the evangelist as saying that we know our every work to be elegant and pleasing in the sight of God if done with a heart of simplicity. Such works are celestial by nature with regard to their intention; they reflect the eye of charity because *the fullness of the law is love of charity.*[82] Therefore, we ought to receive this eye of intentionality ourselves. Then, if whatever we do we do with intention, and if we gaze upon those things which we ought to gaze upon, and if what we do is done with simplicity and purity, then all of our actions will, unavoidably, be good.

The whole body drives a person in every work. This is why the apostle calls men and women to avoid certain works of which he disapproves and why he advises mortification of the flesh: *Put to death, therefore, the members of your body that are of the earth: sexual immorality, impurity, avarice,*[83] and other such evil. It is not what any person does, but rather the contemplative reflection under which the soul carries out the act. Indeed, the fruit of every work consists in a simple integrity of intention. Withdrawing from every worry and weighing the balance of our iniquities in confession, we examine the intention of our thoughts and whatever our thoughts might give birth to in action. With fair and just freedom, we examine a thought's birth in action and inquire as to whether the thought might be full of respectability for the public good, whether it is appropriately heavy with the fear of God, whether it results from an integrated perception, whether it reveals the nature of human affairs or whether it is overburdened with the presumptions of the will, whether the depth of its merit might not in fact be rooted in an empty abyss, and whether it has the pleasure of smiling upon God's glory. So that we might understand the perfection of our intention by worthwhile consideration, the thought ought to be compared to the acts and witness of the prophets and apostles and weighed according to its value in the public sphere. And finally, so that imperfect or condemned thoughts and actions might not mistakenly be considered harmonious, we ought to weigh them with care against worthy models and by public examination and if necessary, diligently refute them.

The Fifth Wing

The fifth wing is the love of neighbor.

In love of neighbor the first feather is to avoid injury to others either by word or by deed. Concerning this very thing scripture says, *Do to others as you would have them do to you.*[84] This feather forms the virtue of innocence. The innocent person is the one who, when it is possible, wishes to do no harm. *Who will ascend*, the psalmist asks, *the mountain of the Lord? The one with innocent hands*, etc. *Who is the one with innocent hands? The one who does no evil to his neighbor. The one who leads no one into the view of evil things.*[85] And who is the personification of these evil things if not the devil? Whoever wishes to do no harm to neighbor, regardless of the time or circumstance, already feels the first stirrings of love.

The second feather is not to avoid injury but rather to do good in every word and deed. *Brother helping brother is like a strong and fortified city.*[86] This feather elevates and carries the virtue of compassion forward to a culmination of perfection. *Blessed are the merciful.*[87] Those who are zealous to do good in all things breathe the living flame of true love.

The third feather is not to become used up or to weep over much in reaching out to an injured friend, rather, by the courage of true courtesy, to avoid feeling so burdened that you are no longer of any value to them. Done from a sense of magnanimity, a series of kindnesses in support of a brother or sister always delights the heart. Those who understand this count up the sacrifices they make toward worthy ends; they do not waste them. Those who are not able to reach out to their friends with a refreshed and gladdened heart suffer sadness. Concerning this feather scripture says, *He who overlooks personal loss on account of a friend is righteous, but the way of the wicked deceives even a friend.*[88] The one who understands these things is a friend of love.

The fourth feather is to lay aside the soul for the sake of a brother or sister. What does this mean, to lay aside the soul for another? It means to abandon one's own will for the salvation of a neighbor, for the eternal salvation of a brother or sister, and as an articulation of friendship to endure freely the partition of death. Concerning this scripture says, *Greater love has no man than this, that he will lay aside his soul for the sake of a friend.*[89] Nothing has a greater capacity to stoke the flames that boil up the fever of love.

The fifth feather is to persevere in all these forms of love. They, in turn, perfect the virtue of perseverance. The fighter is not crowned till the end; those who persevere do not know what it means to quit the battle.

The Sixth Wing

The sixth wing is the love of God.

This wing also has five feathers. Whoever longs for and strives after nothing other than God has the first of these feathers. Longing for and striving after God is the motion of this love.

Whoever distributes this love actively among brothers, sisters, and the world for the sake of God has the second of these feathers. Those with this feather retain a part of this love for themselves and yet bestow a part of their love upon others for their God's sake. Apportioning love to self and others for God's sake is the flame of this love.

Those who, for God's sake, reserve nothing for themselves but relinquish all things in God's name, these people have the third of these feathers. Giving over all things in the name of God is the act of this love.

Those who deny themselves for God alone, these people have the fourth feather. They deny themselves when they abandon themselves completely to accomplishing the will of God alone. Complete self-abandonment is the boiling passion of this love.

Whoever perseveres in these things has the fifth feather. Because *Whoever perseveres until the end will be saved.*[90] Perseverance is the unceasing nature of this love.

These are the wings of which the psalmist said, *Hide me under the shadow of your wings, from the face of the wicked who assail me.*[91] And who said, *I will take hope in the shadow of your wings until the injustice has passed.*[92] These are the feathers of which the psalmist also said, *Who will give me feathers like the dove, that I might fly away and be at rest?*[93] "That I might fly away," the psalmist said, abandoning the earth, striving passionately after heaven, and delighting in the eternal blessing, the true freedom of peace. Amen.

Umiltà of Faenza

De angelis sanctis

Sermons
on the Holy Angels

Introduction

Few saints of the church have had as personal or as intimate a relation with angels as Saint Umiltà of Faenza. Not only does she know the names of two guardian angels given especially to her by Christ, but one gets the feeling from reading her accounts of their presence in her life that she can, as well, touch, smell, and see them as if they were a part of her closest family. Though she is acutely aware of the nine orders of angels and their various functions,[1] she is less interested in those "faceless" orders than in individual, personalized, named angels who seem to be friends, companions, and cherished intimates as well as guides and protectors. She speaks with her two angels about matters as grand as the very nature and speech of God, and about matters as mundane as the burdensome tasks of founding and guiding a monastery. One angel, of overwhelming beauty, adorned in gems and a coat of every color, has been with her from birth. This one's name is Sapiel, the Wisdom of God. The other, from the highest courts of heaven, also of fiery, dazzling beauty and dwelling in the very presence of the Trinity, is named Emmanuel, God is with us. She loves them both, as she says, with a love that is founded in God. They, in turn, guide her in all her ways into an ever-deepening adoration of Mary, the mother of God, and into the clear and cleansing rivers flowing from the throne of the Father, Son, and Spirit.

147

Umiltà of Faenza (Saint Humilitas), foundress of two monasteries for Vallombrosan nuns, was born at Faenza, Italy, in the province of Romagna in the year 1226. Rosanna de Negusanti, called Umiltà (Humility) upon her taking vows and entering the order, was born into a wealthy and high-ranking family. From her *Vitae*, compiled in the fourteenth century, we learn that "from childhood she was intent on divine obedience, occupying her time in constant prayer, and generous alms giving."[2] She had always intended to lead a celibate life, but when her father died, it became necessary for her to marry. Marrying a gentleman of Faenza, one Ugoletto Caccianemici, she had several children, all of whom died at a young age. After her husband experienced a serious illness, Rosanna, with the assistance of her doctors, persuaded him to allow them to lead a celibate life and to allow her to enter a religious vocation. They both joined the double monastery of St. Perpetua, a community of Canons Regular under the Augustinian Rule, he becoming a lay brother and she a choir nun.

Wanting more solitude and austerity, Umiltà withdrew first to a house of Poor Clares and then to a cell adjoined to the church of Saint Apollinaris. As an enclosed recluse devoted to a life of solitude, austerity, and penance, Umiltà interacted little with the world; the only aperture of her cell was a small "squint" that enabled her to follow Mass and receive holy communion.[3] She nonetheless managed to attract followers, who began to build cells next to hers. After Umiltà had lived twelve years as a recluse, with a number of young women wishing to follow her, the Vallombrosan abbot general persuaded her to emerge from her seclusion to organize a foundation for women. The Vallombrosan was a reforming order founded in 1036 by St. John Gualbert, with a Rule based on the Benedictine but with greater stress on austerity and penance. In 1266, at a place called Malta outside the walls of Faenza, she established the first Vallombrosan nunnery, of which she became abbess; it was known as Santa Maria Novella alla Malta. The monastery, dedicated to the Virgin, thrived. In 1282 St. Umiltà founded a second house in Florence, dedicated to Saint John the Evangelist, where she died on May 22, 1310.

St. Umiltà is known for composing and preaching nine Latin sermons and for writing Lauds to the Virgin Mary in verse. Tradition has it that she was illiterate, though it is possible that her lack of knowledge of Latin is an exaggeration. Whether illiterate or trained, from a time shortly after her death her cult presumed that the sermons were given to her miraculously, some from an angel, some directly from God. The first three sermons are primarily doctrinal; the remaining six are closer in form to prayer and meditation. The sixth sermon combines a number of erotic themes, particularly around her love for Saint John the Evangelist. In her "little lamb" meditation, also in the sixth sermon, Umiltà uses motherhood and the desire to nurture as metaphors for the soul's union to Christ.[4] On the basis of the many miracles attributed to her, the process of beatification was begun soon after her death, but her cult was not authorized until 1720, by Clement XI, when her feast day was fixed at May 23. The title of saint was confirmed in 1948.

Umiltà seems to have been guided by a wide range of divine figures. In her sermons she feels herself surrounded at all times and spoken to on occasion by, among others, the Virgin Mary, John the Evangelist, numerous saints, and a panoply of angels—especially two or three to whom she is particularly close. And on occasion she speaks directly with God. Her sermons also exhibit discourses on the Incarnation, the nobility and offices of the angels, and praises for the mother of God, John the Evangelist,[5] and her guardian angels.

Throughout her sermon on the holy angels, Umiltà plays self-consciously with various levels of divine, angelic, and human "speech" and the revelatory "hearing" implied in their reception. One level of this "speech" is the sermon or dialogue between God and the angels. Another level is the sermon or conversation between those same angels and herself. Still another is the sermon or "speech" of *Sermon Four: On the Holy Angels* itself, spoken to her sisters. The implication throughout is that by hearing the "speech" of the angels and by imitating their silent, joyful listening (as she has), or by hearing her own sermon and imitating her own silent, joyful listening, the sisters can hear and imitate the divine sermon itself, thereby participating in holy conversation, in divine speech.

Note on Translation: The following selections are translated from Umiltà, *Sermoni*, ed. Adele Simonetti. An earlier edition by T. Sala, *Sanctae Humilitatis de Faventia: Sermones* (Florence, 1884) is difficult to find in the United States. Portions of Umiltà's sermons and *Vitae* can be found in *Acta Sanctorum, Maii V*, vol. XVIII, *Vita Sanctae Humilitatis Abbatissae, Analecta* (Antverpiae, 1685), 214–16, and *Maii VII*, vol. XX, Appendix ad Diem XXII Maii, *Sermo Sanctae Humilitatis Abbatissae*, 815–26. Italian translations of the sermons can be found in Pietro Zama, *Santa Umiltà: La vita e i "sermones"* (Faenza: Fratelli Lega Editori, 1974). Portions of *Sermon Four* in English translation can be found in Elizabeth Alvilda Petroff, ed., *Medieval Women's Visionary Literature* (New York: Oxford University Press, 1986), trans. Richard J. Pioli, and in Elizabeth Petroff, *Consolation of the Blessed* (New York: Alta Gaia Society, 1979). Simonetti, Sala, and the *Acta Sanctorum* label this sermon on the angels *Sermon Four;* the partial translation by Pioli is given as *Sermon Two.*

 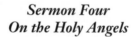

Sermon Four
On the Holy Angels

Whoever wishes to learn by hearing divine speech[6] must be silent with great interior joy. A still heart is a loving heart, which listens with a kind of ardent fever and receives inwardly the sweet allurements of the holy words. Therefore, whoever goes out to gather divine speech ought to do so with wonder and great delight. Even those who suffer great pain or grief, as if in a kind of stupor, even these can be awakened to the melodious cadence of this speech. And those who already delight in the highest celestial forms of love will be strengthened all the more.

This sermon[7] speaks of the angels in common, because there is joy in all the saints. It speaks specifically of two of the most noble creatures who have always remained steadfast. I have been moved by my love for them to point out how sublime is the grandeur by which God, in the beginning, created them, granting them the image of divine beauty. God dignified them with every adornment, placing them above the firmament. God gave them knowledge of every science with which they might be servants and ministers of divine greatness. God gave wings to each, so that those messengers who carry extraordinary news of the most noble magnitude might fly quickly, crossing any barrier, reaching every height. For it is on account of their sublime beauty that they are the ministers of the Trinity. Whenever they unfurl their wings in flight and then gather them gracefully together again, they make their ministry a sweet song. Since they are spirits endowed with the power of the Most High, they make a song that no other creature is able to sing.

These are the angels who are marked in heaven and placed in positions of great strength. They are positioned in orders, of which there are nine, and each order is named initially according to its own greatness. But all of the angels are also named among themselves, having each a personal, individual name of great beauty. The first angels of whom I will begin to speak are two who are familiar to me, who are no less than the others, and who have a name of supreme significance. All the others, which I have named elsewhere,[8] show forth their splendor as well.

I love all the angels of heaven,[9] but two are the most cherished darlings of my joy who give me comfort day and night and offer me their gifts from the bountiful wealth of their riches. My Lord assigned them to me as guardians so that they might protect me from all harm. They have attended perfectly to this divine injunction as they have placed me, as it were, within the protection of their strong fortress. On my right and my left hand[10] both angels hold me close, so that I cannot fall except through my own foolishness. While I hold[11] myself firmly to them, my enemies are unable to harm me. And by the grace of John the Evangelist I know the proper name to call both of them.

One comes from that order of angels who are given to Christians as guardians in this life. And mine is not among the lesser angels. I know this for certain; I learned it through having heard[12] their speech. Her[13] appearance is of overwhelming beauty, like a precious stone or a pearl of great value.[14] And I love her before all

151

others that remain as her companions. She is called the angel Sapiel, a name that reason reveals as meaning divine wisdom. My heart fills with joy every time I hear the name. She has all the rich charms, all of which she bestows abundantly upon me. Indeed, having been present with me steadily from the moment I was born into this life, I know by her courtesy and courtly manners that she is full of piety.

But because I have led a sinful life and troubled her, I accuse myself before her. Yet Sapiel is good. She has spared my sin and my foolishness. She has always been the most faithful advocate for my soul before Christ. And my heart finds great consolation when her love is tested within me,[15] for her love is full of every virtue and through it divine wisdom is established. She is adorned from head to toe with precious stones,[16] and her garment is of every color, for my angel has been blessed with great power. Christ himself has assigned her to me, and thus her companionship is mine in heaven.

The other angel is one of the Cherubim,[17] who have six wings[18] and who sit upon the highest throne, and whose power from the angelic order of the highest magnitude is exulted above all others. This angel remains in the imperial courts of the highest heaven, contemplating the nobility of divine beauty. The clear spark from which divine love is inflamed is always burning within this angel, and since she herself is most beautiful, she remains near the Trinity and must herself burn hot with the fire of beauty. Worthy of the highest realms of heaven, she has been admirably named. Christened from the mouth of John the Evangelist and with the great depth of his wisdom, she is the angel Emmanuel.[19] And that name, which is the verbal expression of her greatness, thrives and grows as the evangelist knew it would. It would be easier to count the drops in the great breadth of the sea than it would be to say or to think or to see the magnitude of her goodness. And that name, her verbal expression, does not begin to be the equal of her supernal magnitude. I cannot tell you of her fullness; my mouth makes only the sounds of a stuttering baby.

This angel, who is full of every breadth and magnitude, was given to me by my Lord after my thirtieth year. It was at that time when I had entered into thoughts of more important matters since my flock was given into my care[20] and I had neither the strength nor power of her might for that work. But the angel Emmanuel opened her wings and helped relieve me of the anxiety of this great labor, for she is in the glory of God and serves as interpreter of the dominion and power[21] descending from the greatest heights. Emmanuel, being compassionate and devoted to God, consoled me, giving always to me abundantly of her many treasures. Clearly, among her treasures, is the praise and glory represented by her blessed name, which is full of beauty of many kinds. Indeed, her power in heaven is such that no likeness of its loftiness can be named. In fact, Emmanuel is baptized in that royal river that always flows forth from the throne of the most high, in which the exalted God the Father remains, and the Son and the Spirit, who flames forth. The rivers, of which there are five, are greater than all seas—and over each river in its great magnitude, God the Most High remains seated. The rivers, of which there are four major ones, all flow to the sea. In their union, what they were as many in multitude becomes one in magnitude. My Emmanuel was baptized in this multitude and magnitude, in this river flowing to the sea from the throne of the Most High.

From
Sermon Two[22]

O archangel Gabriel, messenger of the most high, I entreat you to allow me to receive the most glorious infant Jesus as easily as did the Virgin[23] when you announced to her that she would conceive a child in her precious womb.[24] O holy angels of God and all Archangels, O Emmanuel and Sapiel, who are my angels, I pray to you, most sweet ones, that from all your powers you might assist me to picture the Virgin's inner chamber before my eyes so that I might be able to contemplate Mother and Son and from her lap receive her child into my arms.

From
Sermon Eleven[25]

And you, my ruddy angels, visit me in all my pathways. Rouse your guard to a fever pitch so that my enemies may not advance upon the door of my soul. Since you were given to me from the beginning, put your sword before me, guard me in every season from my enemies.

Put your sword in your right hand at the first gate, the gate of my mouth. Constrain it against vain words, hold it closed against lazy speech, so that when such foolish words do wish to exit, they will not be allowed to escape.[26] Sharpen my tongue with a piercing edge so that it may cut away vices and plant virtues to the praise and glory of the highest king and of his divine mother. Place two seals of love upon my eyes with your holy fingers to correct their vision, so that they will not look with longing upon the things of this world. Keep my eyes continually open and aroused to vigilance lest out of sleepiness they throw the Divine Office into confusion or fatigue the mind when it ought to be praising God. Hold my ears with your holy hands in such a way that they may be firm in the name of Jesus so that no evil word bearing poison to my soul can ever enter them. Again, open, prepare, and excite my eyes to the praise of God, his mother, my angels in their particular heavens, and all of the divine court. Bind my feet in such a chain of love that they are unable to trespass into any path of error, and so that all my steps might honor Christ and his mother. Hold my hands fast between your blessed wings, always prepared and eager for divine worship. Do not permit the wings of evil angels to draw near. They always cause the soul to dwell in wretchedness. Withdraw every deceitful odor so that my nose allows only the fragrance of the most precious flowers from paradise to enter my soul.

O my sweetest angels, perform works of charity through the love of Christ. Give me the guardians I beg for my soul's usefulness. Hold fast to your good guardianship so that my bodily senses become the strong foundation of my spiritual senses, making it possible for my soul to rest in delight with her Beloved. Hold me to the paths of love with such firmness, that when the floods of this world threaten my soul they are unable to engulf it, to draw it down, or to drown it. Always protect my soul with your love.

My most beloved angels, I have been placed under your stewardship. May the protection I beg be made firm in me through his name, because there remains within me something that brings forth the greater traitor who carries accounts in and out at all hours. I could never say to you, "Send him to prison." I cannot capture him; he is of such a condition that he can be killed but not captured, and he is lord of his whole treasure.[27] So who have the capacity to judge themselves? Let him who reads and hears understand the reason. Our heart is our noblest possession, our dearest wisdom, our deepest treasure. The heart can be captured only by the love of Christ. And only Christ can fill it.

Section Two
Commentaries on the
Celestial Hierarchy
of Dionysius the Areopagite

DIONYSIUS THE AREOPAGITE
AND THE *CELESTIAL HIERARCHY*

The following translations represent a variety of genres, all of which comment on the *Celestial Hierarchy* of Dionysius the Areopagite (Pseudo-Dionysius). Dionysius's *Celestial Hierarchy* was most likely written at the end of the fifth century or the beginning of the sixth (though the writings themselves locate the writer in the first century, a companion of Paul). Today, the identity of the writer of the Dionysian corpus is completely unknown. However, Dionysius's apostolic credentials were unquestioned throughout most of the period of writings represented in this volume. Dionysius was considered to be the Dionysius of Acts 17:34. In the *Celestial Hierarchy*, Dionysius's apostolic authority and wisdom were invoked not only on the subject of angels but also on the proper method of interpreting symbols, the process of procession and return to God, the nature of hierarchy, what we might call spiritual enlightenment, the theology of beauty or aesthetics, and even architecture. By the time of the rise of humanism, the authorship of the Dionysian corpus began to be questioned, and it is generally agreed that the denial of Areopagitic authorship by the Italian humanist Lorenzo Valla dealt such a blow to interest in Dionysius that by the time of the Reformation the reformers, as a rule, had little use for him. Today, while there is universal agreement denying the authorship of the Areopagite from Acts (hence the often-used "Pseudo"), interest in the Dionysian corpus is at a near revival pitch, and the literature on the corpus is almost overwhelming.[1]

John Scotus Eriugena

Expositiones in ierarchiam coelestem S. Dionysii

Commentary on the Celestial Hierarchy of Saint Dionysius

Chapter VII

Introduction

A master of Celtic, Greek, and Latin theological and philosophical sources, and a genius of intellectual and cultural synthesis, John Scotus Eriugena's (810?-877) place in the history of Christian spirituality is secure,[1] yet his life and training remain a fascinating enigma. Although he was a ninth-century Irish guest in the Carolingian court of Charles the Bald and director of the palace school, little is known of his family or his early training. In fact, the details of his acquisition of a superb knowledge of Greek in Ireland and later in the Carolingian courts on the continent, his general absorption of Latin theology, philosophy, and culture,[2] and his Celtic inheritance during his stay in Ireland will probably never be known. What we do know is that, through his translation and commentary on the works of Dionysius,[3] Gregory of Nyssa,[4] and Maximus the Confessor,[5] his use of Augustine, and his own synthesis of sources and cultures, Eriugena had a significant impact on later medieval theology, philosophy, aesthetics, symbolic theology, and spirituality.[6]

Eriugena's mature thought is marked not only by his *Commentary on the Celestial Hierarchy*, but by his massive syntheses, the *Periphyseon* or in Latin, *De divisione naturae (The Division of Nature)*, which is recognized by some as the first medieval *summa*. His mature thought is marked also by two exegetical works on John, *Homily on the Prologue of John* and the unfinished *Commentary on*

John. These works were probably all written during the 860s. Overall, the writing of Eriugena is grounded in the natural world, yet it moves finally toward anagogy, contemplation, and mystery. Mysterious too are the actual details of Eriugena's life. Tantalizingly touched by footprints here and vital signs there, the exact contours and historical facts of his life nonetheless remain a mystery. John Scotus Eriugena might well have delighted in the ironic parallel between his own life's unknowability and God's unknowability in this life.

Eriugena's anthropology[7] exhibits dialectical features centered on issues of the knowability of God and self. On the one hand, he denies the possibility of a comprehensive knowledge regarding God and self. On the other hand, he acknowledges positive self-knowledge and knowledge of God, even in this life.[8] In this he is both similar to and dissimilar from his early mentor, Dionysius the Areopagite. As Donald F. Duclow points out, Eriugena responds to and expands Dionysius's teaching on the relation and unitive understanding of humanity, angels, and God:

> Eriugena the metaphysician responds when Dionysius describes God as "the source of illumination for those who are illuminated."…Expanding on Dionysius's text, he then fuses the themes of being, illumination, and vision. "For God and for every rational and intellectual creature, it is not one thing to be light and another to see.…For them it is one and the same thing to be, to give light, and to see: for their being is light and vision."

God, the angels, and humans are thus united in a reciprocal lighting and seeing.[9] But his anthropology also differs from Dionysius, especially with regard to our relation with the angels; as Duclow also points out, "Eriugena presents a direct, unmediated relation between humanity and God."[10] Dionysius describes the angels as themselves the mediating beings between humanity and God. Eriugena often uses Augustine's phrase *nulla interposita creatura* (no creature intervenes)[11] to describe the unmediated relation between the human mind as God's image and the mind's contemplative vision. In the *Commentary on the Celestial Hierarchy*, Eriugena uses the idea that "no creature intervenes" to describe the human mind's contemplation of God in seraphic terms, as an unceasing circular motion around God, again, with no intervening creature. In this way, he suggests "that humans become peers with the highest angels."[12] Dionysius the Areopagite suggests this as well, but for him the angels serve as mediators between humanity and God; the angels do intervene. Men and women may thereby acquire an unmediated vision of God by becoming similar to the various, mediating angelic orders, but they are not "peers" with the angels in the same sense that they seem to be in Eriugena.

Many of these issues on mediation and direct vision of God are addressed in the following chapter from Eriugena's *Commentary on the Celestial Hierarchy*. The chapter, Chapter Seven, discusses the first celestial hierarchy, the hierarchy that is closest and dwells in immediate proximity to God, united with the first, divine essence. The angelic orders within this first hierarchy are the Seraphim, Cherubim, and Thrones, each of which carries its own name and attributes, yet each of which also participates equally in the divine presence. In this chapter questions touching on the issue of the relation between angels and humanity include: How do the angelic names reflect their God-conforming properties? How might we be united with the angelic beings in participation in the divine life? Is it possible to have a vision of the Good itself? Is there a form of contemplation natural to the angels that men and women themselves might acquire? In short, what are the causes, nature, and effects of contact with God?

Several other issues raised in Chapter Seven either diverge significantly from Dionysius or will have significant impact on the reception of Eriugena in the medieval period. First and foremost is the equation of the seraphic attributes—fire, burning, glowing, heat—with love. In Eriugena, the Seraphim thus come to represent the path or *spirituality of love*. They rest in immediate proximity to God's love, exemplifying the purgation, illumination, and perfection of that love in a created being, and serve as guides and exemplars for men and women devoted to the path of love. This seraphic equation to love is not present in Dionysius, but is explicit here in Chapter Seven of Eriugena's commentary, and will have a nearly universal impact on later medieval spirituality.

A second key theme in Chapter Seven is a current found throughout Eriugena's writing. The theme is so pervasive that Bernard McGinn, in his comprehensive four-volume study of Western Christian mysticism, refers to it in the title of his chapter on Eriugena: "The Entry of Dialectical Mysticism: John Scottus Eriugena." The theme is *dialectical mysticism;* Eriugena grounds all his work in dialectical philosophy, in the coincidence of opposites. In Chapter Seven this means, for instance, that the Cherubim, Seraphim, and Thrones "stand" in the divine presence and "circle" it in one and the same moment; both their flight and their mode of contemplation are referred to as a kind of stillness in motion or static mobility.[13] It means also that the angelic hierarchy itself represents both a unity and a diversity and that the angels represent both a descent from and a return to God. And of primary importance to our theme of angelic spirituality and the various paths into God that the angels represent, Eriugena's dialectical thinking also means as well that he can work at one and the same time with both an apophatic anagogy based on unknowing and a cataphatic anagogy based on light, symbols, and an aesthetics of beauty.

A third theme found in this chapter is *symbolic theology.* This theme had a particular impact on medieval spirituality and is represented in this volume by the selection from Hugh of St. Victor's *Commentary on the Celestial Hierarchy.* On the basis of this theme, intellectual and sensible symbols become the starting points of various kinds of contemplation leading, finally, to the contemplation of divine theophanies and the vision of Truth itself. Eriugena explains:

> Both kinds of symbols, intellectual and sensible, are contemplated by a hidden, yet discerning understanding. Sensible symbols are contemplated in the understanding of the celestial beings. These symbols of the senses would include the sacraments of the old law, for example, the tabernacle and all those things that the Lord commands to be done in it....And then there are intellectual symbols. These do not come naturally to mind for us unless we speak of intellectual symbols as theophanies, in which one encounters an appearance of truth invisible in itself, now, however in a manner unknown to us as intellectual symbols. They lack the likeness of any material thing.[14]

Finally, in keeping with his cataphatic emphasis on the angels as light, Eriugena develops a fascinating variation on the traditional depiction of the trinitarian nature of God. Rather than describing God as one essence in three substances or persons, Eriugena describes the "threeness" character of trinitarian unity as "three lights." It is these "three lights" in which the angels, as light, participate in God. The angels, in turn, by participation in this light, draw us into participation with the "Father of Lights."[15]

It must also be noted that Eriugena's *Commentary on the Celestial Hierarchy* is at once philological, doctrinal, and spiritual. Its structure, complex yet coherent, follows this outline:[16] (1) the Dionysian text in translation by Eriugena, broken up into short pericopes, (2) a literal gloss or explanation of each pericope, (3) possible alternate translations, equivalent but slightly variant, inserted in the gloss, and (4) grammatical, philological, doctrinal, and spiritual commentaries, especially on words or phrases that present special difficulties. This flexible outline permits Eriugena to present a translation, possible alternative translations, a gloss on the translations, and a variety of commentary forms that allow him to justify the translation or to explain an alternative. As a genre it is perfectly adapted to interpretation and commentary on Dionysius's complex yet practical work on angels.

Note on Translation: The translation is from *Iohannis Scoti Eriugenae: Expositiones in Ierarchiam coelestem*, ed. Jean Barbet, CCCM XXXI (Turnholt: Brepols, 1975), Chapter VII, pp. 92–117. A Latin edition of Eriugena's translation of Dionysius's *Celestial Hierarchy*, along with Dionysius's Greek and eight other Latin translations, is available in *Dionysiaca* 2:725–1039. The Greek edition of Dionysius's *Celestial Hierarchy* is available in Dionysius, *La hiérarchie céleste*. Section titles are not given in the critical edition but are provided here (contained in square brackets) as an aid to following Eriugena's often complex text. Eriugena's translation of Dionysius is given in italics throughout.

Commentary on the Celestial Hierarchy
of Saint Dionysius

Chapter VII

The beginning of Chapter VII, whose title is *On the Seraphim and Cherubim and Thrones, and on theirs, the first Hierarchy.*

1. Do you notice how the names of these angels have exchanged places in the order? In an earlier chapter, the Thrones were placed first; now they follow the others. Similarly, in that earlier chapter, the Cherubim were placed before the Seraphim; now the Seraphim are placed before the Cherubim.[17] We will examine the reason for this change in a later chapter.

[On the Symbolism of the Names of the First Hierarchy]

Dionysius begins, *Having retained this order of holy hierarchies, we believe that an understanding of every celestial intelligence declares, by the allusions contained within its very name,*[18] *something of the God-conforming properties of each.*[19] That is to say, even before we begin to explain these things, we acknowledge that these orders of holy hierarchies declare, by the etymological allusions within their very names, that each celestial intelligence is conformed or imprinted by divine characteristics. Indeed, a celestial name has no particular power unless it is of a deiform quality itself. That is to say, it has no power unless the name serves to indicate a likeness and property of God. A careful inquiry into the meaning of each of the names reveals both the mutual, interactive participations and the particularities that are derivative of their singular, unique essences.[20] A theology is worked out for us, knowing first and most clearly the particular and communal powers of divine intelligences, then the signifying names through which their power is made known to us.

JOHN SCOTUS ERIUGENA

[On the Seraphim]

The holy name of "Seraphim," for those with a knowledge of Hebrew, signifies "aglow with red-hot heat" or "inflamed."[21] *The name "Cherubim" means "fullness of knowledge" or "a lavish outpouring of wisdom."*[22] That is to say, those who know the particular meanings of the Hebrew words are aware that the holy name of Seraphim signifies glowing or burning; this is implicitly understood. It is therefore an *EKΛEIΨIC*[23] of the word [that is, a substitution of the word Seraphim for the meaning "glowing" or "burning"]. The name Cherubim, however, signifies fullness of knowledge. As with the Seraphim above, it is understood that the name Cherubim stands, in a "veiled" way, for "fullness of knowledge." However, Dionysius let the name of the Thrones pass, either on account of brevity of style or on account of a certain reverent silence. This is certainly due to the fact that the names Seraphim and Cherubim are Hebrew names, while Thrones is Greek, and therefore on that account he has temporarily set aside Thrones from the terms of the present discussion.

This is followed by, *Therefore, it is beautifully conceived that the first of the celestial hierarchies is made holy by the most sublime essences having the highest order of all. That is, those established in immediate proximity around God,*[24] *who is the ground of the operations of divine theophany*[25] *and perfections, convey God's primal operations to the orders beneath them through their very proximity to the divine source.* Now, again, Dionysius praises the three orders of the first hierarchy uniformly, saying clearly that the first hierarchy of the celestial hierarchies is therefore beautifully sanctified, or as it may be understood more clearly, sacrificed by means of the most excellent essences, that is, sanctified by the most excellent essences after which it is placed. Indeed, the Greek reads *"IEROYPΓEITAI"*[26] not *"AΓIACΘAI,"* which most properly reads "sacrificed," and not simply "sanctified." In Greek the word is used to convey both senses: truly, whatever is sacrificed is indeed made holy. Thus this is the sense of that phrase: the first celestial hierarchy is consecrated, sacrificed, and made holy by those most high essences placed within it, or again, they are praised and intimately joined to the First Cause of all things.

But in Greek there are middle verbs, called *"MECA,"* which most often necessitate the form of the passive verb and have a middle voice between the active and passive forms. With the Latin language the passive and middle voices are held in one passive form, so that we might shift the sense of our translation slightly in the following way: "Therefore it is beautifully conceived that the first of the celestial hierarchies sacrifice, having as they do the most sublime essence." Thus the order of the words might be "the first of the most sublime essences of the celestial hierarchies, that is, that which is placed first of the most excellent essences of the celestial hierarchy, sacrifices." Nor is it said unjustly that the first hierarchy "sacrifices" to God, because it is first of all the others. We say these things on account of the ambiguity of the Greek word *"IEPOYPΓEITAI,"* which can be either active or passive and thus can mean either "sacrifices" or "is sacrificed." Thus the word signifies both "sacrifice" and "be sacrificed."[27]

What does the first order sacrifice and sanctify? He immediately adds this: those angels sanctify that have the highest order of all, are established in immediate proximity around God, and who are at the beginning of the active and efficacious theophanies and perfections. And this therefore is what these angels sacrifice: a sacrifice of praise and thanksgiving. This refers to ineffable glory, because these angels have the highest place of all the other celestial essences, that is, they praise the fact that they are employed around God, with no other creature of any kind being placed in between.[28]

This is followed by the "first active theophanies," or, one might say, this hierarchy sanctifies the first active theophanies, or the preoperative theophanies in itself, so that they can be brought down into it as being in close proximity to God. In this hierarchy, beyond all others, every divine theophany and perfection is prepared in an orderly way. Into this hierarchy, as immediately proximate to God, these divine theophanies and perfections are primordially led below and fully distributed to the lower orders.

Again, Dionysius turns to an interpretation of the names saying, *Therefore these beings are called "flaming," or "thrones," or "effusion of wisdom." [For each of the angelic orders], the manner by which they are conformed to God is manifested by their names.* Again, we ought to observe the change in the order of the names. In the previous chapter, where he named all of the celestial essences in order, the most holy Thrones were positioned first, then the many-eyed and feathered Cherubim, and after them the Seraphim. Above, in the introduction to this seventh chapter, on the other hand, the Seraphim are placed first, then the Cherubim, third the Thrones. Here, however, as this chapter progresses "flaming," that is the Seraphim, is named first, the Thrones are placed after them in the middle, and finally "effusion of wisdom," that is, the Cherubim, are last. In this he declared straight away this three-form naming to signify clearly the angels' deiform condition and the unchanging powers of their being.

Now first, concerning the Seraphim, we find Dionysius saying, *Indeed, the name and manifestation of the Seraphim teaches the following: a perennial and incessant circling motion*[29] *around divine realities. [It teaches as well] a penetrating heat and overflowing heat of constant motion, a fervent intention in want of nothing, an unceasing hovering in immobile movement.*[30] *It has the power to lead the lower orders back into an assimilated likeness with themselves, recapturing their divine spark, so to speak, and resuscitating that spark into a flame equal to their own. [And again, they represent] a heavenly flame, exposed on every side and inextinguishable, a flame which purifies by means of total combustion.*[31] *[And finally, the name Seraphim speaks eloquently of] overcoming and making manifest every dark shadow, while always maintaining the property of luminescence and clear illumination.* Looking first at the order of Dionysius's words, the name and manifestation teach that, on the basis of their mobility, the Seraphim always encircle divine realities; they are always moved and they are in eternal motion around the divine mysteries. However, they are in motion with regard to neither place nor time, but rather through the action of contemplation[32] they have been ineffably placed above every place and above every time. Likewise, their motion is an immobile movement, unceasing, afire, keen sighted, intending ever upward into divinity, and in perfection lacking nothing. He teaches that the name Seraphim is understood in all these things and all are understood in it.

With regard to the internal sense of these words, the Seraphim represent eternal motion, which is unceasing, pulsing with heat, penetrating. He teaches that their motion is swift, beyond simply striving, attentive, full, unmoving. Indeed, their motion is unceasing, because they fly rapidly around God without any cessation.

If, however, you ask what it is to move around God, diligently inquire why no celestial essence, or, as I generally say, no rational and intellectual creature, can know what the highest good[33] is. For the highest good exceeds all reason and understanding; it is not definable on the basis of any created thing whatsoever since it is infinite, ineffable, and incomprehensible. However, every rational and intellectual creature is carried in circular patterns around the highest good to the extent that through the things that are after the Good and around it, created by it, they know without hesitation that the highest good exists but are not able to know what the highest good is. In addition, all things are said to encircle the highest good that have been created from it, since the highest good is also the inmost good,[34] around which all creatures have been arranged, not in local motion, but in their particular, cosmological order. By this motion either the pure human soul[35] or the celestial intellect, moving around God in intelligible motion, sees through the contemplative eye of the mind that it is indwelling within it as a principle. They subsist through participation in its goodness; through its wisdom they are ordered; by its gift they are beautiful and full of grace.

Such circular motion, or more clearly, such "spherical" motion around the highest good, as if around an immobile center, is the common property of every visible and invisible creature. However, all creatures are not moved equally, for the more they draw near to God, the more they move; they are most quick, unceasingly hot, and more than most fervently carried around God. And this is what he says about the Seraphim, and the orders equal to them moving closely around God, that through the things that are around God moving their contemplative gaze, they understand not what God is in essence, but that God in fact is. Their motion is unceasing since it never stops; they are hot with flaming fire, stirred up by the inflammation of charity. Keen and rapid, they penetrate all things subtly and clearly. And they are ablaze with intense heat and, above all things that follow them, this first hierarchy of the celestial powers blazes forth in love of the highest good.[36] All that has been said in praise of the Seraphim must also be said in praise of the Cherubim and Thrones.

Dionysius follows with the words, *A power to lead the lower orders back into an assimilated likeness with themselves.* These words teach that all things seek to return to their source. They teach the assimilation of the lower orders to a likeness of the Seraphim, which serve as an exemplar to those beings placed below. Therefore, *ΑΦΟΜΟΙΩΤΙΚΟΝ* is translated "assimilated likeness,"[37] because in order to be assimilated it is necessary that the Seraphim serve as a kind of exemplar. The Seraphim and their coordinate orders serve as such exemplars to the lower orders, thereby leading them back in likeness to the highest good, around which they too may fly. And so it is said, "a power to reassimilate the lower orders."

It then follows, *recapturing their divine spark.* Clearly, this is the process through which the Seraphim, as the exemplar of assimilated likeness, are imitated by the lower orders. This divine spark within the lower orders is said to be *resuscitated into a flame equal in intensity to theirs, radiating the heat of charity.*[38] In the same way the Seraphim, as an exemplar, reignite the lower orders by their own heat and resuscitate or reawaken them by their own intense awareness, causing the lower orders to imitate them (indeed the Seraphim purify the lower orders for these very things). They then radiate heat like the Seraphim. Thus, like the Seraphim they imitate, they are on fire with divine love, so that in the same manner in which the Seraphim burn with love, so do the created orders, which are beneath them, burn with the fire of love.

And Dionysius says, the Seraphim *represent a heavenly flame, exposed on every side and inextinguishable, a flame that purifies by total combustion.* This teaches of the sacrifice that is the purgative power of these celestial flames, of the power that is a total consumption in fire, a complete burnt offering. Such is the power of the seraphic flame. Their power, effective in the lower orders, is an intense boiling over of charity, by means of which the Seraphim purge and totally consume all dissimilarity to them in their fire of love. Indeed, this flame purges the orders that follow them and makes them fit and able to receive the highest wisdom; the flame consumes them, consuming and engulfing them in a glowing flame of charity. And so this seraphic power is itself a heavenly flame, exposed on every side and inextinguishable. From every angle it is unconcealed because it reveals totally all aspects of itself to those beings below. And on the other hand, it is inextinguishable because divine love burns forever within.

And what are all these virtues that are proclaimed concerning the Seraphim? That is, what precisely is their mobility and unceasing motion? What is their burning or keen intellect, their constant, intentional, and ardent desire for God, or their unceasing, hovering motion? What is their power of assimilation or, as we have said, their status as exemplars by which the lower orders follow them? What purifies the lower orders so that the fire of charity is internally received by them? What is proclaimed in the Seraphim's inextinguishable, purgative, and visible heavenly flame, which totally consumes all things in fire? Clearly, these things teach nothing other than the Seraphim's name and the nature of their manifestation— indeed, these things stand for the very essence of "Seraphim." And the name and the manifestation signify the nature of "Seraphim," so that this relation of signification always remains changeless. What, above all, the name and manifestation signify is light.[38] The Seraphim are light.[39] In the illuminating form, likeness, and property of light, they pursue, to the very end, all obscuring shadows that bring darkness through ignorance, permitting darkness neither to dwell inwardly nor to deceive outwardly.

And finally, it ought to be noted that it has been said that one praises the Seraphim through *ΥΠΑΛΛΑΓΗΝ*,[40] that is, according to the use of rhetoric or poetry.[41] An example of the formula of this trope is found in the Poet, where he uses the phrase, "to give the south to the armies," for, to give the armies to the south.[42] And in the Psalms we find, "Will God, in his wrath, shut off his compassion," for, will he shut off his wrath in his compassion?[43] While this way of speaking seems to contradict itself, the mutual exchange is understood as a rhetorical device. Thus, when it is said that the Seraphim's mobility, keen-sightedness, and so forth, instruct us concerning the name and revelatory action of the Seraphim, that is, that they have a likeness to the form and essence of light and the special property of illumination, this can be understood, exchanging "light" for the name, as saying that the name and revelatory action instruct us that the Seraphim belong to the "light," that is, they have the form and likeness of light and participate in the special property of illumination.[44] And what, in addition, does this teach? That without question, on account of their mobility, the Seraphim, because of their continual motion, are *mobility*. And likewise, they are, using the exchange, *incessant circling* around divinity, and so on with the remainder of their powers that were named. Thus he said above that each and every name of the celestial intelligences declares something of their God-conforming properties. Finally [we can say that], it is not angelic virtues or attributes that instruct us concerning the name, but rather that the name itself brings out the nature and quality of the virtues.[45] It should be recalled also that the virtues of mobility, keen intellect, and so forth apply not only to the Seraphim but also to all the orders within the first hierarchy. Indeed, what is declared concerning the one concerns all. In fact, there ought to be no doubt: what is said about the one can be declared concerning the others. And likewise, Dionysius teaches that similarly, in the second and third hierarchy, whatever is said concerning one order ought to be interpreted as having been said concerning them all.

[On the Cherubim]

Dionysius continues, *The name Cherubim*[46] *signifies the aptitude to know and to see God, to receive the highest gifts of light, to contemplate Divine beauty in its primordial operations, to be filled with the traditions*[47] *of wisdom, and to communicate the effusive overflow of their wisdom with generosity to those orders below poised to meet them.* What we said above concerning the Seraphim we may now apply to the Cherubim, that is to say, the name Cherubim and the manifestation of the Cherubim

173

convey the fact of their knowledge of God. In like manner, the name teaches of their vision of God and their reception of the highest gifts of light, or to speak more plainly, it teaches of their reception of and their ability to be taken hold of and transformed by the most transcendent divine illuminations.

Having been clothed in knowledge, they possess the gnostic virtues. They possess a knowledge that allows them to see God, since in considering God they possess the speculative capacity to receive the highest illuminations. They have *theoria*,[48] that is, the power of contemplative knowledge of the primordial operations of divine beauty. They dwell in the transmissions of the fullness of wisdom, the doctrine that makes it possible for human souls to grasp wisdom. They possess the power to communicate this wisdom abundantly to those beings that follow them. Their knowledge is transferred to the lower orders in a most clear way by means of an abundant overflow of the gifts of wisdom. The inner meaning of this is controlled by sequence and diffusion: the Cherubim, from an effusive pouring out, communicate by means of the sequential orderings themselves. Thus, one might say, they communicate by means of the gifts of the first wisdom streaming forth into them, and by a consequent pouring out of their own fullness of wisdom into the angelic intelligences below. First, the contents of the highest wisdom itself, which is God, are poured out immediately into the Cherubim, whereupon the highest wisdom flows down through them into the lower orders like a cascading river.

[On the Thrones]

After the explanation of the significance of the names of the Seraphim and Cherubim, the exposition of the name of the Thrones[49] begins. *The name Thrones, the title of the patterned frameworks of the most sublime Seats,[50] conveys that they are lovingly exalted above every impure degradation, that they are bearing ever upward to the summit of supermundane heights, that they are ineffably separated in a most exalted manner, that they have been arranged unchangingly and with a supreme stability, in the totality of their power, around the one who is*

174

truly the Most High, that they are able to receive divine approach in com-
plete serenity and in a perfectly immaterial way, and that they both bear
God and are open, like a humble servant, to receive God into their being.

Since there are other ways to translate this sentence, it seems
to me of value to repeat the whole in a number of ways. We might,
for example, say that the Thrones suggest seats of the most exalted
and lofty nature raised lovingly above all crawling or walking
things, that they are borne ever upward by supermundane things,
that by their higher position they are inflexibly separated from
every extremity, that they are firmly and unshakably founded, by
the totality of their power, around the one who is truly the Most
High, that they suggest the reception of the divine advent in the
impassibility and immateriality of all things, and that they both bear
God and are humble servants in the divine reception.

The name Thrones, that is, the name of the royal structure of
the most lofty seats, is to be understood from the above description
partially on the basis of the translation of the ambiguous Greek
word, *ΕΠΗΡΜΕΝΩΝ*,[51] which, whether it is derived from the word
ΕΠΑΡΜΟ, that is, "binding together or framework," or from the
word *ΕΠΑΡΟ*, that is, "raised on high," teaches the structure and
meaning of the highest seats.

And what else does the name teach? Clearly, these seats are
exalted, that is, lifted up above every impure degradation, evidently
raised up by the worthlessness of what they see beneath them, or
finally, as expressed earlier, above every crawling or walking thing.
Thus, this is the sense: the name Thrones teaches us of the most
sublime divine seats exalted beyond every impurity. They are
exalted above every temporal thing and physical location, as indicated and articulated by the loving humility of all those multitudes
of lower orders who walk and crawl before them on the soles of
their feet. All such creatures who walk and crawl upon the earth are
humbled in the presence of the Thrones.[52]

These seats are most highly exalted above the assembly of all
who walk or crawl and thus are raised into the most majestic heights
above every impure thing. And through these Thrones, these creatures, like the Thrones themselves, are elevated. And in these

Thrones, God, who is exalted and remote from communion with any humble thing and from every material creature, sits ruling and judging all things. The name Thrones teaches these things most openly. It also teaches of their power, a power that counsels detachment from every corporeal creature, a power that transports those dwelling above earthly things into the highest Good. And though humility seems to be worth little in comparison to the lofty understanding of such things, the name nevertheless teaches that the Thrones, the humble seats of divinity, are ineffably carried into the most sublime things, clearly, that is, into God, who is the most sublime essence and nature. And thus through their humble participation with God, the Thrones are themselves made sublime.

The name also teaches of having been arranged or founded. That is, the Thrones' arrangement or foundation, in the totality of their power, is unchanging and supremely stable. They are firm in their assembly around the Most High, around the highest Good, around the true Good, and so around what truly is the most high God. And the name also teaches the attitude of receptivity, the discipline of receiving God as God comes forward from on high. This receptivity is accomplished without any mediating change or materiality but simply with the permanence of immateriality. The name also teaches that they bear God, that is, the divine origin of their powers. For the Thrones sustain the presence of God as servants, that is, in obedience. They praise God by sustaining and by carrying all things to him. We should say, more precisely, that God is not sustained by the Thrones, but rather God sustains; neither is God technically lifted up, but God is on high; nor does God, whose very nature is "to sit," and whose very essence is "to be at peace," though God made all things, actually "sit" in any "throne."

And finally, the name of the Thrones teaches that they are accessible, raised up in open view for all to see, and dwelling in the receptions of divine light. Indeed, they are the highest thrones, clearly above any other resting place. They teach how the divine presence may be absorbed into their being as open and prepared for receiving divine understandings. They are adapted and ready for having God sit upon them.

2. ...[53]

[A Single Hierarchy]

Dionysius continues, *The first essences, the Seraphim, Cherubim, and Thrones, who are located after their substance-giving Thearchy, who dwell as it were in the vestibule*[54] *of God, who surpass all created power, invisible or visible, ought to be thought of as comprising one uniform hierarchy.* From the manner of these words it ought to be understood, or intelligently judged, that on account of their complete uniformity, there is an equality among these orders forming the first hierarchy. This first hierarchy contains the first celestial essences, which are first after the substance-giving Thearchy[55] itself. They are perfected by divinity and are gathered together to dwell in the vestibules of God, clearly proximate to God. And on the basis of this ordained proximity, and as the first celestial essences gathered and ordained in the first hierarchy, they surpass all invisible or visible created power.

[Purity of the First Hierarchy]

Therefore, they ought to be thought of as pure,[56] *not simply in the sense that they are free of all unclean blemish and stain, nor that they refuse to receive material phantasies, but rather because, by their superior moral purity, they excel the very foundations of every holy place,*[57] *and are established above all other deiform powers.* Now Dionysius begins to treat more fully the praise of the qualities of the first hierarchy.

Purity of those first essences of the celestial hierarchy ought to be thought of as their complete dissimilarity from every profane thing, and as our translation clearly leads us to understand, not necessarily just their freedom from all earthly blemish and stain. Or, if we were to speak openly about this, they are not freed in the same way that our purgation frees us. We mortal humans are freed from inordinate pleasure in every earthly blemish and stain by grace working and cooperating through our earthly nature; they are freed by the very nature of their dissimilarity from impurity.

177

Nor are they pure simply on the basis of their freedom (a freedom we do not possess) from material phantasies, that is, false and vain images of material things by which the soul of the flesh—the soul clearly living carnally—is pressed upon and crushed by the love of temporal things and seduced by the tortuous coil of diverse errors. And what is most pernicious of all is that such a soul is separated from the love and knowledge of the truth. We are restored from such separation by divine grace calling us back; the first celestial essences are already called. These celestial essences were never driven away from the contemplation of the highest good. They were driven away neither by the sordid contamination of pleasure, nor by material phantasies, nor by crushing oppression or depravity. Rather, they are above all created substances, or as it may be expressly translated, above all lower orders, being raised above all material, mortal, spacial, and temporal things. Their unfailing contemplations are of immaterial and immortal celestial essences, contemplations beyond all place and time, contemplations of a loving motion away from vile and outlandish things, a motion around pure and most exalted things.

[These first celestial essences], as it is said in what follows, "excel the very foundations of every holy place." This might be simply translated as "excel the foundations of every sacred thing," for the Greeks use *IEPOC* to indicate anything sacred. But it is most especially in a holy place, a temple, that these holy essences are established above all of the other most deiform powers, that is to say, above all other Godlike powers. [Thus these Seraphim, Cherubim, and Thrones] are securely established beyond the foundation of every holy place, and beyond every perfect, pure, and uncontaminated spirit in whom God dwells and is honored.

Dionysius continues [on why the Seraphim, Cherubim, and Thrones ought to be thought of as pure]: *And because of their permanent attachment to their own self-moved[58] order, a motion immediately received, without modification, according to an eternally ordained love for God.* This ought to be understood as pointing out and leading us to what the first essences receive without modification. It cannot be described how these motions are received without modification in themselves, that is, how they return into themselves. [Thus we could say], as the motion of a circle revolving around itself forms a sphere, they are perpetually, by motion through itself,[59] moved by themselves and with the same movement. Thus their uniform motion is the same, because it is most correct to call God either fixed motion or dynamic stability.[60]

This Dionysius follows by "according to an eternally ordained love for God." Every order loves God without swerving from this ordained love; it is willed that there is no variability, but only uniformity of love and motion around God. But the phrase "self-moved" is worthy of investigation. For if, indeed, all things are moved by God, reason clearly teaches that we must ask how it can be that the celestial essences, even the foremost celestial essences, are moved around God by their own self-motion. For if one were to say that every creature, from the greatest to the least, has its own natural motion under its own personal control, it might as well be said that praise for the celestial and most excellent Thrones applies no less equally to the praise of the simplest worm. Would this not be a just comparison if every creature comes by its motion of its own accord? So perhaps it ought to be said, and not irrationally regarding this question, that a created thing is not itself moved by a more superior creature but rather receives its motion from that same Creator who is the sole, unmediated cause of all first things. This same Creator is said, rightly, to be itself unmoved, because the cause of motion is himself beyond all essence, all motion; it is above all things which are, and above all things which are not.[61]

Clearly though, the rest of the whole created orders, that is, those orders beneath the first celestial essences, however much they are established in the one motive cause of all God's first principles, do not receive their motion immediately from God. Rather, they are moved and administered according to grades, always from the higher to the lower. But it is a beautiful conception and well conceived that these highest of the celestial essences are called *AYTOK-INHTOI*,[62] that is, self-moving. They both are and are called this because they move themselves; they are self-moved. They are moved by nothing higher than themselves, except by God alone, who is moved by no particular principle because God is the universal principle. However, the universal of all things belongs to no one of them. For this reason, not only the primordial causes of all things are *AYTOKINHTOI*, self moving, but also the highest celestial orders are said to be so.

And the human soul,[63] too, is not unreasonably called by the philosophers *AYTOKINHTOC*, that is, self-moved, because no creature is closer to God than the human creature. And if man had not sinned, he would have managed the affairs of his own order without the aid of any superior order, because there would have been no order superior to the human order. And so it will be again when humanity is recalled to the pristine dignity of its nature.

[And they are pure because] *they are completely unacquainted with insulting or humiliating behavior of any kind toward inferior orders.* That is, however much they might have been created by God as the most sublime of all creatures, and however much all things are inferior in their kind to them, they are unwilling and unable to insult or humiliate; they are unable to show contempt in any way. And not only that, they admonish and recall all other orders to communion with their Creator in true love and knowledge.

And so it follows, *They have eternal, unending natures and thus they are also immutable, having as their most pure foundation their own particular deiform properties.* Thus not only are they, from their most sublime position, free of contempt for those beneath them, but they have an eternal and unending nature and thus have an unchanging and most pure foundation based upon their own special deiform characteristics. Of course, it is a most holy foundation, and clearly their foundation is eternally and unendingly ordained since, being completely immutable, it cannot be moved. And what is that foundation? What is that ordination? Clearly, it is their own special, deiform nature. And, as we might want to put it, this pure foundation, which is their own special deiform property, is sought out by every other creature, whether that creature knows it or not. [And in the ordination of this pure foundation] all end and change are absent; it brings no creature injury or contempt simply on the basis of its place in creation.

JOHN SCOTUS ERIUGENA

[On Their Contemplation]

[And the first beings, the Seraphim, Cherubim, and Thrones], are contemplative also,[64] *not simply in the sense that they gaze upon sensible or intellectual symbols.* What ought to be understood first off by this phrase, is that the contemplation of sensible and intellectual symbols by these celestial beings is equivalent to the speculative gaze upon these symbols.[65] The sense of this can be understood in two ways: the meaning also is that the celestial beings are contemplative by means of their speculative gaze upon intellectual and sensible symbols, that is, by means of a hidden[66] understanding. Thus both kinds of symbols, intellectual and sensible, are contemplated by this hidden, yet discerning understanding.

Sensible symbols are contemplated in the understanding of the celestial beings. These symbols of the senses would include the sacraments of the old law, for example, the tabernacle and all those things that the Lord commands to be done in it. Also the visions of the prophets in various forms and figures, and subsequently the ecclesiastical mysteries of the New Testament. The holy angels clearly discern the innermost light of all these things.

And then, there are intellectual symbols. These do not come naturally to mind for us unless we speak of intellectual symbols as theophanies, in which one encounters an appearance of truth invisible in itself *(per se)*, now in a manner unknown to us as intellectual symbols.[67] They lack the likeness of any material thing. And so, in theophanies themselves, that is, in the divine manifestations they contemplate with the eye of understanding, the angels gaze upon the most intimate recesses of divine understanding, just as many things are given to us to know by means of sensible symbols, so that we too are invited to comprehend certain hidden mysteries of God. Now we might understand this further by saying that the contemplation of sensible symbols is to be considered as a meditation upon the most eminent essences. [We might also want to call it, as we said above], speculative contemplation or the understanding of any manner of intellectual thing. On the other hand, we are not compelled to understand intellectual symbols in both ways, but rather absolutely. That is, intellectual symbols, as whatever seems more probable to someone, are understood of things, of hidden things, or of powers or likenesses.

How the celestial essences, given that they are wholly incorporeal, contemplate sensible symbols needs no small investigation, unless perhaps we say that they take on the garments of a spiritual body, so that sensible things can be understood through the senses. It is certainly to be believed that they are able to discern not only intellectual but also sensible things without the support of the corporeal senses. This is illustrated, for instance, in the story of Elisha, who with a spiritual eye saw Naaman the Syrian washing himself in the Jordan, saw with a spiritual eye.[68]

Nor simply in the sense that they are led back[69] *into divinity by the many forms of contemplation*[70] *of sacred scripture, but that they are filled by that highest light,*[71] *higher than all material knowledge, and that they are restored, as far as possible, by the contemplation of that One who is both the form of beauty and who is yet the primordial and superessential*[72] *Beauty manifested in threefold luminosity.*[73] We must not think of the angels as contemplating only sensible symbols or the understanding of intellectual things on the heights of understanding in order to be led back to God by the variety of forms of contemplating sacred scripture. Yet, it is not our own mind that, having abandoned divine understanding, is led back to divine understanding through the variety and manifold forms of contemplation of sacred scripture. It is rather the angelic essence of the first hierarchy that is led back to God. It is led back as filled with the abundance of the highest of all immaterial knowledge, one could say the most divine light, insofar as it is possible for a creature, by the contemplation of the primordial and superessential beauty and threefold luminosity! By means of contemplation these celestial beings have full, supermundane knowledge of the light that surpasses every light;[74] by contemplation they have knowledge of the source of beauty that forms all things. On that account, by the fullness of its contemplation, this hierarchy of celestial essences is said to be superemanating beyond all others. It is superessential, three illuminations, or again, it is the three self-revelations, or simply translated, three heavenly lights.[75] [This threefold heavenly light] beholds the superessential Cause of the foundation of all things before and beyond the lower, inferior essences. Not unreservedly is this called "three heavenly lights," because it illuminates in three ways. Thus God, one in unity of essence in three substances, shines forth to those seeking him in piety and true understanding with the most brilliant, luminous glow. Indeed, this light shines in the Father by whom all things are, this light shines in the Word through whom all things are, this light shines in the Gift by whom all things are blessed.

Note also that we have used the word *beauty* to translate the Greek word *KAΛΛΟΥC*, which can be translated both as "form" and as "beauty." Neither is far from the sense, for the divine Good both forms and gives beauty to all things.

[They are contemplative also because] they have been judged worthy to enter, equally, into communion with Jesus.[76] Or, simply translated, they are equally worthy to be in communion with Jesus. Or again, to complete the meaning from what was said before, these angelic beings have been judged worthy to enter into communion by means of direct participation with Jesus. And Dionysius says "equally" so that we ought to understand that just as with the aforesaid powers, they too enter into communion with Jesus because, as the three orders of the first hierarchy, they have become equally worthy of direct participation with him.[77]

They give expression to the deifying likeness, *not in images of holy forms, but by truly drawing near to God through the first participation of the knowledge of his deifying lights.*[78] They do not give expression to—or to put it better, "re-form" the deifying likeness within themselves through holy forms made through images, nor even in symbols such as we form in a divine way as formative in some evident way. We ourselves are as yet like young children in these matters; we are still being formed within into the divine likeness through holy symbols and by images, so that now we are deified by faith, and only later will be deified in the act of looking.[79] But truly, without any image or symbol whatsoever [the Seraphim, Cherubim, and Thrones] are drawing near to Jesus himself in primary participation of the knowledge of his deifying light; they are being fully deified in the illuminations of Jesus himself.

Clearly, no image, no sacrament, no formal likeness of any kind comes between them and Jesus Christ himself, with whom they dwell in divine proximity.[80] *And it was most humbly given to them to be like God.* What is said above is here repeated, as it is thought, because it has been given to them to be like God. Or to put it another way, the likeness of God has been given them in all humility. Clearly, their subject is near God, because all things have been made subject to God. [And the three orders of the first hierarchy] are in the first, most subject position of all; that is, the triple order of the first hierarchy is the closest to Jesus. *And so in this way they are communicants with Jesus, to the extent that this is possible, in the operation of his deiforming power and his human virtues.* The divine likeness has been given to them as the nearest subject. Therefore, orders of this sort communicate, insofar as it is given them, in the preoperative deifying power of Jesus at work in them and also in his human virtues. Hence, by a certain ineffable likeness, through his deifying and human powers—that is, love and kindness toward humanity— the angels cooperate with and minister to us[81] in the process of our deification and salvation.

[On Their Perfection]

Likewise [the first hierarchy of Seraphim, Cherubim, and Thrones], are perfect, not simply in the sense of illuminating analytical knowledge in holy variety, but rather because they are filled with a primary and supereminent deification, by means of which they have access to the most elevated understanding that the angels are allowed to have of God's works. "Likewise" indicates these celestial orders to have been perfected by prior divine favor. They are perfected,[82] but not in the way that we are, by giving light in a holy variety of symbols to analytical knowledge and discipline.[83] Indeed, *ΕΠΙCΤΗΜΗΝ*[84] (knowledge) signifies both ways of illumination, for it can be interpreted as both knowledge and discipline. Our rational spirit is led back into the supernal heights of deification, by means of this same discipline, by having been illuminated by the wide variety of sacred symbols. The Greeks call this discipline *ΑΝΑΛΥΤΙΚΗ*[85] (analytics). There are two parts to the dialectical method of knowledge and discipline: one is called *ΔΙΑΙΡΕΤΙΚΗ*[86] (division, distinction), the other is *ΑΝΑΛΥΤΙΚΗ* itself. *ΔΙΑΙΡΕΤΙΚΗ* is concerned with the process of division; it divides the unity of the highest genera from top to bottom until it arrives at individual forms and so comes to the end of divisibility. *ΑΝΑΛΥΤΙΚΗ*, on the other hand, reverses this process, moving from the division of parts upward to the beginning through the same grades by which the first method descended. This second method of discipline ascends assembling and collecting the original unity of the highest genera. And so it is called the restorative method of return, or anagogical method.[87] [Through the process of *ΔΙΑΙΡΕΤΙΚΗ*], the rational soul by way of expiation of its sin, which divided it and cut it up, with a kind of diarchic force, in appetites for many and various forms of temporal things, now has reached the end of its partition in the love of temporal things. Below this it cannot go. Again, through the Creator's grace going before it, saving, assisting, calling it back, the rational soul is first re-gathered into itself by some analytical steps. Then, by the power of deification, it is restored to the unity of its Creator, that unity which it divided by sinning.

But it is not so in celestial essences, especially in the most eminent [Seraphim, Cherubim, or Thrones], who have never separated from the unity of the Creator. They do not use *ΑΝΑΛΥΤΙΚΗ*, that is, restorative or anagogical knowledge. Rather, having been filled with the first and most superabundant light of deification, they are, as much as it is given to angels, perfect participants in the highest knowledge of divine operations. And for these things we ought to honor them, because through their unmediated participation in divine works, they are illuminated and perfected by God's power.

And Dionysius follows this with, *And it is not through other holy essences, but from Divinity*[88] *itself by which the Seraphim, Cherubim, and Thrones are sanctified.*[89] *They are extended, without mediation, into God by a power and order beyond all things. Hence they are drawn together into the strength of the highest, most sublime purity and are led (to the extent that it is possible) into contemplation and into immaterial and invisible Beauty. The knowable causes of divine works, as the first essences are turned around God, are made holy by the highest source of perfection itself.*

These sentences need no further exposition, except for some potentially ambiguous translations. For instance, what we have translated as "the strength of the highest, most sublime purity," might also be translated here as "the inflexibility of the highest, most sublime purity," since *APPEΠEC*[90] means both strength and inflexibility in the Greek. But neither meaning alters the sense, since what is truly strong does not suffer movement. Similarly, where we have translated "invisible Beauty," we could say "intelligible elegance"[91] with the same meaning. The true understanding of invisible beauty is nothing other than intelligible elegance; the Greek word *EYΠPEΠIA*[92] indicates both beauty and elegance. Where we have translated "to the extent that it is possible," one might say "to the extent that it is allowed" or "to the extent of the law" or "extent of justice." From the one Greek word *ΘEMITON*[93] are to be understood at once such terms as permitted and allowed, law and justice. And where we have translated "the essences are turned around God," one might use phrases such as become "perfected" or "instructed" or "initiated" or "saturated" as they are turned. All these things are contained in the Greek word, which is *MYOMAI*,[94] and whose third person plural is *MYONTAI*, which, in so many previous translations of this word, agrees with how it is used here. But I do not see *MYONTAI* as being appropriate in this sentence if it is understood simply as "they restrain their eyes." And where we have translated "are sanctified," we might have, maintaining the same sense and meaning, used terms such as "are sacrificed" or "are immolated." However, the "highest source of perfection," which in Greek is called *TEΛETAPXIA*,[95] is the same "highest" divinity who in the height of all things sanctifies, sacrifices, and immolates the highest of all the orders, those of the first hierarchy.[96]

Hugh of St. Victor

*Commentariorum in hierarchiam coelestem
S. Dionysii Areopagitae
secundum interpretationem Joannis Scoti*

*Commentary on the Celestial Hierarchy
of Saint Dionysius the Areopagite
(According to the translation
of John Scotus Eriugena)*

Introduction

Hugh of St. Victor (ca. 1096–1141) was the first great master of the order of Canons Regular at the house of St. Victor in Paris. Already introduced in this volume as the author of a portion of *On the Six Wings of the Cherubim,* he is also the author of the massive *De sacramentis christianae fidei (On the Sacraments of the Christian Faith),* considered by many to be the first Scholastic *summa.* His *Didascalicon* serves as an outline for training Christian scholars in philosophy and theology, as well as a methodological guide for reading scripture.[1] Hugh of St. Victor is known as well for his profound spiritual writings and for being the teacher of the second great Victorine spiritual master, Richard of St. Victor. Through the inspiration and guidance of Hugh, all Victorine writing reflects a healthy integration of contemplation, biblical exegesis, theology, liturgy, and charity. This Victorine integration serves as a model for Christian spirituality today.

Hugh of St. Victor's *Commentary on the Celestial Hierarchy of Saint Dionysius the Areopagite*[2] is, in major part, a treatise on symbols and how they function in contemplation and the anagogical journey into God. As such, it represents an extremely important medieval resource for reflection not only on angels, but also on the sacramental view of the world, contemplation of images, and what might be called "visual spirituality."[3]

Chapter One from Book I of Hugh's *Commentary* begins this discussion on symbols by making a distinction between philosophy (what he usually calls "mundane philosophy") and Christian theology (what he usually calls "divine theology"). The distinction is made through Hugh's concentration on Christ as the center of Christian theology. Hugh's particular emphasis here is on the humility of Christ crucified and Christ as the light of the Father.

By making a further distinction between the symbols of nature (available to philosophy) and the symbols of grace (available only to theology), Hugh is able to link the work of Christ to the angels. The angels, through the symbols of grace in the "humility" of their various missions on earth, reflect and imitate the humility of Christ. As symbols of various anagogical paths into God, they also parallel and reflect the *victory* of Christ's humility. Hugh's introduction to his *Commentary* on angels and symbols is thus, in effect, an exegesis of 1 Corinthians 18–31, which reads in part:

> And God made the wisdom of this world foolish, since the wisdom of God is not found in this world. God showed another wisdom which seemed to be foolishness, yet it was not. And what was this wisdom? This wisdom was Christ crucified, of whom we preach so that truth might be sought through humility.

The angels, in their missions of love and knowledge and justice also participate in the humility and "sheer folly" of the Christian message. Yet they participate as well with Christ in its victory.

The angels also participate with Christ as the light of the Father. As theophanies, the angels are light and are made known through light as a symbol of grace. Hugh, in the second book of his *Commentary*, paraphrasing Dionysius, says:

> Let us, then, invoke Jesus, the light of the Father, who is that truth who "enlightens all humanity coming into the world" [John 1:9], through whom we have access to the Father, the original light [Eph 2:18; cf. Rom 5:2]. As much as it is possible, we should look back to the enlightenments handed down by the Father in the most holy eloquence of scripture....This is the light, by way of the various figures of symbols, through

which that most blessed and immaterial hierarchy of angels is manifested to us.[4]

In Jesus as the light of the Father all things, visible and invisible, are manifested to us through symbols.

Hugh of St. Victor defines symbol as, "a collection of visible forms for the demonstration of invisible realities."[5] As mentioned, there are two kinds of symbols that together illustrate the double aspect of divine mystery. First, there are the symbols of nature illustrating the mystery of the grandeur of creation. These symbols are available to natural philosophy. They make known the existence of the Creator by preaching that God is, but fail to illuminate the mind beyond the reality of divine being. Second, there are the symbols of grace illustrating the mystery of the humility of redemption, the "foolishness" of the cross. The symbols of grace are accessible only to the person of faith and thus are useful guides to Christian theology. They make known the humanity of the Word, thus showing God not only to be, but also to be present. Symbols of grace participate in the restoration of creation by showing the humility of Christ to be the source of all wisdom and his life to be an exemplar of healing and teaching.

For Hugh, all symbols can function anagogically, passing the soul beyond signs or figures or shapes in order to restore it to Wisdom and Truth. But it would be wrong to think of Hugh's contemplative anagogy as disengaged from the body or out of touch with the natural world. For the soul is restored to Truth as a concrete "thing" (res) intimately integrated with an "image" (imago). This, in fact, is a christological truth, the restoration of the humble "thing" and the victorious "image," the restoration of the flesh and the spirit. In fact, for Hugh of St. Victor, whoever practices this anagogical contemplation dwells in the ultimacy of this concrete and christological "thing" and "image."[6]

Both the symbols of nature and the symbols of grace are given to people by God for the demonstration of invisible realities. Hugh of St. Victor uses Book One of his *Commentary on the Celestial Hierarchy of Saint Dionysius the Areopagite* to prepare the reader for his teaching on the guidance of angels into the light of God. The angels, as represented in their various orders, assist in demonstrating the invisible mysteries of God through the visible attributes they manifest. In representing and manifesting the visible realities of, for instance, love, knowledge, justice, and joy, they guide the soul into the invisible realities of the Father of Lights, who is the source of every good and perfect gift.

Note on Translation: The following selection is translated from Hugh of St. Victor's *Commentariorum in hierarchiam coelestem S. Dionysii Areopagitae secundum interpretationem Joannis Scoti,* found in *PL* 175:923–1154.

 Commentary on the Celestial Hierarchy
of Saint Dionysius the Areopagite

Book One, Chapter One
Concerning the distinction of mundane and divine theology
and demonstrations of the distinctions.

Jews seek signs while Greeks seek wisdom.[7] Certainly, there was a kind of wisdom that appears as wisdom to those who do not know true wisdom. And the world found this kind of knowledge and began to be puffed up, swelling with pomposity, and imagining themselves great because of what they had found. Taking what they had found, and having complete confidence in it as if that knowledge were an effective path, the ancient philosophers thought to proceed beyond these things to an even higher wisdom.

And in fact they did ascend, indeed they were even lifted up, so that they reached the secret things of the heart. The Greek philosophers made themselves, as it were, a ladder, based upon the outward appearance[8] of creatures, thereby climbing up to the invisible things of the Creator. Then, when those invisible things had been manifested to them by God, they moved forward into illumination. These invisible things did indeed became known, but they were made known through an impure heart. Yes, those invisible things that they saw were known, yet there were in fact other things that

190

were not known to them. They thought by means of those invisible things that had been clearly manifested to them to enter even into those more secret things that are hidden.[9] But in this manner, in the falsehood of their fictions,[10] their minds failed to attain the highest possible truth, because what they apprehended on the basis of outward appearance is not, finally, the fullest truth to be found.

Thus God made the wisdom of this world foolish,[11] since the wisdom of God is not found in this world. God showed another wisdom, which seemed to be foolishness, yet it was not. And what was this wisdom? This wisdom was Christ crucified, of whom we preach so that truth might be sought through humility.[12] But the world despised the healer and was thus unable to come to know this truth. Worldly philosophy, certainly, wished to contemplate the wondrous works that God had made, yet was not willing to venerate the works that God had put forth for imitation. Neither did the world attend to his death but rather sought healing through pious devotion. It dedicated itself to false healing, presuming to investigate strange, unsuitable things through vain curiosity.[13]

Now this philosophy seemed to be proficient with things outside itself but deficient with regard to things within themselves, and totally unable to find any of those things that were beyond the self. And worldly philosophy put forth opinions concerning false healing that began with a heart filled with pride. They seemed to ignore the truth and eagerly followed a road of errors, pursuing many things opposed to the full truth. This philosophy aspired as well to many things contrary to the honor of Divinity, many things that were a travesty to God's most eminent majesty, so that error came into being. Now certainly at first there was truth in worldly philosophy, and it seemed great. Yet it fell into falsehood just at that moment when truth ought to have been consummated. Thus, for example, just as certain kinds of light are often described by means of their equal but opposite portion of dense darkness, so within worldly philosophy there grew a deep mist of ignorance whereby a trap of errors was laid down in the deceitfulness of pride. Again, there is no doubt that these philosophers saw where the light was, yet they were not able to see the darkness. In not seeing the darkness, they were entrapped by deception on account of the audacity of their presumptions. Thus they fell headlong only into those things having been clearly manifested. Yet still, how great are those excellent and vast monuments that these philosophers left behind whereby so many investigations into the secrets of nature and the hidden things[14] of the world's foundation were carried forward so that we might regard the efficacy of these same things, bringing them to light by means of every kind of study.

We read the arts, the studia, the disciplines, and the many rules of reason that those philosophers had carefully examined and found by the gift of understanding itself and by their own natural mental abilities.[15] Having discovered these things they wrote of them and in so doing handed down to posterity logic, ethics, mathematics, and physics concerned with the forms of reason, life, and death. They wrote of these things and handed down the institution of natural decency, the disposition of order, the causes, and the providence of all things. No, they were not weak in these areas; they apprehended the truth, but only a partial truth, to which they became servants. And this partial truth had to be served; it was not the truth that leads to life, and they were not the sons of life.

This life is a gift for our account, which will be given in full at the consummation and will be made obedient as well to the beginning of things. The labor of this gift was appointed to them; its fruit serves us. They perceived light by means of the whole of their understanding, by the incisive nature of their genius, and by the virtuous sensibility of their example. Through these things they subtly discussed the power of creatures, and the means and ways of inferior natures according to the forms of innate reason.[16] Lastly, they were theologians in that they applied their reasoning to divine things; by their deep scrutiny of invisible things they surrendered themselves to wisdom as if to be perfected through it. Indeed, on this account the ancients thought themselves to be perfected. But they were, in fact, about to lose the truth; truth was not to be found by these paths. Instead, they began to sink down into the false nature of images.[17] They claimed that visible appearances were the likeness of divine things, so that by means of these visible appearances they saw what seemed to them to be invisible things. Indeed the visible appearance was significant. But that which was sought in this way concerning divine manifestation turns out to be not light poured out upon the eyes but rather the spreading out of a dark mist. Certainly, nature shows forth its Creator. But nature offers only a remote resemblance[18] to the Creator's excellence and majestic power. Philosophy has been unable to find an evident demonstration [of the Creator's excellence and majestic power] in all these outwardly visible appearances. This is because nature, through which many things become clear in contemplation, was not in itself completely healthy.[19]

Indeed, nature itself does not contain the models[20] formed through grace for the health of our internal vision. Worldly philosophy does not know the ark of wisdom,[21] or the foundation of all things, or the flesh of the eternal Word in the humanity of Jesus. This philosophy therefore contemplated only in the cloudy light of half-blind insight using the created world as a model.[22] This form of contemplation leads only to the observation of the outward appearance[23] of creaturely things. On that basis the ancient philosophers wandered and passed away from the truth, when in fact they had hoped that, with their mind, they would pass beyond the outward appearance of things to truth. They wished to pass beyond what they had learned by investigation alone yet beyond those things they were not able to see. Thus those who thought themselves able to see were, in the end, found to be blind. Their procedures were images of errors[24] that their theology (as indeed they called their study, by which they believed themselves to be thoroughly investigating divine things), venerated emptiness and deception. Through this they went far beyond truth, beyond what is correct, and beyond the true nature of the good; they were deceived and ought now to blush. To be sure, there is a kind of justice in the fact that, as to the highest things by which pride made their understanding firm, they also despised the humility of faith in the death of a Savior. Yet they marveled in recognition of the nobility of the Savior's creation.

Two images[25] were proposed to humanity by which it was possible to see invisible things: one is the image of nature, and one is the image of grace. The image of nature was the outward appearance of the things of the world. The image of grace is the humanity of the Word. By both means God is shown, but God was not understood in both ways. Nature certainly demonstrates its art by means of its outward appearance, but it is not able to illuminate completely the eye of contemplation.[26] Truly then, the humanity of the Savior was the healing through whom the blind received light and teaching, so that seeing they might know truth.[27] The Savior made mud from spittle and smeared the eyes of the blind man, and the blind man washed his eyes and saw.[28] And what happened after? The blind man, seeing but not yet understanding, Jesus said: *"I am the one who spoke to you, the same one is the son of God."*[29] Therefore, first Jesus illuminated, then he clearly demonstrated.[30] Nature is able to demonstrate, but it is not able to illuminate completely. The world preaches its Creator on the basis of nature's outward appearance, but again this understanding of truth is not poured into the hearts of humanity. But while the Creator is signified through the many images of nature, in the images of grace God is revealed to be present. The images of nature were created so that God might be understood to be, while the images of grace were created so that God might be known to be present.[31]

This is the distance of this theology of the world from that which is called divine theology. It is impossible to demonstrate the invisible world unless it is demonstrated by visible things.[32] On that account all theology must necessarily contain visible demonstrations for the open expression of invisible realities. But worldly theology, we might say, adapted the work of creation and the elements of this world according to the created, outward appearance of things. It hoped in this way to make its demonstration by means of these visible realities alone. Divine theology, on the other hand, has chosen the work of restoration[33] according to the humanity of Jesus and his sacraments,[34] which were from the beginning of the world, adding natural symbols in due measure as they conform to his teaching. However, as we have said, a greater declaration of divinity is revealed in the sacraments of grace, in the flesh of the Word, and by mystical operation, than is ever preached by the outward appearance of natural things. And for this reason mundane theology, using a demonstration that in the end clarified little, did not have the power to bring forth incomprehensible[35] truth unstained by error. Divine theology, however, understood the need to preach humility by simple and pure assertions.

Now, the nature of divine theology ought to be clarified, and the clearest depths and the beginning of things ought to be discussed. All philosophy is divided into three principle parts: logic, ethics, and theory.[36] A fourth, to which we will direct our minds at the proper time, is to recount divine theology from the standpoint of its overflowing abundance. So philosophy contains three parts. The first is logic, through which, by the power and harmony of reasoning, attention is given to the discernment of true things from false. The second is ethics, by which a way of correct living is ordered and a form of discipline established according to which virtue is maintained. The third is theory, by which only the truth in all things, that is, what truly is and what truly is not, is selected for careful observation. There are three parts to this theoretical aspect of philosophy: first is mathematics, second physics, third theology, in which, by contemplation of truth, one ascends to the summit by means of degrees of contemplation. In the first, mathematics, the visible forms[37] of visible objects are contemplated. However, in the second, physics, invisible things are observed through visible causes. Only the third, theology, contemplates invisible substances and the invisible natures of invisible substances. And there is in these invisible things a kind of progression and a certain perfection of mind rising to a knowledge of truth. Indeed, by the visible forms of visible things one arrives at the invisible causes of visible things. And through the invisible causes of visible things one ascends to invisible substances and a knowledge of their natures. This latter, however, is the summit of mundane philosophy and the perfection of its truth; no higher truth is possible to the contemplative soul alone. In this way the wise ones of this world were made foolish proceeding, as we have already said, by the pattern of nature alone according to the elements and the outward appearance of things of the world. These wise yet foolish ones did not have the exemplars of grace,[38] through which the outward appearance of things was humility, and through which the demonstration of truth was presented more clearly. Such is the manner in which God has rendered the wisdom of this world foolish.[39] The world on its own is not able to recognize truth, since its mundane knowledge has contemptuously rejected the form of humility.

We are now in a position to speak more fully regarding theology based on the hierarchy of Dionysius, about which we now, by the grace of explanation, undertake to say a few words. Indeed, all things are placed under the hierarchy of theology, and so it is necessary to place before the reader something introducing the theology of hierarchy. We ought also to define its material, which consists totally of invisible substances, and similarly, using visible patterns, to demonstrate something of the nature of invisible things.

Alan of Lille

Hierarchia Alani

Treatise on the Angelic Hierarchy

Introduction

There is some question as to whether Alan of Lille's *Treatise on the Angelic Hierarchy* draws more directly from the angelic spirituality of Gregory the Great or from Dionysius the Areopagite. But there is no question that this short treatise is an imaginative and comprehensive commentary on the angelic orders that serves to rupture restricted notions of the life of Christian faith. For, as Alan of Lille says in explaining his concept of the angels as "theophanies" of God, each angelic order represents a particular earthly ministry as well as a genuine spiritual path into God.[1] A theophany, as he makes clear, is an appearance of God, a "God-light," a way of seeing divinity, a divine revelation, a "voice" of God. So listen and look, says Alan of Lille, the life of Christian faith is complex and multifaceted, for "many are the ways and forms of seeing God." For one soul the way is love, for another the way is knowledge, for yet another the form is discernment, for another the form is justice. Put simply, drawing from Gregory the Great, the many angelic ministries parallel and exemplify the many human ministries, and drawing from Dionysius the Areopagite, each ministry is its own pathway into God, a form of seeing divine operation and mystery. For Alan of Lille, the angelic hierarchy assists and guides one in watching, listening for, and following the pleasure of God.

Known as Doctor Universalis because of his vast knowledge, Alan of Lille (c. 1114/20–1202) was one of the most original personalities of the twelfth century. He was a philosopher, theologian, historian, naturalist, poet, preacher, and spiritual writer. He was never throughout his long life totally identified with any one school. We know nothing of his first forty years. His productive years teaching in Paris, Montpelier, and perhaps Le Puy are sketchy. And we know next to nothing of his later years, except that before his death he retired to the Cistercian community at Citeaux and was never heard from again. Fortunately his writings survive. He is perhaps most widely known for his poetical works, especially *De planctu naturae*, half verse and half prose, which presents nature as a poet out to correct moral disorders. One of his greatest works, the poetic epic *Anticlaudianus*, which inspired Dante and Chaucer, depicts nature as she attempts to create the perfect man. A number of Alan of Lille's works examine angelic spirituality. In addition to the *Treatise*, translated here, there is his *Expositio Prosae de angelis*[2] (the *Prosae* being a composition in rhythmic prose, written as a sequence for the feast of St. Michael), which has material on the archangels not present in the *Treatise*. Also containing material on angelic spirituality are the *Summa*, *Quoniam homines*, and the *Anticlaudianus*, both of which make references to the celestial hierarchies, with brief descriptions of each angelic level, but which add little to the material found in the *Treatise*. And, as noted in the introduction to *On the Six Wings of the Cherubim*, Alan of Lille was long thought to be the author of that work as well, but the attribution is now suspect.

In his *Treatise on the Angelic Hierarchy* Alan of Lille develops a number of complex categories and terms to explain the function, nature, and spiritual ministries of the angels. Among these terms are numerous words compounded from the Greek *phania* or *phany* plus a prefix. *Phania* can be variously translated as "light," "vision," "apparition," or "manifestation." The prevalence of this root is due to the fact that the angels themselves are "light" and represent various ways of "seeing" God. The following chart helps to make some of his terms and categories more accessible. It also outlines the

location of the angels in Alan's cosmology according to their placement in the *Treatise*. Not detailed in the outline, but spelled out in
the *Treatise*, which follows, are the various spiritual paths of the
angelic orders and the relation of those paths to the human order.

Mode of Wisdom:	**Theosophy** (wisdom of God, *Dei sapientia*)	**Theophany** (angelic knowledge, *scientia angelica*	**Theology** (human knowledge, *humana scientia*)
Corresponding Hierarchy:	supercelestium "above the heavens" i.e., the Trinity	celestium "the heavens" i.e., the Angelic Order	subcelestium "below the heavens" i.e., the ecclesial or human order

The Expanded Angelic Hierarchy
(Theophany)

Epiphany	Hyperphany	Hypophany
Seraphim	Dominions	Virtues
Cherubim	Principalities	Archangels
Thrones	Powers	Angels

Within this cosmology, each individual order within a hierarchy has
its own separate identity but at the same time functions as a part of
the larger whole. This has two effects in Alan's *Treatise*. The first
effect is an intimate connection between the whole and the parts so
that, for instance, the work and spirituality of the angels are likewise
the work and spirituality of human persons. The ministry of the
angels is thus intimately connected to the ministry of humans,
which in turn is intimately connected to contemplation of God.

The second effect of the balance between the whole and the
parts is what might be called a noetic connection. That is, within a
given hierarchy, each order or member has a particular ministry or
path into God, yet that particular charism, that particular gift, does
not block empathy with or a noetic knowledge of other spiritual
paths within the hierarchy. The old story of the ten blind men and
the elephant illustrates this. Each blind man touches a part of the

elephant, getting something of his "part" correct, but totally misreading the "whole" of the elephant. For instance, one blind man touches the elephant's tail and declares it to be a broom, which in fact is not totally wrong, for it has the shape of a broom and certainly functions as a broom to sweep off flies. But a partially correct conclusion about the part leads to a totally erroneous conclusion concerning the whole. However, if the ten blind men had touched their part of the elephant, compared notes, pieced the parts together with a bit of creative intuition, they may very well, through their contact with the parts, have determined the whole. This is how Alan of Lille's celestial hierarchies work, and it is also how knowledge of God functions across hierarchies. Each angel touches or reveals a part or attribute of God. For instance, the seraphim reveal love. But in noetic connection with the other angels, the seraphim connect with the knowledge, wisdom, power, discernment, and justice of God as well. And the angels, of course, are not blind; their noetic, intuitive, and creative charisma are full of light, serving to open the eyes of men and women to the full range of active and contemplative ways and forms of seeing God.

Two other issues, in addition to Alan of Lille's depiction of the spiritual paths of the angels and their relation to people, deserve notice. Though not unique to Alan, they are highlighted here in his *Treatise on the Angelic Hierarchy* and given particular clarity. The first is how the angels, especially those of the first angelic hierarchy, the Seraphim, Cherubim, and Thrones, represent and clarify the issue of mediated *vs.* unmediated participation with God.[3] For Alan, the Seraphim, whose mode of divine union is love, hold out the possibility of a direct, pure, simultaneous, and immediate relation to God. With the Cherubim, whose mode of union is knowledge or intellect, the possibility of immediate union begins to dissolve, but for good reason. The Cherubim, as fullness of intellect, see or understand God by means of symbol or representation or likeness *(similitudo)*, which mediates the divine reality. Likewise, as Alan explains, through the use of dialectic, they are the first order to manifest and understand difference *(dissimilitudo)*. The Cherubim are "different" from God in a way that the Seraphim are not. And yet at the same time, through reason and intellect, they are "similar" to God. They are similar/different as well from the Thrones. With the Seraphim, by means of love, one pursues the path of immediate enlightenment or union with God. With the Cherubim, representing knowledge, one's path follows the way of symbolic representation and dialectic, which requires similarity and difference.[4] Thus, for Alan, the love of the Seraphim models a kind of immediate union and participation with God, and the knowledge of the Cherubim models a union through image, symbol, language, and culture, but which nonetheless is therefore able to dwell comfortably in the dialectical tension of unity and diversity within the Trinity.

The second and final issue is what Alan of Lille calls the *exordo*. *Exordo* is Alan's term for orders (or the dis-orders) of demons or fallen angels that attempt to counteract the good angels and to work within the earthly realm to direct humanity's passion away from love of God and neighbor and toward love of the world. Thus, within the *exordo* and working against the Seraphim are the Antiseraphim, against the Cherubim the Anticherubim, and so on. This *exordo* represents a shadow hovering within the course of angelic spirituality, a darkness that can conceal the many pathways to the Father of Lights. His use of the forms of the *exordo* and his warning against it make it clear that Alan of Lille was aware of this darker, chaotic spirit world.

Note on Translation. The *Treatise on the Angelic Hierarchy* is translated from *Alain de Lille: textes inédits avec une introduction sur sa vie et ses oeuvres*, ed. Marie-Thérèse d'Alverny (Paris: J. Vrin, 1965), 219–35 (references to d'Alverny's introduction will be d'Alverny, *Textes inédits*; references to Alan's treatise will be Alan, *Hier. Alani*). Though d'Alverny's critical edition gives this treatise the title *Hierarchia Alani*, she also cites the manuscript variant *Tractatus de angelica yerarchya*. This latter is a more appropriate title for our purposes and conveys the content of the work well. Bold section titles (contained in square brackets) are added as an aid to following the text and are not present in the d'Alverny edition.

Treatise on the Angelic Hierarchy

This is a reflection on the angelic orders. We will look first at what hierarchy is, second why it is called hierarchy, and third at the nature of its outward appearances.

Hierarchy is legitimate exercise of authority by divine nature in and through divine forms by means of order, knowledge, and action.[5] Note the elegance of this description and the intricate relation of order, knowledge, and action. This is because the exercise of authority, unless it is ordered, is weak and fearful and is not legitimate. Likewise, if there is order in the exercise of authority but no knowledge, foolishness abounds; if there is order with knowledge but without action, the exercise of authority is listlessness; if there is action without knowledge it is idleness; if there is action without order it is presumption; and if there is knowledge without order the exercise of authority ends in ruin. Again, how gracefully are the words in this definition of hierarchy set forth.

The phrase "divine nature," which is a part of this definition, refers to the supercelestial hierarchy, which consists of the trinity of persons. The phrase "in and through divine forms" refers to the celestial hierarchy, which consists of the angels that are created in the image and likeness of God,[6] or to the subcelestial hierarchy, which consists of the people of the body of the church who, through likeness to divinity, are conformed to God.

Hierarchy is also called the "sacred beginning"[7] or "origin" from *archos*, which is the first, and *iereos*, which is interpreted as holy. Hierarchy is divided into three forms: supercelestial, celestial, and subcelestial.[8]

Concerning the Supercelestial Hierarchy. The supercelestial hierarchy is one, simple, of uniform dominion, without grade, without differentiation, without comparison, the highest, eternal, perfect, and true, creating and re-creating in all its works its own omnipotent power, allowing access to nothing extraneous, dismissing nothing of itself.

The supercelestial hierarchy is called "one" because only the One has divine dominion, "simple" because it banishes every manner of composition, "uniform" because the Father, Son, and Holy Spirit are alike in every way. The supercelestial hierarchy is said to be "without grade," because by comparison there is nothing more equal or less equal among the three Persons, "without differentiation" because divinity is perfected unity, "without comparison" because nothing bears resemblance to divinity. It is "highest" because it is the highest good, "eternal" because it has neither beginning nor end. With regard to both action and nature it is said to be "perfected" because nothing in it is superfluous or diminished, and "true" because it is one and perfect and immutable.[9] The supercelestial hierarchy is said to "create and re-create in all its works its own omnipotent power" because it requires no higher assistance, and that it "gives access to nothing extraneous, dismissing nothing of itself" because nothing is added to it nor is anything taken from it. It is without change or any shadow of vicissitude.[10]

Concerning the Celestial Hierarchy. The celestial hierarchy is the dominion of the celestial spirits who, balanced in equilibrium, are secondary in likeness only to the most sublime hierarchy. This hierarchy has grade, sustains differentiation, and admits of comparison. Members of this celestial hierarchy are distinguished from, yet related to the highest Trinity in three ways: (1) by adoption, (2) by participation, and (3) by the supreme worthiness by which they are fit to their tasks. This second hierarchy proceeds from the first supercelestial hierarchy, it never recedes from the first, it is under obedience to the first, and it looks back[11] constantly upon the first.

It is said, and rightly, that the spirits composing the celestial hierarchy are "balanced in equilibrium," because the angels have their gift, office, and power proportionally. They are said to be "second" to the most sublime likeness because the first likeness is the Trinity, while the second likeness is in the angels. The celestial hierarchy "has grade" because there are various degrees and differentiation among the angels. It is said to "sustain differentiation and admit of comparison" because some angels are greater than others. It is "distinguished from yet related to the highest Trinity in three ways" because it is collected into and distinguished by nine orders of angels in three hierarchies. This hierarchy shares in "adoption" because the angelic nature is adopted through grace, it shares in "participation" because it is a true partner with the goodness of divinity, and it participates in the "supreme worthiness by which they are fit to their tasks" because the highest honor is from God who distinguishes and graces the angelic nature with so many gifts. The celestial hierarchy "proceeds from the first supercelestial hierarchy" because it goes forth from God by means of creation, re-creation, and preservation; It "never recedes from the first hierarchy" into dissimilarity from God because in whatever place it is sent an angel is still encompassed within the divine immensity. It is "under obedience to the first" because all angels are spirits of divine administration[12] and in all of their duties they dwell in God. And finally, it "looks back upon the first" because whatever they do, they do under the gaze and in the contemplation of God.

Concerning the Subcelestial Hierarchy. The subcelestial hierarchy is power and strength ordered in human nature. Following the first and of subordinate place to the first, it imitates the highest image and the superexcellent likeness by receiving from the center or celestial hierarchy and thereby being drawn back to the first, supercelestial hierarchy.[13] The whole of creation is therefore from the one, and the whole returns to the one, and thus the one is the whole.

The human, or subcelestial hierarchy, is said to "follow the first and be of subordinate place to the first" hierarchy and "imitating" because imitation of angelic nature brings humanity to imitation of divinity. Thus humanity, meditating upon the goodness of divine governance is instructed by angelic nature so that God might be imitated in God's self and so that humanity might receive the "highest image and the superexcellent likeness." That is, humanity becomes the image and likeness of the highest and superexcellent God so that therein the whole of human creation might be returned to its source. Humanity, in fact the whole of creation, is thus "drawn back to the first principle"; it "is from the one" as from the highest Creator, it is "to the one" as to the certainty of a final end, and "the one is the whole" because all the saints with the holy angels are as one through the order, knowledge, and activity[14] of their imitation of God.

[The Angelic Order]

Now we ought to investigate the reasons why the celestial hierarchy is divided into nine orders or nine hierarchies.[15] Each separate hierarchical order can be described according to these divisions. The nine orders, by each participating in the one hierarchy, are said each to express a spiritual likeness to the first hierarchy. Dionysius the Areopagite grouped these nine orders together into three hierarchies.

In considering these orders of angels, our agenda will be as follows. First, we ought to consider what an angelic order is; second, we will consider matters pertaining to the question of angelic nature; third, we will investigate how the angelic orders can be distinguished; fourth, we will assign appropriate names to each order; and fifth, we will seek out the nine orders, neither more nor less, and whether at any time there were ten orders.[16]

[Definition]: An angelic order is a simple and non-imaginary theophanic character[17] containing a multitude of uniform celestial spirits. Each spirit is characterized by a pure and singular form and without mediation or intervening image.[18] We ought to note what manner of "singular form" is operative in this description: it is a singularity dependent on the fact that without plurality there is no order within the celestial community.

In this definition the collection of individual spirits is together called a "multitude." The term "spirits" is added to distinguish the angels from humanity, which can likewise be seen as multitudinous or many. And since the spirits of evil are also multitudinous, "celestial" is needed. And since the plurality of good angels is able to exist in a contemplative mode yet not in a mode that combines or mixes in form with God, it follows that they are "a theophany characterized by a pure and singular form." That is, they come together and combine, but in their own unified mode of contemplating God. "Imprint" is also a theophanic aspect of the mode or symbolic manifestation of each angelic order. In the word *theophany*, *theos* means God, and *phanes* is interpreted as vision;[19] and indeed, the "theophanic imprint" indicates the way or form of seeing God. Theophany is thus the pluralistic uniformity of the various angelic orders designated by the phrase "theophanic imprint." That is, theophany is the way or form of the vision of divinity.

Many, however, are the ways or forms of seeing God.[20]

Indeed, at any time we can comprehend the ground cause, God, through the visible nature of the various things of the universe.[21] However, each theophany is composed in its own particular way having its original design from God, the initial ground cause. Thus a given vision of God is composed in a given way depending upon the grace of a particular word or the unique visual capacity of a given body.[22]

For instance, when a visible ray is detected for comprehension by the bodily eye, a beam of the ray strikes against an object and its parts are diffused around the obstacle. The object is returned to the eye as a kind of reflection and an image of the object is retained. In this way the soul is stimulated, as it were, to comprehension of objects by the senses. Therefore, as we have said, this kind of comprehension is ordered in its own particular way by means of the properties of bodily vision. The vision of reason, on the other hand, presents another form of comprehension by which we contemplate God. When we are directed toward comprehending God through reason, we gaze attentively upon the primary nature of creatures. Creatures inhere to their Creator; they are turned to their Creator by reason to consider their own primary nature, the form of their Creator. By such a route we are consequently led by the guidance of reason to contemplation of God.

Angels, however, look upon God not according to these theophanies[23] but according to the simple, unmixed theophany, because the all-encompassing light of God is simple. The angels themselves contemplate God through themselves without mediation, without image. Vision becomes mediated, however, when we comprehend one thing through another. Thus, for instance, since the beauty of Atalante[24] finds its echo in Parthenopaeus,[25] we see the beauty of the mother in the son, yet only indirectly. In the same way we comprehend the invisible things of God by a likeness through those things that have been made.[26] Thus we infer the power of God[27] through the essence of God's creatures. We infer the wisdom of God through their order and beauty. We infer the benevolence of God through these things that persevere and are sustained in their own being.[28]

But lest we seem to describe the unknowable only on the basis of our simple ignorance, we ought first to investigate the difference between theosophy, theophany, and theology.

Theosophy is the wisdom of God, what God is in God's self. Theophany is angelic knowledge by which the angels contemplate God. Theology is human knowledge by which God is understood by humans. Our temporal vocabulary is called theology, not theosophy or theophany. This implies that God, in the present time, is seen by humanity as if through a mirror, in an enigma.[29] In the same way humanity has not named its knowledge wisdom, but rather philosophy or philology or physiology to signify again that, in the present time, humanity is not able to have full and perfected knowledge of God. And since the angels contemplate more perfectly than do men or women, their knowledge is called theophany.

Theophany is further defined as arising from a sequence of signs, not from the substance of spirits. A theophany is received by a mind cleansed of images, it is of a superessential and definitive origin, it is a simple and immediate[30] manifestation.

Now, notice that sometimes knowledge concerning effect is prepared beforehand by understanding the cause, while at other times understanding of the effect stands before knowledge of the cause. Thus, for instance, because the moon is placed between [the earth and] the sun, a solar eclipse is witnessed. In this case understanding of the effect is shown by [understanding] the cause. In a similar way, because we see the sun undergoing an eclipse, we know the moon to be [between the earth and] opposite the sun. In this case, the cause is shown by the effect; that is to say, in the showing of the effect, understanding of the event is obtained.

Thus, the definition of theophany above notes the "substance of spirits," that is, the essence of nature. Indeed, the spirit of nature is often called the natural "god." However, this manner of manifestation pertains to natural philosophy, which treats of natural things. Natural philosophy does not, however, have knowledge concerning

God based upon the essence of nature because the superessential cause has no cause. But through a "sequence of signs," that is, knowledge concerning God is possible through the effects of the supreme cause, which are themselves sequenced by that same supreme cause. Theophany concerns these sequenced manifestations, whence at the beginning of the above definition we said "a sequence of signs, not from the substance of spirits." This in turn indicates the difference between philosophy and theophany. And in this they are different: the philosophy of nature begins from the intellect and descends from there to a perception of the senses and from thence to the experience of a thing. Thus by natural philosophy, the fact that pepper burns is first perceived naturally by the intellect and only afterward is experienced by the senses. Theophany, on the other hand, begins from the senses and then extends to the intellect. Thus we see that, by what was said above,[31] we understand God through the beauty, magnitude, and order of things. Our understanding now, however, is only partial, not full. But, what has been until now an imperfect mode of understanding will be perfected in the future. True theophanic understanding of God, however, is already consummated in the angels.

The definition of theophany follows with the statement "a mind cleansed of image." That is, the mind is purged of chaotic imagining. For instance, when we contemplate God (so it is testified by the great Boethius in his book on the Trinity), it is not necessary that we be led into images in such a way that we are led to believe, by a strange metamorphosis of imagination, that God is somehow a kind of corporal figure begirded by angels on some kind of military exercise.

This is followed in the definition by the phrase "of a superessential and definitive origin." God is called "origin" because from God's very singularity comes the multiple manifestations of being, "definitive" because through God, at any place whatever, a thing is, as a fixed class of things, completed as to its essential nature, and "superessential" because divinity exceeds the customary understanding of eternity, of immutability, and of the essential property of its substance.

And finally it is added that theophany is "a simple and immediate manifestation." That the manner by which the manifestation we have concerning God is "simple" is evident from what is said above. However, the vision is also called "immediate," which means that it is not brought about through mediation of any kind but rather is spontaneous, direct, instant. In humans a "manifestation" of God occurs only through mediation, as we have already said. In angels this truly is not necessary, because angels see God as God is in God's self, and they see themselves in God.

Theophany is divided into three kinds: Epiphany, Hyperphany, and Hypophany.[32]

On the Nature of Epiphany: Epiphany is that superexcellent vision of God by which the most superior orders of angels, the Seraphim, Cherubim, and Thrones, contemplate God. The word is composed of *epi*, which means beyond and *phany*, which means vision. Thus epiphany means the most superior vision of God. Epiphany is also the ministry of burning affection, and the highest understanding resulting in the free distribution of justice. This description suggests a threefold aspect to the ministry of angels: a triple gift, a triple power, and from these conditions a triple clothing[33]—love, knowledge, and discernment.[34]

Among these three orders of angels the Seraphim have preeminence. Concerning this order we will look first at what the Seraphim are, second at why they are called Seraphim, and third, what we ought to consider concerning those beside them in the celestial order.

Seraphim are the supereminent ones of the society of celestial spirits. They are fiery, mobile, keen-sighted, discriminating, delicate, illuminated by an unmediated fountain of lights, in turn illuminating the center orders by mediation. The spirits that constitute this order have preeminence among all the celestial orders. The Seraphim are thus called "supereminent"; and because they burn with great love for the divine they are called "fiery"; and because they have a most subtle nature, which provides them with the ability to choose the good freely, they are called "mobile"; because they penetrate the most remarkable celestial mysteries, they are called "keen-sighted"; and because they have a more refined and subtle nature than other spirits, they are called "discriminating" and "delicate." Thus this order is most elegantly called Seraphim, which means burning, because they glow with great love for the divine.

This is followed by a "fountain of lights,"[35] that is, from God, who is the Father of Lights.[36] The Seraphim are "illuminated" in an "unmediated" way because God illuminates nothing of God's own essence by mediation. The Seraphim are irradiated by God's brilliance, receiving God's radiance with immediate understanding. On the other hand, the Seraphim are said to illuminate the center orders[37] by mediation because the center orders, through the mediation of the Thrones, illuminate divinity by means of revelation.[38]

...

Therefore, those angels who are burning most fiercely with divine love are specially delegated to this office so that they in turn can allure humanity to a similar burning with divine love. These spirits constitute the first angelic order.

Through the ministry of this seraphic order of angelic spirits, there are those contemplative men and women who give themselves in all things to the love of God. These are the cloistered men and women.[39] Opposite to these are the disordered order of demons,[40] or rather more truly the *exordo*, who are delegated to this office (as are the Seraphim to theirs) so that through them humanity is shut off from love of God and neighbor and lured into love of the world. This same demonic assembly[41] speaks falsehood and lies against the Seraphim, they are Antiseraphim, they are the assembly who puts forth the love of the world as the love of God. However, that order called the Seraphim, the first division in this description of Epiphany, oppose the Antiseraphim with their "ministerial office of glowing affection."

Now, because after love the most worthy and fruitful thing is knowledge, it is necessary to take up that order which, after the Seraphim, has the fullest comprehension of divinity. Thus, in consideration of this order, we will look first at the nature of those spirits called Cherubim, second at why they are called Cherubim, and third at what we ought to investigate concerning them.

The Cherubim is the angelic order fit first for the fullness of knowledge. Preceding the Thrones, whom they resemble and yet at the same time from whom they differ, they are like the Seraphim, whose likeness they impart to the Thrones. Because the Cherubim are after the Seraphim, they receive their fullness of knowledge from this higher order. The Cherubim are thus truly in concord with the first order and precede the third. The first likeness within the angelic orders occurs in the Cherubim because they imitate the first order, receiving from them their knowledge and charity. This likeness, however, also represents the first dissimilarity as well. The Cherubim are like the Seraphim, yet unlike the Thrones; they receive from the Seraphim but do not pass on all knowledge and love to the Thrones. The first dissimilarity is also said to be found in the Cherubim since, with respect to the Seraphim, the first diminution in the order of good nature and grace is found in them. This dissimilarity between the Seraphim and Cherubim is, at the same time, a likeness between the Cherubim and Thrones. And so it goes throughout the angelic hierarchy; the center order is always less than the first, and so dissimilar, yet like the first, and so similar. In this manner those things revealed by the first order to the second are in turn revealed by the second order to the third.

Therefore those angels that, after the first order, are filled most with knowledge and have been given the ministry of leading men and women into knowledge of God are those spirits that compose the order of Cherubim. Named according to the full capacity of their wisdom, the Cherubim are called "fullness of knowledge." There are thus those holy men and women who, through the ministry of this order of the Cherubim, contemplate God by means of the zeal of their attention to holy scripture.[42] However, those demonic assemblies who attempt to shut humanity off from knowledge of God are in direct opposition to the Cherubim. This assembly is made up of the "Anticherubim." These Anticherubim are those evil spirits who seek the understanding of a given age or the praise of contemporaries more than they do the overriding wisdom of God. Opposed to them, as was said before, is the order of the Cherubim, whose name means "of the highest understanding."

Then there are those spirits who possess knowledge for discerning or judging between good and evil. Such spirits are, by a special selection, given the office of ministry to men and women who are themselves summoned to the task of discerning between good and evil. These third spirits constitute the order called Thrones. These are given the name Thrones not only because they judge but also because of their ministry of judging. That is, their ministry to human judges and to those concerned with discernment. Indeed, the Thrones are themselves seats of discernment.

The Thrones, in addition, represent the celestial place of assembly for supercelestial discernment in which justice is examined. Thrones are those spirits through whom men and women are likewise invited to pursue justice, and indeed, that order through whom God (who is accomplishing all things in heaven and on earth) reveals divine justice. God also calls humanity to discernment through the Thrones so that men and women might judge and not deviate from the balance of justice. Such men and women, through the ministry of the Thrones, are led to a clear determination for justice and do not fall away from the paths of righteousness. The order opposed to the Thrones is that assembly of demons who condemn righteousness in order to seduce men and women and to cause them to fall away from balanced judgment between good and evil. It is through the work of these malicious demons that some prefer earthly rulers who do not in fact observe the order of justice.

The third order of Thrones demonstrates discernment "with balanced judgment" from our definition of Epiphany. On the other hand, the phrase "with the results distributed" describes the nature of the manifestation of all three orders. This latter phrase is used to indicate that the presence of each divine theophany is clearly and equally brought forth, but in different ways. For instance, the highest love for an object makes the object of affection lovingly present; full knowledge brings forth the beauty of an object to us and exhibits it clearly; and in like manner the discernment of justice is that practice around which our own judgment is manifested.

Therefore these three manifestations of the three highest orders contemplate God, but in diverse ways, and thus are fittingly described as manifesting God "with distributed results."

And note that the Seraphim and Cherubim are not placed before the Thrones because love is more worthy than reason but because it is more fruitful. Love is more fruitful because in love we follow after the fruit of blessedness. Thus love and the first position are given to the Seraphim. Likewise, since discernment emanates from knowledge and we have justice because knowledge walks before it, the Cherubim necessarily occupy second place.

On the Nature of Hyperphany: Hyperphany refers to the three central orders, that is, the Dominions, Principalities, and Powers, who have come together in contemplation of God. Celestial secrets are revealed to them by the three superior orders. These orders are called Hyperphany from *hyper,* which means after,[43] and *phanes,* which is an appearance or visible manifestation. Thus after the first vision comes the manifestation of the second.[44] Hyperphany is the divine illumination of God's self distinguished in three ways: by participation in an ascending ladder of reverence, by teachings on spiritual practices, and by protection against secret, opposing forces.

On the Dominions: There are certain greater, listening spirits who have the official duty to govern lesser spirits in such a way that the lesser spirits are obedient to them. These greater spirits have as their function to show humanity the nature of obedience and reverence as well. This fourth order is composed of those spirits called Dominions because the lesser orders are in fact ruled by them and are taught by the Dominions how they ought best to give reverence to the Lord. It is due to this order of spirits that there are people who regularly obey their leaders and who govern those below them rationally. The orders opposed to the Dominions are those assemblies of demons who lure people into disobedience. On account of this demonic assembly certain individuals become obstinate toward their superiors and irrationally govern those less fortunate.

Dominions demonstrate the first part of the definition of Hyperphany, that is, "of God's self distinguished by participation in an ascending ladder of reverence." Indeed, reverence ought to be considered to be composed of various grades. Some owe their reverence to the greatest things, others to middling things, still others to lesser things. These grades of reverence bring to mind the Dominions as described above and show forth divinity to men and women on the basis of just governance and obedience. This is brought about either by means of exhibiting the diversity of orders of reverence, or by that diversity itself exhibiting an illumination.

On the Principalities: There are those orders of angels, after the Dominions, who rule the lower orders and who are deputized to this ministry in order to summon men and women into the spiritual practice of leadership, and as spiritual leaders to teach the practice and forms of spiritual devotion to others. Thus, because these spirits have as their function to rule the lower orders and to teach humanity good governance of the less fortunate, they are called Rulers or Principalities. It is on account of this order of spirits that there are some people who govern those subject to them with justice. There are opposed to this order of spirits various assemblies of demons who suggest that tyranny, not just rule, is the proper exercise of power over subjects. On account of this demonic partnership, there are those men and women who wish rather to stand before and preside over their subjects than to protect them. Thus the point addressed in the definition of Hyperphany concerning "the spiritual practice" of leadership applies to the order of spirits called Principalities.

On the Powers: There are other spirits who are chosen on account of their power. They have as their function to deter demons from practicing great evil on men and women and thereby tempting human beings beyond what they are able to bear. Indeed, the ministry of such good spirits is to teach humanity to resist the temptations of the demons. Those that make up this order are called Powers. They are called Powers on the basis of their function and office of ministry to humanity. On account of this order of spirits there are some people who are able to defend the good against evil powers, resist the depraved suggestions of demons, and instruct others in resisting evil. Opposed to this order of spirits are certain assemblies of demons who are able to put up great resistance to the

Powers. These are the Antipowers on account of whom evil is offered up to humanity.

These final two orders are also signified in our definition of Hyperphany. Thus the "spiritual practice" of just governance applies to the Principalities, while "guarding against opposing forces" applies to the Powers.

On the Hypophany:[45] Hypophany is divine participation occurring by means of natural law for the discernment of celestial secrets by means of a capacity for revelation. This portion of the celestial hierarchy pertains to the three lower orders: the Virtues, Archangels, and Angels. The phrase "divine participation" is used because in this way knowledge, which these same three orders have concerning God's very self, comes into being for us by means of their participation in God. Of these three orders, the first is called the Virtues.

On the Virtues: There are certain angels who have as the function of their ministry to bring miracles into being and who, by mediating goodness, do in fact bring miracles into the world for humanity. These spirits, which constitute the order called Virtues are, for instance, believed to be present in the altar when the bread is changed into the body of Christ. These are the fellowship of spirits who are specifically gifted with the special function of working miracles and wonders.

On the Antivirtues: There are opposed to the Virtues certain gatherings of demons, the "ministry" of which is to become full of deceitful tricks and illusions in order to deceive humanity. On account of these gatherings there are those who turn to tricks by means of divination. The Virtues, however, demonstrate the point of the above definition, which indicates that they perform miracles "by means of the natural law." The Virtues work their ministry in accordance with the natural law, performing their many miracles in the context of this law.

On the Archangels:[46] There are other angels who have as their function the ministry of receiving, revealing, and displaying the highest celestial secrets to humanity. These spirits are the messengers of God's foremost mysteries. Such angels make up the order called the Archangels, since they announce the highest and first order of things. They are named from *archos*, which means the first, and *angelus*, which means messenger. "Angel" is the name of the office, not of their nature. On account of this order of spirits there are those who, with the highest and purest intentions, prophesy of God for humanity.

On the Antiarchangels: The order that is against the Archangels is that assembly of demons who suggest to humanity the errors of heresy. On account of this assembly of demons there are those heretics who shape abominable doctrines concerning God.

On the Angels: There are other orders of angels who receive from the Lord, as their function, the ministry of revealing lesser things and of announcing these things to humanity. These angels are sent to assist men and women in the course of their various duties and hardships. This order of spirits is believed to be deputized as watchful guardians of humanity. These spirits constitute the order called Angels. Indeed, Angel means messenger. On account of this order there are those who keep the welfare of their brothers and sisters foremost in their minds.

On the Antiangels: Opposed to the order of Angels are those demonic assemblies who, though less abominable, nonetheless suggest false things to humanity concerning God. On account of this order of demons, lesser heretics are ensnared by the worst heretics.

These last two orders of angelic spirits were described in the above definition when it was stated that the spirits of the Hypophany deal with "celestial secrets with the capacity for divine revelation." Indeed, this description applies to the Angels and the Archangels. And so, concerning these things, this is sufficient.

Thomas Gallus
(Thomas of Wales, Canon of St. Victor, Abbot of Vercelli)

Extractio

Extract
on the Celestial Hierarchy

Introduction

Thomas Gallus (d. 1246), founder and abbot of the celebrated monastery of St. Andrew at Vercelli, joins that remarkable group of medieval contemplatives, including Bernard of Clairvaux, Catherine of Sienna, and Teresa of Avila, who not only wrote about and practiced mystical theology, but who were also involved in an intense and active life of political engagement. A contemplative teacher and practitioner, Gallus nonetheless continued with the active administration and direction of the abbey and hospital at Vercelli throughout most of his life. He was known and revered from the thirteenth through the sixteenth centuries, primarily as a commentator on the Dionysian writings and as an exegete of the Song of Songs. However, from the seventeenth century until the early part of the twentieth century, Thomas Gallus (also known as Thomas of St. Victor or Thomas of Vercelli) was largely forgotten. In recent years he is being rediscovered.[1]

Thomas Gallus was born in France shortly before 1200. He was teaching and writing in Paris by 1218, where he was an Augustinian canon of the abbey at St. Victor. In 1219 he left Paris to found the abbey of St. Andrew at Vercelli in the Piedmont province of northern Italy. An indication of the effect of his writings and of his work as prior and abbot of St. Andrew's is that, largely on Gallus's account, the Franciscans transferred their *studium generale* from Padua to Vercelli in 1228. However, Gallus's involvement in quarrels between popes and the Emperor Frederick II eventually forced him into exile in Ivrea in 1243, where he continued writing until his death in 1246.

Representing some of the finest articulations of the integration of speculative and affective strands of mysticism found in the Christian spiritual tradition, it is appropriate that Thomas Gallus is receiving renewed attention. Gallus's integrative sensibility is inherited from a number of medieval and pre-Christian sources. Included among these are the Neo-Platonic metaphysics of *eros*,[2] the speculative anagogy of Dionysius the Areopagite, monastic theological preoccupations including a theology of history and eschatological biblical hermeneutics,[3] the insights into divine theophany and human holiness in Eriugena, especially in his *Commentary on the Celestial Hierarchy*, Hugh and Richard of St. Victor's work on symbols, aesthetics, and angelic spirituality,[4] and the Christian strand of affective mysticism exemplified in particular by twelfth-century Cistercian writers. Gallus's *Prologue* to his *Commentary on the Song of Songs*, presented in the following section of this volume, serves as a primary example of his ability to weave these strands together into a cohesive whole. Giving equal authority, for instance, to the intellectual vision of Dionysius and the affective lyricism of Solomon (the supposed author of the Song of Songs in the thirteenth century), the *Prologue* presents the work and wisdom of both these writers in such a way that they are shown to be dialectically divergent, on the one hand, yet mutually complementary, on the other.

Thomas Gallus's writings include three commentaries on the Song of Songs,[5] a *Commentary on Isaiah 6*,[6] two mystical treatises, *On the Seven Grades of Contemplation* and *The Mirror of Contemplation*,[7] and two major works on the Dionysian corpus. These include *The Explanations*, an extended exposition, phrase by phrase, of the full Dionysian corpus, finished in 1243, and *The Extract*, finished in 1238.[8]

The Extract on the Celestial Hierarchy,[9] a part of which follows, is neither a paraphrase, nor a commentary, nor a translation in the strict sense. Rather, it was composed in order to furnish a brief, more comprehensible compendium of Dionysius's texts for his

Latin readers. As such, *The Extract* is sometimes abridged, often peppered with short paraphrases, and illuminated throughout with some of Gallus's own interpretations. Among all Gallus's works, *The Extract* was certainly the most widely known and utilized. Introduced at the University of Paris as a part of the semi-official Dionysian corpus, which included as well the translations of Eriugena and Sarracenus, the *Scholia*, and the commentaries by Eriugena and Hugh of St. Victor, it quickly became a vehicle for Gallus's own ideas throughout the medieval period.

A number of these ideas are of particular interest to the development of angelic spirituality. One, alluded to above, is Gallus's affective use of love and charity, and the Seraphim as representative of that love and charity, as driving forces in the soul's spiritual journey into God. This theme, present here in *The Extract*, is even more apparent in the *Prologue to the Third Commentary on the Song of Songs*, found in the next section of this volume. A second theme, present in Dionysius but emphasized more fully in Gallus, is that of the angels, along with Jesus, scripture, and the tradition of the fathers, as "signs" or "symbols" that lead the soul back to God. Gallus writes:

> Just as we were first inwardly illuminated by the Lord Jesus himself, let us then, according to our ability, look upon the anagogic illuminations of the sacred scriptures handed down by the holy Fathers. Afterwards, let us contemplate, according as we are able, the angelic hierarchies manifested to us by the illuminations themselves as anagogical signs.[10]

By means of these angelic forms the soul is led through contemplation and then, not back to contemplation of angels themselves (which are always in some way symbolic coverings of divine reality), but to contemplation of the simplicity of divine reality itself. That is, the angels lead the soul into an unmediated, un-enveloped participation in pure divinity. A final theme, one related to the idea of the angels as anagogical symbols lifting the soul to God, is Gallus's overriding conviction that by imitating the angelic orders, the soul (to the extent that it is able, as Gallus is fond of saying) is conformed to God; in fact, the soul is deified.

The following *Extract* on Dionysius's *Celestial Hierarchy* is evidence of the rich and deep tradition of devotion to and contemplation of angels in the Latin West. This *Extract*, as well as the complete corpus of Gallus's work, reflects the integration of monastic, metaphysical, theological, and spiritual themes as they developed within that tradition of angelic devotion. His work also serves to highlight the seminal work of Dionysius the Areopagite and its influence on subsequent centuries of Christian contemplative thought and practice.

Note on Translation: The Latin text of Gallus's *Extractio* on the *Celestial Hierarchy* is available in *Dionysiaca* 2:1040–66. The following *Extract on the Celestial Hierarchy* is translated from that edition. The *Extractio* is also available in *Dionysii Cartusiani Opera Omnia*, vols. xv–xvi, Tournai, 1902. Much of Gallus's *Extractio* is an exegetical commentary on James 1:17, which refers to God as the "Father of Lights." Where Gallus comments on God as the "Father of Lights," the translation of pronouns referring to God will be consistent with the gender of "Father," i.e., male. The pronouns in the Latin are, in any case, consistently masculine. References to God that are not commentaries on James 1:17 will be translated neutrally with regard to gender.

Extract
of the Abbot of Vercelli, Thomas Gallus, on the Celestial Hierarchy[11]

Chapter One

Even though in various ways every divine enlightenment proceeds, out of its goodness, toward those provided for, it not only remains simple in itself, but also unifies those it enlightens.[12]

Every good blessing of the natural world and every gift perfecting the natural order is from above,[13] coming down upon creatures from the eternal Father who generates light most simple in its essence and most complex in its efficacy. And the universal light proceeding from the Father himself admits not only celestial minds[14] to communicate knowledge and participation of itself, but also advances to us through the distribution of goodness. Again, [this is] as if the unifying virtue so fills us with itself that it arouses those who are separated from the depths to a knowledge and desire for the light itself. And once the distraction of the mind has been removed, the light turns us back to the unity of the eternal Father, who gathers together the dispersed of Israel and [turns us to] the simplicity that to some extent conforms [us] to the supremely simple God.[15]

So that we may be perfected by this univocal light, let us call with the most pure prayers upon Jesus who is truly the light of the Father. Jesus is the *true light who illuminates everyone coming into this world*,[16] and it is he *through whom we have obtained access*[17] to the Father, the author of lights. Just as we were first inwardly illuminated by the Lord Jesus himself, let us then, according to our ability, look upon the anagogic illuminations of the sacred scriptures handed down by the holy fathers. Afterward, let us contemplate, according as we are able, the angelic hierarchies manifested to us by the illuminations themselves as anagogical signs.[18]

And so we are inwardly receiving, with acts of understanding that are pure and strengthened by practice, the principle (or rather super-principle) gift from God, the Father of Light, which manifests to us through the formal symbols of scripture the most blessed hierarchies of angels. Let us lastly, because of that participation in the light, be lifted up to contemplating the unitive, simple ray of the Father himself, that is, the Word of wisdom that radiates eternally from the Father.

That ray, although it pours itself out in various ways, is never, however, deprived of its proper and singular unity. Rather, communicating itself in multiple ways to the uplifting activity[19] and unifying conjunction of the elect (insofar as the good befits them), it nevertheless within its very self is singularly fixed by its immobile identity. It extends upward to those who are turned to it and [who are] reaching out as much as they are able, according to their ability,[20] and it unifies them to itself in accordance with its own proper, simplified imitation of others things.

For it is not possible for this divine principal ray to shine in its fullness[21] for us in this life in any other way save being wrapped round with the various coverings of sensible forms according to what is suitable and advantageous for our uplifting activity, and [unless] through the fatherly providence [it is] linked to those things which are known by us in a way natural for us yet suitably adapted to itself.[22] On this account the holy ordination of God, which is the foundation of perfection, deigns to make our most holy hierarchy a supermundane imitation of the angelic hierarchies, which are in themselves immaterial. The [holy ordination] sets this forth in the sacred scriptures by various material figures and composite forms so that we (as we are able) might be drawn back through the holy symbols of sensible forms to the contemplation of simple supernal powers, which are not of things capable of being formed. They are always the same.

For it is not possible for our soul to be aroused upward toward that immaterial imitation and contemplation of celestial hierarchies unless our mind itself, in keeping with its condition of present blindness, makes use of the guiding hand[23] of material symbols. This happens by reflecting in some inner evaluation that the most beautiful things we can sense are but images of invisible beauty, and that the pleasing odors we can sense are expressions of the variety of odor beyond what we can sense, and that material lights are but images of the intelligible light, and that the cognitive understanding of the sacred scriptures is but an image of that comprehensive contemplation which satisfies souls just as [it is said], *I will be satisfied when your glory appears.*[24] It also happens by reflecting on the fact that the ordinations of sensible congregations arranged in order are images of ordinations and conditions that are in the heavenly orders, ordered after the imitation of God, and that the receiving of the most divine Eucharist in life is but an image of our full participation in Jesus, which is perfected in the Fatherland. And it happens by reflecting similarly upon all manner of things that agree with the heavenly substances in a supermundane way and are handed down to us under sensible symbols in scripture.

In order, therefore, to obtain this likeness to God according to the varied ability of mortals, the beneficent author of total perfection represented supercelestial minds by sensible images in the composite forms of sacred scripture. In doing so, this author of total perfection manifested celestial hierarchies to us and is making our hierarchy (according as we are able) a co-worker of the celestial hierarchies themselves through the God-forming assimilation by which these hierarchies are conformed to God. He did this insofar as he would lead us through sensible things to a knowledge of intelligible things, and from catholic signs or symbols to contemplating and imitating the highest celestial hierarchies.[25]

Chapter Three[26]

What a hierarchy is and what its benefit is.

According to our view, hierarchy[27] is a holy congregation of rational persons properly divided by order through grade and ministerial office; a holy congregation assimilated to conformity with God, as far as possible, by knowledge and activity fitting itself; a holy congregation raised up to an imitation of God (according to the capacity of each) through divine enlightenments pouring down upon it. Divine beauty, to which the hierarchies of angels and humanity must be assimilated, is simple and good and the principle of perfection, just as it is completely cleansed of all that is not fitting[28] and generous with its own light in accordance with the capacity of each of those illuminated. Through the distribution of the light itself it is perfected by that perfection which makes the perfect assimilated to God. And in accordance with their intransmutable conformity to God, they are perfected in a way that befits the divine beauty that is the divine inheritance.[29]

A hierarchy reaches to God by means of constant gazing, desiring,[30] insofar as it can, to be made like and united to God. It has God himself as leader of all holy knowledge and activity. It looks in unwavering fashion to divine beauty and, by contemplating it, is shaped by this as if it were forming beauty itself. It makes persons who have praises of God within themselves divine signs and most clear and spotless mirrors,[31] receptive of the primal ray and the God-initiated light.[32] It is filled with holy divine clarity poured upon it through the same ray so that the higher orders copiously and with splendor pour the brightness upon those lower according to what was divinely established for them.

It is inappropriate for either the superior beings who are working at perfection or those lesser beings who are being perfected by them to engage in any activity beyond what is ordained by God, who is the first principle of perfection. Indeed, observance of the divine order is necessary for them. This is so in order that they may persist in a state of happiness, and so that they may enjoy fully the divine clarity that is making them Godlike,[33] and thus be reformed in a manner similar to the capacity of any one of the holy minds, a thing they highly desire.

It is clear from what is said above that the name hierarchy generally designates a certain holy assembly representing divine beauty within itself and exercising special activities commensurate with its own virtue in accordance with the measure of power and knowledge of its holy preeminence, and made similar, according to its possibility, to its own origin, namely, God. For the perfection of each person of the hierarchy is to be led back to the imitation of God according to what is proper and fitting, and to become a *fellow worker with God*.[34] This implants an effective divine conformity upon all things and in itself represents a manifestation of divine activity according to the capacity of each. Thus it is said, *Indeed, we are co-workers with God*.[35] Thus within the order of a hierarchy, the lesser orders are purged, illuminated, and perfected by the superior orders while the superior orders purge, illuminate, and perfect the lesser.[36] Purgation, illumination and perfection, the active [work of the superior orders] and the passive [work of the lesser orders], conform hierarchical persons to God to the degree possible.

Divine blessedness, according to what is able to be praised by all people, is indeed cleansed of everything dissimilar to its eternal fullness. Hierarchical persons are in some way made similar insofar as they are purged. Divinity is full of eternal light, to which hierarchical persons are made similar insofar as they are illuminated. It is perfect and so lacks nothing of divine perfection. Hierarchical persons are made similar insofar as they are perfected. Thus divinity is purging, illuminating, and perfecting. Or rather, it is itself the highest purging beyond all purging, it is the enlightenment above every light, and it is the perfection beyond every perfection. Perfect in itself, it is the beginning of perfection and the cause of every hierarchy. According to its transcendence, it is set apart from every sacred thing. Hierarchical persons are made similar to it insofar as they cleanse, illuminate, and perfect their inferiors, and insofar as the hierarchical persons have above themselves the first principal of purgation, illumination, and perfection. They do not receive any light from lower beings but flow into them from divine fullness and are sublimely present to them.

Consequently, it is necessary that all those who have been purified be totally cleansed and that they be free from all that is not luminous. By the same token, it is necessary that those who have been illuminated be filled with the divine light, becoming uplifted in understandings and sighs that purely and supremely desire the divine light in order to obtain more fully and possess more firmly the divine contemplation. It is necessary that those who have been perfected be led across from imperfection, or a lesser degree of perfection, and grasp fully an increase of perfect knowledge, a knowledge that experiences the taste of intimate wisdom.[37] Those who have been purified of other things ought to hand down something of the abundance of their more pure purgation to the lower orders. Those who have been illuminated, since they are more intimately joined to the divine light and more abundantly filled with the same light, ought to allow that light to flow down upon others, according to the capacity of each to receive. And those perfected, just as they are more experienced in the perfective tradition through their experience of internal tastes of perfect wisdom, ought to perfect the orders beneath them with a holier teaching.

On account of this everyone constituted in a hierarchical order is raised upward to divine cooperation according to proper proportion. And in a certain manner in themselves and by means of their own work through grace and power divinely conceded [to them], that cooperation represents those things that are in the holy Trinity naturally, or rather supernaturally, and which transcendentally[38] come into being from the Trinity. That is to say, the Father is fullness in terms of essence, of life, wisdom, goodness, and power, and is completely the fullness of all desirable fullness, taking from no one, but subsisting transcendentally by his own and only authority. All this same fullness the Father supernaturally and transcendently gives the Son by generating him, and Father with the Son give the same fullness supernaturally to the Holy Spirit by transcendently breathing[39] the Spirit. [These are accomplished] since in the holy Trinity itself there is no superior or inferior grade, but there is a certain superintellectual and transcendental exemplar of superiority and inferiority, namely, authority and subauthority. Therefore, those things that are and take place in Divinity transcendentally are manifested within the hierarchies, so that the holy minds situated in them, which love God, may be able in some way to imitate divine knowledge.

Chapter Six[40]

What is the first rank of the heavenly beings, what is the middle, and what is the last?

God alone manifests the number and worthiness and glory and arrangement of the substances of the celestial hierarchies. God knows well the nature of powers and illuminations and of his own invisible ordination. For us, however, it is impossible to know the mystery and perfection of those essential natures except as we are instructed by divine dispensation and from the celestial beings themselves, who know well [their own] special characteristics. Therefore we will have nothing of our own to say in this treatise concerning them, but rather, as much as we are able, we will explain those things that the apostles, disciples, and holy persons who have written concerning the status of angels have thought out.

As collected from various testimonies of sacred scripture, there are nine orders of angels, each designated by a distinct name. These the holy apostle Paul, our teacher, divided into three groups of three hierarchies.[41] The first hierarchy, he says, is gathered around the very substance of God before any others and is united attentively to God without mediation. And he says that from scripture we know that in this hierarchy three orders are collected principally and immediately around God. The last is called the Thrones, the middle in Hebrew is called Cherubim (which is also called the "many-eyed" on account of the multiplicity of its knowledge), and the highest in Hebrew is called Seraphim. Seraphim are associated with wings because they fly above every other. The apostle has taught us that this hierarchy, containing three orders, is, as it were, a single one and is coordinated as the first of all angelic hierarchies, since no other is more conformed to God or closer to God where the illuminations of the divine hierarchy are emanating at first, as it were, from the principal fount. The apostle says that the second hierarchy is made up of three orders, of which the first is the Dominions, the second the Virtues, and the third the Powers. And he says the third and final hierarchy contains three orders, of which the first is the Principalities, the second is the Archangels, and the third and final is the Angels, as is clear below.

Chapter Eight[42]

Concerning the Dominions, Virtues, and Powers, and theirs, the middle hierarchy.

After the first hierarchy we ought to consider the middle by contemplating with discernment the three orders comprising this hierarchy: Dominions, Virtues, and Powers.[43] Each of these three names signifies something of the properties of the order through which the substances of the order conform to God.

The name Dominions signifies that substances of this order, free from every shameful servitude and unworthy subjugation, are lifted up to God through the first hierarchy. And the name signifies that this order is not held down by the violence that characterizes the various miseries of this world, but that it has an indissoluble dominion which rises supereminently above all undue slavery. It is not subject to any form of violent subjugation, and it is separate from and exceeds all mutability because its dominion is one. Through an unending desire for God, who is the true source of dominion, they mold both themselves and the lower orders into a likeness and imitation of God insofar as is possible through good graces and works. And as their name signifies, they fashion the lower orders as well. And through contemplation and total longing they are converted not to that which simply appears as the good, but to the true existing good, and, as far as they are able, they always participate by conformity in God, who is the first source of all dominion.[44]

The name Virtues[45] truly signifies something robust, and unshakable strength. This strength is for accomplishing every work that is suitable for this order in keeping with grace and virtue through which the substances of this order are conformed to God. This strength is subject to no debilitating infirmity by which it might be less able effectively to receive whatever divine illuminations are conferred upon it. Rather, powerfully imitating the divine operations in accordance with their ability, without small-spiritedness, they never abandon the motion that conforms them to God but firmly reach out to God's virtue, which stands above all substances and is the author of every form of virtue. Thereby they realize (to the extent possible) an image of that same divine virtue. (In the process it conforms those orders beneath it to the same divine virtue.) This order is strongly turned back toward divine virtue, which is the principal virtue, and proceeds to the lower orders by the distribution of the God-forming virtue.

The name Powers signifies the regular power of the substances of this order, which is coordinated by the Dominions and Virtues. That is, they are ascribed a position in the same hierarchy as Dominions and Virtues in order to receive divine illuminations without any confusion or disruption. The name also signifies that an invisible and supermundane arrangement of the power of understanding exists among these powers that are lifted upward in proper order, not by misusing their own tyrannical strength toward the inferior orders, but powerfully and kindly lifting up the lower hierarchy (containing the Principalities, Archangels, and Angels) to a fuller knowledge, love, and imitation of God.[46] And the Powers assimilate them to God, who is the chief of all power and causes all power. And the Powers reflect God back to the lower angels insofar as the angels themselves are able to receive the reflection; these angels are in the three orders of the lower angelic hierarchy, which is well ordered by the Powers. Having these deiform properties, the middle hierarchy of celestial minds, as has been said, is purged, illuminated, and perfected by the Deity by means of illuminations passed on to the second hierarchy by the first, the illuminations descending from God with the first hierarchy mediating through the light-filled second.

By examples from scripture we will make known that one celestial mind is illuminated by another mind mediating above it. For just as those men and women who heard the words of the Savior directly were taught more perfectly than those who learned through the mediation of these same holy apostles and disciples of the Lord, so it is with celestial minds. Those celestial beings who dwell in the immediate presence of God are illuminated more clearly and perfectly than are those who are illuminated by God through those who dwell nearest God as mediators. Hence the tradition of the apostles teaches that primary intelligences exist, and that they are said to have a role in the purgation, illumination, and perfection of the lower orders.[47] This is because these same primary orders lift up the lower orders to God, who is the transcendent source of all things, and because they make them each according to their own capacity participate in divine purgating, illuminating, and perfecting. Generally, it has been ordained by God that [it is] through superior beings that inferior beings participate in divine illuminations. This can be collaborated by supporting examples from the scriptures.

We read in Zechariah, for example, that the generous justice of God converted Israel back to God through salvific trials and punishments, promising release from the Babylonian captivity.[48] This example illustrates how all of the elect are corrected by the adversities of the world and led back to a more faultless and purgative life. It is also found in Zechariah that one angel, whom I judge to be from the first order, which circles immediately around God, received gracious and comforting words[49] from God concerning the restitution of the captives and their dwelling in Jerusalem. Another angel, learning divine council from this first angel as if from his hierarch, taught Zechariah that Jerusalem would be rebuilt and would be inhabited by a multitude of people.[50]

A similar thing is found in Ezekiel, when (so it is said) the fatherly kindness of God judged that the children of Israel who had been punished by the discipline of divine justice needed to be absolved from the penalty that had been inflicted. The judgment of Divinity concerning this was revealed first to the Cherubim, and after the Cherubim to the angel who, in keeping with the meaning of the hierarchical symbols, is said to be clothed in linen and to have an ink stand by his side.[51] The angels, designated here by the six men having weapons of war in their hands intended for destruction,[52] are instructed by God through the symbol of a man clothed in linen and are taught God's judgment concerning transgressors to be punished and those to be saved, who were marked with a Tau[53] upon their foreheads when he said: *"Pass through the city following, and strike; do not spare your eye,[54] show no pity. Kill old people, adolescents, and virgins, young children and women until there is total destruction. But strike no one upon whom you see the mark."*[55]

It can also be read in Daniel that the same angel who revealed to him the mysteries of the incarnation of the Lord,[56] said to Daniel: *"The word went forth, and I have come to make it known to you."*[57] This indicates that the word went forth to one angel, which in turn is made known to Daniel through another angel. And again, in Ezekiel it is read that one angel took the fire from the midst of the cherubim[58] and that he gave this fire into the hand of a second angel who is designated by the man clothed in linen.[59] It is shown by this that one higher cherub has influence upon a lower cherub and that this cherub has influence on another. And yet in Daniel again it is read that a certain angel (as the superior angel) came in contact with

Gabriel (as the inferior angel) in order that Daniel might under-stand the vision.[60] Thus a superior angel taught Gabriel so that Gabriel might teach Daniel.

We can gather the same message from other illustrations that might be collected from the testimony of scripture that treat of the understanding of the deiform, good, and properly ordered celestial hierarchies. The order of our hierarchy has been made similar (as far as the possibility of our mortality allows) to these celestial orders, and, representing the angelic beauty in itself through images, it is lifted up through it to God, who is the transcendent principle of every hierarchy.

Chapter Ten[61]

Repetition and Conclusion Concerning the Angels' Ordination.

We said above that the highest hierarchy of celestial minds is governed by Divinity itself insofar as it extends without mediation to Divinity itself by a more hidden and yet brighter illumination of the principal Deity,[62] purged, illuminated, and perfected. It is more hidden, as if very intimate and very simplified and unified. It is brighter as if from the first emanating from divine brightness, appearing at first to celestial minds and very universal and very much poured out to the first principle.[63]

By this [process] the second hierarchy is truly lifted up to God by the first hierarchy, according to its possibility. And the third is lifted up to God by the second. And our own hierarchy is in turn lifted up by the third hierarchy to God, the first and principal foun-dation and consummation of every hierarchy. And this [happens] according to the same law that the divine preeminence ordains in the lifting up of angels, which is in keeping with what is fitting for God and possible for our hierarchy.

But all the celestial spirits are successive manifestations of the ones above. To illustrate: The lower Angels are manifestations of the Archangels and the higher orders, and the Archangels are man-ifestations of the Principalities and the higher orders, and so forth. Again, the highest angels (that is, the Seraphim) are manifestations of the very Deity who sets them in motion;[64] and the Cherubim are manifestations of the order of Seraphim; and so successively, according to the rank of the individual orders. The individual orders are able to accomplish this properly because the divine fullness, by arranging all things in harmony, makes provision and distribution in the areas of knowledge and virtue to any and every hierarchy or order of angels and humans, in order that each and every order or hierarchical person may successfully complete the holy uplifting action and work established for it.

It is clear from what is said above that any hierarchy can be divided into three orders, that is, the first, the middle, and the lowest. Further, each order is divided into three parts containing within it the first, the middle, and the ultimate virtues.[65] Thus might it be understood from what Isaiah said of the Seraphim, that *"one cried out to another."*[66] This shows plainly that the one who cried out instructed another who cried out. Isaiah reveals that one distributes divine understanding to the other within the same order, just as do the superior orders to the inferior.

Let me add, from much that I could say, something that is not out of place. Any well-ordered human soul or angelic mind[67] has, within its own separate person, its special primary and middle and ultimate orderings and virtues assigned to each individual hierarchical person. And it has within itself the uplifting actions of hierarchical illuminations clearly separated and ordered in keeping with the proportion of their natural powers. Twenty years ago, in the cloister of St. Victor in Paris, I carefully considered the opening words of Isaiah's vision, *"I saw the Lord,"*[68] according to the new translation of Jerome. Through these uplifting actions, any angel or hierarchical human participates (each according to its capacity) in the super-pure cleansing of God, in the super-full light of God, and in God's perfection, which comes before and causes every created perfection. Indeed, there is nothing that is perfect in and of itself. Nor is there anything that does not need perfection from someone else, except God alone, who is complete fullness and contains complete fullness by means of his own virtue, nature, and authority. All of which God contains before all things and above all things.

THOMAS GALLUS

Chapter Twelve[69]

Why human hierarchs are called "angels."

Those practiced in seeking to understand holy scripture desire
to know why our human hierarchy is called *the angel (or messenger) of
the Lord of Hosts,*[70] when it was mentioned above that the inferior
orders do not participate in the same fullness of divine illumination
as those in the superior orders. We would respond that this is not
actually contrary to what was said above. Granted, while the inferior orders do not participate in the same fullness as the higher
orders, they nonetheless do participate in the same light.[71] Some
orders participate in a sublime way, others less so; for that reason
they can be named in the same way. For instance, the order of the
Cherubim participate in the wisdom and knowledge of God more
sublimely than do the inferior orders. However, even these inferior
orders, all of them, participate in divine wisdom and knowledge.
Indeed, they participate in their own particular way by gazing upon
the higher orders. The common feature of all minds conformed to
God is to share wisdom and knowledge simply, but to participate in
a particular understanding granted to a grade of the first order, or of
the second order, or of whatever lower orders, is not a common feature of all conformed souls.[72] Rather, they participate according to
their appropriate levels.

What we said about the angelic orders is rightly perceived to
concern all divine minds. Just as the superior minds have virtues
and knowledge that the inferiors have, but in a more abundant way,
so in turn do the inferiors participate and share in the virtue and
knowledge of the higher orders, not equally but in a lower way.
Therefore, it is not unsuitable that our hierarch[73] in sacred scripture
is called an "angel." According to his virtue, our human hierarch
participates in the virtue of "announcing," which is, to be sure, the
peculiar quality of angels. Having acquired the property of angels,
our hierarch teaches men to imitate the various manifestations of
angels in a divine and celestial way.

It is found as well that sacred scripture calls "gods" not only certain celestial powers,[74] but also men of special holiness and excellence

most beloved of God,[75] although the divine substance in itself is superessentially separated and elevated above all things and from all communion with things. No existing being is comparable with God in any way whatsoever. Yet every celestial and human mind that according to its virtues is converted back to a unifying communion of the one, and that according to its possibility is incomprehensibly expanded toward the divine illuminations[76] (insofar as it is able), is worthy [of the title] through imitation of God and by means of a divine equivocation.

Chapter Fourteen

What the traditional number of angels signifies.

This agrees with what is said in Daniel concerning the angels: *A thousand times a thousand served him, and ten thousand times ten thousand stood by him.*[77] Here the largest simple number, that is, "thousand,"[78] is compounded and multiplied by itself. Through this we clearly know that celestial substances are innumerable. Indeed, so numerous are the blessed celestial minds that they exceed the feeble and constricted measure of our numbering system and are cognitively defined only by a heavenly understanding and knowledge given to them by a divine sanctification of infinite comprehension. For this divine transcendence is the essential principle above all substances, the underlying cause of all things, the power energizing all things, and the uniting goal of every like being.

Thomas Gallus
(Thomas of Wales, Canon of St. Victor, Abbot of Vercelli)

Prologus, Commentarii in Cantica Canticorum

Prologue to the Third Commentary on the Song of Songs

Introduction

In the *Prologue* to his *Third Commentary on the Song of Songs*,[1] Thomas Gallus uses a simple metaphor to summarize the profound complexities of language, love, and mystical union. This metaphor is the kiss; not the kiss obtained, but the kiss remembered and the kiss achingly longed for. For Thomas Gallus, the kiss is a metaphor of language, or more precisely, language silenced; the lips that must be silent in a kiss are the same lips that speak. Yet the silence of the kiss, which represents the death of the intellect, the ineffable cessation of speech, is also the birth of passion and charity. Thus, for Gallus, the kiss is a metaphor of love; the same lips that speak in silence spark passion. And the kiss is a metaphor of union with God, of deification. The mouth of the soul that speaks, the lips of the Bride that kiss, are joined as one to the Bridegroom, to Christ. They separate and, in longing, join again, even as the Bride repeats, *"Oh, that he might kiss me."*[2]

This kiss and Thomas Gallus's *Prologue* in general function as an outline of his mature theology and spirituality. The *Prologue* provides an anthropology of the soul that combines Dionysius the Areopagite's speculative and anagogic metaphysics with Solomon's practical wisdom of love to teach a path of assimilation and union with God. What is unique in the *Prologue* is Thomas Gallus's formulation of angelic spirituality. In effect, Gallus transfigures the

235

angelic hierarchy into a kind of angelic anthropology. That is, he uses the orders of angels as a means of describing the nature and goals of the human person *and* as a diverse but comprehensive path into God. For Gallus, the soul is, in effect, ontologically structured by the angelic orders. The angels become the prism hues of God's *agape*, the (in)visible icons of God's revelation, the gatekeepers through which love comes into being. If the kiss serves as a multivalent metaphor for Gallus, the angels are the ontological keys to its understanding.

Utilizing Dionysius, Solomon's Song of Songs, and his own synthetic imagination, Thomas Gallus employs the angels to describe three basic themes in his angelic spirituality: (1) the relation of love and knowledge,[3] (2) the nature of the soul's union with God, and (3) the contemplative and active paths and practices leading into that union.

The relation of love, or affect,[4] and knowledge is at the heart of Gallus's angelic spirituality. All of the angelic orders, from the order of Angels to the Seraphim, contain and exemplify the various hues and mixtures of heart and mind. All possible permutations of their relation and integration are considered. Thus, for example, Gallus considers the love of knowledge as well as the knowledge of love, making a distinction between what he calls *scire* and *nosse*. *Scire* is love of knowledge—to know, to understand, to be cognizant. *Nosse* is the knowledge of love. It is a more practical, experiential, and affective knowledge, but it is knowledge nonetheless. The highest form of *scire* is found in the Cherubim (or what Gallus calls the "Cherubim of the soul"). The highest form of *nosse* is found in the Seraphim of the soul, where every other form of knowledge is eradicated in the purely immediate, existential kiss that the Seraphim, in their burning passion, exemplify most clearly.

But for Gallus every angelic order exemplifies something of the relation between intellect and affect. For example, he uses the angelic Dominions to discuss free will and its relation to intellect and affect. As "authentic authority," the Dominions of the soul engage intellect and affect profoundly, allowing the soul to choose between good and evil. The immediate effect of this "authentic decision" is Gallus's idea of suspension *(suspendium)*. Suspension, at the level of the Dominions, aids in the soul's meditation on God's divine emanations. The angelic Thrones add another dimension to mind and heart exemplified in the soul's suspension in meditation. The Thrones of the soul represent the "death" of the intellect in "ecstasy" of mind *(excessus mentis)*. Thus suspension in the Thrones of the soul represents separation from mind, leading to the possibility of the reception of divine love through grace. In Gallus, the Cherubim of the soul balance intellect and affect most perfectly. Intellect is perfected in this balance and, in fact, comes in contact with God, but it can go no higher than a simple touch. Thus in the Cherubim of the soul, even the perfected intellect is unable to participate in the deepest divine mystery.

Only at the level of the Seraphim is the soul able to enter the purity of affect or love and so enter into complete and deiforming union with God. Gallus equates the seraphic soul with immediate proximity and circling union with God, based on the theoretical vision of mystical theology from Dionysius and with the kiss of union based on the practical wisdom of Solomon's mystical theology.

In *Prologue*, Y,[5] Gallus uses the Seraphim to describe the apex of the affective faculty of the soul and the affective spark within the soul that serves as the modality of divine fusion. Describing the seraphic, affective faculty at the apex of the soul as *apex affectualis*, he uses the term "spark of consciousness" *(scintilla synderisis)* to characterize the highest and most pure form of human love.[6] The *scintillae* of *Prologue*, Y, are the highest "order" of the soul; they are the sparks of the fullest manifestation of human affection. The Seraphim thus represent a supreme and pure participation in divine Goodness, a flowing of light that descends from God into God's image. The Seraphim thus also represent *theoria* as contemplative life, an ineffable separation from all that is not divine light, and a passing, so to speak, into the divine life itself. But, as noted, it is a "passing" beyond simple silence, represented in Gallus by the Cherubim. It is a "crossing over" *(transitas)* and "return" to the active, ethical life of faith, hope, and charity represented so passionately in *Prologue*, Z, as a kiss.

As with all writers on angelic spirituality since the time of Dionysius and Gregory the Great, Gallus uses the angelic orders as symbols and theophanies of spiritual paths into God. For Gallus, the celestial hierarchy is a comprehensive, mandalic map of the spiritual journey that is internalized within the human soul; he develops, as it were, an angelic hierarchy of the soul. This angelic anthropology, as we have called it, clarifies how we experience God, dares to imagine what it would be like to know God more intimately, and teaches a form of prayer based on the unity of God manifested in a variety of adaptations to our human nature. And, according to Gallus, as the angels themselves clarify, dare us to imagine and teach us to become more human and at the same time more Godlike through them.

But even taken as a whole, the full celestial city does not represent the most comprehensive route to God. For Gallus, the angels are mediators between humanity and God, but they are not the Mediator. Christ alone is the Mediator, the supreme hierarch, reflected most fully, perhaps, in the comprehensive activity of the angelic orders. But the angelic orders simply reflect "as in a mirror"; they are not historically present, as is Christ. Running throughout Gallus's *Prologue*, like a shy shadow, is the assumption that there is no other way to the summit of unitive contemplation than through the *imitatio humanitatis Christi*, through affective meditation on the suffering humanity of Christ. Thomas Gallus's project in the *Prologue* is in part to use the angels as a touchstone for a depiction of the human soul quickened and brought to life by the fullest realization of its natural and grace-given powers. But finally, as it is Christ who restores and heals, so it is Christ who mediates human union with God.

Just a few decades before Gallus, using the Cherubim as a symbol of the highest route into God, Richard of St. Victor had extended the contemplative aspects of the *imitatio* of Christ to its intellective limits.[7] And just a few decades after Gallus, Bonaventure would propose that Christ as the supreme hierarch, incorporating all the angelic theophanies while dwelling in the fullness of his humanity, is, through the burning love of his crucifixion, the door, the way, and the goal of the contemplative and active lives.[8] Gallus, however, writing between the time of Richard of St. Victor and Bonaventure, is mostly silent in the *Prologue* with regard to Christ as hierarch. In the *Prologue* the pattern of ascent into God is an angelic one; its realization in Christ is only hinted. Elsewhere, however, Gallus is more explicit concerning the affective, unitive path into God through devotion to the humanity of Christ:

> It is through the careful consideration of the blessed, beautiful and wounded Christ. For among all the mind's exercises for the ascent of the spiritual intelligence, this is the most efficacious. Indeed, the more ardent we are in his most sweet love, through devout and blessed imaginative gazing upon him, the higher shall we ascend in the apprehension of the things of the Godhead.[9]

Represented by the soul ontologically structured according to the pattern of the angels, Gallus teaches that there are many ways and forms of seeing God that are accommodated to our nature. But there is but One door into the Godhead. And, according to Gallus, love and the kiss, as symbolized by the Seraphim of the soul, are the key to that door.

Note on Translation: The following *Prologue* is translated from the critical edition found in Thomas Gallus, *Commentaires du cantique des Cantiques*, Texte critique avec introduction, notes et tables par Jeanne Barbet, Textes philosophiques du moyen age, XIV (Paris: J. Vrin, 1967). A portion of the *Prologue* is available in Denys Turner, *Eros and Allegory: Medieval Exegesis of the Song of Songs* (Kalamazoo, Mich.: Cistercian Publications, 1995). Though Gallus will, on occasion, use the Latin translation of the Dionysian corpus by John Scotus Eriugena, his overwhelming preference is the translation of Sarracenus. Thus the Latin of Dionysius found in Gallus, *Comm. Cant.*, is mostly from Sarracenus, but where a comparison might shed some light on the translation, I have given the Latin of Sarracenus and Eriugena as well as Dionysius's Greek. All of these are available in *Dionysiaca*. Gallus's *Prologue* is full of citations from scripture and from Dionysius. In keeping with manuscript practices, Barbet's critical edition often indicates these citations with first and last words only. I have supplied the full citation. The letters beginning each section are present in the critical edition; the section headings (in square brackets) are added for convenience of reading.

Translation of *Mens*: *Mens* is translated variously, though consistently, throughout this volume as "mind" or "soul." In referring to angels, it is always translated as "mind." For human persons, either "mind" or "soul" might be appropriate depending on the context. But even as "mind," it should be remembered that *mens* is painted from a much broader anthropological palate in Gallus's time than in ours. The anthropological trichotomy usually used to describe the medieval conception of *mens: sensus-ratio-intelligentia*, is even richer in Gallus's work expanding to include, in this work alone, *sensus-imaginatio-ratio-intellectus-intelligentia* (drawn from Isaac of Stella, *Epistola de anima*, probably by way of Pseudo-Augustine, *De spiritu et anima*). In addition, in this work Gallus is expanding the meanings even farther to include an anthropological "hierarchy of the soul" *(hierarchia mentis)* that correlates to the hierarchy of angels. Thus, for instance, within the human person there is an anthropological category of "Seraphim of the soul," "Cherubim of the soul," and so on. Still further, the final three angelic orders of the soul—Thrones, Cherubim, Seraphim—moving toward love at the level of the Seraphim, are not described in terms of the category of mind (though they are sometimes defined negatively as beyond mind, for instance, the term ecstasy of mind—*excessus mentis*). And the final order, the Seraphim, burning with love alone, actually incinerate *all* anthropological categories, including mind, in a flaming kiss of union (cf. *Prologue*, Z). These final three orders of the soul are defined in total by Gallus as affect *(affectus)*, again, not generally a category of mind. As such they demonstrate three levels of the knowledge of God as *nosse* (see *Prologue*, B). This knowledge is a "union achieved through unknowing" according to Dionysius, a union that surpasses mind. This wisdom exceeds even the human heart. These higher levels of Gallus's anthropological schema center these affective hues in the very "bones" (*Prologue*, W) of the contemplative soul. As a finishing flourish to this colorful anthropological palate, at the apex of affect, love colors and illuminates the soul with super-brilliant rays of divine enlightenment. And it is, finally, the mind, but more important, the soul, that receives this full enlightenment.

Prologue to the Third Commentary
on the Song of Songs

[Knowledge of God: *Scire et Nosse*]

A. *But let the one who glorifies glory in this, that he understands (scire) and knows (nosse) me, that I am the Lord who is compassion and justice, and righteousness in the earth. I delight in these things says the Lord.*[10] This verse from Jeremiah indicates that there are two forms of the knowledge of God. The first, intellectual understanding[11] of God (that is, *scire*), is acquired through consideration of the created order as taught in the exposition on Ecclesiastes by the venerable doctor, Master Hugh, a canon of our church of St. Victor in Paris.[12] Concerning this type of understanding, the apostle says, *"Since the creation of the world God's invisible nature, that is his eternal power and divinity, is beheld, having been clearly understood through the things that have been made."*[13] And concerning this type of knowledge Solomon teaches, *"Foolish and vain are all men in whom the knowledge of God does not dwell. They are not able to know He Who Is from the good things that are seen, nor are they able to recognize the craftsman*[14] *while attending simply to his works,"*[15] and, *"Their creator is able to be seen intuitively from the greatness and beauty of created things."*[16] Dionysius has said, writing to Titus: "Every visible operation of the world manifests the invisible nature of God."[17] And in *The Divine Names* Dionysius says: "It is true to say that we know God not from God's nature in itself, for God is unknowable and beyond all reason and mind, but we know God from the ordering of all things—which is the work of God alone. Images and likenesses of God's divine exemplars[18] show forth by which we ascend, as far as our capacities allow us, to that which is above all life and order."[19] This form of the knowledge of God is speculative and enigmatic.[20] It is spoken of and taught universally as much by meditating, as by hearing and reading. It is only this kind of knowledge that the pagan philosophers were able to grasp. Thus the apostle says, *"What is known of God is made clear to them."*[21] These things are knowable by a kind of preexistent knowledge of the sensible world.

B. But the second kind of knowledge of God [that is, *nosse*] is a kind of knowledge that incomparably exceeds the first described above. This second kind of knowledge is described by the great Dionysius: "It is the most divine knowledge of God, which is knowledge attained through unknowing.[22] It is achieved in a union which surpasses mind. It occurs in the mind receding from all things, later the mind abandons even itself, having been united with the most super-brilliant rays, and illuminated by profound, impenetrable depths of wisdom."[23] This illumination is *"The wisdom of the Christians that is from above[24]...descending from the Father of Lights."*[25] Indeed, this more superior wisdom exceeds what is in the human heart, hence "the heart does not ascend to it."[26] But as mentioned above, the wisdom of the intellect *(scire)* does in fact ascend from the sensual nature, as it were, into understanding. But the knowing *(nosse)* that is beyond intellect, [the wisdom of the heart], *is the servant of the throne of God.*[27] This is the secret and hidden wisdom of which the apostle spoke to the mature at Corinth.[28] And from this doctrine of the apostle, the great Dionysius the Areopagite writes of the theoretical aspects of this super-intellectual wisdom, to the extent that it is possible to write of such things, in his little book, *The Mystical Theology.* I commented carefully on this little book ten years ago.[29] Solomon, on the other hand, in the Song of Songs exposes the practical [rather than the theoretical] aspects of this same mystical theology. This is made clear through the important material narrated throughout the whole book.[30]

[On the Human and Angelic Hierarchy]

C. In order to come to an understanding of Solomon's practical wisdom, it is necessary, by way of a preface, to give an explanation of the following sentence from Dionysius: "I add this, and not unreasonably I believe, that each and every celestial and human spirit possesses its own orders and its own powers according to three levels: primary, middle, and ultimate. By such order and power every human and celestial spirit becomes, by direct participation, the illuminative manifestation of the hierarchies, participating—to the extent that it is possible—in that purification beyond the most sublime purity, in the fullness of superabundant light, and in the perfection that surpasses all perfection."[31] Dionysius speaks [of this joint participation of human and celestial spirits] after having investigated the angelic orders. He discusses the assembly of celestial orders in the seventh, eighth, and ninth chapters of the *Celestial Hierarchy*, looking first at the three hierarchies and then at the triple orders within each.

D. Just as there are distributed within a single hierarchical soul three hierarchies each with three orders, so it is with the angelic distribution. Clearly, the lowest hierarchy contains the orders of Angels, Archangels, and Principalities; the middle contains the Powers, Virtues, and Dominions; and the summit or principal hierarchy contains the Thrones, Cherubim, and Seraphim.[32] I treated this subject in detail twenty-seven years ago in the abbey at St. Victor in Paris, commenting on Isaiah 6[33] in the passage that begins: *"I saw the Lord sitting upon a throne, high and exalted."*[34] This material is for the most part repeated at the end of my commentary on Chapter Ten of the *Celestial Hierarchy*.[35] As for the present, I briefly repeat the preliminary remarks that seem necessary for this treatise, because the Bride of the Song of Songs speaks at one time in one hierarchy of the soul, now in another; now in one order, now within another.

E. The lowest hierarchy of the soul consists of its very own nature; the middle hierarchy of the soul consists in effort, which incomparably exceeds nature; and the highest hierarchy of the soul consists in the ecstasy of mind.[36] In the first hierarchy of the soul, only nature is operative; in the highest, only grace; in the middle, grace and industry are jointly operative.[37]

[The Angelic Soul]

F. The lowest order of the lowest hierarchy of the soul is called the angelic order.[38] The angelic hierarchy of the soul contains the essential and simple natural means of apprehension of both knowledge and affect[39] without any judgment as to propriety or impropriety [of one over the other]. This is just like the Angels, that is, the messengers who simply bring news to the soul.[40]

G. The middle order[41] contains natural judgments about things understood, whether they seem advantageous or disadvantageous. They communicate from a region closer to the source than do the first order.

H. The third angelic order contains attractions to and flights from natural judgments according to the dictations of propriety or impropriety. Indeed, their flights are away from evil and their attractions are toward the good.[42] Thus this order reaches out to guide the lower orders to the divine. This order is known by the name of Principality.

I. The fourth order, which is the lowest of second hierarchy of the soul, contains the voluntary motions of both the intellect and affect, already received from free choice between good and evil. This hierarchy of the soul, by examining and ordering the mind through the discernment[43] of reason, commits itself to an appropriate distinction between good and evil, and to the extent that it can, sets the mind in order. Here the intellect and affect of the ordered soul, through a definitive disposition, are committed to desire and seek the highest good with all their strength, and to reject all obstacles to that Good. According to Dionysius, the Powers signify this ordering.

J. The fifth order, which is the middle of the middle hierarchy, contains the robust energies of the soul, those of the natural[44] and gratuitous[45] virtues. What the Powers have ordained to be the correct course of action, these virtues help to carry through to the end with a resolute will. This order is known by the name of Virtues.

K. The sixth order, which is at the summit of the middle hierarchy, contains the authentic exercise of the discipline[46] of free will. By the exercise of the authentic authority of the free will, the very summit of the affect and intellect is suspended to receive divine visitations from on high insofar as is possible for a free will aided by grace.[47] The sublimity of this suspension and of this exercise of discipline and of this freedom is designated by the name Dominions. In this order the as yet sober mind is extended and exercised to the highest rays, to the highest ends of its nature.

L. The seventh order, through ecstasy of mind, is totally receptive to the highest divine visitations.[48] Hence this order is known by the name of Thrones. And there are as many Thrones as there are hidden places of the mind or capacities for receiving that super-substantial ray which is totally simple in essence yet multiple in its effects.

M. The eighth order contains every mode and manner of intellectual knowledge that is drawn toward divine worthiness. Yet the intellect does not have the strength to ascend on its own.[49] And the affect as well is similarly drawn by divine attraction, yet it is not drawn beyond the height and attraction to which intellect is drawn.[50] Intellect and affect walk hand in hand, as it were, and indeed are drawn all the way to the final point at which the weakened intellect passes away; at this point, where intellect reaches its summit, is the order of Cherubim. In this order the intellect, although it has been thus drawn upward into its completion, does not pass beyond its capacities. Rather, understanding here reaches the consummation of its knowledge and light. Hence this order is called Cherubim.[51]

N.[52] The ninth order contains the highest longing sighs for God, the extensions and deep penetrations that go beyond understanding, the burnings of brilliant radiance and shinings of fiery ardor.

The intellect is not able to be drawn into sublime ecstasies or into the excesses of all these lights, but only the highest love, which can unite the soul to God.[53] In this order the *most holy prayers*[54] are offered, by which we are drawn into the presence of God. This order lovingly embraces God and is wrapped in the loving embrace of the Bridegroom. This is no knowledge in a mirror;[55] it takes *Mary's good portion, which will not be taken from her.*[56] In this order a bed is laid out for the Bridegroom and the Bride. From this order a flood of divine light, cascading through the correct sequencing of the orders, flows in succession through all the lower angelic orders.

[On Angelic Contemplation]

O. We have made clear the names of the nine orders referred to above according to the exposition of Dionysius, who speaks, for example, concerning the Seraphim, in the *Angelic Hierarchy*, chapter 7b; on the Cherubim, 7c; on the Thrones, 7d; on the Dominions, chapter 8a; on the Virtues 8b; on the Powers 8c; on the Principalities, chapter 9a; on the Archangels, 9b; on the Angels, 9c. We have shown this in a diligent study of the *Angelic Hierarchy*. Accordingly, anyone who will read these glosses will be ready, so to speak, to return freely to those ranks when necessary, most readily to the higher ones. However, a frequent and penetrating consideration[57] of these orders is most useful in every way. It is through such consideration that the soul is led through the ninefold pattern of both the angelic and ecclesiastical orders into the divine oneness; from this enfolding of the one and holy Trinity that the soul goes forth into the Trinity itself. Thus Dionysius says in *The Divine Names*, "And the celestial souls also are said to move. First they move in a circle when they find themselves united to those illuminations emerging, without beginning or end, from the Beautiful and the Good. The soul too has circular movement when it turns within itself and away from what is outside, and by uniform revolution returns into its intellectual faculties."[58]

P. In commenting now for the third time on the Canticle, but not having those commentaries in hand that I sent before, I will now follow as usual only those occurrences of meditations[59] that shine from above by means of discerning comprehension,[60] extending the soul to the highest rays. Dionysius has followed the same approach in the *Ecclesial Hierarchy*, saying, "And for you, I have no doubt, more splendid and more divine beauties will illuminate you in all things; my words will serve as guides in ascending to the highest divine rays."[61] I believe nothing of what I am about to write contradicts the aforesaid.

Q. And so the contemplative soul, moving through the levels of the six grades of contemplation, at the height of the sixth insight fixing its gaze and attaching itself there to the order of the Dominions of the soul,[62] strives toward meditative ecstasies, longing to be assumed into the order of the Thrones of the soul.[63] And the contemplative soul is in that place in order to be near that divinity *who is present to all things, though all things are not present to it*, as the great Dionysius teaches in *The Divine Names*.[64] There are three spiritual arts practiced in the Canticles:[65] the art of most holy and chaste prayers, the uncovering of the mind, and the capacity for union.

[On the Spiritual Arts]

R. Holy and chaste prayer[66] requires obtaining advantageous, temporal things and removing inappropriate, temporal things. As scripture says, *Pray for that*, and, *Pray to me.*[67] More holy and chaste prayer is for spiritual things; the Psalms say, *Avert your face from my sins, and count all my iniquities as nothing. Create in me a clean heart, God, and place a new and right spirit within me. Do not cast me away from your face, and your Holy Spirit take not from me.*[68] The most holy and chaste prayers are not just the gifts of the Bridegroom, they demand the Bridegroom himself. Such prayers are constant and in rapid succession in the Canticles: *Kiss me,*[69] *Draw me after you,*[70] *My lover is...resting between my breasts; My lover is to me a cluster of henna blossoms,*[71] etc., *Who is from you for me?*[72] etc.

247

S. Uncovering the mind means putting aside all exterior considerations and obstacles.[73] So *The Mystical Theology* says, "With strong contrition abandon all perceptible and intellectual works, all that can be perceived by the senses, and all non-being and all being,[74] and by unknowing strive upward to a union with him who is above all substance[75] and understanding. And by abandonment of your very self and a detachment from all things and by an absolutely pure ecstasy of mind, you will ascend beyond every attachment to the ray of divine darkness beyond any being or substance."[76] In the Song of Songs, Solomon says, "*I had put off my garment.*"[77] Elsewhere Dionysius says, "The body [of men and women] is naked and their feet are bare, signifying detachment, easy disentanglement from restraints, not wishing to be held back, purification from any exterior opposition, and the greatest possible assimilation into the divine simplicity."[78]

T. However, a capacity to adapt to union is achieved through an abundant, overflowing, and fluid devotion and resolution of the mind.[79] A fluid soul is promptly unified. As Solomon says, "*My soul became like liquid.*"[80]

U. And so after that the soul *is turned to know and consider and seek wisdom and the reason of all things,*[81] longing to be separated from the whole universe of being and to be successfully united, beyond any substance, with the Bridegroom. So Dionysius says, "But my discourse now ascends from the lowest to the final, transcendent thing, so that as our discourse ascends, its capacity is diminished. And after ascending beyond all, it will be totally without voice,[82] totally united with that ineffable One about whom nothing can be spoken."[83] Such a mind asks for a kiss, that is, a conjunction or union beyond mind, though one still capable of separation.[84] Dionysius has also written of these things in *The Divine Names*[85] and *The Mystical Theology.*[86]

V. This is what Job says: "*My soul would choose suspension and my bones death.*"[87] Suspension[88] is the expansion of the mind all the way to the summit of the order of Dominions into superluminous contemplations. Dionysius says concerning this: "They are extended firmly and unswervingly to that super-resplendent ray that enlightens them. And in a measure commensurate with their love, they become as light as the light that is given to them, raised up toward God as if on wings, with holy reverence, with temperateness, opening to holiness through holiness."[89] The soul chooses this grace before all others because it is not able to go into the most sublime things on its own. One enters the sublime only through the Spirit.[90]

W. And as Job continues above, *"And my bones [choose] death."* "Bones" are the most robust powers of the soul; they represent the contemplative life of the intellect and the very core of the affections. The mind has no stronger powers in relation to divine things. Death, here, is distinguished by two marks: (1) extinction, and (2) separation. And so here, in the Dominions of the soul, these "bones" have [reached] the ultimate summit of [their] spiritual powers.

X. Thus, when the soul is assimilated into the order of the Thrones to kiss the Bridegroom, every effect and every operation of the intellect and affect cease. As the prophet says, *"My Lord, by reason of your vision, pains are set loose upon me; no strength remains in me. How is it possible that the servant of my Lord might speak to my Lord? For no strength remains in me, and my breath is shut off within me."*[91] In the order of the Thrones, intellect and affect are separated from the mind through ecstasy. In *The Divine Names*, Dionysius says, "The mind, drawing back from all things, and after abandoning even its very self, is united to rays of clarity beyond any light, permitting the mind to obtain the inscrutable depths of illuminated wisdom."[92] And Hebrews says, *Living and effective and more penetrating than any two-edged sword is the word of God. The word of God is piercing, so that it divides soul and spirit, joints and marrow; it discerns the thoughts and intentions of the heart.*[93] And again, Dionysius says that, "To us death is not only the complete destruction of being,[94] as some others might imagine, but a true separation of unity."[95]

Y. The spark, seeing that it is the apex of the affective faculty,[96] is the principle and most pure participation in the divine goodness, which flows out from truth into the image. This spark is ineffably separated from all inferior realities and crosses over, so to speak, into the divine life. In doing so, in some ineffable way, it is deified. Dionysius says, "The source of this hierarchy is the fountain of life, the being of goodness, the one cause of all existing things, the Trinity, who on account of goodness brings being and well-being into existence. This blessed Trinity, existing beyond the most divine summit of all things, who is three and also one, who truly is, wills, for reasons incomprehensible to us but clear to its design, the salvation of rational beings. The blessed Trinity wills the salvation of rational beings like us and of rational beings of a substance and existence beyond us. This is only possible with the divinization of those who are saved, and divinization is, to the extent that it is possible, assimilation to and union with God."[97] Thus Origen, commenting on the beginning of the Gospel of John, claims John himself to have been deified when he said, "In the beginning was the Word."[98]

Z. Thus the Bride is sighing with passion for this deifying union. She has been suspended[99] in the order of the Dominions of the soul, and, still placed in the mirror, she says of him as of a person absent: *"Oh, that he might kiss me."*[100]

Notes

General Introduction

1. Martin Luther, *The Babylonian Captivity* in *Luther's Works*, American Edition, 55 vols., ed. Pelikan and Lehmann (St. Louis and Philadelphia: Concordia and Fortress, 1955–), 36:109. Of course, in other contexts, Luther could be more generous, for instance, in the touching conclusion of the evening blessing in Luther's *Smaller Catechism*, "Thy holy angel be with me, that the evil foe have no power over me! Amen. And then quickly and happily to sleep."

2. Cf. *Sermons on the Psalms*, 12.7.

3. Cf. *Treatise on the Angelic Hierarchy*, "The Angelic Order."

4. Three great poems in which angels play a central role are Dante's *Divine Comedy*, Milton's *Paradise Lost*, and Goethe's *Faust*. Studies that address the issue of angels in literature in general include Gustav Davidson, *A Dictionary of Angels* (New York: Free Press, 1967); Peter Lamborn Wilson, *Angels* (New York: Pantheon Books, 1980); Clara Erskine Clement, *Angels in Art* (New York: L. C. Page, 1898).

5. Cf. Henry Corbin, *Avicenna and the Visionary Recital*, trans. Willard R. Trask (London: Routledge and Kegan Paul, 1960); Morris B. Margolies, *A Gathering of Angels: Angels in Jewish Life and Literature* (New York: Ballantine Books, 1994); Muhammed Abdul Rauf, *Islam, Creed and Worship* (Washington D.C., 1974).

6. See Walter Wink, *Unmasking the Powers: The Invisible Forces That Determine Human Existence* (Philadelphia: Fortress Press, 1986); C. G. Jung, *Answer to Job*, trans. R. F. C. Hull (London: Routledge and Kegan Paul, 1954).

7. The best example of this approach applied primarily to Satan but containing material on angels as well is Elaine Pagels, *The Origin of Satan* (New York: Random House, 1995).

8. The material in these areas is vast, of course. Studies of particular note include the following: in history, Jean Daniélou, *The Angels and Their Mission: According to the Fathers of the Church*, trans. David Heimann (Westminster, Md.: Christian Classics, 1976); Jeffrey Burton Russell, *A History of Heaven: The Singing Silence* (Princeton, N.J.: Princeton University Press, 1997); in philosophy, Mortimer J. Adler, *The Angels and Us* (New York: Macmillan Publishing Co., 1982); Robert Avans, *The New Gnosis: Heidegger, Hillman, and Angels* (Dallas, Tex.: Spring Publications, 1984); R. L. Clark, "Where Have All the Angels Gone?" *Religious Studies Review* 28 (1992): 221–34; John Locke, *Essay Concerning Human Understanding* (Oxford: Clarendon Press, 1967), especially Book I and Book II, X.9, XI.11, XXIII.5, 15, 18–22, 30–37; Jacques Maritain, *Three Reformers* (New York: Charles Scribner's Sons, 1932); George MacDonald Ross, "Angels," *Philosophy* 60 (1985): 495–511; in theology, Roman Catholic sources of angelology to be examined include Augustine, *City of God*, a portion of which is included in this volume; Bonaventure, *Breviloquim*, especially II.6–8, 12; Aquinas, *Summa Theologica*, especially Part I, questions 50–64 and 107–14; among Protestant theologians, essential works include Martin Luther, *Table Talk*, in *Luther's Works*, vol. 54, ed. and trans. Theodore G. Tappert (Fortress Press, 1967); John Calvin, *Institutes of the Christian Religion*, ed. J. T. MacNeill (Philadelphia: Westminster Press, 1960), especially I.II.14. The most thorough survey on Roman Catholic and Protestant thought on angels, as well as his own remarkable contribution to the subject, can be found in Karl Barth, *Church Dogmatics*, ed. G. W. Bromiley and T. F. Torrance (Edinburgh: T. & T. Clark, 1960), 3.3:369–531.

9. A sampling of works that support this first source includes Bradley C. Hanson, ed., *Modern Christian Spirituality: Methodological and Historical Essays* (Atlanta: Scholars Press, 1990); Bernard McGinn, "The Letter and the Spirit: Spirituality as an Academic Discipline," *Christian Spirituality Bulletin* 1 (1993): 1, 3–9; Walter Principe, "Spirituality, Christian," in *The New Dictionary of Catholic Spirituality*, ed. Michael Downey (Collegeville, Minn.: The Liturgical Press, 1993): 932–38; Sandra Schneiders, "A Hermeneutical Approach to the Study of Christian Spirituality," *Christian Spirituality Bulletin* 2 (1994): 9–14; Sandra Schneiders, "Spirituality as an Academic Discipline: Reflections from Experience," *Christian Spirituality Bulletin* 1 (1993): 10–15.

10. While it is impossible to summarize fully the features and content of the medieval belief in angels—a belief both rich and complex, and often intermingling facts of faith with picturesque fables—it is nonetheless possible to identify some common characteristics. These include the following facts: (1) a general belief in angels was firmly rooted during the period, especially during the eleventh to fifteenth centuries, when intellectual curiosity concerning angels was at its height; (2) faith in angels was a universal conviction—from Greek to Islamic and Judaic to Asian religions; belief in the existence of angels was never doubted; (3) faith in angels is a dynamic element of medieval spirituality, not a mere passive reception of ancient tradition; and (4) the medievals characterized the role of angels as active spirits within the cosmos and as having an effect on humanity and history. The depiction of this latter effect was varied. Bonaventure, for instance, focused on the aid angels bring to humanity; Rupert of Deutz focused on the role of angels in salvation history; and Aquinas explored the limits of diabolic spirits on the action of men and women in the world (see Arturo Blanco, "The Influence of Faith in Angels on the Medieval Vision of Nature and Man," in *Mensch und Natur im Mittelalter*, ed. Albert Zimmermann [Berlin: Walter de Gruyter, 1991], 456–67).

11. The development of angelic spirituality in the early church and in Patristic writings will not be addressed directly. It will be addressed indirectly within the introductions, particularly where issues in the theology and philosophy of angelic spirituality are highlighted. In general, the fathers and mothers of the church Christianized pagan angelology by (1) subordinating angelic ministry to Christ's unique mediation, though early on Christ himself was equated with the Angel of Great Counsel; (2) decidedly opposing syncretistic efforts to identify angels with the pagan messengers of gods; and (3) developing a theology of angels that studied, in the light of divine revelation, the invisible world of spiritual intelligences (good angels) created by God who assist humanity in the attainment of salvation and share with men and women the divine call to grace and glory. On the general subject of angels in Patristic literature, see Steven Chase, *Angelic Wisdom: The Cherubim and the Grace of Contemplation in Richard of St. Victor* (Notre Dame, Ind.: University of Notre Dame Press, 1995), especially chapter 1 under "The Greek Patristic Influence" and "The Latin Patristic Influence"; Jean Daniélou, *The Angels and Their Mission*; Dionysius, *Hiér. cél.*, lvii–lxiii; *DS*, vol. 1, "Anges: la dévotion aux anges," by Joseph Duhr; Stephen Gersh, *From Iamblichus to Eriugena* (Leiden: E. J. Brill, 1978), 167–77; Andrew Louth, *Dionysius the Areopagite* (Wilton,

Conn.: Morehouse-Barlow, 1989); Geddes MacGregor, *Angels: Ministers of Grace* (New York: Paragon House, 1988), 73–81.

12. Ultimately, the question of the existence of angels is a matter of faith. The question has, of course, often been approached as one of theological methodology rather than one *de fide*. A good summary of theological descriptions of angelic existence can be found in Paul M. Quay, S.J., "Angels and Demons: The Teaching of IV Lateran," *Theological Studies* 42:1 (March 1981): 20–45. Quay's summary includes theological descriptions of angels (1) as created self-manifestations of God's will, (2) as having a strictly metaphorical existence referring to God and God's acts, (3) as personifications of the overawing and "sacral" aspects of nature, society, or our own psychic experiences, and (4) as having a hypothetical existence as elements of long-gone world views that once served as vehicles for revealed truth but that now have no reference in the real world. Quay's typology, of course, does not cover all options. Many theological descriptions assume the *de fide* approach of the existence of angels and describe the angels as existent, created beings who assist in the economy of salvation.

13. More will be said concerning this issue in the conclusion of this General Introduction.

14. Pagels, *The Origin of Satan*, xv–xvi.

15. This distinction between angels "in" revelation and as existent beings in the content "of" revelation is a distinction that matters only within the realm of *religious belief*. Within that realm they are consistent and mutually affirmable. Outside that realm, within, say, science or some forms of philosophy, the distinction may legitimately be made that, affirming the possibility of revelation *per se*, affirms that angels are present "in" Christian revelation but denies the possibility of angelic existence as a content "of" revelation. A recent and rather curious article on angels treats revelation in an oddly literalistic and non-hermeneutic way, denying the existence of angels as a content "of" biblical revelation, without considering the important category of faith. The entry's distinctions concerning biblical assertions and assumptions are also curious and do not help. See Bob Hurd, "Angels," in Downey, *The New Dictionary of Catholic Spirituality*, 38–41.

16. For a wider survey of the biblical location and function of angels, see Stephen F. Noll, *Angels of Light and Powers of Darkness: Thinking Biblically About Angels, Satan, and Principalities* (Downers Grove, Ill.: InterVarsity Press, 1998). See also T. L. Fallon, "Angel: In the Bible," in *The New Catholic Encyclopedia* (1966); T. H. Gaster, "Angel," in *The Interpreter's Dictionary of the Bible* (1988); A. B. Davidson, "Angel," in *A Dictionary of the*

Bible (1988); Duane F. Watson, "Angels," in *The Anchor Bible Dictionary* (1992); Wesley Carr, *Angels and Principalities* (Cambridge: Cambridge University Press, 1981); Duane A. Garrett, *Angels and the New Spirituality* (Nashville, Tenn.: Broadman and Holdman Publishers, 1955), 10–26; William George Heidt, *Angelology of the Old Testament: A Study in Biblical Theology* (Washington D.C.: Catholic University of America Press, 1949); Louth, *Dionysius the Areopagite*, 33–35.

17. It was only in the Vulgate that a systematic distinction was made between angelic messengers (Latin, *angelus*) and human ones (Latin, *nuntius*). It was, of course, this Latin Vulgate that the writers in this volume had access to.

18. On the use of the angelic Cherubim and Thrones in scripture, especially as they are interpreted by Augustine, see Anne-Marie La Bonnardière, "Anima justi sedes sapientiae dans l'oeuvre de saint Augustin," in *Epektasis: Mélanges Patristiques offerts au Cardinal Jean Daniélou*, ed. Jacques Fontaine et Charles Kannengiesser (Paris: Beauchesne, 1972), 111–21.

19. For a good summary of angels and demons in Paul, see Pierre Benoit, "Pauline Angelology and Demonology: Reflexions on the Designations of the Heavenly Powers and on the Origin of Angelic Evil According to Paul," *Religious Studies Bulletin* 3:1 (1983): 1–19.

20. For a more comprehensive survey of angelic functions and ministries, especially in the context of angelic contemplation, see Chase, *Angelic Wisdom*, 70–75, 91–96.

21. See Hadewijch, *Visions*, in *Hadewijch: The Complete Works*, trans. Mother Columba Hart (New York: Paulist Press, 1980); Birgitta of Sweden, *Angelic Sermon on the Blessed Virgin (Sermo angelicus)*, in *Sancta Birgitta, Opera minora II, Sermo Angelicus*, ed. Sten Eklund (Uppsala, 1972).

22. Umiltà of Faenza, for instance, names one of her guardian angels Emmanuel, meaning "God with us," thus signifying that the angel represents the presence of God.

23. Richard of St. Victor treats the Cherubim in this way in his treatise *The Mystical Ark* (see Chase, *Angelic Wisdom*, 129–36).

24. On the use of symbols in angelic spirituality in the medieval and contemporary period, see Chase, *Angelic Wisdom*, "Symbolic Theology," 48–60, and "Contemplation and the Cherubim as Symbol," 61–96.

25. See Denys Turner, *The Darkness of God: Negativity in Christian Mysticism* (Cambridge: Cambridge University Press, 1995), 121–24. Arturo Blanco explores the question of the assimilation of human attributes in angels, raising the question of the origin of such anthropomor-

phism in writers such as Duns Scotus, Bonaventure, and Aquinas, in "The Influence of Faith in Angels on the Medieval Vision of Nature and Man," 456–67. For a list of other medieval writers who outline the relationship between humanity and the angels, see Giles Constable, *Three Studies in Medieval Religious and Social Thought* (Cambridge: Cambridge University Press, 1995), 291ff.

26. Gregory also uses beauty (in his illustration, the beauty of nine precious stones) as the means by which angels are made visible (*Homily 34*, Section 7).

27. *Homily 34*, Sections 8, 12.

28. Umiltà of Faenza, *Sermon Four,* "On the Holy Angels."

29. John Scotus Eriugena, *Commentary on the Celestial Hierarchy,* "On the Seraphim."

30. This is particularly true of the Apocryphal literature, in which a single angel heads a hierarchy and various groups and classes of angels perform unique tasks. But in the Hebrew Bible as well particular angels have their own unique responsibilities, as Michael in Daniel 12: 1, or the Cherubim as guardians of the gates of paradise in Genesis 3, or as guardians of the place of God's presencing in Exodus 25. In the New Testament also, Pauline angelology seems to indicate that there are different orders of angels with different functions (see Col 1:16; 2:10; 2:15; Eph 1:21; 3:10; 6:12).

31. On the philosophical history of the development of Christian angelic spirituality, especially its Neo-Platonic influence, see Adler, *The Angels and Us,* 99–144; Dionysius, *Hiér. cél.,* lvii–lxiii; Gersh, *From Iamblichus to Eriugena,* 167–77; Paul G. Kuntz, "The Hierarchical Vision of St. Bonaventure," in *Jacob's Ladder and The Tree of Life: Concepts of Hierarchy and the Great Chain of Being,* ed. Marion Kuntz and Paul Kuntz (New York: Peter Lang, 1986), 83–100; D. E. Luscombe, "Conceptions of Hierarchy Before the Thirteenth Century," in *Soziale Ordnungen im Selbstverstandnis des Mittelalters,* ed. Albert Zimmermann (Berlin: Walter de Gruyter, 1979), 1–19; D. E. Luscombe, "The Reception of the Writings of Denis the Pseudo-Areopagite into England," in *Tradition and Change,* ed. Diana Greenway, Christopher Holdsworthy, and Jane Sayers (Cambridge: Cambridge University Press, 1985), 115–41; René Roques, *L'univers Dionysien* (Aubier: Editions Montaigne, 1954).

32. Origen, in *De principiis,* II, 9; III, 5–6, appears to be the first to make a distinction between angels and archangels. In both the East and the West until the time of Gregory the Great, the interpretation of the

names of the archangels was unsettled (see Joan M. Peterson, "'Homo omnino Latinus'? The Theological Background of Pope Gregory the Great," *Speculum* 62/3 [1987]: 534–35, 537).

33. Ambrose, *Expositio in Lucam* 7.210.

34. Jerome, *Adversus Iovinianum* 2.28.

35. This list is from Gregory's *Moralia* 32.48. The list is slightly different from that of Gregory's *Homily 34*, included in this volume.

36. Dionysius, *CH* 7.1, 8.1, 9.1.

37. A famous passage in Dante's *Divine Comedy* gives preference to Dionysius's ordering. Dante has Gregory the Great look upon the angelic orders in paradise and recognize, graciously, that Dionysius had been right all along (see the introduction to Gregory's *Homily 34* in this volume for the text of Dante's comment. The introduction also discusses whether Gregory knew of or read Dionysius).

38. By the twelfth century the common Latin translation of "hierarchy" was *sacer principatus*.

39. The second section of this volume is devoted to commentaries on Dionysius the Areopagite's *Celestial Hierarchy*. For a brief outline of Dionysius's work and its influence, see the introduction to Section Two of this work.

40. Dionysius, *CH* 3.1, 2. The concept of hierarchy being arranged triadically—in three sets of threes, hence the nine orders of angels in three groups of three—is also important for Dionysius. The famous triad of purgation, illumination, and union is a stamp of the angelic hierarchy through which the human soul is led into God.

41. For an excellent study on the function and use of mandalas in religious practice and as aids in deepening religious consciousness, see Giuseppe Tucci, *The Theory and Practice of the Mandala*, trans. Alan Houghton Brodrick (London: Rider, 1967).

42. The dialectical principle thus employed was that of the *coincidentia oppositorum*, the coincidence of opposites. Briefly, in this particular form of dialectic, opposites coincide while maintaining the integrity of their opposition, yet the intensity of their opposition is at its height precisely in the fact that they coincide. The clearest explanations of this dialectic can be found in Ewert Cousins, *Bonaventure and the Coincidence of Opposites* (Chicago: Franciscan Herald Press, 1978) and H. Lawrence Bond, *Nicholas of Cusa: Selected Spiritual Writings* (New York: Paulist Press, 1997).

43. *Teresa of Avila: The Interior Castle*, trans. Kieran Kavanaugh and Otilio Rodriquez (New York: Paulist Press, 1979).

44. Cf. Huston Smith, "Come Higher My Friend?: The Mysticism of Meister Eckhart," in *Doors of Understanding: Conversations in Global Spirituality in Honor of Ewert Cousins*, ed. Steven Chase (Quincy, Ill.: Franciscan Press, 1997), 201–18.

45. David Bohm, *Wholeness and the Implicate Other* (London: Routledge, 1980), 177. Cited in Smith, "Come Higher My Friend?"

46. This conception of play is discussed in some detail by Hans Georg Gadamer. His use of play as a metaphor for the to-and-fro or conversational "play" of meaning between text and reader is particularly apt in this context. The angels themselves are "hermeneuts" in the Gadamerian sense: they are messages at "play" between God and the human soul (see Hans Georg Gadamer, *Truth and Method*, trans. J. Weinsheimer and D. G. Marshall [New York: Crossroad, 1989], 101–34).

47. For a number of other illustrations and analogies of hierarchy, see Steven Chase, "Angels: The Classical Christian Tradition and Contemporary Spiritual Direction," *Listening: Journal of Religion and Culture* 32:2 (Spring 1997): 91–103.

48. Dionysius the Areopagite, *The Ecclesiastical Hierarchy*, 1.1, in *Pseudo-Dionysius: The Complete Works*, ed. Colm Luibheid (New York: Paulist Press, 1987).

49. *Respiciens*. Alan uses words formed from the verb *specio*, meaning "to see or observe, to regard or consider," throughout this treatise to describe the relation of the angels to the Trinity.

50. Alan of Lille, *Treatise on the Celestial Hierarchy*, "On the Celestial Hierarchy."

51. Portions of the following section were published in slightly altered form in Steven Chase, "Angels: The Classical Christian Tradition and Contemporary Spiritual Direction," *Listening: Journal of Religion and Culture* 32:2 (1997): 91–103.

52. Still, angelic spirituality allows for a re-imagining, one might say, of possibility. Christ, for instance, *is* the divine nature in its fullness, yet the angels are theophanies of divine attributes. Christ took on, shows us, and *is* human nature in its fullness, yet angels can expand our vision and appropriation of human nature. Christ *is* the message of divine grace, yet angels do deliver that message as well. Christ *is* the mediator between humanity and divine holiness, yet angels mediate something of divine holiness to the world. Augustine, for example, is very clear on this. Angels

assist in the economy of salvation, but only Christ is sufficient for salvation, and only Christ can mediate between humanity and the God (cf. *City of God*, IX.15).

53. Dionysius notes that Seraphim, Cherubim, and Thrones are in "immediate proximity to God"; that the Dominions, Powers, and Authorities are in complete "conformity to God"; and that the Principalities, Archangels, and Angels participate in "divine revelations" to the world.

54. Gregory the Great, *Homily 34*, Section 11.

55. Gregory names and gives the appropriate ministry of three of the archangels as follows: Michael means "who is like God"; Gabriel means "the strength of God"; and Raphael means "the healing of God."

56. See *Bonaventure: The Soul's Journey into God, The Tree of Life, The Life of St. Francis*, trans. Ewert Cousins (New York: Paulist Press, 1978). Bonaventure borrows heavily from Bernard of Clairvaux in outlining angelic orders and corresponding spiritual paths (Bernard of Clairvaux, *On Consideration*, V.5.12). But where Bernard had not explicitly internalized the angelic orders within the human soul, Bonaventure accepts and utilizes this interiorization without question. Bonaventure is indebted to Thomas Gallus's *Prologue* to the *Commentary on the Song of Songs* for this interiorization of the angelic hierarchy within the human consciousness.

57. Bonaventure, *Soul's Journey into God*, 4.4.

58. Bonaventure says that in the human soul the first three levels (angels, archangels, virtues) correspond to human nature, the next three (powers, principalities, dominions) correspond to human effort, while the last three (thrones, cherubim, seraphim) correspond to divine grace.

59. Alan says, "the angelic hierarchy is a theophany of the multitude of celestial spirits, each characterized by a pure and singular form." He adds, "In the word 'theophany,' *theos* means God, and *phanes* is interpreted as vision; and indeed, the character of theophany indicates the way or form of seeing God."

60. The word is composed of *epi*, which means "beyond," and *phany*, which means "vision." Alan adds that *uperphany* is composed of *uper*, which means "after," and *phany*, which means "vision," while *upophany* is composed of *upo*, whcih means "before," and *phany*, which means "vision."

61. Alan describes the first three orders as participating in the triple gift, triple power, and triple clothing of love, knowledge, and discernment; the middle three orders as reflecting a divine illumination of God in God's self through their attributes; and the lower three orders'

attribute as allowing divine participation through the discernment of secrets and divine revelation.

62. Gallus's angelic analogues to the human soul, what might be called his angelic anthropology, are subtle and complex. A few examples are given in what follows, but a chart would not do justice to the full range of Gallus's spiritual analysis. The reader is referred to the full text of the *Prologue* provided in this volume and to the introduction and notes that accompany it.

63. For a variety of reasons discussed in the Introduction to this treatise, though the critical Latin edition of the text refers to "Cherubim" in the title, the author no doubt intended "Seraphim." "Seraphim" will thus be used in the discussion that follows.

64. The author notes that satisfaction comforts, cures death, corrects evils, is the path to health, and restores all wounds. The first and second wings, the author says, together form compunction of heart.

65. Gregory the Great, *Homily 34*, Section 11.

66. *On the Six Wings of the Cherubim*, Section One. As noted in the introduction to this treatise, this first section is written by Hugh of St. Victor.

67. Gallus, *Extract*, One.

68. The *Celestial Hierarchy* is, in effect, a medieval handbook of light-mysticism. Josef Koch documents the connection between Eriugena and Dionysius and their influence on the medieval period with regard to the metaphor of light in "Über die Lichtsymbolik im Bereich der Philosophie und der Mystik des Mittelalters," *Studium Generale* 13 (1960): 653–70.

69. On God named as light in scripture, see John 8:2; cf. John 1:4–9; 9:5; 1 John 1:5.

70. Dionysius, *CH* 1.3.

71. Gregory the Great, *Homily 34*, Section 7.

72. In a similar way Shadrach, Meshach, and Abednego were protected from the fiery furnace by the angel (Dan 3).

73. Dionysius, *CH* 1.3.

74. Exod 33:20. We see the full glory of God only in the face of Christ (2 Cor 4:6).

75. Dionysius, *CH* 1.1. Biblical citations are from John 1:9 and Romans 5:2.

76. Dionysius, *CH* 1.2.

77. Gallus, *Extract*, One.

78. Hugh, *Com. hier. coel.*, chap. 2 (*PL* 175:941B).

79. Dionysius, *Divine Names*, 4.1, in Luibheid, *Pseudo-Dionysius: The Complete Works.*

80. See ibid., 4.2.

81. Eriugena, *Commentary on the Celestial Hierarchy*, "On Their Contemplation."

82. Alan of Lille, *Treatise on the Angelic Hierarchy*, "The Angelic Order." Alan of Lille also defines theophany as "angelic knowledge" *(scientia angelica)* in counter-distinction to theosophy, which is "wisdom of God," and theology, which is "human knowledge."

83. Ibid.

84. See Dionysius, *CH* 3, on the nature of hierarchy in which the triad purification, illumination, and perfection or union is woven throughout. Not only the individual angelic orders themselves, but the very quality and structure of the hierarchy participates in this threefold process of spiritual formation.

85. Umiltà of Faenza, *Sermon Four,* "On the Holy Angels."

86. Dionysius the Areopagite, *The Mystical Theology*, 1.1.

87. Dionysius, *Divine Names*, 7.3.

88. On the necessary integration of the positive and negative way in Dionysius and Richard of St. Victor, and on the two cherubim as representing each of these ways, see Chase, *Angelic Wisdom*, 28–47. In Richard of St. Victor's *Mystical Ark*, one of the cherubim atop the ark of the covenant represents the positive way, the other represents the negative way. For Richard, both cherubim (both ways) assist in the understanding and acknowledgment of God's presence for the people of Israel.

89. Gallus, *Prologue*, N.

90. See Richard of St. Victor, *The Mystical Ark*, IV.vi.

91. Gallus, *Prologue*, B; cf. 1 Cor 2:6–11.

92. Gallus, *Prologue*, L, M.

93. An example of the Seraphim leading into the Trinity as love can be found in Gallus's *Prologue*. An example of the Cherubim leading into the Trinity as incomprehensibility is Richard of St. Victor's *The Mystical Ark*. It could be argued that Gallus's "seraphic mystical consciousness" ends in a new form of cataphatic awareness, that awareness being love, while Richard's "cherubic mystical consciousness" remains an awareness of apophasis.

94. Daniel C. Matt, ed. and trans., in *The Essential Kabbalah: The Heart of Jewish Mysticism*, "Creation: Concealing and Revealing." (San Francisco, Calif.: HarperSanFrancisco, 1996), 91.

95. See Dionysius's Letter Nine in *Pseudo-Dionysius: The Complete Works.*

96. Dionysius's method of ascending negations and descending affirmations is as much a spiritual exercise or practice aimed at cleansing the mind of false notions about God as it is a metaphysical system. The method is most clearly described in his *Mystical Theology*, 3, where he says, "Is it not closer to reality to say that God is life and Goodness rather than that God is air or stone? Is it not more accurate to deny that we can apply to God the terms of speech and thought?" For a relatively clear explanation of this difficult but effective method, see *Pseudo-Dionysius: The Complete Works*, 140 n.17.

97. René Roques, *Structures théologique: de la gnose à Richard de Saint-Victor* (Paris: Presses Universitaires de France, 1962), 142.

98. Thus, sensible symbols are realities grounded in scripture (tabernacle, the law, etc.), while intellectual symbols are theophanies, the vision of truth in itself.

99. Eriugena, *Commentary on the Celestial Hierarchy*, "On Their Contemplation."

100. On symbolic method applied to angels as found in Dionysius the Areopagite, Hugh of St. Victor, and Richard of St. Victor, see Chase, *Angelic Wisdom*, 48–60; on typologies of symbol in the medieval period in general, see especially ibid., 58–60.

101. Hugh says, relating angels as symbols to the ascent from the visible to the invisible world, "a symbol is a juxtaposition, that is, a joining together of visible forms set forth to demonstrate invisible things" (*Com. hier. coel.* III [*PL* 175, 960D]). Hugh of St. Victor's work in Section One of *On the Six Wings of the Seraphim* (also translated for this volume) is also an excellent example of angels mediating the deep mysteries of God to humanity. Based on Isaiah 6, Hugh interprets the Seraphim as an exemplar of divine incomprehensibility, enfolding the "body" of God as church, Christ, Eucharist, world, and time within its wings. Yet it is in this very "covering" of God that the Seraphim reveals (in the sense of uncovering) the deeper mystery of God's incomprehensibility.

102. This, at least, is the primary direction of movement in the Latin West. In the East, the primary direction of movement is God's trinitarian diversity grounding God's unific simplicity. Of course, the strongest statement of trinitarian doctrine recognizes the paradox of the one and the many grounding each other and at the same time moving in both directions.

NOTES

103. Richard of St. Victor, *The Mystical Ark*, I.xii. Richard of St. Victor, in fact, uses the two Cherubim "hovering" atop the ark of the covenant to signify this incomprehensible trinitarian wisdom. He says, "These two cherubim look at each other mutually, because we say that one and the same God is one according to substance and three according to person. According to the first cherub, we say that the Father, and the Son, and the Holy Spirit are united in one substance, in one essence, and in one nature. According to the second cherub, we say the Father is one in person, the Son is another in person, and the Holy Spirit is another in person" (*The Mystical Ark*, IV.xix).

104. See Bernard McGinn, "Love, Knowledge, and *Unio Mystica* in the Western Christian Tradition," in *Mystical Union and Monotheistic Faith: An Ecumenical Dialogue*, ed. Moshe Idel and Bernard McGinn (New York: Macmillan, 1989), 59–86.

105. It should be noted that the association of the Seraphim with love was not an immediate association; it evolved over time. Dionysius the Areopagite, for instance, said simply that the Seraphim, as fiery and burning, represented a perennial circling around divinity or a penetrating warmth. It was John Scotus Eriugena, in the ninth century, who made the connection between the Seraphim as "burning" and love. In *Commentary on the Celestial Hierarchy*, Chapter Seven, represented in this volume, he says, "Their motion is unceasing since it never stops; they are hot with flaming fire, stirred up by the inflammation of charity *(caritatis)*. Keen and rapid, they penetrate all things subtly and clearly. And they are ablaze with intense heat and, above all things that follow them, this first hierarchy of the celestial powers blazes forth in love *(amore)* of the highest good" (cf. section entitled "On the Seraphim"). And writing more than likely outside of the Dionysian tradition, Gregory the Great had, as early as the sixth century, noted that "the Seraphim burn with incomparable love *(ardent amore) (Homily 34*, Section 10).

106. Gregory the Great, *Homily 34*, Section 10. As noted in the above section on the theme of spiritual paths, Gregory goes on to relate all of the angelic orders, including Cherubim and Seraphim, to men and women. He says, "Clearly, there are ways of human life that coincide with single orders of angelic bands. By means of correspondence in virtue, these people are counted worthy of sharing in the angelic nature" *(Homily 34*, Section 11). Seraphim, for instance, are men and women set on fire by love, contemplatives who love, burn, and rest in love by their burning.

107. Alan of Lille, *Treatise on the Angelic Hierarchy*, "On the Nature of Epiphany." As with Gregory the Great, in Alan of Lille the angels lead humanity into ministries that parallel the angels' own ministries. The Cherubim, as is apparent from the citation, lead men and women into "knowledge of God." The Seraphim are "those angels who are burning most fiercely with divine love, who are specially delegated to this office so that they in turn can allure humanity to a similar burning with divine love."

108. Again, as pointed out in the introduction to *On the Six Wings*, the treatise is *not* on the Cherubim but rather on the Seraphim.

109. Hildegard of Bingen, *Scivias*, Book One, Vision Six, "The Choirs of Angels," 9 and 10, in *Hildegard of Bingen: Scivias*, trans. Mother Columba Hart and Jane Bishop (New York: Paulist Press, 1990), 142.

110. Hadewijch, *Visions*, "The Six-Winged Countenance," 13.252, in *Hadewijch: The Complete Works*, trans. Mother Columba Hart, O.S.B. (New York: Paulist Press, 1980), 302.

111. Richard of St. Victor, *The Mystical Ark*, 1.xii, in *Richard of St. Victor: Twelve Patriarchs, The Mystical Ark, Book Three of the Trinity*, trans. Grover Zinn (New York: Paulist Press, 1979), 172.

112. From the vast literature on Francis, see Ewert Cousins, *Christ of the Twenty-First Century* (Rockport, Mass.: Element, 1992), 140–50; Ottaviano Schmucki, *The Stigmata of St. Francis: A Critical Investigation in the Light of Thirteenth-Century Sources* (St. Bonaventure, N.Y.: Franciscan Institute, 1991); Bernard McGinn, "Was Francis of Assisi a Mystic?" in *Doors of Understanding: Conversations in Global Spirituality in Honor of Ewert Cousins*, ed. Steven Chase (Quincy, Ill.: Franciscan Press, 1997), 145–76.

113. Bonaventure, *The Soul's Journey into God*, V.1, in *Bonaventure: The Souls's Journey into God, The Tree of Life, The Life of St. Francis* (New York: Paulist Press, 1978), 94.

114. Alan of Lille, *Treatise on the Angelic Hierarchy*, "The Angelic Order."

115. Obviously, these are the roles of Christ in most Christian spiritual writing. In Bonaventure, for instance, the burning love of Christ crucified is the way, door, and goal of his *Soul's Journey into God*. Often, as here in Bonaventure's great work, the role of love and the role of Christ come to be closely, if not perfectly, identified.

116. On Gallus's distinction between understanding and true knowledge, or wisdom of the heart, see *Prologue*, A, B. Denys Turner describes Gallus's shift from knowledge that is "speculative and enigmatic" to wisdom of the heart as a shift from the intellectual and visual mysticism

of Dionysius to a "mysticism of affectivity." Unlike Dionysius, Turner claims, Gallus's intellectual knowledge of God is cataphatic and runs throughout the first eight angelic hierarchies of the soul, while apophasis is reached only at the level of the Seraphim in the transcending state of "knowing" love. The insight concerning the apophasis of love in Gallus is good, though apophasis of the intellect is present in Gallus's first eight levels as well (Turner, *The Darkness of God: Negativity in Christian Mysticism* [Cambridge: Cambridge University Press, 1995], 186–94).

117. *Prologue*, L.

118. *Prologue*, M.

119. *Prologue*, N. Gallus is careful in his exploration of the relation between love and knowledge to make a distinction between the work of humanity and the grace of God. His contemplative method moves first through six grades of contemplation, represented by the first six angelic orders. This initial contemplative effort integrates human nature and divine grace, culminating in the sixth insight fixing its gaze upon the Dominions of the soul. From there, grace alone leads the soul through the levels of the Thrones, Cherubim, and Seraphim and into the ninth sublime insight, which one enters, Gallus says, "only through the Spirit" (*Prologue*, V).

120. Bernard of Clairvaux, *Sermons on the Psalm, "He Who Dwells,"* 12.7.

121. Alan of Lille, *Treatise on the Angelic Hierarchy*, "Concerning the Celestial Hierarchy."

122. Ibid., "Concerning the Subcelestial Hierarchy."

123. Bernard McGinn, *The Foundations of Mysticism*, vol. 1 of *The Presence of God: A History of Western Christian Mysticism* (New York: Crossroad, 1991), xvii.

124. See footnote 3 in the introduction to Alan of Lille's *Treatise* for contemporary essays exploring the issue of mediation in mystical consciousness. Two excellent sources that explore the issue in the context of angels are Joseph Duhr, "Anges," *DS*, 1:580–625; and Roques, *L'univers Dionysien*, 135–67.

125. Here the "language" of mediation becomes important. To speak of an "immediate presence," for instance, is just one of many ways of codifying divine union. Given the complexities of the mystery of God, "mediated absence" could just as easily be used. "Touch," "embrace," and "vision" of God are likewise examples of the many possibilities. Thus,

because they directly affect one another, languages of union and deification are discussed together.

126. Alan of Lille, *Treatise on the Angelic Hierarchy*, "On the Nature of Epiphany." For a more extensive discussion of Alan's use of the Cherubim and Seraphim on the issue of mediation, see the introduction to his *Treatise* in this volume.

127. Gregory the Great, *Homily 34*, Section 10.

128. The phrase "no creature intervenes" *(nulla interposita creatura)* is from Augustine and is also used by Eriugena in this volume. See footnote 11 in the introduction to Eriugena's *Commentary*, and the section in the *Commentary* entitled "On the Seraphim."

129. Gallus, *Prologue*, M.

130. Ibid., N.

131. Augustine, *City of God*, IX.15.

132. Umiltà of Faenza, *On the Holy Angels*, Sermon Four.

133. Bernard of Clairvaux, *Sermons on the Psalm "He Who Dwells,"* 12.4.

134. Gallus, *Extract*, One.

135. Eriugena, *Commentary on the Celestial Hierarchy*, 7.4.

136. For a detailed discussion of "angelization," see Chase, *Angelic Wisdom*, 115–28.

137. Richard of St. Victor, *The Mystical Ark*, IV.iv.

138. Raimundo Panikkar, "The Contemplative Look: An Old Vision of Reality," *Monastic Studies* 19 (1991): 169.

139. For an excellent history of this tradition in classical philosophy and Patristic spirituality, see Pierre Hadot, *Philosophy as a Way of Life*, ed. Arnold I. Davidson, trans. Michael Chase (Oxford: Blackwell Publishers Ltd., 1995).

140. Gregory the Great, *Homily 34*, Section 13.

141. Bernard of Clairvaux, *Sermons on the Psalm "He Who Dwells,"* 11.2.

142. Alan of Lille, *Treatise on the Angelic Hierarchy*, "Angelic Order," "Concerning the Subcelestial Hierarchy."

143. Augustine, *City of God*, XI.25. On the use of dogma or doctrine in general for the devotional life, especially its pastoral application, see Ellen T. Charry, *By the Renewing of Your Minds: The Pastoral Function of Christian Doctrine* (New York: Oxford University Press, 1997).

NOTES

144. Eriugena, *Commentary on the Celestial Hierarchy*, "On Their Contemplation." This entire section focuses on the contemplative, deifying nature of the Seraphim, Cherubim, and Thrones.

145. Alan of Lille, *Treatise on the Angelic Hierarchy*, "The Angelic Order."

146. Richard of St. Victor, *The Mystical Ark*, I.1. Anagogy and tropology, two of the three traditional "spiritual" methods of biblical exegesis, are roughly equivalent to contemplation and action respectively. Anagogy has to do with "ascent" to God by means of scriptural symbols (or material forms, the visible world, etc.), leading ultimately to God-consciousness or God-centeredness. Tropology is the moral sense; that is, the *praxis* or virtue or charity to which an interpretation of scripture leads. Tropology can also be fed by anagogy, as the active life can be fed by the contemplative. Section Two of *On the Six Wings of the Cherubim* is an example of a tropological application of angelic wisdom.

147. Gallus, *Prologue*, F, N. While each of the sections in the *Prologue* that focuses on a particular angelic level teaches on contemplation, sections O-Q are on contemplation *per se*. These sections also lead into Gallus's teaching on the three spiritual arts that provide context for both contemplation and action.

148. Umiltà of Faenza, *Sermons on the Holy Angels*, Sermon Two.

149. Augustine, *City of God*, IX.15.2. The scriptural allusion is to Philippians 2:7.

150. On the variety of ways, all important to distinguish, in which Christ might be spoken of as an angel, see Joseph W. Trigg, "The Angel of Great Counsel: Christ and the Angelic Hierarchy in Origen's Theology," *The Journal of Theological Studies* 42 (1991): 35–51.

151. The Angel of Great Counsel comes from the Latin of Isaiah 9:6 and from subsequent liturgical texts, *angelus magni consilii*. Christ as the Seraphim was used to give a trinitarian dimension to Isaiah 6. One wing represented Christ, the other the Holy Spirit, while the Father stood between (see Günther Juncker, "Christ as Angel: The Reclamation of a Primitive Title," *Trinity Journal* 15 [1994]: 221–50).

152. Juncker, "Christ as Angel," 234.

153. Eriugena, *Periphyseon*, V, in *PL* 122, 846C, D, cited in Donald F. Duclow, "Isaiah Meets the Seraph: Breaking Ranks in Dionysius and Eriugena?" in *Eriugena East and West*, ed. Bernard McGinn and Willemien Otten (Notre Dame, Ind.: University of Notre Dame Press, 1994), 233–52.

154. On this christological interpretation and its application in Richard's teaching on contemplation, see Chase, *Angelic Wisdom*, especially chap. 5, "Apophatic Christology."

155. In Hugh of St. Victor, *On the Six Wings of the Cherubim*, Section One. These comments come after the material by Hugh of St. Victor and are thus the words of the anonymous writer/redactor of the treatise.

156. Eriugena, *Commentary on the Celestial Hierarchy*, "On Their Contemplation."

157. See Ewert Cousins, "The Humanity and the Passion of Christ," in *Christian Spirituality II*, ed. Jill Raitt, vol. 17 of *World Spirituality: An Encyclopedic History of the Religious Quest*, ed. Ewert Cousins (New York: Crossroad, 1987), 375–91.

158. Bonaventure, *The Soul's Journey into God*, 4.5. See also Turner, *The Darkness of God*, 125ff. on Bonaventure's reconciliation of the angelic hierarchies in Christ. Turner also discusses the issue of why Christ became human, not angelic, in the context of Bonaventure's reconciliation. Where Augustine had argued this issue on the basis of the relation between good and evil, Turner bases his argument on the mediating quality of the angels *vs.* Christ as the supreme Mediator (cf. Augustine, *City of God*, IX.15; Turner, *The Darkness*, 118–20).

159. Bonaventure, *The Soul's Journey into God*, Prologue, 3.

160. Ibid., 1.

161. Barth, *Church Dogmatics*, 3.3:484–86.

162. Karl Barth summarizes these movements and their effect on theologians and angelology in *Church Dogmatics*, 3.3:401–18. He summarizes the modern attitude to angels by quoting G. Spinner, "The reality of angels is questionable; their influence none; their revelations to us none. We shudder at the empty spaces which open at this point." Barth himself concludes that "these modern thinkers are not prepared to take angels seriously. It does not give them the slightest joy to think of them. They are plainly rather peevish and impatient at having to handle the subject" (ibid., 413, 415).

163. This "fluttering across our vision" is in part exemplified by the vast literature on angels available today. No complete bibliography is available at this time. A reasonably helpful though incomplete bibliography of recent literature can be found in Duane A. Garrett, *Angels and the New Spirituality* (Nashville, Tenn.: Broadman and Holdman Publishers, 1995).

164. See David C. Steinmetz, "The Superiority of Pre-Critical Exegesis," *Theology Today* 37 (1980): 27–38.

NOTES

165. George Steiner, *Real Presences* (Chicago, Ill.: University of Chicago Press, 1989), 146. M. Foucault's observation that every discourse is a discourse of power, even discourses of charity, compassion, or hosting, is certainly true. Every discourse is a discourse of power, but it is also, potentially, more than that.

Section One
Augustine
City of God

1. The literature on the life, writing, spirituality, episcopate, and influence of Augustine is monumental. His *Confessions* are the first place to go for information on his life, especially the period around his conversion. A good summary of his life, writings, spirituality, and influence can be found in the introduction of Mary T. Clark, *Augustine of Hippo: Selected Writings* (New York: Paulist Press, 1984).

2. *City of God*, XI.1.

3. On Neo-Platonic theurgy—the invocation of the power or even direct presence of the gods through the use of mediating spirits through prayers, incantations, trances, or other practices—against which Augustine is here reacting, see Gregory Shaw, *Theurgy and the Soul: The Neoplatonism of Iamblichus* (University Park, Pa.: University of Pennsylvania Press, 1995).

4. Cf. Philippians 3:19; Colossians 3:2. Augustine uses Paul's phrase, *terrena sapimus*, literally "to mind earthly things."

5. The evil angels, of course, are able to mediate, not between humanity and God, but between humanity and evil.

6. Above, Christ leads humanity through (*perducat*) to blessed immortality from mortal misery; here evil angels have the power of leading humanity down or seducing (*seducerent*) to immortal misery from mortal misery.

7. Cf. John 1:3.

8. Augustine's statement here depends on such passages as 1 Corinthians 8:5–6 and 1 Timothy 2:5, which practically forbid the invocation of saints or of any other intermediaries between the soul and God.

9. *Conpendium*, "a direct means," literally, "a short cut."

10. Once again Augustine associates the guiding hand of Christ's mediation with *perducit*, we are "led through" to participation with God.

11. *Cuius et angeli participatione.* Cf. *City of God* IX.21–22, where Augustine says that the angels are among the blessed "participating" in God for eternity.

12. Cf. Philippians 2:7.

13. The word here is not based on the root word *latreia* but rather *cultus*. In not using *latreia* in the context of angelic worship, Augustine emphasizes the importance of the full force of *latreia* in its proper context. Only worship of Christ affords that true context. There must be no hint of confusion. While the angels can exemplify *cultus*, the sacrifice of Christ discussed below, teaches, makes possible, and asks for true worship as *latreia*.

14. Psalm 87:3.

15. Ibid.

16. This word, *peregrinatur,* is the same word used by Augustine to describe his famous heart that "is wandering till it finds rest in Thee."

17. Cf. Acts 7:53; Galatians 3:19.

18. In the following chapter Augustine lists miracles, including Sarah giving birth at a barren age, the angel's prediction of the destruction of Sodom by fire, how Lot was rescued and his wife turned to salt, Moses' rescue of his people from Egypt, and others.

19. The word Augustine uses here is *serviunt*, the angels "serve" the will or providence of God. This, for Augustine, is the closest Latin equivalent to *latreia* (cf. *City of God* X.1, 3). As noted, *latreia* is the word that for Augustine conveys the fullest sense of our relationship with God, conveying worship, service, religion, *cultus*, and piety. Thus here, through their ministry, the angels "serve," while in *City of God* X.7 they participate in the "cultus" of service and worship around God. By making this distinction Augustine emphasizes that the direction of our own love and worship ought to be oriented toward God and not toward the angels.

20. Acts 7:53.

21. In this case, worship as *cultus.*

22. *Lex in edictis angelorum daretur.* Augustine uses *edictis* here in the sense of a proclamation or edict. The Vulgate at Acts 7:3 uses *dispositione* of the angels, which would indicate more a sense of an orderly argument than of a general proclamation.

23. The idea of the poetic representation of the divine that equated God's manifestation to human thought and speech was discussed by Proclus and is developed by Augustine in this section into a theory of divine expression. Through angelic mediaries, who receive communications from God non-discursively, God's self-expression here proceeds "syllable

by syllable, each with its tiny duration, in the words of human speech" (cf. Robert Lamberton, *Homer the Theologian: Neoplatonist Allegorical Reading and the Growth of the Epic* [Berkeley and Los Angeles: University of California Press, 1989], 258–59).

24. Again, this is not the full worship of the Christian of the one, true God, that is, *latreia*, but the worship of the one God possible to non-Christians when they observe the obedience of creation to the Creator (cf. Rom 1:20). Thus, for Augustine, the Neo-Platonists are partially correct, but to distinguish this worship from true worship of the true God he again uses the word *cultus*. This worship of the eternal through the temporal sacraments or signs is thus the *Dei cultus*.

25. Matthew 23:26.

26. Continuing Augustine's exegesis of Psalm 73.

27. Psalm 73:26.

28. Psalm 73:27.

29. Psalm 73:28.

30. Psalm 73:28.

31. Romans 8:24–25.

32. Augustine is playing on the word *annuntiem*, "I might announce." For all the Latin writers, the angels are the beings whose ministry is "to announce." Thus in his exegesis of Psalm 73, the soul who "announces the Lord's praises" is naturally an "angelic" soul. In the lines above this quotation Augustine also uses the same play on words: we ought to become angels or messengers *(nuntii)* of God, announcing *(annuntiantes)* God's will.

33. Psalm 73:28. The Vulgate, at the equivalent Psalm 72:28, adds "the gates of the daughters of Zion" *(in portis filiae Sion)*. Welldon notes that there are no such words in the Hebrew (in *De civ. Dei*, ed. Welldon, 1:442 n.17). They appeared in the Septuagint, from there they passed to the Vulgate, and from the Vulgate into the Prayer Book Version of the Psalter.

34. The Holy City consists of (1) the angels, (2) the saints in heaven, and (3) Christians on earth. Only the angels are, in some sense, citizens of both.

35. *Quod numquam peregrinata*, whereas the life of the City of God on earth is essentially a *peregrinatio*.

36. Genesis 1:1.

37. Genesis 1:2.

38. Cf. Daniel 3:57–58.

39. Psalm 148:1–5.

40. Job 38:7.

41. In his translation Dods notes at this point that "the Greek theologians and Jerome held, with Plato, that spiritual creatures were made first, and used by God in the creation of things material. The Latin theologians and Basil held that God made all things at once."

42. John 1:9. Bettenson, *St. Augustine: City of God*, p. 440 n.17 notes, "There is an irreproducible pun here on *mundus* (world) and the adjective *mundus* (pure) with its opposite, *immundus.*"

43. Ephesians 5:8.

44. *Mali enim nulla nature est; sed amissio bond, mali nomen accepit.* Bettenson notes, "Cf. Plot., *Enn.*, 3,2,5. 'Evil is to be defined as the lack of good'; cf. also ch. 22, and *Enchir.* 4, 'What is called evil is really the privation of good'" (*City of God*, 440 n.19).

45. See *City of God*, XI.7.

Gregory the Great
Forty Homilies on the Gospels, Homily 34

1. There is an allusion to this at the beginning of *Homily 34*, where Gregory explains that a delay in his gospel exposition was caused by illness brought on by the severity of summer.

2. For the most complete doctrinal study of Gregory's angelology, see Patrick Verbraken, "Le commentaire de Saint Grégoire sur le Premier Livre des Rois," *Revue Bénédictine* 66 (1956): 159–217.

3. Joan M. Petersen, "'*Homo omnino Latinus*'? The Theological and Cultural Background of Pope Gregory the Great," *Speculum* 63:3 (1987): 529–51. Petersen also presents a thorough discussion on the exact translation of Gregory's verb *furtur*, "it is said."

4. Ibid., 536–37. For an excellent bibliography of Latin lists of angels, see ibid., 536 n.27. For additional bibliography on Gregory and angelic ranking, see Rorem, *P-D*, 85 n.11. In fact, Gregory has two slightly different angel lists:

Homily 34	*Moralia* 32.48
Angels	Angels
Archangels	Archangels
Virtues	Thrones
Powers	Dominions
Principalities	Virtues

Dominations	Principalities
Thrones	Powers
Cherubim	Cherubim
Seraphim	Seraphim

5. Nevertheless, d'Alverny claims that, Dante notwithstanding, Gregory the Great had a deeper influence on medieval angelology than did Dionysius (cf. Alan of Lille, *Hier. Alani*, 86). Against Petersen, d'Alverny also is convinced that Gregory had Dionysius's *Celestial Hierarchy* translated into Latin (cf. ibid., 86–91).

6. Dante, *Paradiso* 28.130–35, trans. John Ciardi (New York: Norton, 1977). For further bibliography on the role of Dionysius in Dante's angelology, see Rorem, *P-D*, 84 n.9.

7. *Homily 34*, Section 11.

8. See especially Gregory's discussion of the attributes of the Cherubim and Seraphim in ibid.

9. Ibid., Section 13.

10. See ibid, Section 7, on the nine precious stones.

11. See ibid., Section 9, on the names Michael, Gabriel, and Raphael and what these names signify and how this signification renders the angels visible.

12. Gregory also discusses the two cherubim from Exodus 25 in his *Homily 25* on John 20:11–18. There the two cherubim are allegories of the Old Testament and the New Testament, and Gregory emphasizes the harmonious contemplation of the two cherubim (Testaments) of the mystery of the Incarnation (see Chase, *Angelic Wisdom*, 17–18).

13. Gregory's phrase "does charity cease to burn" *(ardere charitas cessavit)*, referring to his own burning love, foreshadows his description of the Seraphim themselves: they are inflamed by or burning with love. His silence and his burning love also foreshadow all of the angelic orders as an example of angelic, contemplative adoration of God. The ministry of each particular angelic order will become its "speaking"; its service in the world will be the "active" counterpart to its silent contemplation (cf. Section 10, in which Gregory describes the Seraphim as *ardent amore, ardentes vel incendentes, flamma amor est, amore flammescunt.*) Gregory describes charity through images of burning or fire throughout this first section. I will continue to make a distinction in translation between charity *(charitas)* and love *(amor* or *dilectio)*. *Charitas* is an archaic variant of *caritas*, which can mean "love" or "charity." In addition to reasons mentioned above in this note, my warrant for making the distinction between "charity" and "love"

is based on Gregory's apparent access to and use of *"charitas"* in Romans 13:10 rather than the more standard *"dilectio"* of the Latin Vulgate. See note 59 below.

14. Though charity is entangled by preoccupations and the sun is covered by clouds, still, both charity and sun continue to burn in heart and in heaven. Likewise, Gregory makes the case that the Seraphim, Cherubim, and Thrones have unlimited and unmediated proximity and consciousness of divine presence. The highest angelic orders thus dwell in God's presence obscured by neither cloud nor preoccupation.

15. The outward "revelation" of charity is here related to speaking.

16. The love of the community inflames Gregory, returning the outward "flames of work," in his case, speech. This paragraph, then, has "burned" with images of flame related to charity. Gregory claims that charity never ceases to burn *(ardere charitas)*, it blazes *(flagrat)*, the sun too burns *(ardet)*, charity has the power of burning *(ardoris)*, it is not revealed outwardly in flames *(flammas)*, and the community's zeal inflames him *(accendunt)*. As Gregory makes clear, the Seraphim also burn with the flame of this love.

17. Luke 15:8.

18. The shepherd of Luke 15:1–7, which Gregory has just commented upon.

19. That is, Christ.

20. Psalm 22:15 (Vulgate, 21:16).

21. That is, the "choir of angels" *(angelorum choros)*. Gregory is referring to his earlier interpretation of Luke 15:6, the parable preceding the parable of the woman and the lost coin. Gregory had said, "The sheep having been found, the shepherd returns home, since our Shepherd, having restored humanity, returned to his heavenly kingdom. There he found his friends and neighbors, those choirs of angels who are his friends since by their stability they keep constantly to his will. And they are also his neighbors, since by means of their continual presence and clarity of vision they enjoy the Shepherd to the full" *(PL* 76, 1247D–48A).

22. Gregory uses the word *figuratur,* meaning "formed, molded, shaped." In the context of his discussion on angels, especially as they are used to comment on the theology and method of symbolism, the word can be taken broadly as signified or symbolized. This will become clearer in the various commentaries on *Celestial Hierarchy.*

23. *Similitudinem*. Cf. Genesis 1:26, "Let us make humanity in our image and likeness." In the Vulgate, Genesis 1:26 reads, *"faciamus hominem ad imaginem et similitudinem nostram."*

24. Gregory also uses the allegory of the ten coins and the "ten" orders of angels and humans in his commentary on the First Book of Kings (see Verbraken, "Le Commentaire de Saint Grégoire," 203–4).

25. As noted in the introduction, Gregory uses a slightly different angelic order in his *Moralia* 32.48. In addition, as with the Greek lists of Cyril of Jerusalem and John Chrysostom and the Latin lists of Ambrose and Jerome, Gregory arranges the angels in ascending order from Angels to Seraphim. Alan of Lille, on the other hand, lists the angels in descending order, starting with the Seraphim. See d'Alverny's treatment in Alan of Lille, *Hier. Alani*, 85–90, as to why he would name the orders in descending order.

26. *Esse*.

27. Ephesians 1:21.

28. Colossians 1:16.

29. *Esse*.

30. Ezekiel 28:12. Sign or seal of a likeness *(signaculum similitudinis)* echoes the Genesis 1:26 passage and foreshadows the use of angels in the medieval period as anagogic symbols. Gregory makes the points here that, like humanity, angels are created beings, but that unlike humanity, they are created of a finer substance and more "like" their creator.

31. Ezekiel 28:13.

32. Here, as elsewhere, Gregory wrestles with the issues of how the angels, essentially invisible beings, become visible to us. Here they come into presence or "existence" (earlier he had expressed their presence as *"esse,"* here the angel *"exsistavit"*) through a covering of stones. That is, the invisible is made visible by natural beauty. We might liken this to "seeing" the wind as it moves through trees or "seeing" our breath in the frigid winter air. Gregory continues to use visual metaphors to express the angelic presences—metaphors that express both their presence to us and God's presence to them—but he also comes to rely on their ministry, service, or act in the world as our primary way of "seeing" them.

33. *Ministeria*.

34. Revelation through scripture seems to evoke the angel's essential nature *(esse, exsistavit)*, while its name evokes function, ministry *(ministeria)*, or service *(nomen est officii)*.

35. Psalm 104:4, Vulgate 103:4.

36. Cf. Luke 1:26–27.

37. *Plena scientia,* an early reference to the name given to the Cherubim.

38. They come to us with a name signifying their active function; in heaven they are without a name signifying their contemplative function.

39. Gregory's source for interpreting these names is most likely through Jerome's *Commentary on Daniel* and his *Book of Interpretation of Hebrew Names* (see Petersen, *"Homo omnino Latinus?"* 534–35; *Gregory the Great: Forty Gospel Homilies,* trans. Dom David Hurst [Kalamazoo, Mich.: Cistercian Publications, 1990], 299).

40. Isaiah 14:13–14.

41. Revelation 12:7.

42. Not the "heavenly" sphere above the earthly air in Gregory's cosmology, but the *aereas,* the lower air or atmosphere where evil powers, those relying on *superbia,* or pride, dwell.

43. Psalm 24:7–8, Vulgate 23:7–8.

44. Psalm 24:10, Vulgate 23:10.

45. Tobias 11:13–17.

46. The "names of angels" *(angelorum nomina)* and the "words [we use to indicate] their duties" *(ipsa officiorum vocabula)* are two separate means by which angels become "visible" to us. In the first instance, it is their *essence* that lends the angels particularity and thereby "visibility." Gregory will now describe their *functions* and in the process claim that their *functions* also render them "visible."

47. *Virtues adversae.* Powers combating opposing Virtues allow Gregory to hint here of the existence of a parallel order of opposing angels. Alan of Lille will develop this idea more fully.

48. That is, the Principalities are the middle order of angels; four orders are arranged above them, four below.

49. Gregory uses the verb *discerno* here, meaning to sever or to separate, or in the language of spiritual wisdom, to discern (by "cutting" good from evil). Thus, for God, the Thrones are the agents of God's judgment as well as agents of our discernment.

50. Psalm 9:4, Vulgate 9:5.

51. *Plenitudo scientia.*

52. On the Cherubim as a model and object of contemplation in Latin spirituality and theology, see Chase, *Angelic Wisdom,* especially chaps. 1 and 4.

53. *Ardent amore.* Note again the opening of *Homily 34*, in which Gregory describes himself as burning with compassion and ignited by the love of his community.

54. *Conjuncta sunt.*

55. Deuteronomy 32:8.

56. That is, from the different orders of angels and their separate activities and ministries.

57. What follows is the development of a correspondence between angelic orders and human virtue based not on ontology *(analogia entis)*, as in Aquinas or Bonaventure (see F. Copleston, *A History of Philosophy*, vol. II, *Medieval Philosophy* [New York: Doubleday, 1993], 266–64; 352–58), but on ministry or service. Alan of Lille will also draw a specific correspondence between angelic and ecclesial ministries (see his *Treatise on the Angelic Hierarchy* in this volume). Richard of St. Victor, whose teaching on contemplation of angels is intended to guide the pilgrim into the "secret places of divine incomprehensibility," draws together both the ontological and the ministerial correspondence in *De arca mystica* (see Chase, *Angelic Wisdom*, chap. 6 on "angelization").

58. Exodus 7:1.

59. Gregory's term here for "fullness of love" is *dilectione pleni sunt.* Note that the Cherubim, formerly referred to as the fullness of knowledge *(plenitudo scientiae)* now represent the fullness of knowledge as equivalent to the fullness of love. Gregory bases this proximate relation between love and knowledge on Romans 13:10, which in Gregory's text *(PL* 76:1253C) reads: *plenitudo legis est charitas.* Romans 13:10 in the Latin Vulgate reads: *plenitudo ergo legis est dilectio.*

60. Romans 13:10.

61. As he does above with the Cherubim, Gregory blends heart and mind here at the level of the Seraphim. It is the fire of love that illuminates the mind; likewise, it is the Cherubim who are so filled with love of God that they are "fullness of knowledge." As with other medieval figures, Gregory is not so intent on distinguishing and separating the categories of heart and mind as he is in advocating and illuminating their relation.

62. See the introduction for a discussion of this tantalizing reference to Dionysius. The Migne edition of Gregory's *Homily* cites the reference to Dionysius as *De cael. hierarch.*, chap. 7.9, 13, which does not exist. Dionysius indicates throughout the *Celestial Hierarchy*, however, that angels and archangels interact with humanity (cf. *CH* 9) and implies the same by saying that the first hierarchy, comprising Thrones, Cherubim,

and Seraphim, who are in immediate proximity to God, "ceaselessly dance around an eternal knowledge of him" (*CH* 7.4).

63. It is important to note that, in the context of Gregory's sermon stressing charity and virtue within the dual communities of the monastery and of heaven, monks and angels withdraw neither from intimacy with other spirits nor with God.

64. Isaiah 6:6–7.

65. That is, the service, or duty, or ministry they perform is the outward sign by which we recognize them and through which they are named. Again, Gregory focuses on action, Dionysius on being.

66. Daniel 7:10.

67. Gregory has not really succeeded here in explaining how the angel having contact with the very human Isaiah could be called seraphim. Indeed, the angel burns and purifies, and thereby deserves the name associated with its activity, but Gregory's answer never addresses the hierarchical issue of how or why the seraphim would encounter a human. Dionysius, in fact, goes on at some length in an attempt to explain the same problem (see *CH* 13). He proposes two solutions, preferring the second: first, that "when the passage refers just to seraphim what is not meant is one of those enthroned beside God but one of those powers assigned to purify us" (*CH* 13.2); and second, that "this mighty angel, whoever he was, caused a vision so as to initiate the theologian into the divine things, then he attributed to God and, after God to the senior hierarchy his own sacred work of purification" (*CH* 13.3). The different answers to the problem of the seraphim in the Isaiah passage, finally, signify the different set of assumptions and questions each author brings to the discussion. Gregory is interested in the angelic orders primarily as models for human virtue; thus he addresses the issue from the standpoint of their ministry. Dionysius focuses on issues of hierarchy and the angelic orders as beings participating in the glory of the celestial realms.

68. Zechariah 2:3–4.

69. Gregory is setting up an equivalency between being sent and standing, on the one hand, and action and contemplation on the other. Both are integrated, and ideally each flows in and out of the other.

70. This metaphor of thrones, chairs, or seats of God should be taken in the larger sense of God's habitation, dwelling, or resting place.

71. Psalm 80:1, Vulgate 79:2.

72. Thus the Thrones, and the human person imitating the Thrones, "see" God by God's dwelling in their minds. For Gregory,

God sits *(praesidet)* upon the Thrones, and God dwells or sits *(praesideat)* within the mind.

73. Exodus 33:13.

Bernard of Clairvaux
Sermons on Psalm 90

1. For an introduction to Bernard of Clairvaux's spirituality and a selection of his spiritual writings, see *Bernard of Clairvaux: Selected Works*, trans. and foreword G. R. Evans (New York and Mahwah, N.J.: Paulist Press, 1987).

2. See *On Consideration*, V.5.12. Bonaventure also quotes this text in the *Soul's Journey into God*, 4.4, as an instance of how the human spirit is made hierarchical and can thus mount upward to the "heavenly Jerusalem." Thomas Gallus's *Prologue*, in this volume, also uses the angelic hierarchy as a model of the hierarchical soul.

3. An introduction to the *Sermons* can be found in *Bernard of Clairvaux: Sermons on Conversion*, trans. and intro. Marie-Bernard Saïd, Cistercian Fathers Series 25 (Kalamazoo, Mich.: Cistercian Publications, 1981), 83–109. Concerning the genre of the *Sermons*, Saïd concludes that the "intrinsic structure is that of a methodical plan of the spiritual combat, but the extrinsic form is that of the sermon…a treatise written in the literary genre of a sermon" (94).

4. The Book of Wisdom, relying on traditions of Alexandrian Judaism, says, "You fed your people with the food of angels and gave them bread from heaven prepared without labor, having in it all that is delicious and the sweetness of every taste" (Wis 16:20). On the "bread of angels" in Origen and other Patristic writers, see Jean Daniélou, *The Angels and Their Mission: According to the Fathers of the Church*, trans. David Heimann (Westminster, Md.: Christian Classics, 1976), 8–9.

5. Bernard of Clairvaux, *Sermons* 12.7.

6. Ibid., 11.7.

7. Ibid., 12.7.

8. Dante, *Paradiso*, xxxiii, line 145. See also Ewert H. Cousins, "Preface," in Evans, *Bernard of Clairvaux: Selected Works*, 5–11.

9. In the Vulgate system of numbering familiar to Bernard, this was Psalm 90. Direct references to the Psalms in the text of the *Sermons* that follow have been left in the form known to Bernard. Scriptural references

cited in the notes conform to the numbering of the Hebrew text familiar to us today, that is, to the psalm "He Who Dwells" as Psalm 91.

10. Psalm 91:10. This verse is also the subject of Bernard's previous Sermon in *He Who Dwells*. In Section 1 of *Sermon Eleven*, Bernard spoke of the Lord's ever watchful eye over us. The Lord's watchfulness is essential, Bernard says, because he who assails us (the devil) "neither slumbers nor sleeps."

11. Psalm 55:6.

12. Psalm 37:27.

13. Matthew 3:7.

14. The remainder of this sermon is essentially a commentary on these many "ways" *(Multae sunt viae, et genera multa vearum)*. As Bernard mentions soon in Section 3 below, there are the ways of humanity, the ways of demons, the ways of angels, and the ways of God. He uses a variety of phrases and words to describe these ways; in addition to *via* (way) here, he also uses and expands on the meaning of such words as *iter, semitalis*, and *vestigia* and their function in the spiritual life. *Via*, in addition to "way," can also mean "path," or "road" or "journey" and will be translated accordingly as appropriate.

15. Bernard here uses *viatori* from *viator*, which was also the title of Mercury as the protector of travelers. It is notable that he does not use *perigrinatio*, "wanderer," which is a common term in this tradition for the spiritual pilgrim.

16. Isaiah 47:15.

17. In Sections 4 and 5 Bernard proceeds to look first at the ways or paths of the "sons of Adam," that is, the ways of men and women. We, he says, are led by necessity and greed. There are many pathways and no shortcuts along the routes of necessity and greed. The roads of both necessity and greed end only in the depths of hell. Thus, for instance, sorrow and unhappiness are the ways of men; "sorrow in necessity, unhappiness in greed." "Necessity," Bernard says, "arises from the weakness of the flesh; greed proceeds from the penury of heart and forgetfulness." After the ways of human persons, Bernard examines the ways of demons. We ourselves can fall into these pathways of the demons by steps. The first step is when people persuade themselves that they are more than what they are. The second step is self-ignorance. The third step is the presumption of trying to defend oneself. The fourth step is contempt, leading to impenitence, which leads in turn to stubbornness, leading finally to the

pride that does not fear God. Finally, Bernard says, whoever walks with the devil in all these ways is "made one in spirit with him."

18. John 1:18.

19. John 1:51. Vulgate reads: *videbitis caelum apertum et angelos Dei [ascendentes et descendentes supra Filium hominis]* (You will see heaven open and the angels of God [ascending and descending upon the Son of Man]).

20. Matthew 18:10.

21. Psalm 25:8.

22. Psalm 25:9.

23. Psalm 106:7.

24. Psalm 85:10.

25. That is, Christ (see Psalm 76:2).

26. Psalm 78:3.

27. Psalm 44:1.

28. Psalm 40:14. Vulgate reads *semper susceperunt* (They have always supported).

29. Psalm 26:3.

30. Psalm 89:24.

31. Vulgate: Psalm 83:12.

32. Psalm 98:3.

33. Psalm 96:13.

34. James 2:13.

35. Based on the Vulgate text that immediately follows, Bernard shifts slightly from "way" *(via)* to "pathway" or "journey" *(iter, itinera)*. This has more to do with the act of traveling or a journey or the road along which one proceeds on the spiritual journey than with the "way" or "path" of that journey. This will be alternately translated as "pathway" or "journey" as appropriate.

36. Habakkuk 3:6.

37. Psalm 103:17.

38. Psalm 117:2.

39. John 12:31.

40. Ephesians 6:12.

41. Here Bernard again shifts his vocabulary. He moves from the word "way" *(via)* to *semita*, which connotes more a sidetrack, path, or alleyway. It was also the name of a footpath or wayside for deities.

42. John 8:44.

43. Ibid.

44. Sirach 14:5.

45. Wisdom 5:6.

46. 1 Corinthians 7:25.

47. Hosiah 14:10.

48. Isaiah 60:14.

49. Here Bernard again makes a slight shift in his commentary on the "ways" *(via)* of humanity, angels, demons, and God. The word here is *vestigia*, meaning "footprint" or "track," the trace or indication of a presence; it also means the movement of the foot in walking or where one has set one's foot on a sure foundation. This last nuance is especially appropriate in opposition to the "winding and digressive steps that are not so much pathways as precipitous descents" above. Finally, it can mean a mode of behavior appropriate for imitation or example. It is appropriate then that Bernard would use *vestigia* as the "footstep" of a behavior fit for imitation, that is, the "footprint" of God.

50. In keeping with the metaphor of the soul's spiritual journey and the "ways" of humanity, demons, angels, and God, Bernard here speaks of the soul's first "step" on that journey. Using the Latin *gradus* for "step," Bernard invokes not only the image of walking but of a stage or step in the soul's spiritual progress.

51. Luke 1:77–78.

52. Isaiah 49:15. The son of his mother *(filio matris suae)* would be the person himself.

53. Sirach 30:24.

54. Isaiah 46:8. In the Vulgate the recollection of transgressions is in the "heart," not the "mind" as in RSV and New Oxford.

55. Numbers 21:22.

56. Romans 10:10.

57. Psalm 85:8.

58. Matthew 18:3.

59. Cf. Vulgate, Psalm 72:22.

60. Psalm 16:11.

61. Hebrews 1:14.

62. John 13:15.

63. Matthew 20:28.

64. Luke 22:27.

65. Jeremiah 21:8.

66. Terence, *Andria*, 310. Cf. Bernard, *In Psalmum*, 456.

67. Luke 10:27.

68. Lamentations 3:41.

69. From the Preface to the Eucharistic Canon.

70. Psalm 4:2.

71. Psalm 84:12. Here Bernard associates the unburdened and lightened heart of confession with the unburdened angelic ascent or "lifting up" (*lightened* and *lifting up* enjoy the same Latin root). Bernard says, *cor leve levatur* (the lightened heart is lifted).

72. Luke 24:49.

73. Bernard here uses yet another word cognate with his theme of wandering or journey. In this case, and associated with the demons, it is *vagantur*, which forms the English word *vagabond*. In Latin it has the sense of wandering from place to place at will but without definite direction, straying, being carried on a meandering way to and fro, proceeding without rules or form, fluctuating, wavering, vacillating. These are the forms of the demons' journey.

74. 2 Corinthians 3:5.

75. James 1:5.

76. Romans 9:5.

77. In Sections 1 and 2 of Sermon Twelve, Bernard expands on what he said in Sermon Eleven concerning the ways of the demons. He says that he continues to "track down" *(vestigare)* their ways. For Bernard, the pattern of the devil's ways are a "circuit" *(circuitio)* and a "circumvention" *(circumventio)* in the sense of encompassing or enclosure by hostile forces through cheating or trickery. On these circular pathways the devil is "always being raised up and always being thrown down; he is always climbing up by pride, and always being humiliated. Is that not a circuit?…Woe to the man who follows this circuit." This is, of course, the parallel but opposite and malicious side of the angels' ways of ascent by contemplation and descent by compassion. But circumvention, which the devil does far more regularly, is worse. By circumvention the evil spirits imitate or copy *(aemulari)* the angelic ways. Such evil spirits "ascend by eager vanity and descend by jealous spite. Their ascent is counterfeit and their descent is cruel."

78. Psalm 40:12.

79. Bernard is here making reference to Satan's use of this psalm text in the temptation of Jesus in Matthew 4:6–7.

80. Romans 8:28.

81. Psalm 107:8.

82. Psalm 126:3.

83. Psalm 144:3.

84. Job 7:17.

85. 1 Maccabees 16:14.

86. Luke 10:35.

87. 1 John 4:9.

88. Psalm 104:30.

89. Psalm 89:15.

90. Hebrews 1:14.

91. Psalm 104:4. That is, in English, you make the "winds your messengers." In the Vulgate, the "winds" are *spiritus*, thus the spirits are angels, that is, messengers.

92. Matthew 18:10.

93. Ephesians 2:9.

94. Bernard completes this section by reminding his hearers that humanity is insignificant in relation to God, and yet God is mindful of us, and for the sake of his elect God nonetheless gives the angels charge over us. He then tells the parable of the provident householder (God) sending his servants (angels) to gather the scattered weeds (humanity) among the wheat (Christ), asking finally, how is the wheat is to be preserved among the weeds.

95. Matthew 3:12.

96. Song of Songs 2:2.

97. Or "watchmen," but the same root word in Latin as the "give the angels charge of you to *guard* you" of Psalm 91 (cf. Isaiah 62:6).

98. Galatians 2:9.

99. Ephesians 5:15.

100. Hebrews 11:1.

101. Psalm 116:12.

102. 1 Timothy 1:17.

103. James 1:17.

104. 1 Timothy 1:17.

105. Vulgate, Psalm 138:17.

106. Romans 13:8.

107. Romans 13:17.

108. 1 Peter 4:11. Bernard's phrase here is *"non modo prae omnibus, sed in omnibus."* God, for Bernard, is thus transcendent (before and above all things), and at the same time immanent (in all things).

109. Mark 12:30.

110. Romans 8:17.

111. 1 John 3:2.

112. Galatians 4:1–2.

113. Isaiah 8:14; Romans 9:32.
114. Psalm 91:13.
115. 1 Corinthians 10:13.
116. Matthew 8:25.
117. Psalm 121:4.
118. 1 Corinthians 10:13.
119. Isaiah 8:14.
120. Matthew 21:44.
121. 1 Peter 2:6.
122. Psalm 55:8.
123. 2 Corinthians 4:17–18.
124. Psalm 78:49.

Hugh of St. Victor/Anonymous
On the Six Wings of the Cherubim

1. See, for instance, Marie-Thérèse d'Alverny, *Alain de Lille: textes inédits avec une introduction sur sa vie et ses oeuvres* (Paris: J. Vrin, 1965), 154–55.
2. D'Alverny, *Alain de Lille*, 155.
3. John 15:13.
4. Psalm 55:6.
5. See the drawing entitled "Cherubim Mysticus." This drawing, reproduced in Migne, *PL* 210:267–68, is, according to d'Alverny *(Alain de Lille*, 155), reproduced and interpreted by C. de Visch in an accurate fashion from several manuscripts. It serves as a pictorial representation of the Seraphim described in Section Two.
6. The nearly verbatim excerpt from Hugh of St. Victor's *De arca Noe morali*, or *On the Moral Ark of Noah* begins with the next sentence (see *De sex, PL* 210:269A; *De arca, PL* 176:622D; *Hugh of Saint-Victor*, 52). The editorial insertions will be pointed out as they occur in the text.
7. Isaiah 6:1.
8. See Augustine, *City of God*, XXII.29–30 on joy and peace as the reward of the souls of the holy.
9. Isaiah 6:3c.
10. Jeremiah 23:24.
11. Isaiah 66:1.
12. Isaiah 6:1b. Hugh of St. Victor here follows the Vulgate, though he slightly alters it by not describing those things that were under

God and filling the temple as the "train of his robe" but simply as those things that were under God (*quae sub ipso erant*) filled the temple.

13. In this shift from mind to heart, Hugh draws a parallel between the immensity of divine labor (*operum divinorum immensitas*) and the immensity of the things (*immensitas eorum*) that his heart considers. The parallel finds a connection both by the failure of either mind or heart to comprehend immensity and by the fact that both heart and temple are filled by divine incomprehensibility.

14. Isaiah 57:15.

15. Hugh is surveying divine attributes, or names of God. Having discussed God as immensity, perfection, and fullness, he now adds and will continue to discuss eternity, and will shortly add omnipotence.

16. A *circuitus temporum*, or a complete circle of "time" and a *ambitus saeculorum*, or circuit or revolution of the "ages."

17. That is, time in its fullness returns to its beginning, but *also*, in making the circuit (around the temple) gives birth to (*generando*) something new. Time both stabilizes (returns to the beginning) and produces new life in the context of the temple (the fullness of the works of God). Here Hugh of St. Victor meditates upon the static and dynamic natures of time and the spiritual journey.

18. Isaiah 6:2a. See Grover A. Zinn, Jr., "Hugh of St. Victor, Isaiah's Vision, and *De arca Noe*," in *The Church and the Arts*, ed. Diana Wood (New York: Blackwell Publishers, 1992), 106 n.16 on why "*super illud*" here ought to be translated "upon it" (the throne) rather than "above it" as in *Hugh of Saint-Victor.*

19. As mentioned in the Introduction, *On the Six Wings of the Cherubim* is really about the Seraphim. As described in Hugh's text, they have all the attributes that the tradition has ascribed to the Seraphim (burning, six wings, and so on), and as a commentary on Isaiah 6, the text is certainly about Seraphim. Here, however, according to the allegorical tradition, Hugh says Seraphim but really means Cherubim. The tradition has looked not to the seraphim of Isaiah 6 but to the two cherubim above the ark of the covenant in Exodus 25 as the allegorical representation of the two testaments. On the two cherubim as allegories of the two testaments, see Chase, *Angelic Wisdom*, 14–27.

20. With this parenthetical comment on the seraphim, Hugh of St. Victor begins a word play on the metaphysics and spirituality of light and burning, the primary attributes of the seraphim. In three short sentences he manages to use eight words in eleven ways related to burning, illumination,

fire, and light *(ardens, illuminat, ardere, ardet, incendit, ardentem, ardentes, lucere).* By participating in the radiation of divine love and knowledge, the seraphim serve as a theophanic link between the eternal and omnipotent fullness of God and the temple which God fills and where created creatures dwell. Hugh of St. Victor elaborates the mediatory quality of the seraphim by connecting the metaphor of "burning" as a kind of angelic anthropology to the "burning" of the human heart and mind.

21. 2 Peter 1:19.

22. *Divinitas deitatis.* This might also be rendered as "the divinity of the Godhead," or "the divinity of the deity," or simply "the divinity of God."

23. Here Hugh focuses on the perfection of deity. For him, such divine perfection cannot advance in virtue, give birth to wisdom, become more full than full, or divide eternity into units of time. For these operations the angels come into play. For instance, divinity does not give birth to wisdom *(nec sapientia crescit)*; angels do. Richard of St. Victor uses the same phrase, *sapientia crescit,* to describe the birth of wisdom between the two cherubim. For Richard of St. Victor, wisdom is born between two cherubim; here for Hugh of St. Victor, wisdom is born of the Seraphim (see Chase, *Angelic Wisdom,* 15–16, 72–73, 90–95, 121–26).

24. Cf. Romans 8:15–17; Galatians 4:3–7; Ephesians 1:3–14.

25. Isaiah 6:2b.

26. Zinn, "Hugh of St. Victor," 106–7, points out that Hugh here "follows neither biblical text nor exegetical tradition when describing the seraphs' wings." Hugh's major departures are (1) covering the bodies of the seraphs and (2) covering Christ's *head* but not his *face.*

27. Hugh takes this phrase, "the one to the other," directly from the Vulgate. The text is from Isaiah 6:3a and reads *alter ad alterum.* The scriptural context is that the seraphim are shouting "holy, holy, holy" one to the other and as models of love, fly, the one to the other, as two lovers while in the highest service of the Lord.

28. As noted above, much of the tradition uses the Cherubim, not the Seraphim, as allegories of the two testaments of scripture. However, because Hugh here takes the two seraphim to be an allegory of the two testaments, he could not have missed the implication that the two testaments also "fly one to the other," *alter ad alterum.*

29. Thus forming the "six wings" of scripture. The six wings are thus the two wings that cover their bodies, which are the historical reading; the two wings that cover the head and feet of the Lord, which are the

allegorical reading; and the two wings with which they fly, which are the tropological or moral reading.

30. Hugh of St. Victor uses this phrase, *excessum mentis rapimur,* to describe the ecstatic mystical vision of God. Another translation for *excessum mentis* is "ecstasy of mind." Thus the phrase *excessum mentis rapimur* indicates a "force" that seizes or steals the mind outside itself, resulting in an ecstatic vision of God. The mind in a sense becomes inebriated and finally "alienated" from itself (the phrase *alienatio mentis* is also, in fact, used in writings on angelic spirituality to describe this ecstatic vision). The moral aspect of this ecstatic vision is laid out by Hugh in what follows. The important aspect of this moral implication is that the soul no longer follows the angelic contours of "mind," which are integrated and transcended, but rather the contours of charity or "love." *Excessum mentis* is also one of the phrases used by Richard of St. Victor to describe the modes of contemplation at the sixth and final level of contemplation symbolized by the cherubim (see *De arca mystica,* V.v.).

31. On angelic "flight into the secret places of divine incomprehensibility," see Richard of St. Victor, *De arca mystica,* IV.iv, *PL* 96, 140D.

32. See drawing. The incense burners, or censers, *thuribula* in the text, referring to frankincense, were originally flutes played while incense burned during sacrificial rituals.

33. This sentence, beginning with "The incense burners," is an editorial insertion by the anonymous writer/redactor. Hugh of St. Victor's text begins again with the following sentence (see *De sex alis, PL* 210:271C; *De arca Noe, PL* 176:624D; *Hugh of Saint-Victor,* 57).

34. Isaiah 6:2c.

35. Exodus 32:20.

36. 1 Corinthians 13:12.

37. Ibid.

38. Here the dynamic of the *apophasis* of hidden and revealed is more apparent in the Latin. Hugh says that the face of God in heaven is *non veleta, sed revelata;* God is no longer garmented or veiled but rather uncovered and revealed. In this life the angels alone see the revealed face of God; we see only the seraphim and the veil.

39. Matthew 18:10.

40. The text in *De sex alis, non immutantes,* is obviously wrong (cf. *De arca Noe, PL* 176:625B, *non mutantes*).

41. Hugh of St. Victor is referring to a picture, now lost, of the ark and the cosmic Christ. *De arca Noe morali* and *De arca Noe mystica* describe

NOTES

the picture and use it as a focus for meditation and contemplation. The picture becomes then, both an object intended to aid in meditation and a kind of visual exegesis. For reproductions of what the drawing might have looked like and a discussion of Hugh's two texts, see Zinn, "Hugh of St. Victor," 99–116; Patrice Sicard, *Diagrammes médiévaux et exégèse visuelle le Libellus de formatione arche de Hughes de Saint-Victor* (Turnhout: Brepols, 1993).

42. Isaiah 6:2c.

43. Isaiah 6:3b.

44. That is, *in aperto.* Hugh now takes his earlier theme of the hidden and revealed things of God, the things that are open and closed to us. Note that this leads him directly into his contemplation of that which is intermediate between the beginning and end times, that is the *visible* "body" of God, the Church.

45. In Latin, *hoc corpus est.* This reference to the Mass and to Christ is also, in another sense, the church.

46. The preceding two sentences are not in Hugh's *De arca Noe* text (see *PL* 176:625D). The next three paragraphs, to the sentence ending "upon the sea of life," are greatly altered (cf. *De sex alis, PL* 210:272C–D with *De arca Noe, PL* 176:625D–626B).

47. The writer/redactor ends the copying of a portion of Hugh of St. Victor's *De arca Noe morali* here (cf. *De arca Noe, PL* 176:626B; *De sex alis, PL* 210:272D). The sentence that follows in *On the Six Wings of the Cherubim* text above is also from Hugh, though from another location (see De arca Noe PL 176:629D–630A). The remainder of Section One of *Six Wings* is from the writer/redactor and, as we are assuming, Section Two begins the work of the anonymous writer.

48. Here the writer/redactor is probably referring to the picture of the seraphim, the *"cherubim mysticus,"* as well as to Section Two, which can be thought of as a "verbal picture" of the seraphim, the exemplar of Christ.

49. Psalm 117:29.

50. James 5:16.

51. Imitation *(simulationem)* is used here not to indicate image or metaphor but to claim true self-understanding and true knowledge as an aspect of the confession of sin. Genesis 1:25 is echoed but given a different twist in that sin, which destroyed our original likeness or similitude to God, is now truly confessed without the conceit of image or likeness.

52. Cf. Augustine, *De vera et falsa poenitentia*, IV.15.

53. James 4:6

54. The Latin, *satisfactio*, also has strong christological connotations, referring theologically to the satisfaction and compensation of Christ's work of redemption. Christ's work "satisfies" the justice and love of God. In the spiritual journey of the believer, satisfaction is linked with comfort.

55. Joel 2:13.

56. Psalm 4:4, Vulgate 4:5.

57. The "fear of God" here means "knowledge of God." The anonymous author is saying that unless you really know who God is, and because of that knowledge fear God due to the radical discontinuity between your creatureliness and God's creative power, unless you *know* this, you will not have compunction or contrition of heart.

58. Psalm 31:19, Vulgate 30:20.

59. Psalm 37:3, Vulgate 36:3.

60. Psalm 37:5, Vulgate 36:5.

61. Judith 13:17.

62. Psalm 2:12, Vulgate 2:13.

63. Cf. Ezekiel 28.

64. Psalm 44:21, Vulgate 43:22.

65. 1 Corinthians 4:5.

66. Psalm 130:8, Vulgate 129:8.

67. Cf. Ezekiel 33:10–20.

68. Cf. Luke 3:8; Matthew 3:8.

69. Psalm 37:27, Vulgate 36:27.

70. Psalm 26:4–5, Vulgate 25:4–5.

71. *Maceratio*, a steeping, soaking, or maceration in order to make soft or tender in preparation for healing.

72. Philippians 3:19.

73. Gregory the Great, *Rule of Pastoral Care*, IV.xxv.

74. Luke 21:34.

75. Romans 6:19.

76. 2 Samuel 13.

77. Psalm 37:4, Vulgate 36:4.

78. Luke 10:42.

79. Isaiah 48:22.

80. Luke 2:14.

81. Matthew 6:22.

82. Romans 13:10.

83. Colossians 3:5.

84. Matthew 7:12.

85. Cf. Psalm 24:3–4, Vulgate 23:3–4. Here the author is quite free with his quotation from Psalm 24.

86. Proverbs 18:19.

87. Matthew 5:7.

88. Proverbs 12:26.

89. John 15:13.

90. Matthew 10:22.

91. Psalm 17:8–9, Vulgate 16:8–9.

92. Psalm 57:1, Vulgate 56:2.

93. Psalm 55:6, Vulgate 54:7. The Vulgate does refer to feathers, rather than the wings of the dove.

Umiltà of Faenza
Sermons on the Holy Angels

1. See *Acta Sanctorum, Maii VII*, vol. XX, Appendix ad Diem XXII Maii, "Sermo Sanctae Humilitatis Abbatissae" (Antverpiae, 1685), 820 B-E.

2. A portion of the *Life of St. Umiltà of the Vallombrosan Order in Florence* is available in translation in Elizabeth Alvilda Petroff, *Consolation of the Blessed* (New York: Alta Gaia Society, 1979), 121–51.

3. Elizabeth Alvilda Petroff, *Body and Soul: Essays on Medieval Women and Mysticism* (New York and Oxford: Oxford University Press, 1994), 110–38, points out that Umiltà, along with other Italian women saints of the period, was given specific images of behavior associated with the desert by her biographers. Using the trope of the desert, not the monastery, Umiltà represents a paradigm of holiness and transformation, making her an exemplum of asceticism, which includes silence, prayer, solitude, and abstinence.

4. On this sixth sermon, see Elizabeth Alvilda Petroff, *Medieval Woman's Visionary Literature* (New York: Oxford University Press, 1986), 236.

5. Saint Umiltà considered Saint John the Evangelist to be her special patron and maintained a devotional attachment to him from an early age (see Petroff, *Consolation of the Blessed*, 142–43). Translating an unnamed Sermon of Saint Umiltà's, Petroff gives a flavor of her attachment to the evangelist: "St. John the Evangelist is my teacher and my master, without whom I would wish to learn no doctrine. After Christ and his

blessed Mother, he is my glory, my hope, and my refuge, my counsel and the joy of my soul" (142).

6. *Divinum sermonem.* See introduction on the relation of divine, angelic, and human speech in this sermon.

7. Saint Umiltà here again conveys a humble comparison between her sermon *(iste sermo)* and the divine sermon or speech *(divinum sermonem)* discussed in the paragraph above. From the first paragraph we learn that the way to "listen" to divine speech is in silence, silence tempered with great internal joy or delight. Now, and for the rest of her sermon, she will speak of the angels, those celestial beings who are exemplars for those who listen silently and with great joy. Thus humanity also may imitate the angels and in so doing "hear" the words of God.

8. See *Sermon I,* line 170, in Umiltà, *Sermoni,* 9. There Umiltà names the archangel Gabriel as well as the angels Emmanuel and Sapiel; see also *Acta Sanctorum, Maii VII,* vol. XX, cited above in note 1, where Umiltà discusses the names and functions of the nine orders of angels.

9. The *Acta Sanctorum, Maii VII,* edition begins here, 816; the *Acta Sanctorum, Maii V,* edition also begins here, 214.

10. Exodus 14:29; Matthew 25:33.

11. The Lord's injunction to the angels to guard Umiltà functions reciprocally: the angels both hold *(tenent)* Umiltà as she holds *(teneam)* tightly to them. *Teneo* here should be taken in the sense not only of "to hold" and "to preserve" or "persevere," but also in the sense of "to hold in the mind, to understand, to grasp, to know." Thus both the angels and Umiltà and the angels "hold" by contemplating the other.

12. Her claim to learn through hearing *(per auditum)* the angels echoes the opening of this sermon, where Umiltà claims that it is possible to "hear" *(audire)* divine speech through silent and still joy. Thus again, the angels are both exemplars of the contemplative mode—silent and still joy—necessary to hearing God's divine word, and exemplars of the form of speaking that word that Umiltà has in mind.

13. Though the masculine form of the third person possessive adjective is used here *(eum),* I am translating it as feminine based on its actual name, Sapiel, which is derived from *sophia.* The personification of *sophia* is generally female. The gender of the adjective or pronoun referring to an angel often appears to be a matter of convention. Our present-day convention calls for attention to other than strictly grammatical considerations.

14. Matthew 13:46. Gregory the Great, *Homily 34*, compares the nine orders of angels to nine precious stones or jewels.

15. In the tradition of the later examen of conscience, Saint Umiltà realizes that to be tested or examined, or even, to be put on trial *(examinatur)* by Sapiel's love is not to risk coming up short according to some test of "perfect love" but rather to risk being clarified and even transformed by that love.

16. Revelation 21:19; Psalm 20:4; Exodus 28:13.

17. Though the critical text has *cherubin*, from the allusion to Isaiah 6:2, the claim that the angel is from the highest order of angels, and the language that follows associating the angel with fire, flame, and purification, Umiltà is clearly describing the seraphim.

18. Isaiah 6:2; Revelation 4:8.

19. Or "God with us." Umiltà finds this name appropriate because the angel Emmanuel, as a cherubim/seraphim, would have been in immediate proximity to God. To be in conversation with such an angel would signify as well that God is "with us." The depth and mystery of this presence is, as she says below, only partially understood by her and but poorly expressed. The name Emmanuel is given in Isaiah 7:14 and 8:8 with a messianic overtone. Matthew 1:23 picks this up as well. Emmanuel is not referenced in either Saint John's gospel or in Revelation, which Umiltà would have assumed was written by Saint John. Therefore, she must be implying that the name was revealed to her directly from the mouth of the apostle.

20. Umiltà refers here to her founding and taking on the responsibilities of abbess of the Vallombrosan monastery in 1266. She would have been forty at the time.

21. As noted above, Umiltà was very aware of the nine orders of angels. Thus Emmanuel, from the order of Cherubim/Seraphim, who dwells in the glory of God "interpreting" God's dominion and power *(dominatio, aut potestas)*, is also, in Umiltà's mind, "interpreting" the angelic orders of Dominions and Powers as she spreads her wings and assists Umiltà with the chore of guiding her flock.

22. Umiltà, *Sermoni*, 24. A partial translation is available in Petroff, *Consolation of the Blessed*, 142.

23. See the *Magnificat*, Luke 1:46ff.

24. Luke 1:31.

25. Umiltà, *Sermoni*, 150ff. Also available in part in *Acta Sanctorum, Maii VII*, 816–17. Partial translations are available in Petroff, *Consolation of the Blessed*, 141, and Petroff, *Body and Soul*, 221 n.14.

26. Cf. Psalm 141:3–4. This is also an allusion to Genesis 3:24, where, after the banishment of Adam and Eve, God placed cherubim with flaming swords at the gates of the Garden of Eden to guard the way to the tree of life.

27. Cf. Matthew 6:21.

Section Two
Commentaries on the *Celestial Hierarchy* of Dionysius the Areopagite

1. A few recommended works on Dionysius that focus especially on the *Celestial Hierarchy* and are particularly helpful are Paul Rorem's commentary on the *Celestial Hierarchy* and his survey of Dionysius's reception in the medieval period in Rorem, *P-D*, 47–90; Andrew Louth's helpful volume, *Dionysius the Areopagite* (Wilton, Conn.: Morehouse-Barlow, 1989), 33–51; the introductory material and notes in Classics of Western Spirituality Series volume on Dionysius, *Pseudo-Dionysius: The Complete Works* (New York: Paulist Press, 1987); and Chase, *Angelic Wisdom*, especially the sections on Dionysius's symbolic theology, apophatic methodology, and angelology. Helpful studies on the subject in French include Dionysius, *Hiér. cél.*, lviiff., on the Christian sources of Dionysian angelology, and René Roques, *L'univers Dionysien* (Paris: Aubier, 1954), 135–67, on angels and intellectual hierarchies.

John Scotus Eriugena
Commentary on the Celestial Hierarchy of Saint Dionysius

1. On the spirituality, mysticism, and angelology of Eriugena, see Deirdre Carabine, "Eriugena's Use of the Symbolism of Light, Cloud, and Darkness in the *Periphyseon*," in *Eriugena: East and West*, ed. Bernard McGinn and Willemien Otten (Notre Dame, Ind.: University of Notre Dame Press, 1994), 141–52; Paul A. Dietrich and Donald F. Duclow, "Virgins in Paradise: Deification and Exegesis in 'Periphyseon V,'" in *Jean Scot Écrivain: Actes du IVe Colloque International, Montréal*, ed. Guy Allard (Montréal: Bellarmin, 1986), 254–78; Donald F. Duclow, "Isaiah Meets the Seraph: Breaking Ranks in Dionysius and Eriugena?" in *Eriugena: East and West*, ed. Bernard McGinn and Willemien Otten (Notre Dame, Ind.: University of Notre Dame Press), 233–52; Maurice de Gandillac, "Anges et hommes dans le commentaire de Jean Scot sur la *Hiérarchie céleste*," in *Jean Scot Érigène et l'histoire de la philosophie* (Paris: Éditions du centre

national de la recherche scientifique, 1977), 393–403; Stephen Gersh, *From Iamblichus to Eriugena: An Investigation of the Prehistory and Evolution of the Pseudo-Dionysian Tradition* (Leiden: Brill, 1978); Nikolaus M. Häring, "John Scottus in Twelfth Century Angelology," in *The Mind of Eriugena*, ed. John J. O'Meara and Ludwig Bieler (Dublin: Irish University Press, 1973), 158–69; David Luscombe, "The Reception of the Writings of Denis the Pseudo-Areopagite into England," in *Tradition and Change*, ed. Diana Greenway, Christopher Holdsworth, and Jane Sayers (Cambridge: Cambridge University Press, 1985), 115–43; Bernard McGinn, *The Growth of Mysticism*, vol. 2 of *The Presence of God: A History of Western Christian Mysticism* (New York: Crossroad, 1994), 80–118; Dermot Moran, *The Philosophy of John Scottus Eriugena: A Study of Idealism in the Middle Ages* (Cambridge: Cambridge University Press, 1989); René Roques, "Jean Scot Érigène," in *DS* 8:735–61; Rorem, *P-D*, pp. 77–81. For further bibliographies on the growing research on Eriugena, see McGinn, *The Growth of Mysticism*, 454 nn.3, 6; Rorem, *P-D*, 85 n.14, 87 n.20.

2. For a brief but detailed description of Eriugena's Greek and Latin philosophical and theological sources, see McGinn, *The Growth of Mysticism*, 88–92.

3. About 860, Eriugena was asked by Charles the Bald to retranslate Hilduin's poorly done translation of the Dionysian corpus. His commentary on Dionysius's *Celestial Hierarchy* was done between 865 and 870.

4. A treatise on theological anthropology called *The Image*.

5. These included the *Questions to Thalassius* and *Ambigua to John*. Maximus was a seventh century Byzantine monk.

6. On the impact, particularly, of Eriugena's *Commentary on the Celestial Hierarchy*, see Rorem, *P-D*, 74–81. It should be noted, however, that by the middle of the thirteenth century Eriugena was enjoying less and less popularity, to the point where Aquinas denounced him as an originator of heretical views concerning the angels. As H. F. Dondaine has shown, however, the texts Aquinas assumed to be Eriugena's were in fact not his (Häring, "John Scottus in Twelfth Century Angelology," 163).

7. Recent critical reflection on Eriugena's anthropology include Willemien Otten, *The Anthropology of Johannes Scottus Eriugena* (Leiden: E. J. Brill, 1991); Dermot Moran, *The Philosophy of John Scottus Eriugena* (Cambridge: Cambridge University Press, 1989), 154–211.

8. Donald F. Duclow succinctly defines these two poles of ignorance and knowledge as "(1) a self-ignorance whereby humanity knows only *that* it is, not *what* it is, which reflects God's unknowable transcendence, and 2)

a self-knowledge that embraces all creation, visible and invisible, in which the humanity becomes—in Maximus' phrase—'The workshop of all things,' faithfully mirroring God's creative Wisdom" ("Isaiah Meets the Seraph," 241).

9. Duclow, "Isaiah Meets the Seraph," 237. However, it is not simply through light and illumination that perfect equality of angels and humanity is affirmed in Eriugena, but rather *in spe*, in hope (Gandillac, "Anges et hommes," 396–97).

10. Duclow, "Isaiah Meets the Seraph," 241.

11. "Between our mind, by which we know the Father, and the Truth, that is to say, the inward light through which we know Him, no creature intervenes" (Augustine, *De vera religione* 55, 113 [CCSL 32:259], cited in Duclow, "Isaiah Meets the Seraph," 250 n.45).

12. Duclow, "Isaiah Meets the Seraph," 242. Duclow goes on to point out that in his *Periphyseon* Eriugena spells out this relation in detail. For a summary of the similarities and differences between Dionysius and Eriugena, see ibid. 246–47.

13. On the theme of motion and rest in Neo-Platonism and Eriugena, see Gersh, *From Iamblichus to Eriugena*, 67–70, 243–50.

14. Eriugena, *Commentary on the Celestial Hierarchy*, "On Their Contemplation."

15. Cf. James 1:17. A distinction here, however, is necessary. For Dionysius, the celestial hierarchies truly are a means of access to the Father. For Eriugena, it is only through humanity and the wisdom of Christ that we have such access. The wisdom of Christ is, however, in the scheme of Eriugena, roughly equivalent in some sense to the created world plus the full celestial hierarchy (see Gandillac, "Anges et hommes," 395–96).

16. This structural outline follows that of the Latin editor of Eriugena's *Expositiones in Ierarchiam coelestem*, Jean Barbet, in Eriugena, *Exp. coel.*, x–xi; see also xi n.1.

17. Eriugena is referring to Chapter VI of the *Celestial Hierarchy*, where Dionysius had first listed the nine orders of angels, starting with the angels in the first hierarchy in the most immediate proximity to God, and listing them as Thrones, Cherubim, Seraphim (see Dionysius, *CH* 6.2, 160–61). Eriugena had commented that with regard to "nearness" to God, these three orders are indistinguishable, the first hierarchy being a kind of trinity in which the individual orders are reflective of the three persons of the Trinity, yet none is essentially different or foremost. Thus, in *CH* 6

there is a kind of ascending movement from Thrones to Seraphim that nonetheless maintains a kind of unity in diversity, while in *CH* 7, Eriugena following Dionysius says something about the "light" or divinity that descends through the angelic realms to our understanding, and so begins with the "first" order nearest to God, the Seraphim. On Eriugena's commentary on *CH* 6.2, see Eriugena, *Exp. coel.*, 89–91.

18. Eriugena uses *cognominationes* here for Dionysius's Greek term, ἐπωνυμία. Sarracenus, for instance, had used simply *nominatio* (*Dionysiaca* 2:835). (The *Dionysiaca* contains Dionysius's Greek text along with nine different Latin translators, including Eriugena and Sarracenus. While Eriugena, *Exp. coel.*, is the critical edition used for this translation, *Dionysiaca* will, from time to time, be consulted for comparison.) Eriugena's rendering indicates more the meaning of a name derived from some personal characteristic, achievement, attribute, or the like. Its derivation is thus allusive; the word itself highlights the idea that the very name of an angelic order indicates the manner in which God has imprinted or characterized it. The word, interestingly, was also used as the title of a god, where again the name would convey something of the god's divine attributes.

19. On the common ancient and Patristic principle by which the "names" signify something of the quality of the "thing" itself, or that the name serves as a kind of mirror of the essence of a being or god, see *Dionysius l'Aréopagite: La hiérarchie céleste*, intro. René Roques, critical text Günter Heil, trans. and notes Maurice de Gandillac, Sources Chrétiennes, no. 58 (Paris: Les éditions du cerf, 1958), 105 n.4.

20. Using a strong dialectic of commonality and specificity or unity and particularity, Eriugena indicates here that an angelic name, which expresses divine characteristics, renders a particular angelic order both unique in its conformity to the divine essence (*specialitates*), and at the same time holding something of the divine essence in common with all celestial intelligences (*communiones*).

21. *Incendentes aut calefacientes.* Dionysius's words here are ἐμφαίνειν and Θερμαίνοντας, also indicating light and heat. On additional references to Seraphim within the Dionysian corpus, see Dionysius, *CH*, 161 n.71. On the etymology of Seraphim, see Dionysius, *Hiér. cél.*, 105–6 n.5.

22. On additional Dionysian references to Cherubim see Dionysius, *CH*, 161 n.72. On etymology and exegetical tradition concerning the Cherubim, see Chase, *Angelic Wisdom*, chap. 1. On "abundance of knowledge" and "effusion of wisdom" signifying a christological turn—those attributes signifying the very Word of God itself—which is not present in

Dionysius, see Duclow, "Isaiah Meets the Seraph," 240. Duclow also points out how Eriugena sees all the angelic ranks as symbols for the second Person of the Trinity: "By a kind of wonderful metaphor the Wisdom of God [i.e., Christ] is intimated in Holy Scripture by the names of all the heavenly essences" (*Periphyseon*, V, 864D, cited in Duclow, "Isaiah Meets the Seraph," 240).

23. Here, and in what follows, Eriugena inserts Greek words within the gloss or within the gloss's equivalents in order to make a philological, grammatical, or etymological point. If the word comes from Dionysius's text, I will give a footnote indicating Greek lower case and Eriugena's Latin translation. In this case the word is not in Dionysius but is brought in by Eriugena. In Patristic Greek this is the eclipse that took place during the Crucifixion. It can mean "defect" as a figure of speech but is here used reverentially in the sense of "veiling."

24. On the hierarchical structure of the world and celestial realms as a concentric circle around God, the angels standing immediately before God, see Hans Urs von Balthasar, *The Glory of the Lord: A Theological Aesthetics*, vol. 2, *Studies in Theological Style: Clerical Styles*, trans. Andrew Louth et al., ed. John Riches (San Francisco: Ignatius Press, 1984), 191–203.

25. Elsewhere Eriugena describes theophanies as "divine apparitions that are comprehensible to the intellectual nature" *(comprehensibiles intellectuali naturae quasdam divinas apparitiones) (Periphyseon* I 444C, cited in Otten, *The Anthropology of Johannes Scottus Eriugena*, 66). Otten adds that Eriugena uses the term in an attempt to reconcile the opinion that "the angelic nature was established before every other creature, and can therefore correctly behold the eternal reasons in God, with statements of St. Paul, e.g. Romans 11:54 *(quis intellectum Domini cognovit?)* and Philippians 4:7 *(pax Christi quae exsuperat omnem intellectum)*, which irrefutably deny the possibility of direct knowledge of God" (ibid., 66–67). Theophany is thus a mediating vision.

26. Which Eriugena translates first *sanctificatur*, "made holy." He will now broaden the meaning to include "sacrificed" in a special sense. Dionysius's Greek: ἱερουργεῖαι (see *Dionysiaca* 2:836).

27. Eriugena, rather nicely here, shapes a grammatical discussion into a commentary on the ontological nature of the celestial hierarchy and, in a larger sense, of sanctity. The first angelic order, Seraphim, Cherubim, and Thrones, holds a mediatory position between God as the essential ground of being and "other" beings. As such they can, in a similar way to

the Greek middle voice, both sanctify and make God holy (active) and be sanctified and made holy by God (passive). Eriugena is careful to point out that this is just and warranted, though on the surface it seems absurd: how can any lesser being "sanctify" God? The answer, in a sense, is in the grammar: the ontological relations of sanctity are ambiguous, as is the Greek middle voice. From our position as observer, we are able, in a sense, to hold the ambiguous grammatical tension and also, perhaps, the ambiguous ontological tension. Surely the angels are sanctified, yet from our perspective, they sanctify God as well in that their "sacrifice" is a kind of consecration; we, as beings "below" the angels, actually "see" the holiness of God through the sanctifying ontology of the Seraphim, Cherubim, and Thrones. This sanctifying circle is complete, however, only in the sense of sanctity as sacrifice: we are sanctified as we sacrifice ourselves (or are sacrificed) in an oblivion of personal will into the will of God.

28. A phrase from Augustine, *nulla interposita creatura*, used often by Eriugena to indicate a direct, unmediated relation between, in this case, the Seraphim and God, and elsewhere, the possibility of an unmediated relation between humanity and God. As such, "image and archetype differ only 'in relation to the subject' (*Periphyseon*, IV 778A)—i.e., as creature and creator—but in all other respects are identical" (Duclow, "Isaiah Meets the Seraph," 241–42).

29. On the circular movement around a divine or holy center in Plato, Proclus, and Aristotle, see Dionysius, *Hiér. cél.*, 106 n.3. Dionysius also speaks of angelic movement in relation to the Good and the Beautiful in *Divine Names*, 4.8, 78. There the divine intelligences move in three ways: in a circle, in a straight line, and in a spiral. Those moving in a circle do so "while they are one with those illuminations which, without beginning and without end, emerge from the Good and the Beautiful." Richard of St. Victor, in *De arca mystica*, uses these motions in a slightly altered way to describe the movement of the human soul. The soul, in contemplation of objects, he says, moves in a straight and random line, in a circle, or in a hovering motion (*De arca* I.v). See also, Stephen Gersh, *Kinesis Akinetos: A Study of Spiritual Motion in the Philosophy of Proclus* (Leiden: E. J. Brill, 1973), 73–83; idem, *From Iamblichus to Eriugena*, 217–28 on circular activity (alternately ἐνέργεια and κίνησις in Proclus) as the representative name of the whole Neoplatonic cycle of remaining, procession, and return.

30. On the paradox of the coincidental opposites (*coincidentia oppositorum*) of stability and mobility in Christian mysticism, especially with regard to angelic "movement" in relation to God, see Chase, *Angelic Wisdom*,

xx–xxiii, 131–33; see also Dionysius, *Hiér. cél.*, 106–7 n.1. Stephen Gersh also points out the dual nature of time in Proclus, who speaks of time as immobile according to its internal activity but in motion according to the external one (Gersh, *"Per se ipsum:* The Problem of Immediate and Mediate Causation in Eriugena and His Neoplatonic Predecessors," in *Jean Scot Erigéna et l'histoire de la philosophie,* ed. René Roques [Paris, 1977], 370).

31. *Holocauste.* On this "total combustion" as a sacrificial prayer of thanksgiving, or "complete burnt offering," see Dionysius, *Hiér. cél.,* 107 n.2; as a sacrifice of appeasement, see Leviticus 1:6–9. The purifying aspect of this burning flame, signifying one of the primary "names" of the Seraphim, also echoes Eriugena's discussion of the relation of sacrifice and sanctity above.

32. The "action of contemplation" is another coincidence of opposites similar to the dialectic of motion and immobility given above.

33. The *summum bonum.*

34. That is, going higher in the hierarchy is equivalent to going inward in contemplation.

35. This is the first instance in this chapter of Eriugena explicitly linking angelic attributes, contemplative practices, or the life of holiness to the human soul. While he weaves his exposition in and out of the purely angelic realm, the reader is expected to intuit something of the possibility of human purification, illumination, and perfection in all that he says concerning the angels.

36. This equation of the seraphic attributes of fire with charity *(caritatis)* and heat with love *(amore)* is not present in Dionysius. Eriugena's equation was to have tremendous influence in the medieval period, an influence that would equate the Seraphim with love explicitly. Since the Seraphim are in the same hierarchy, yet somehow "higher" than the Cherubim, who symbolize knowledge, the affective powers of love were thus often thought to be equal to the intellective powers of mind, if not superior.

37. Eriugena, *Exp. coel.,* 95, l. 150, has *assimulatiuum* as the translation of "assimilated likeness," while *Dionysiaca* 2:838, has Eriugena's translation as *exemplativum* and Sarracenus's as *assimulatiuum.*

38. Again, Eriugena interposes the phrase "of charity" *(caritatis)* into his translation of Dionysius and will continue to equate "fire" with love or charity throughout the remainder of his commentary.

39. For an excellent discussion on the use of the metaphor of light in Eriugena as (1) a creative movement of self-manifestation of the hidden,

(2) the epistemological ascent from the darkness of unreality to the light of truth, and (3) an expression for the diffusion of all things from their causes to created effects inspired by James 1:17, see Carabine, "Eriugena's Use of the Symbolism of Light, Cloud, and Darkness in the *Periphyseon*," 141–52. Duclow also cites Eriugena, *Exp. coel.*, 13: "For God and for every rational and intellectual creature, it is not one thing to be and another to be light; nor is it one thing to be light and another to see....For them it is one and the same thing to be, to give light, and to see; for their being is light and vision." Duclow notes, "God, the angels, and humans are thus united in a reciprocal lighting and seeing" ("Isaiah Meets the Seraph," 237). On the simile of light in Proclus's system of the spirituality of motion, see Gersh, *Kinesis Akinetos*, 90–94.

    40. This Greek word, ὑπαλλαγή, literally meaning "interchange" or "exchange," is also a rhetorical figure of speech. As Eriugena uses it here, it is the rhetorical equivalent of metonymy, whereby the name of one thing is exchanged for that of another, or the use of one word for another word that it may be expected to suggest. Servius Honoratus (d. 390), in *In Vergilium commentarius*, uses the exact example from Virgil that Eriugena uses here.

    41. Eriugena had earlier occasion to use the *ars poetica* and had referred to Dionysius as a *summas rhetor* (Eriugena, *Exp. coel.*, 4, l. 272, p. 72).

    42. Virgil, *Aeneid*, III, 61. That is, *dare classibus austros*, for "dare classes austris." As a metonymy or *hypallage*, or the exchange of one word for another, one might say, "lands belonging to the *crown*," or "demand action by *city hall*." Likewise, the metonymic trope here is, "to give the *south* to the armies."

    43. Psalm 77:9, Vulgate, 76:10.

    44. In this and what immediately follows, Eriugena attempts to restore the proper relation of the signifier to the signified. As he makes explicit, the virtues or attributes signify the name.

    45. Here Eriugena refuses to separate the etymology of the name from its referent. Duclow suggests that elsewhere, in the *Periphyseon*, Eriugena does isolate the etymology from the referent, with the result that "what matters is no longer the mediating chain of the angelic command, but semantics and allegory." Grammar, rhetoric, and semantics are certainly evident here as well, but again, the refusal to separate name from referent is also at work (Duclow, "Isaiah Meets the Seraph," 239–40).

46. On the Cherubim in Greek and Latin Patristic exegesis, on their use as a trinitarian metaphor, and on their medieval use as objects of knowledge and contemplation, see Chase, *Angelic Wisdom*, 14–20, 70–90, 115–28.

47. Literally *traditionis*, in the sense of handing over, passing on, surrendering, teaching, or transmitting knowledge. In a sense it is a gift, but important within its family of meanings is the idea that "tradition" is itself a passing on of wisdom. Thus the Cherubim are filled with the wisdom of the passing on of wisdom.

48. Eriugena, for the most part, uses "contemplation" *(contemplatio)*, but on occasion uses "theoria" *(theoria)*. The translation will follow Eriugena's use, employing "contemplation" or "theoria" as he does. From Greek philosophers as early as Plato and continuing through Plotinus, and Greek theologians as early as Clement of Alexandria, *theoria* meant simply the vision of God. It came to be equated as well with divine union, contemplation, and speculation. While *praxis* meant "doing," *theoria* meant "watching," and was generally thought of as comprising two components: scientific theorizing and contemplative gazing or vision of the divine world. On *theoria* in the mystic tradition, see McGinn, *The Foundations of Mysticism*, especially 104–7, 124–25, 150–56, 178–79, 256–57.

49. Although the Cherubim also, at times, act as "thrones," Colossians 1:16 describes the Thrones as a separate order. On the thrones of God and the Cherubim as thrones, see Anne-Marie la Bonnardière, "Anima iusti sedes sapientiae dans l'oeuvre de saint Augustin," in *Epektasis: mélanges patristiques offerts au Cardinal Jean Daniélou* (Paris: Beauchesne, 1972), 111–20. On the use of the image of the thrones in Neo-Platonism and Patristic writers, see Dionysius, *Hiér. cél.*, 108 n.2.

50. Of the nine Latin translations of Dionysius's work given in *Dionysiaca*, Eriugena's is the only one to use *sedium* here instead of *thronorum*. Actually, his translation is felicitous, as *sedes* conveys in the Latin not only a seat or a place to sit but also a seat or center of emotions or particular activity, and also a dwelling place, and in particular a dwelling place of the gods.

51. Dionysius's Greek: ἐπηρμένων; Eriugena's Latin: *compactarum*. Cf. *Dionysiaca* 2:841.

52. By focusing on the metaphor of the feet of the lower orders, including earthly creatures, Eriugena is contrasting those who sit and rule (symbolized by the throne) with those who walk (as symbolized by the feet) and are ruled. In addition, the feet indicate direct contact with and

dependence upon earth; those who sit upon a throne may be raised to celestial realms.

53. At the beginning of Section 2 (text not included), Eriugena continues with his commentary on Dionysius's motif of purification, illumination/contemplation, and perfection after first reiterating that the aim of every hierarchy is to imitate God. Dionysius then proposes to explore what holy scripture reveals concerning the angelic hierarchies of Seraphim, Cherubim, and Thrones.

54. On Proclus's use of the angels dwelling in the vestibule of God, the soul dwelling in the vestibule of the *Logos*, and the physician dwelling in the vestibule of philosophy, see Dionysius, *Hiér. cél.*, 109 n.2. Dionysius speaks of the "vestibule of the Trinity" in *Divine Names*, 5.8.

55. In addition to descriptions of angels as "deiform" *(deiforma)* or "Godlike" *(deisimilito)*, Eriugena variously uses *divina, Deus,* and *Thearchia* for "God."

56. Dionysius here begins to apply the characteristic pattern of purification, illumination, and perfection that is a primary functional characteristic of both angelic and human hierarchies. Cf. Dionysius, *CH* 3.2, 154–55, on this pattern as the goal of hierarchy. Eriugena adjusts the second feature of this pattern by transposing contemplation for illumination. But as he makes clear, contemplation, at least on the angelic level, is simply the practice of recognizing, receiving, and participating in divine illuminations.

57. Eriugena is the only Latin translator to use *templum* instead of some form of *sanctus* (cf. Dionysiaca 2:846).

58. Dionysius uses ἀυτοκίνητον, Eriugena *se motu* for self-moved. On the self-moved or "ipsomotrice" in Platonic and Neo-Platonic thought, see Dionysius, *Hiér. cél.*, 110 n.2. Dionysius himself uses the circle as a model of self-motion in the notion of descent and return in *Divine Names:* "a simple self-moving power directing all things to mingle as one, that it starts out from the Good, reaches down to the lowliest creation, returns then in due order through all the stages back to the Good, and thus turns from itself and through itself and upon itself and toward itself in an everlasting circle" (*Divine Names*, 4.17).

59. That is, motion *per se*, "through itself." Eriugena uses the phrase *per se* twice in this sentence, and *ex semetipsis*, "from itself with itself," once. On the notion of autokinesis as *"per se,"* see Gersh, *"Per se ipsum,"* 367–76.

60. Eriugena here emphasizes the divine poles of motion and rest in coincidental opposition. As God is *"motus stabilis et status mobilis,"* so too are the angelic first essences that move stably around God. On the

metaphor of "hovering" as exemplifying this notion of motion and rest, both in God and in contemplation as exemplified by the Cherubim, cf. Chase, *Angelic Wisdom*, pp. xx–xxiii, 61–2; 88–91.

61. This is an allusion to Eriugena's classic definition of nature or the created world. In his masterpiece and first medieval *summa*, the *Periphyseon* (in Latin, *De divisione naturae*, or in English, *The Division of Nature*), we find an account of all reality, or nature, defined as "the general name of all things that are and those that are not" (*Periphyseon* 1 [441A], cited, for example, in McGinn, *The Growth of Mysticism*, 82–83).

62. See note 59 above on Greek and Latin equivalents of the term *autokinetic*.

63. On the human soul in Eriugena purified by grace, in order both to be returned to the ancient dignity of its nature, as here in Chapter VII, and also, so that the human soul polluted by human sin might recover the secrets of the angels, as in Chapter II of his commentary, cf. Gandillac, *"Anges et hommes,"* 399. This also serves as a reminder that, as usual, in talking here about angelic purification, Eriugena is also teaching at the same time on human purification.

64. That is, in addition to "pure," explained above, and "perfect" explained below.

65. Eriugena here wants to establish a relative equivalency between contemplation *(contemplativa)* and the art of the speculative gaze *(speculationis)*.

66. *Occulte*.

67. Thus, sensible symbols are realities grounded in scripture (tabernacle, the law, and so forth) while intellectual symbols are theophanies, the vision of truth in itself.

68. 2 Kings 5.

69. Eriugena uses *reductas* here as a translation of ἀναγομένας, having as its root to bring, lead, or take up and as its later Latin equivalent, anagogy. Eriugena's sense, more than simply a lifting up, implies a return as well as a "leading" of the contemplative through and by means of perceptible and imperceptible symbols. The leading back or taking up echoes a dominant theme within Eriugena, based on the Neo-Platonic doctrine of emanation and return, of procession and return *(processio et reditus)*. While here Eriugena's pattern involves a theophanic *processio* and symbolic *reditus*, elsewhere the return or *reditus* is explicitly christological.

70. Here, Eriugena uses *theorie*, a particularly anagogical form of contemplation.

71. In this section Eriugena elaborates on light as a metaphor of divinization. Indeed, the angels are light, the trinitarian Godhead manifests light in three Persons, and *theoria* and contemplation are flooded in light. Christ himself, the light of the world, becomes the highest intellective symbol. On the *Celestial Hierarchy* as the medieval handbook of light symbolism, documenting the connection between Eriugena and Dionysius on this metaphor of light, see Josef Koch, "Uber die Lichtsymbolik im Bereich der Philosophie und der Mystik des Mittelalters," *Studium Generale* 13 (1960): 653–70.

72. On the language of God being both "within and beyond" the created world and its capacities and the use of *superessentialis* as indicating language that is positive in form but negative in content to mark that dialectic, see McGinn, *The Growth of Mysticism*, 98ff. Eriugena's translation and naming of the first celestial hierarchy also uses this language of superessentiality: the Seraphim, Cherubim, and Thrones are *supercelestibus essentiis*.

73. On the relation of the Good and the Beautiful in Dionysius, see *Divine Names*, 2.1 and 4.7, and on the relation of divine unity and trinitarian multiplicity, see *Divine Names*, 2.1 and 13.3. It should be noted that neither Dionysius nor Eriugena speaks of the trinitarian nature of God as "three Persons" (as Gandillac, for instance, incorrectly translates Dionysius: "*manifestée* en trois *Personnes*," cf. Dionysius, *Hiér. cél.*, 111), but rather as "three lights" or "threefold luminosity," as Eriugena makes clear in his commentary.

74. Dionysius had earlier commented on the "light that surpasses every light" as a primary attribute or metaphor of the Good, itself a primary name of God. Eriugena echoes many of Dionysius's themes in this discussion on illumination, contemplation, and the cycle of emanation and return. Cf. Dionysius's discussion of light as the visible image of the Good, and the conceptual content of light applied to the Good in *Divine Names*, 4.4–6. Dionysius says, in part, "So it is with light, with this visible image of the Good. It draws and returns all things to itself, all things that see, that have motion, that are receptive of illumination and warmth, that are held together by the spreading rays."

75. As noted above, Eriugena speaks here of trinitarian nature not in terms of "persons," but of "lights." His phrase, trying three ways to describe the three lights is *ter lucens, vel ter apparens, vel, ut simpliciter transfertur, trilucea*. The word from Dionysius's text, also most simply "three appearances," is τριφανοῦς.

76. On the relation of Jesus to the angelic hierarchy, see Dionysius, *Hiér. cél.*, 111 n.4. On Dionysian Christology, see Chase, *Angelic Wisdom*, 225 n.18.

77. The philosopher Stephen R. L. Clark, in a compelling article entitled "Where Have All Angels Gone?" in *Religious Studies* 28 (1992): 221–34, points out the value of seeing angels as Plotinian *logoi* that must be united in and subordinate to the one *Logos*, and the tradition of equating angels as *logoi* with divine names and attributes. Eriugena, in following Dionysius, certainly continues the tradition of equating the nine angelic orders with divine theophanic qualities. And here the Seraphim, Cherubim, and Thrones function in the *logoi* tradition, being both subordinate to and in participatory union with Christ as divine *Logos*. But, as Clark points out and Eriugena seems to be keenly aware, angelic *logoi* in union with Christ as divine *Logos*, can serve as revelatory icons, while *logoi* outside that union can only serve as idols (see especially 228–31). On the relation of idol and icon in revelation and reason, see Jean-Luc Marion, *God Without Being*, trans. Thomas A. Carlson (Chicago: University of Chicago Press, 1991), especially ix–xv, 7–24.

78. On Neo-Platonic theurgy (θευργία) and its relation to light, see Dionysius, *Hiér. cél.*, 111–12 n.5. See also translations of Augustine in this volume, and especially, Gregory Shaw, *Theurgy and the Soul: The Neoplatonism of Iamblichus* (University Park, Pa.: The Pennsylvania State University Press, 1995).

79. On the use of this sentence as a point of entry for discussion of Eriugena's concept of deification or *theosis*, see McGinn, *The Growth of Mysticism*, 114ff.

80. Eriugena, in explaining the relation and difference in contemplation of sensible symbols as opposed to intellective symbols, has moved from the mediating contemplation of images, symbols, language, rhetoric, and so on, to the non-mediated contemplation where the "clothing" of material things, hidden things, virtues, or images of any kind do not intervene. In order to accomplish this, the contemplative being must become deiform, Godlike, not in an imitative way, but identically in nature, essence, and being. This is accomplished, for Eriugena, through the "medium" of light: the three trinitarian substances of Father, Word, and Gift are light, and the Seraphim, Cherubim, and Thrones are themselves light. Thus illumined and so deformed, the angels are free to communicate, dwell, and essentially participate in God "unfettered" by images, symbols, and cultural artifacts. But this is not the final shape of consummation: there is one

"image/thing" in which, by which, and through which even these angels participate in divinity, and that is Jesus Christ, humble in his humanity (the Seraphim, Cherubim, Thrones are themselves "first" in celestial humility) and exalted in his humanity and divinity (as the angels are likewise exalted). But again, Jesus Christ is not himself a formal likeness, not a symbol, not a "modulation in the voice" of God; Jesus Christ *is* the power of divinity and the love of humanity; he *is* the primary participant.

81. Commenting on that section of the Lord's prayer, "Thy will be done on earth as it is in heaven" (Matt 6:10), Maximus the Confessor develops a similar context and sense of our cooperation with angels. As the angels in Eriugena find their source and return to Christ as *Logos*, so Maximus finds intelligences (as *logoi*, whether angelic or human) returning to Christ: "There is only the intelligence naturally leading intelligent beings toward the source of intelligence, the Logos Himself." There, those who "worship God mystically…become in all things a co-worshipper and fellow-citizen with the angels, conforming to St. Paul's statement, 'Our citizenship is in heaven' (Phil. 3:20)…for if we imitate the heavenly angels in this way, we will find ourselves always worshipping God, behaving on earth as angels do in heaven" (cf. St. Maximus the Confessor, *On the Lord's Prayer*, in *Philokalia*, trans. G. E. H. Palmer, Philip Sherrard, and Kallistos Ware [London: Faber and Faber, 1981], 298).

82. The discussion here on the perfection of angels ought to be understood as an implicit discussion on the perfection, to the extent that it is possible, of the human soul. Throughout, Eriugena moves imperceptibly from his discussion of the purification, illumination, and perfection of angels to an analogous teaching on the same process in the human soul. Section 4 below begins to make this connection more explicit, but the connection ought to be made throughout. Dionysius himself is clear on this connection: "Everything having to do with the hierarchy of heaven, namely, the angelic purifications, the illuminations that occur beyond the cosmos, and the achievements that are a part of the perfection of the angels, all comes from the universal Cause and Source of goodness. From this Source it was given to them to exemplify the Good, to manifest that hidden goodness in themselves, to be, so to speak, the angelic messengers of the divine source, to reflect the light glowing in the inner sanctuary. Next to these sacred and holy intelligent beings are the souls, together with all the good peculiar to these souls. These too derive their being from the transcendent Good. So therefore they have intelligence, immortality, existence. *They can strive toward angelic life. By means of the angels as good*

leaders, they can be uplifted to the generous Source of all good things and, each according to his measure, they are able to have a share in the illuminations streaming out from that Source" (cf. *Divine Names*, 4.2).

83. This latter, "discipline" *(disciplina)*, should be understood somewhat as we understand "praxis" today. It was "instruction, teaching, or training," the result of which was a disciplined or ordered way of life. It also indicates a body of knowledge, a science, or a rhetorical or philosophical system. Eriugena would have had many if not all of these meanings in mind. It is *theoria* in the widest sense, contemplative knowledge and spiritual practice co-existing in the same teaching and way of life. The contemporary separation between theory and praxis loses the necessary interrelation of practice or discipline with knowledge or theory.

84. Dionysius's Greek: ἐπιστήμην; Eriugena's Latin: *scientiam* (cf. *Dionysiaca* 2:850).

85. Dionysius's Greek: ἀναλυτιήν; Eriugena's Latin: *analyticam.* Here Eriugena applies the method of procession and return at the analytical, philosophical level; in doing so in what follows, *analytica* will correspond to *reditus*, or return, while *diairetica* (division) will correspond to *processio* or procession. Earlier (see Section 1 above), he had applied the same method at the grammatical level during his discussion of the middle voice of the verb "to make holy."

86. This is not in Dionysius's text, but is brought in by Eriugena to discuss two forms of discipline as found in dialectics, or the logical method, primarily of the Academy. Eriugena's Latin translation for the method is *diaeretica*, actually a simple transliteration.

87. Thus, as Bernard McGinn notes, in Eriugena deification is "as much philosophical as it is spiritual and theological (remember that 'the true philosophy is true religion and vice versa'" [quoting D. Moran]). See McGinn, *The Growth of Mysticism*, 114.

88. Dionysius has Θεαρχίας, more properly translated as "thearchy," which Sarracenus uses in his text.

89. In this context the angels are sanctified in the sense of being "made hierarchical" as Dionysius's Greek would indicate, and as Eriugena notes elsewhere in his discussion of sanctification (see the section "On the Seraphim" above).

90. Dionysius's Greek: ἀρρεπές; Eriugena's Latin: *fortitudinem* (see *Dionysiaca* 2:851).

91. *Decorem*, which Sarracenus uses (cf. *Dionysiaca* 2:852).

92. Dionysius's Greek: εὐπρέπειαν (cf. *Dionysiaca* 2:852).

93. Dionysius's Greek: Θεμιτόν; Eriugena's Latin: *fas* (cf. *Dionysiaca* 2:852).

94. Dionysius's Greek: μυοῦνται; Eriugena's Latin: *flectuntur* (cf. *Dionysiaca* 2:852).

95. Dionysius's Greek: Τελεταρχίας; Eriugena's Latin: *perfectionis principe*. Sarracenus, in fact, translates *Teletarchia* (see *Dionysiaca* 2:852).

96. In Section 3 Eriugena continues to translate and comment on Dionysius's work. In this section Dionysius extends his discussion of the nature and function of the hierarchy and the Seraphim, Cherubim, and Thrones' place within that hierarchy as transmitters of divine understanding to the lower orders. He summarizes his ongoing discussion of the purifying, illuminating, and perfecting work of the hierarchy ("the task of every hierarchy is to receive and to pass on undiluted purification, the divine light, and the understanding that brings perfection," *Celestial Hierarchy*, VII.2) and also summarizes how the angelic essences participate in this work, and how, again, the three orders of the first hierarchy are the first to receive and be initiated (or shaped) by purifying, illuminating, and perfecting understandings of the Godhead. Gandillac, "*Anges et hommes*," p. 399, makes the case that Eriugena transposes the hierarchy as order, knowledge, and action (as defined by Dionysius, cf. *CH* 3) upon these various aspects of the Godhead, so that order is associated with purification, knowledge with illumination and contemplation, and action with perfection.

In Section 4 Eriugina explores a variety of themes associated with the Seraphim, Cherubim, and Thrones. First, he uses a series of coincidental oppositions based upon the "immobile movement" and "mobile stability" of the angels to emphasize the paradoxical relation of stillness and action in contemplation. Later, echoing Augustine, he comments on the proximity of the Seraphim, Cherubim, and Thrones to God; they circle immediately around God, he says, "without any created thing intervening" *(nulla creatura interposita)*. Angelic "union" with God is further explored as Eriugena notes that the highest celestial hierarchy is assimilated to God "by imitation of the good things in God's habits and acts." Here "habits *(habitus)* is more than just habits, customs, or practices; *habitus* includes the training in, art of, and embodiment of a life of virtue. Eriugena emphasizes that it is the first angelic hierarchy alone that is worthy to participate intimately with God by receiving the effusions and communications of God. These communications are, in turn, then passed on to the lower orders. Through contemplative comprehension and imitation of the Good reflected in God's habits and acts, the "rational and discerning soul" communes with God and shares in God's work. "Soul," by this point in Eriugena's treatise, ought to be taken as indicating both the angelic and the human soul. He is, of course, explicitly talking about angelic cooperation and communion, but the habit of the "rational or discerning soul" *(rationalis aut intellectualis animi)* is a description that does not exclude the human soul. This, together with the phrase *quantum nostre scientie, humane videlicet* at the beginning of Section 4, indicating the clear relation between human and angelic knowledge, shows something of Eriugena's intent in shifting from an explicit description of angelic purification, knowledge, contemplation, virtue, and perfection to an implicit acknowledgment of the application of these angelic insights to the human soul as well. In another theme of Section 4, Eriugena develops a theology of celestial hymns of praise or, as he says, "theodoxic *(theodochis)* blessings that flow into the heavenly intelligences." Eriugena spends some time exploring these hymns, noting that they are made manifest to humanity by two means, either (1) through sensible and perceptual images or (2) immediately without intervening image. In either case those discerning minds who receive these celestial hymns of praise, or for that matter any divine communication, also in some sense receive God (they are "God-receiving," or in Dionysius: Θεοδόχων [cf. *Dionysiaca* 2:866]. In Barbet's edition, Eriugena, *Exp. coel.*, l. 935, p. 116, the word is *Theodochis;* in *Dionysiaca* 2, the phrase is *Deum recipientibus*). Another metaphor of divine union that Eriugena uses is that of the heavenly throne. Intelligences, to the extent that they conform to God, become the "thearchic" *(thearchice)* location, as scripture says, of God's divine rest. Thus, for instance, Eriugena makes reference to the image of the cherubim on the ark of the covenant and God's sitting enthroned upon them. Cf. Psalm 80.1, Vulgate, 80:2: "You who are enthroned upon the cherubim"; Psalm 99:1, Vulgate, 99:2: "The Lord sits enthroned upon the cherubim." Isaiah 66:1 also picks up the images of throne and rest: "Heaven is my throne and the earth is my footstool; what is the house which you would build for me, and what is the place of my rest?" The image is, of course, extended to include the pure human soul, who, as Eriugena points out, also receives God and therefore becomes God's resting place. (See also John 14:23 and Dionysius, *CH*, 166 n.85, for additional biblical references. On the use of these images in the Patristic tradition, see la Bonnardiére, "Anima justi sedes sapientiae," 111–20.) Another theme of Section 4 is the process by which the first hierarchy passes its received understanding of the mystery of the Trinity to humanity. Eriugena uses the dynamic relation of the first hierarchy to God as an illustration of the relation of unity and personhood within the Trinity. Having established the correlation between the mystery of angelic proximity to God and the mystery of the Trinity itself, he goes on to say that divinity "is a monad *(monas)* or unity *(enas)* in three substances." The Seraphim, Cherubim, and Thrones are also, in their way, three "substances" in communion with divine union. The Latin here for "substances" is *substantialiter*, which refers to substance as a quality of being real or having an actual existence; it is an underlying or essential nature. This expression, "in three substances," is classic trinitarian language from Athanasius on, but this trinitarian terminology is often rendered as "in three persons," or "tri-hypostatic." Eriugena's is the only Latin translation of the nine in *Dionysiaca* to use "three substances." The other eight use "three persons." The term is a translation of τρισυπόστατος (see *Dionysiaca* 2:867). Finally, in Section 4 Eriugena teaches that the first hierarchy, in praise of divinity, also passes on an understanding of God's good providence. This "providence" (πρόνοια), is *not* divine activity or operation, that is, the whole cycle of procession and return, but rather "before intellect" (πρὸ νοῦ, *anti intellectum*). That is, providence transcends the unity of the intellect, having its source in the Good (cf. Gersh, *Kinesis Akinetos*, 93ff.). Eriugena claims that "God's providence for all extends from the most sublime celestial beings to the lowliest creatures of the earth....[It] extends into all creatures and penetrates all creatures....Or so that it might be more easily understood [God's providence], 'binds round about.'" This is the translation of the Greek participle ΠΕΡΙΔΕΔΡΑΓΜΕΝΗ, characteristically translated as "tying together," as tying the shoots of a vine or "holding together" in the hand. Thus the meaning might more clearly be: "God superessentially ties all things together as vines from a single shoot" or "God holds all things together, superessentially, as it were, in God's hand" (cf. Barbet, ed., *Exp. coel.*, 7, 4. 967–69, 981–86).

Hugh of St. Victor
Commentary on the Celestial Hierarchy of Saint Dionysius the Areopagite (According to the translation of John Scotus Eriugena)

1. The *Didascalicon* also serves as an outline for reading any "holy" literature. Hugh, in fact, uses the methods described in the *Didascalicon* to read and comment on Deny's *Celestial Hierarchy*. Thus, following his outline in the *Didascalicon*, Hugh's *Commentary* traces (1) the *littera:* not the "literal sense," but clarification using word studies, linguistic observations, etymologies, grammar, and so forth; (2) the *sensus:* a restatement or simple

311

paraphrase for the "meaning" of the text; and (3) *sententia:* the deeper meaning of the text based on allegorical, tropological, and anagogical interpretations.

2. There has been little scholarship in English on this important treatise. Important works in French on the subject include Roger Baron, "Le commentaire de la 'Hiérarchie Céleste' par Hugues de Saint-Victor," Chapter VII in *Études sur Hugues de Saint-Victor* (Paris: Desclée de Brouwer, 1964), 133–218; Jean Châtillon, "Hugues de Saint-Victor critique de Jean Scot," in *Jean Scot Érigène et l'histoire de la philosophie* (Paris: Éditions du Centre National de la Recherche Scientifique, 1977), pp. 415–31; René Roques, "Connaissance de Dieu et théologie symbolique d'aprés l' 'In hierarchiam coelestem sancti dionysii' de Hugues de Saint-Victor," Chapter II in *Structures théologique: de la Gnose á Richard de Saint-Victor: Essais et analyses critiques* (Paris: Presses Universitaires de France, 1962), 294–364.

3. A recent work on Hugh of St. Victor, for example, develops the idea of "visual exegesis" as a component of this emphasis on visual spirituality (see Patrice Sicard, *Diagrammes médiévaux et exégèse visuelle le* Libellus de formatione arche *de Hugues de Saint-Victor* [Paris: Brepols, 1993]).

4. Hugh of St. Victor, *Com. hier. coel.*, PL 175:933C–934B; see also Dionysius, *CH* 1.1.

5. Ibid., *PL* 175:941B: "*Symbolum est collatio formarum visibilium ad invisibilium demonstrationem.*"

6. Cf. *De sacramentis christianae fidei, PL* 176:342D: "*Qui contemplationem habent, rem et imagem habent.*"

7. Cf. 1 Corinthians 1:22.

8. The word used here is *speciem.* Throughout Hugh's discussion on the ability of symbols to lead one into God, he employs a variety of words that serve to describe different aspects of symbol. As he uses them, the notes will comment on the Latin word used and the shade of meaning Hugh might have intended. *Species* comprises two related word groups: (1) a seeing or look, and (2) an outward appearance, an idea or notion, a vision or likeness.

9. That is, the wisdom of the Greeks allowed them, through the ladder of the created world, to enter into the invisible things *(invisibilia)* of God, but not into the hidden things *(abscondita).* As Hugh points out, to "see" the hidden things of God requires theology of a kind not available to the "mundane philosophy" of the Greeks. Yet René Roques observes that divine revelation is required in both cases. In the case of the Greeks it is

the divine mystery of the grandeur of creation *(creatio sublimis)*; in the case of theology as Hugh develops it, the divine mystery of the humility of redemption *(redemptio humilis)*—the work of Christ—is required (see René Roques, "Connaissance de Dieu," 296–302).

10. Another word from the group connoting the nature of symbol, the word used here is *figmentorum*. This word, while in various contexts means likeness or image, has in the context of Hugh's use, a meaning of a fictive or concocted image, a fantasy creation or invention.

11. Cf. 1 Corinthians 1:20.

12. Cf. 1 Corinthians 1:23. On Hugh's distinction between the humanity of the Word and the humility of the Crucified, see Chase, *Angelic Wisdom*, 226 n.37; on wisdom as the humility of Christ, see ibid., 112–13. Also, on the life of Christ as the source and criterion of true wisdom, and on the humility of Christ teaching the wisdom of healing and teaching humility as well, see Roques, "Connaissance de Dieu," 300–301.

13. On this false wisdom or healing *(falsa sanitate)*, see Roques, "Connaissance de Dieu," 301.

14. Once again, as above, mundane philosophy can "see" the invisible things of creation but not those things, as Hugh will explain later, that are hidden to all but the humble. Here Hugh uses the secrets of nature *(secreta naturae)* and the hidden things *(abdita rerum)* of creation. That these are the hidden *things* should also be noted. For Hugh, the *res*, or thing, is the Word of God to humanity; *verbum* is simply the words of humanity. The "thing" is therefore closer to the image *(imago)* or symbol itself, being linked finally as thing and image in Christ (cf. Sicard, *Diagrammes médiévaux et exégèse visuelle*, p. 160).

15. On the arts (logic, mathematics, physics), the studia including the *trivium* (grammar, rhetoric, dialectic), and the *quadrivium* (mathematics, including arithmetic, music, geometry, and astronomy), the mechanical sciences (fabric-making, armament, commerce, agriculture, hunting, medicine, theatrics), physics, ethics, theory, and philosophy, see Hugh's *Didascalicon*, especially Book Two. Hugh endorses all of these arts and sciences, accessible by natural reason, as important and preparatory to theology.

16. *Formam rationis insitae*, that is, the innate powers of reason that govern humanity as well as creatures. They are "lower" because, for Hugh, there are "higher" powers that direct creatures, powers not governed by or observable by reason alone.

17. Hugh here begins a series of words relating to symbol that he uses in a negative way. That is, the mundane philosophers have only false images of the truth. The word for images here is *figmentorum*, used above. In the next sentence he uses *species*, outward appearance, also used above, and likeness, *simulacra*. *Simulacra* can have a positive sense as in image, likeness, or portrait. It can also have a slightly negative connotation, such as Hugh employs here, meaning phantom or imitation.

18. *Similitudo peregrina. Similitudo* is also a word from the family group of symbol. It means likeness, similarity, resemblance.

19. *Sana.* Roques notes that the adjective *sana* designates at the same time, moral health (absence of sin) and vigorous understanding (as opposed to *insanitas*) ("Connaissance de Dieu," 304 n.1).

20. *Exemplaria*, another word in the family n of symbols, meaning model, ideal, and example.

21. An aspect of Christian wisdom explored by Hugh in his *Mystical Ark of Noah* and *Moral Ark of Noah* (see *On the Six Wings of the Cherubim* in this volume for a portion of the latter text) and by Richard of St. Victor in his *Mystical Ark.*

22. *Documento.*

23. *Specie.*

24. *Simulacra errorum.* This is the clearest of many examples Hugh uses to claim that symbols or images used in an incorrect way lead not to truth but to falsehood.

25. In what follows, *simulacrum* is translated "image," and *species* is translated "outward appearance."

26. On the three eyes and the resulting visual spirituality of Hugh, see Sicard, *Diagrammes médiévaux et exégèse visuelle,* 187ff.

27. On the humanity of the Word as the wisdom of Christians, see Roques, "Connaissance de Dieu," 297–301; Chase, *Angelic Wisdom,* 112–13, 127, 226 n.37.

28. John 9:6–7.

29. Cf. John 9:35, 37. The Vulgate has *Filium Dei*, Son of God, as does Migne. The RSV, from the Greek, has "Son of Man."

30. This distinction will be expanded below to illustrate Hugh's distinction between symbols of nature and symbols of grace. Nature and the symbols of nature demonstrate or imply (from *demonstrare*) Christ, while grace and the symbols of grace illuminate Christ.

31. Cf. Sicard, *Diagrammes médiévaux et exégèse visuelle,* 241.

32. Hugh's definition of symbol is echoed here. As noted in the introduction, later in the *Commentary* he defines symbol as "a collection of visible forms to show invisible realities" (see Hugh, *Com. coel.* 941B: *"symbolum est collatio formarum visibilium ad invisibilium demonstrationem."*)

33. On *opera conditionis/opera restaurationis*, or the works respectively of creation and restoration, see Hugh's *De sacramentis*, especially the Prologue and Book One, Part One.

34. Here then, is the final form of symbol, *sacramenta*. It is available only to divine theology using the full range of the symbols of grace. Thus the full range of the symbols of grace are drawn from nature, scripture, and the sacraments.

35. It is the "ark of wisdom," mentioned above, that brings forth the unstained, *incomprehensible* truth. Cf. Richard of St. Victor, *The Mystical Ark*, IV.iv, where the cherubim symbolize and even ritualize this passage through the ark of wisdom into the secret places of divine incomprehensibility.

36. See Hugh's *Didascalicon*, II.18, where Hugh also divides the theoretical into theology, mathematics, and physics.

37. *Formas.* That is, the form, figure, shape, even beauty of an image or likeness. Hugh's definition of symbol, given above, is of a collection of these visible forms, for the demonstration of invisible things.

38. The *exemplaria gratiae*, Hugh's final variation on the family group of symbol, by which the contemplative finally sees that the highest truth or wisdom is humility, stamped upon creation by Christ.

39. Cf. 1 Corinthians 1:18–31. The entirety of Chapter 1.1, which introduces Hugh's *Commentary on the Celestial Hierarchy of Saint Dionysius*, can be seen as an extended exegetical commentary on these verses, also quoted in part at the opening of the commentary.

Alan of Lille
Treatise on the Angelic Hierarchy

1. Alan of Lille's work here is in part an attempt to visualize pagan authors as one possible alternative route to Christian truth. P. G. Walsh points out that this attempt withered in the schools under the attack of orthodox theologians but reemerged in the creative imagination and literature of the Renaissance (see P. G. Walsh, "Alan of Lille as a Renaissance Figure," in *Renaissance and Renewal in Christian History*, ed. Derek Baker [Oxford: Basil Blackwell, 1977], 117–35).

2. This work can be found in Latin in the same edition used for the translation of the *Treatise*, Marie-Thérèse d'Alverny, *Alain de Lille: textes inédits avec une introduction sur sa vie et ses oeuvres* (Paris: J. Vrin, 1965), 194–217.

3. For contemporary discussion of this issue, see the volumes edited by Steven Katz, who holds the position that there is *no* unmediated experience or intuition of God, and the volume edited by Robert Forman, who advocates the *possibility* of such an experience (Steven Katz, ed., *Mysticism and Philosophical Analysis* [Oxford: Oxford University Press, 1978]; idem, ed., *Mysticism and Religious Traditions* [Oxford: Oxford University Press, 1983]; Robert Forman, ed., *The Problem of Pure Consciousness* [Oxford: Oxford University Press, 1990]).

4. Throughout much of the literature on angelic spirituality the Seraphim, and their primary name, which is love, evoke just such a discussion of issues centered around the nature of mediated *vs.* unmediated contemplation and union. On the other hand, the Cherubim, and their primary name, which is knowledge, evoke a discussion of dialectical issues centered around the nature of similar and dissimilar symbols and apophatic and cataphatic methodologies.

5. On hierarchy as order, understanding, and activity, see Dionysius, *CH* 3.1: "In my opinion a hierarchy is a sacred order, a state of understanding, and an activity approximating as closely as possible to the divine." See also the translation and commentary of Eriugena on this passage in Eriugena, *Exp. coel.*, 3, 1, lines 5–49.

6. *Ad imaginem et similitudinem.* Cf. Genesis 1:26.

7. This definition, *sacer principatus* in the Latin, is commonly used by authors of the twelfth century (see Hugh of St. Victor, *Comm. in Hier. cael.*, *PL* 175:931).

8. Alan tells us elsewhere that at least two of these divisions are from Eriugena. See his *Summa Quoniam homines*, ed. P. Glorieux, cited in Nikolaus M. Häring, "John Scottus in Twelfth-Century Angelology," 167 n.37; the distinction is also made in Lille's *Expositio prosae de angelis*. On the possible identity of the "Eriugena" in Alan's work, see d'Alverny, *Textes inédits*, 93–95.

9. Alan describes similar divine attributes also in *Regulae theologicae*, Rule V., *PL* 210:626.

10. Cf. James 1:17.

NOTES

11. *Respiciens.* Alan uses words formed from the verb *specio*, meaning to see or observe, to regard or consider, throughout this treatise to describe the contemplative relation of the angels to the Trinity.

12. Cf. Hebrews 1:4.

13. Here, and in what follows, Alan is much closer to Dionysius's use of the angels as mediators between humanity and God than he is to Eriugena's. As was apparent in his *Commentary on the Celestial Hierarchy*, mediation based on the emanationist metaphysics of procession and return is certainly present in Eriugena's work, but so as well is a more immediate relation between persons and angels and persons and God. This latter, more immediate relation, often discussed in apophatic language, is the alternative "pole" to Eriugena's dialectical mysticism.

14. The definition given above of "hierarchy." Thus the hierarchy itself participates in this procession and returns to the one. Hierarchy also participates in the dialectic of the many in the one and the one in the many.

15. Throughout his works Alan cites Augustine, Gregory the Great, Isidore of Seville, and Bede the Venerable on the creation and nature of angels. On the celestial hierarchy itself, Alan cites Dionysius and Dionysius's commentator Eriugena. However, based on a discrepancy in the ordering of the angelic choirs in the hierarchy, and Alan's commentary on Eriugena with a consistent and creative *"liberté,"* d'Alverny claims that Alan of Lille relies more heavily on Gregory the Great than on Dionysius on matters relating to the celestial hierarchy (see d'Alverny, *Textes inédits*, 85–90, 107–8). Also on Alan's use of Eriugena and Dionysius, see Häring, "John Scottus in Twelfth-Century Angelology," 159, 161–63.

16. Alan does not follow up on the second section of this fifth point. He is very likely following Gregory the Great's interpretation of Luke 15:1–10. There, the woman (wisdom) has ten coins. She loses one (humanity) and goes in search of it while she keeps the nine (the nine orders of angels) by her side (see *Homily 34* in this volume).

17. *Caractere.* This might mean as well a branded or impressed stamp or imprint, a mark, an impression, a likeness of some form etched upon some substance. As Alan goes on to explain, an angelic order, especially the Seraphim, is a special kind of theophany, one without mediation, simple, pure, uniform, and of the "character" of its originator.

18. Häring points out that this definition is "hardly understandable" without the commentary that follows ("John Scottus in Twelfth-Century Angelology," 160). What is clear, however, is that the angelic orders are

theophanies which, in some sense, are in simple, unmediated "contact" with the divine.

19. Eriugena defines theophany simply as *dei apparitio*, a vision or appearance of God (cf. Häring, "John Scottus in Twelfth-Century Angelology," 160, 166 n.25).

20. This important phrase, *"Multiplex autem est modus vel figura videndi Deum,"* allows Alan of Lille to develop an angelic spirituality based on the various ways of seeing. Each angelic order represents a way or form of seeing God, an imprint of divine light. In their own way, people imitate these various angelic orders, thus themselves pursuing "many ways or forms of seeing God." Bernard of Clairvaux, though without the detailed metaphysics of theophany and angelic forms, develops a similar spirituality of "ways" or "paths" into God via the angels (cf. *Sermons on Psalm 90, "He Who Dwells,"* in this volume).

21. Cf. Romans 1:20.

22. As he will explain below, Lille is referring to the capacity of given bodies to "see" God with the physical or bodily eye, or to "see" God with the interior eye by means of reason. The angelic "bodies" see God by means of contemplation. These different ways of seeing, or different "eyes," were a common medieval way of speaking of the different, usually ascending, ways of seeing God. Hugh of St. Victor, for instance, spoke of the "three eyes": the eye of the flesh, by which we see those things in the world outside ourselves; the eye of reason, by which the soul sees within itself; and the eye of contemplation, by which the soul sees both what is within and what is above the self in God (see Sicard, *Diagrammes médiévaux et exégèse visuelle,* 187–88). Richard of St. Victor expanded on Hugh by suggesting the eye of the flesh; the eye of reason or the intellectual eye; the eye of understanding, seeing by means of ecstasy of mind; and the eye of faith (Chase, *Angelic Wisdom,* 148, drawing on Richard's *Mystical Ark,* III.ix, IV.xxi).

23. That is, the theophanies available to the bodily eye or to the eye of reason.

24. Daughter of Atlas, known for her beauty, wife of Meleager.

25. Son of Meleager and Atalante, one of the seven who went against Thebes.

26. Cf. Romans 1:20.

27. On the medieval distinction between the absolute power of God *(potentia Dei absoluta)* and the ordered power of God *(potentia Dei ordinata)* see Amos Funkenstein, *Theology and the Scientific Imagination: From the*

Middle Ages to the Seventeenth Century (Princeton, N.J.: Princeton University Press, 1986), 11–17, 121–24.

28. Alan is here formulating the medieval notion of the trinitarian God reflected in the natural world. As Augustine had developed the trinitarian analogy reflected in the human soul as memory, intellect, and will, so in medieval theology and spirituality is the trinitarian analogy reflected in nature as power, wisdom, and goodness. One of the best examples of this can be found in Bonaventure's *Soul's Journey into God* in *Bonaventure*, ed, Ewert Cousins (New York: Paulist Press, 1978), especially chaps. 1 and 3.

29. Cf. 1 Corinthians 13:12.

30. The word is *reciproca*, an important word for Alan, used to describe the relation of the angels to God. Not only does it indicate something of their immediate, unmediated relation, but it is also evocative of a reciprocal relation or, more precisely, a relation that echoes and reverberates with reciprocal identity.

31. That is, concerning the effect proven by the cause or the cause proven by the effect using the eclipses of sun and moon as a demonstration. Lille's point is that through divine manifestation or theophany we know God as cause, while through natural philosophy we know God only as effect. The argument is sometimes difficult to follow but is intended to lead into his discussion of the theophanic nature of angels.

32. The following definitions, attributed elsewhere by Alan to Eriugena and to Eriugena by several other twelfth-century commentators, have, according to d'Alverny and Häring, very little to do with the definitions he worked with. D'Alverny claims that they are "in conformity with neither the style nor spirit of Dionysius or Eriugena" (d'Alverny, *Textes inédits*, 95–96; cf. Häring, "John Scottus in Twelfth-Century Angelology," 161.

33. On the use of the metaphor of "angelic clothing" to describe angelic theophany, see Chase, *Angelic Wisdom*, especially chap. 6.

34. *Caritatem, scientiam, discretionem.* These in turn will be described as the ministries of the three highest angelic orders. Thus the Seraphim minister through love, the Cherubim through knowledge, the Thrones through discernment.

35. Cf. Dionysius *CH* 1.1.

36. Cf. James 1:17.

37. That is, the Hyperphany, or Dominations, Principalities, and Powers.

38. A short section follows in which Alan discusses the plural and singular forms and the gender of seraphim(n) and cherubim(n). His

319

remarks, however, contradict what he says elsewhere in *Expositio Prosae de angelis*. Of interest is his claim that when the names end in "m," as in cherubim, the reference is plural with regard to number and masculine with regard to gender; when it ends in "n," as in seraphin, the reference is plural and neuter.

39. The *viri contemplativi* (contemplatives) and the *viri claustrales* (the cloistered). Alan begins here to describe the human or ecclesial orders whose ministries are parallel to the ministries of each angelic order. The human orders are drawn into these ministries by their angelic counterpart and echo the power, wisdom, and goodness of those ministries as they are exemplified by the angels. At the same time Alan describes the *exordo* or demonic order, which likewise parallels the "loveless" ministries of evil humanity.

40. That is, the *ordo demonum inordinatus*. Recalling Alan's use of Dionysius's definition of hierarchy—knowledge, activity, order—the fallen angels imitate all the celestial hierarchies, except that they lack order. Their work is a knowledge and activity in disorder. Following Augustine, the primary inordinate characteristic of the demons is their inordinate love.

41. Alan here uses *conventus*, a medieval word often used to describe the assembly, covenant, or union of evil or demonic spirits.

42. *Sacre pagine student*. Elsewhere Alan refers to those directed by the Cherubim as the teachers or masters of holy scripture, the *magistri in sacra pagina* (see d'Alverny, *Textes inédits*, 85–106).

43. This is Alan's translation. *Hyper*, from the Greek, ὑπέρ actually has a variety of meanings. But since it is between *epi* and *hypophany*, it was translated by many of Alan's contemporaries as *inter*, between, or as *iuxta* or *medium*. It is probably most properly *super* or *supra*, over or above, but Alan's translation, *post*, after, is probably the best of the possible translations, given the context. However Häring condemns Alan for his translation. The condemnation is a bit harsh (see "John Scottus and Twelfth-Century Angelology," 160).

44. Thus, for Alan, the Epiphany is the first vision of the divinity beyond vision, while the Hyperphany, is, in a sense, the afterglow, the apparition or appearance visible after the primary vision: his phrase is *post primam visionem apparitio secunda*.

45. Alan does not give the definition of the Greek terms here as he does with Epiphany and Hyperphany. He does do so, however, in his *Exposi-*

tio prosae de angelis, where *hypo* is *sub,* under or inferior (see d'Alverny, *Expositio Prosae de angelis,* 210).

46. Alan discusses the archangels Michael, meaning "who is like God," Gabriel, meaning "the strength of God," and Raphael, meaning "the healing of God," at length in d'Alverny, *Expositio prosae de angelis,* 212–17.

Thomas Gallus
Extract on the Celestial Hierarchy

1. The Dominican scholar Gabriel Théry, who died in 1959, has been the person most responsible for the renewed interest in Gallus. Jeanne Barbet, in fact, in her article on Gallus in the *Dictionnaire de spiritualité,* calls Théry the "inventor" of Thomas Gallus (*DS* 15, "Thomas Gallus," 800). Théry said of Gallus that he "transposed into theology that which Dionysius said in philosophy. In a word—and this is our deep conviction—he Christianized Dionysius" (quoted in Rorem, *P-D,* 229 n.24). For a bibliography of Théry's work, see Barbet, "Thomas Gallus," 815. Other important scholarship on Gallus, including some of the earlier French scholarship, includes Jeanne Barbet's introduction in her critical edition of Thomas Gallus, *Commentaires du Cantiques des Cantiques,* (Paris: J. Vrin, 1967); idem, "Thomas Gallus," in *DS* 15:800–16; Daniel A. Callus, "An Unknown Commentary of Thomas Gallus on the Pseudo-Dionysian Letters," *Dominican Studies* 1 (48): 58–67; Jean Châtillon, "De Guillaume de Champeaux à Thomas Gallus: chronique d'histoire littéraire et doctrinale de l'Ecole de Saint-Victor," *Revue du moyen âge, réforme de l'eglise, spiritualité et culture* 8 (1952): 139–62, 247–73; Robert Javelet, "Thomas Gallus ou les Ecritures dans une dialectique mystique," in *L'homme devant Dieu* (Paris: Aubier, 1963), 99–110; idem, "Thomas Gallus et Richard de Saint-Victor, mystiques," *Recherches de théologie ancienne et mediévale* 29/30 (1962/1963): 206–33/88–121; Rorem, *P-D,* especially 214–19; Denys Turner, *Eros and Allegory: Medieval Exegesis of the Song of Songs* (Kalamazoo, Mich.: Cistercian Publications, 1995), especially 317–40; idem, *The Darkness of God: Negativity in Christian Mysticism* (Cambridge: Cambridge University Press, 1995); James Walsh, "Thomas Gallus et l'effort contemplatif," *Revue d'histoire de la spiritualité* 51 (1975): 17–42. Research on Gallus was also undertaken by James Walsh in an unpublished 1957 Gregorian University dissertation. Walsh also provides some excerpts of Gallus's writing in English in his introductions to *The*

Cloud of Unknowing (New York: Paulist Press, 1981) and *The Pursuit of Wisdom* (New York: Paulist Press, 1988), although they are not always well cited. Finally, Professor Bernard McGinn was kind enough to send me his chapter on Thomas Gallus, which is especially good on the relation of affect and intellect in Gallus, later published in his *The Presence of God: History of Western Christian Mysticism*, vol. 3, *The Flowing of Mysticism* (New York: Crossroad, 1998), 78–87.

2. See Denys Turner, *Eros and Allegory*, 71–73.

3. Ibid., 35–43.

4. Although the claim has been made that Hugh of St. Victor was the first Western commentator to transform Dionysius's etymology of Seraphim as "fire-makers" and "carriers of warmth" to the more affective "fire of love" (see Rorem, *P-D*, 217), it is clear from Eriugena's *Commentary on the Celestial Hierarchy* that the identification of the Seraphim with affective attributes including love and charity was made as early as the ninth century (Eriugena, *Exp. coel.*, 7).

5. These include (1) a lost first commentary from 1224, (2) a second commentary written at Vercelli in 1237–38, and (3) a third commentary written at Ivrea in 1243, the *Prologue* of which is translated in the following section in this volume. Further comments on the three commentaries can be found in the introduction to the *Prologue to the Third Commentary on the Song of Songs* in the following section.

6. Written in 1218, a surviving fragment of this *Commentum super Isaiam 6* has been edited by G. Théry, "Commentaire sur Isaïe de Thomas de Saint-Victor," *La Vie spirituelle* 47 (1936): 146–62.

7. *De septem gradibus contemplationis*, written in 1224–26, and the *Spectacula contemplationis*, written in 1243.

8. *The Explanations (Explanatio)* is currently available only in manuscript form. *The Extract (Extractio)* is available in two Latin editions (see "Note on Translation").

9. As he did with *The Explanations*, Gallus used the Latin translation of Jean Sarracenus (sometimes with the corroboration of Eriugena) for *The Extract*. Sarracenus commented on the *Celestial Hierarchy* and translated the entire corpus. For the little that is known on this twelfth-century commentator, see G. Théry, "Documents concernant Jean Sarrazin, reviseur de la traduction érigénienne du Corpus Dionysiacum," *Archives d'Histoire Doctrinale et Littéraire du Moyen Age* 18 (1951):45–87. On Sarracenus as the source of Gallus's *Extract*, see Barbet, "Thomas Gallus," 804, 812.

NOTES

10. Cf. *The Extract*, Chapter One.

11. Except for a few examples noted in the footnotes, it is left to the reader to examine the many places where Gallus's *Extract* differs from Dionysius's *Celestial Hierarchy*. The careful reader will be rewarded with numerous convergences and divergences within these two texts.

12. These chapter headings are not in Gallus's text, but are added from Dionysius, *CH*, as an aid to the reader. On the doubtful authenticity of the chapter headings, see *Pseudo-Dionysius: The Complete Works, Divine Names*, 1, 49 n.2, and *The Ecclesiastical Hierarchy* 1, 195. Additionally, none of the edited texts of the commentaries on the *Celestial Hierarchy* used for this volume employs chapter headings.

13. Cf. James 1:17. The Vulgate reads *"omne datum optimum et omne donum perfectum desursum est,"* which is usually translated "every good endowment and every perfect gift is from above." Gallus thus emphasizes the gift and blessing from above in the context of the natural order and emphasizes as well the active, ongoing perfect*ing* work of gift. James 1:17 is, of course, the scriptural entry point into the celestial hierarchy for Dionysius (cf. *CH* 1.1), and of all commentaries on his work. Bonaventure, too, uses the same verse to introduce his seraphically structured journey into God (*Itinerarium in mentis Deum*, Prologue, 1).

14. *Mens*, referring to angels or "celestial" beings, will be translated as "mind." Referring to human beings, *mens* will, for the most part, be translated as "soul." It will be translated as "mind" if the context suggests "mental" or "cognitive" activities according to contemporary usage. See Gallus's *Prologue* for a more detailed examination of *mens* and its medieval content and meaning.

15. On the theme of procession (emanation or *proodos;* here in Latin, *prodiens*), and return (conversion or *epistrophe;* here in Latin, *convertat*) described here and detailed throughout the *Celestial Hierarchy*, see Dionysius, *CH*, 145 n.4; A. Louth, *The Origins of Christian Mysticism* (Oxford: Clarendon Press, 1981), 38–40; McGinn, *The Foundations of Mysticism*, vol. 1 of *The Presence of God* (New York: Crossroad, 1994), 46–47, 58–59, 114–18, 166–70.

16. John 1:9.

17. Romans 5:2.

18. Thus, as mentioned in the introduction, according to Gallus we may be illuminated in four ways: (1) inwardly by Jesus himself; (2) by "looking upon" *(respiciamus)* the anagogical illuminations of scripture; (3) by "looking back" to the illuminations handed down by the fathers, and

(4) by contemplation of the angelic illuminations as anagogical signs. The first way, "illumination" by Jesus, is not in Dionysius. Though nested in a passive voice, it may also be a veiled reference to the more "active" devotion to the humanity of Christ as a form of illumination, which did not begin in the Latin West until at least the late eleventh century (see Ewert Cousins, "The Humanity and the Passion of Christ," in *Christian Spirituality II: High Middle Ages and Reformation*, ed. Jill Raitt [New York: Crossroad, 1987]; Giles Constable, "The Ideal of the Imitation of Christ," in *Three Studies in Medieval Religious and Social Thought* [Cambridge: Cambridge University Press, 1995], 143–248; McGinn, *The Growth of Mysticism*, 141–42, 174–77, 315–16).

19. Here the "uplifting activity" *(sursumactionem)* corresponds to the overall uplifting effect of the hierarchies through order, knowledge, and activity. Gallus details this activity through the hierarchies in Chapter Three. On Dionysius's anagogical use of symbols, see Paul Rorem, "The Uplifting Spirituality of Pseudo-Dionysius," in *Christian Spirituality: Origins to Twelfth Century*, ed. McGinn et al., vol. 16 of *World Spirituality* (New York: Crossroad, 1989), 132–51.

20. In partnership with the unifying work of the divine light, a human element is present as well in those "who are turned to it" *(ad se conversos)* and in those who are "reaching out" *(intendentes)* to it. God, or the divine light, "leads" *(duco,* and variously *reducamur, manuductione, inducat* in this chapter). There is thus a sense of personal effort in conjunction with divine action and guidance. The human effort is one of turning one's mind toward, and straining into, the guiding or leading light.

21. *Supersplendere.*

22. On the sacred envelopments or coverings as scriptural and liturgical symbols, see *Pseudo-Dionysius: The Complete Works*, 146 n.7. In this section Gallus attempts to explain the various forms of transcendent enlightenments as various accommodations to our nature.

23. In Latin, *manuductione.* On the use of symbols as the guiding hand *(manuductio)* in anagogic contemplation and as the guide of the soul's entry into the presence of God in Victorine spirituality, see Chase, *Angelic Wisdom*, chap. 3.

24. Psalm 17:15. Not in Dionysius's text, this is an insertion by Gallus.

25. In this paragraph Gallus uses a number of terms to indicate "union" with God: assimilation to God *(Dei assimilationem);* God-forming assimilation *(assimilationem deiformem);* [they are] conformed to God *(Deo conformantur).* In this chapter the *process* of that "union" is, finally, contem-

plating and imitating the highest celestial hierarchies *(contemplandum et imitandum summas caelestes hierarchias)*.

26. On the Dionysian use of hierarchy, see Dionysius, *Hiér. cél.*, xxxix–xlviii; René Roques, *L'univers Dionysien, structure hiérarchique du monde selon pseudo-Dionysius* (Paris: Aubier, 1954), 30ff. For a commentary on this chapter in Dionysius's *Celestial Hierarchy*, see Rorem, *P-D*, 57–59.

27. On human and angelic intelligences and how they are related through these hierarchical attributes of order, knowledge, and activity, see D. E. Luscombe, "Conceptions of Hierarchy Before the Thirteenth Century" in *Miscellanea Mediaevalia*, Band 12/1, pp. 1–19; and idem, "Thomas Aquinas and Conceptions of Hierarchy in the Thirteenth Century," in *Thomas von Aquin: Werk und Wirkung im Licht Neuerer Forschungen*, ed. A. Zimmermann (Berlin: Walter de Gruyter, 1988), 261–77.

28. Gallus does not use *dissimilitudo* (the negative form of similarity, or *similitudo*), as might be expected from Dionysius's other commentators, but rather *omni non se decente*, a cleansing of all that is not becoming or decent with respect to God.

29. Throughout this paragraph, Gallus has used cataphatic language emphasizing light mysticism as the anagogic route to God. Unlike what would be expected from Eriugena, other Victorines, Bonaventure, and especially Dionysius himself, Gallus uses *no* apophatic language to this point.

30. The goal in Dionysius, assimilation and union, is to be found as well here in Gallus. But note the important additions in Gallus of an affective element, "desires" *(desiderans)*, which is not present in Dionysius. As mentioned here, and earlier in Chapter One, contemplation, anagogical illuminations of scripture, and the inward work of Jesus are the routes to this assimilation and union. On the goal of assimilation and union in Dionysius see Dionysius, *Hiér. cél.*, 88 n.1.

31. Cf. Wisdom of Solomon 7:26; See also 2 Corinthians 3:18.

32. *Radii principalis et thearchici luminis.*

33. As a present participle, *deificante*, the implication is that deification is here an ongoing process.

34. Cf. 1 Corinthians 3:9; 1 Thessalonians 3:2.

35. 1 Corinthians 3:9. Gallus uses two terms in this paragraph to indicate that hierarchical participants with God are in fact "co-workers" with God. Here he uses *adjutores* from the Vulgate, and above *cooperatricem*.

36. On the origins of the triadic notion of purgation, illumination, and union, see Andrew Louth, *The Origins of the Christian Mystical Tradition*, 44–47, 66–74, 87–97, 108–13.

37. Gallus here manages to hold affective desiring and intellective knowledge in tension, a tension that leads finally to perfection in wisdom. In the process of illumination the soul is uplifted by understanding *(intellectibus)* through desiring *(desiderantibus)* while holding firm to contemplation. While in the process of perfection, it is necessary that the soul be led across *(transductos)* to perfection in knowledge *(scientiae)*, leading finally to the soul's experiencing the taste of profound, intimate Wisdom *(experientis intimae gustum sapientiae)*. Richard of St. Victor had laid the groundwork for the hierarchical and angelic contemplation leading to the kind of wisdom Gallus describes here. For Richard, wisdom is a container of both affective and cognitive elements, and accessible in an explicit form of angelic contemplation that he teaches. See Chase, *Angelic Wisdom*, 72–73, 87–88, 90–95.

38. *Supersubstantialiter.*

39. In Latin, *spirando*, in the sense of "breathing," "living," "manifesting," and thus, the "living breath" or "breath of life." Gallus's description of the Spirit as the breath between the Father and Son is reminiscent of Richard of St. Victor's description of the Spirit as the love between the Father and Son (see Richard's *De Trinitate*, Book III).

40. On the three triads that make up the celestial hierarchy, see Dionysius, *Hiér. cél.*, xlviii–lvii. For a contemporary commentary on this chapter, see Rorem, *P-D*, 62–63.

41. Gallus here gives the credit for the three groupings of three to Paul, as he naturally would, assuming Dionysius to have been a follower of Paul. Dionysius himself refers only to his own "sacred initiator," whom most have assumed to be Hierotheus. See Dionysius, *CH*, 160 n.68. In any case, the triadic arrangement of the nine names is not scriptural.

42. For brief contemporary commentaries on Chapter Eight, see Dionysius, *Hiér. cél.*, lii–lv; Rorem, *P-D*, 65–66.

43. In Latin, *dominationes, virtutes et potestates*, which will be translated throughout as Dominions, Virtues, and Powers. In Chapter Six the Powers come first, followed by the Dominions and Virtues. The standard order described in this chapter is also used in Chapter Nine. Note the translation in *Pseudo-Dionysius: The Complete Works, Celestial Hierarchy*, Chapter Eight, is Dominions (Κυριότητες), Powers (Δυνάμεις), Authorities ('Εξουσίαι). See Dionysius, *Hiér. cél.*, 121–22 n.2, for a justification

for translating δυνάμεις as "Virtues." Gallus was, of course, already working under the assumptions of that justification: the Latin translation of δυνάμεις, which he was using for his *Extractio* was *virtus*. On the Dominions, Virtues, and Powers of the second triad of the hierarchy, see Ephesians 1:21; 3:10; Colossians 1:6; 2:10; 1 Peter 3:22; Romans 8:38.

44. This paragraph is notable again for its lack of "dissimilar," apophatic language. Also of note are the three verbs at the end of the paragraph used to describe the relation of the angelic Dominions to God: fashion (or mold), converted, participate *(informant, convertuntur, participant)*. Gallus is here working with a variation of the dynamic of the growth of mystic consciousness depicted within the celestial hierarchy itself as purgation (fashion), illumination (conversion), and perfection (participation).

45. *Virtus*, which Gallus uses here for the "Virtues." He uses *Potestas* for the "Powers." Both are translated here according to Gallus's usage. Normally, *virtus* would be translated as "power," but it also carries the sense of *worth, value, goodness, moral perfection* and hence *"virtue."* *Potestas* would also normally be translated as "power," but it also carries the sense of *political power, dominion, rule, sovereignty, authority* and hence would be appropriate to the function of the angelic Powers.

46. Here Dionysius's "things of God" *(τα Θεια)* is expanded and specified in Gallus to include "knowledge, love, and imitation of God" *(Dei cognitionem, amorem, et imitationem)*. Here, as elsewhere, Gallus expands the nature of the anagogic ascent beyond Dionysius's uplifting use of intellect and liturgical symbols to include both an affective component and a component based on virtue or ethic (imitation). It is thus clear here, in Gallus, that by the end of the twelfth century the incorporation of angels as models into the devotional and spiritual life had grown to include ethical, affective, and intellective components.

47. Gallus teaches here, on the one hand, complete knowledge of salvation in the person of Jesus Christ available to the first hearers of Jesus' words, and on the other hand, complete knowledge of God as illuminating first principle available to the first, unmediated celestial orders (particularly the Seraphim, but also the Cherubim and Thrones). He is a bit unclear as to whether the first apostles, with the first celestial orders, also have complete knowledge of God, or conversely, whether the first celestial orders also have complete knowledge of the person and work of Christ. But the implication is that they do; his explicit point is that both angelic and human orders, operating on the basis of mediated understanding, pass

on or hand down their most illuminating knowledge to other beings, whether human or angel.

48. Cf. Zechariah 1:3.

49. Zechariah 1:13.

50. Zechariah 2:4. Gallus gives an example of what he had spoken of above: that the higher orders pass what they have received without mediation to the lower orders by means of mediation. For Gallus, the angel who speaks with God and receives comforting words for Jerusalem is not the same angel who passes this on to Zechariah. The first angel mediates the words of God to the second, who passes the message on to Zechariah, who in turn passes the words on to the captives of Babylon. On this hierarchical transmission of the divine message, cf. Dionysius, *Hiér. cél.*, 124–25 n.2. On the difficulties raised by this hierarchical understanding, see Dionysius's own comments in Chapter Thirteen of the *Celestial Hierarchy*.

51. Ezekiel 9:1–3; 10:1–8.

52. Ezekiel 9:2.

53. The Greek letter T. That is, for Gallus, the sign of the cross.

54. That is, *"do not overlook anyone."*

55. Ezekiel 9:5–6.

56. That is, Gabriel; cf. Luke 1:26–38.

57. Daniel 9:21–23. On the importance of Daniel in the history of angelology, see Dionysius, *Hiér. cél.*, 126 n.3, 127 n.3.

58. On the fire or wisdom of God shining forth from the midst of the cherubim *(in medio cherubin)*, see Richard of St. Victor's interpretation of the two cherubim atop the ark of the covenant in Exodus 25 in his *De arca mystica*, and Chase, *Angelic Wisdom*, chap. 4.

59. Ezekiel 10:1–8; see also 9:1–3.

60. Daniel 8:16–17.

61. For a commentary on this chapter, see Rorem, *P-D*, 68. J. Barbet notes that on the basis of his work on this chapter, Gallus developed a "hierarchy of the soul" in which the soul is structured ontologically according to the three orders of three hierarchies and based upon the nine angelic orders. Thus the virtues and powers of the soul are cast to resemble the angelic orders. Cf. Barbet, "Thomas Gallus," 806.

62. Here Gallus, following Dionysius, establishes one of the most basic *coincidentia oppositorum* in anagogic literature, that of the hiddenness yet revelatory clarity of divine illumination. The angelic orders, of course, participate in both hiddenness (incomprehensibility, invisibility, darkness) and brightness (visibility, light, revelation).

63. Gallus clearly extends his conception of the hidden and revealed nature of God beyond that of Dionysius. In Gallus, God is hidden because, paradoxically, God's illuminations are so intimate *(magis intima)* that, in a sense, they blind one's sight. This "intimacy" is a relational aspect of Gallus's spirituality not brought out in Dionysius. And though Dionysius does employ the emanationist metaphysics common to Neo-Platonism, Gallus focuses on the overflowing fountain-fullness of the Godhead, noting that God's clarity and emanating *(emanente)* illuminations have been poured out *(effusa)* through the celestial souls into our own human hierarchy, as noted in what follows.

64. On the motion of divine intelligences (angelic and human) around God see Dionysius's *Divine Names*, 4.8. With reference to God, the intelligences may move in a circle, a straight line, or a spiral. Richard of St. Victor uses three slightly altered patterns of motion to describe bird flight, ways of human thinking, and forms of angelic contemplation: linear, circular, hovering. Bird flight (the natural world), thinking (human reason), and contemplation (angelic knowledge) are thus united by these patterns of motion and are considered by Richard to be each in its way patterns representative of divine realities (cf. Richard of St. Victor, *De arca mystica*, I, i; v; xii).

65. *Virtutes.* See note 45 above for the explanation for translating *virtus* as "virtue" and *potestas* as "power." *Virtus* is translated as "virtue" throughout this chapter.

66. Isaiah 6:3: "And one called to another and said, 'Holy, Holy, Holy is the Lord of Hosts, the whole earth is full of God's glory.'"

67. *Mens* in both cases. See note 14.

68. Isaiah 6:1. This tantalizing bit of autobiography is, of course, not in Dionysius's text.

69. The previous chapter, Chapter Eleven, raises an exegetical difficulty. It asks why it is that all heavenly beings are called "heavenly powers (or hosts)" (cf. Dan. 3:61; Ps 24:10; 46:11; 103:21) in common, when one angelic order is named "power" in particular. For commentary on this issue, see Dionysius, *Hiér. cél.*, 142–43 n.2, and Rorem, *P-D*, 68–69. Chapter Twelve addresses a second exegetical difficulty. For a commentary on Chapter 12 see Rorem, *P-D*, 69–70.

70. Cf. Malachi 2:7 (LXX). Following the Greek Septuagint, the same word—*angelus*—is used for "angel" and "messenger." Gallus is thus asking how a member of the human hierarchy, which is lower than the celestial hierarchy, can be called by the name from the higher hierarchy.

71. In interpreting this passage from Malachi 2, which appears to Dionysius and Gallus to indicate that Levi is an "angel of the Lord," the authors are exploring the general question of deification and the possible similarity in deification of human and angelic natures. For an excellent discussion of differences and similarities in Dionysius and Eriugena, reflected here in Gallus, concerning the possibility of the deification of human nature by becoming co-rational and co-equal with angelic nature *(corrationabilem et coequalem angelice nature)*, see Maurice de Gandillac, "Angels et hommes dans le commentaire de Jean Scot sur la 'Hiérarchie Céleste,' in *Jean Scot Erigène et l'histoire de la philosophe* (Paris: Editions du centre national de la recherche scientifique, 1977), 393–403, especially 397–99.

72. This principle was noted earlier in Chapter Five of the *Extractio*. Where Dionysius focuses on the relative "intensity" of participation by divine minds in the light from the Father—the higher orders participating more directly in the various divine attributes, the lower participating but in an ever more "reflected" way—Gallus adds gazing back upon *(respectu)* and imitation *(imitatio*, cf. also Chapter Nine) as primary modes of this participation.

73. From Malachi 2:7, Levi and the priests who follow his example.

74. See Genesis 32:28–30; Psalms 82:1; 95:3.

75. Exodus 4:16 (Aaron); Exodus 7:1 (Moses); cf. Psalms 45:6; 82:6.

76. Here again, Gallus expresses a coincidence of opposites not present in Dionysius *(ad divinas ipsius illuminationes incomprehensibiliter extenduntur)*. Dionysius speaks only of Divinity's divine enlightenments, not, as in Gallus, their illuminating incomprehensibility. Richard of St. Victor, writing on the Cherubim as objects of contemplation, also makes extensive use of the revelatory (illuminating) nature of entering the "secret places of divine incomprehensibility" (cf. *De arca mystica* IV.vi; I.iv, x; IV.xvii, xviii).

77. Daniel 7:10. On the exegetical tradition that makes a distinction between the superior angelic orders that wait upon and contemplate God and the inferior yet more numerous angels that stand before God to accomplish God's will, see Dionysius, *Hiér. cél.*, 162 n.2.

78. Since the Latin language of the time had no name for a number larger than 1,000 (e.g., no word for "million"), anything greater must be a multiple of it.

NOTES

Thomas Gallus
Prologue to the Third Commentary on the Song of Songs

1.   The *First Commentary on the Song of Songs*, dated in later works of Thomas Gallus's as having been written in 1224, is available only in fragments. The anonymous treatise *Dieformis animae gemitus* had been thought, until quite recently, to have been this *First Commentary*. Jeanne Barbet has concluded that this treatise is definitely not the work of Gallus: "Nous ne partageons absolument pas leur (G. Théry and Dom Bernard Pex) conviction. Selon nous, *D[ieformis] a[nimae]* ne peut pas être une oeuvre de Thomas Gallus et nous allons essayer de le montrer." Cf. Abbas Vercellensis (Ps. Thomas Gallus), *Le Commentaire du Cantique des Cantiques "Dieformis animae gemitus,"* Etude d'authenticité et édition critique par Jeanne Barbet, Publications de la Sorbonne, Série "Documents," 21 (Paris: Bétrice-Nauwelaerts, 1972), 5–6, 57–70. The *Second Commentary on the Song of Songs* was composed by Gallus between 1237 and 1238, and the *Third Commentary on the Song of Songs*, of which this Prologue is a part, was written in 1243. In addition to the text, the critical edition contains chronology of texts, manuscript, and doctrinal information on the commentaries (see Gallus, *Com. Cant.*).

2.   Song of Songs 1:2.

3.   The really extraordinary thing about Gallus in this work is his ability to combine the apophatic, speculative tradition of *intellectus*, the more linguistically cataphatic, imagistic tradition of *affectus*, and the angelic, devotional tradition of *contemplatio*. Cherubic contemplation represents *intellectus* and seraphic contemplation represents *affectus*, but in Gallus the categories interpenetrate: the height of intellective contemplation is regulated by *attracti*, a category of affect, the *apex affectus* is informed by *excessus*, a category of intellect. Gallus says, "The intellect does not pass beyond touch or a simple surface contact with the divine." This indicates that the intellect encounters God but is not united with God. The affective portion of the soul, however, is fully united with God (see *Prologue*, Y, Z).

4.   Throughout most of this translation, *affectus* will be rendered as "affect." It is often translated in works from this period as "love," which is certainly not wrong. But Gallus has much more in mind with *affectus* than the word "love" has for us today. For Gallus, *affectus* would include meanings that shade into what we would call "feelings," "perceptions," "sensations," as well as "love." In a similar way Gallus uses the word *mens* to

331

indicate much more than what, today, we would call "mind" (see "Translation of *Mens*," 240).

5. Sections of the *Prologue* are lettered from A to Z. The letters, though not present in all the existing manuscripts, have been retained in the critical edition.

6. What Gallus describes as the apex of the affections had been described earlier by both Cassian and William of St. Thierry as the principal affection, which alone is capable of union with God. On Gallus, Cassian *(principale cordis)*, and William's *(principale mentis)* use of these terms, see *The Pursuit of Wisdom: And Other Works by the Author of The Cloud of Unknowing*, trans. by James Walsh, S.J. (New York: Paulist Press, 1988), 66–67; 85 nn.59–60. The prevailing Scholastic tendency was not to make a distinction between *synderesis* and *scintilla* (see Aquinas, *De Veritate*, 17, a. 2, ad 3., cited in James Walsh, "Thomas Gallus et l'effort contemplatif,": *Revue d'histoire de la spiritualité* 51 [1975]: 36 n.62. See also Bonaventure, *Itinerarium*, 1.6: "[Parallel to the six stages of ascent to God are the six stages in the powers of the soul]...the senses, imagination, reason, understanding, intelligence, and the summit of the mind or spark or conscience [*apex mentis seu synderesis scintilla*])." The terms are related, but Gallus does seem to make a distinction. He does not give a direct definition of *synderesis*, but he places it in opposition to the "inferior" part of the soul, *ratio*, and in the context of the order of the Dominations, relates it to *ratio superior* which encompasses the apex or highest spark *(apices)* of the intellect. In his *Commentary on Isaiah 6, 1–4*, and the end of Chapter Ten of the *Explicatio* on the *Celestial Hierarchy*, both of which comment on the order of the Dominions, Gallus says on *synderesis:* "Sextus continet imperia liberi arbitrii, et inflexibiliter precipit in illam eternam plenitudinem totis viribus tendi. Unde et ipsam synderesim tota virtute ad eius suscepcionem expandit et suspendit." (The sixth order of Dominations encompass the commandments of the free will, and the order ordains, inflexibly, a movement of all of its forces toward the eternal plenitude. It therefore expands and suspends itself with all its power in order to receive the *synderesis* itself.) Cited in Walsh, *"Thomas Gallus et l'effort contemplatif,"* 35.

7. Cf. Chase, *Angelic Wisdom*, chap. 5.

8. Cf. Bonaventure, *Itinerarium*, 1.1, 1.6, 4.4, 7.6.

9. Cited in Walsh, *The Pursuit of Wisdom*, 189–90, from Gallus's first *Commentary* on the Canticles.

10. Jeremiah 9:24. Gallus uses this verse to discuss two ways of understanding God: *scire* and *nosse*. In the verse and in what follows, *scire* is

translated as "understands" and *nosse* as "knows." The first describes the knowledge of God as "intellectual" *(intellectus)* understanding, the second as "beyond intellectual" or affective *(affectus)* understanding (cf. Barbet's comments in Gallus, *Com. Cant*, 44). Though Gallus spends some time distinguishing between the two, it might be helpful initially to think of *nosse* as affective knowledge, knowledge that is practical, personal, experiential, of the heart and, as he says in *Prologue*, W, of the "bone." *Scire*, for the moment, can be linked to *mens* or mind. Indeed, *scire* from *scio* is to know in the sense of being cognizant of something by way of reason, while *nosse* from *nosco* is to know in the sense of becoming personally acquainted with, to learn the character of something, to become familiar with through practical experience.

11. *Intellectus*. On the use of this word in Gallus see Robert Javelet, "Thomas Gallus ou les écritures dans une dialectique mystique," in *L'homme devant Dieu: mélanges offerts au Pére Henri de Lubac* (Paris: Aubier, 1963), 99–100. On the larger category of *mens* used by Gallus in this work, a category that includes *intellectus*, see "Translation of *Mens*," 240 above.

12. "Master Hugh" is Hugh of St. Victor. Before moving to Vercelli, Gallus had been a canon at St. Victor in Paris as well, and can be considered a third-generation heir in the contemplative tradition at St. Victor, which extended from Hugh to Richard of St. Victor. Hugh of St. Victor's exposition on Ecclesiastes, *In Salomonis Ecclesiasten, Homiliae XIX, Homilia Primus*, can be found in *PL* 175:115C–133C. Hugh says there that "there are two kinds of contemplation. One, which comes first, is contemplation through consideration of the created world. The second, which follows the first and perfects it, is contemplation of the Creator. In Proverbs Solomon advances toward meditation. In Ecclesiastes he ascends to the first kind of contemplation. In the Song of Songs he is transported to the highest realms of contemplation" *(PL*:117B; see also *Homilia XI, PL*:183A–190C). Hugh of St. Victor also describes these two forms of knowledge as mundane theology *(mundana theologia)*, describing *scire*, and divine theology *(divina theologia)*, roughly equivalent to *nosse* in his *Commentary on the Celestial Hierarchy*, 1.1, in this volume. On the abbey of St. Victor in Paris during the twelfth through the fourteenth centuries, see Steven Chase, "Into the Secret Places of Divine Incomprehensibility: The Symbol of the Cherubim in *De arca mystica* of Richard of St. Victor" (Ph.D. dissertation, Fordham University, 1994), Appendix A, pp. 289–94.

13. Romans 1:20.

14. *Artifex. Artifex* is also used below in *Prologue*, Q, to describe the three spiritual arts practiced in the Song of Songs by which the contemplative soul may rest in God. These practices are most holy and pure prayers, a naked spirit, and the capacity to adapt to union. Gallus elaborates on these three in *Prologue*, R–T. Thus in Solomon, who according to Gallus teaches the practical aspects of mystical theology (cf. *Prologue*, B), we encounter not only the Craftsman who creates those things by which we might see the Good, but also the crafts by which the Good might be sought.

15. Wisdom of Solomon 13:1. "To know" here is *intelligere*, the kind of understanding related to *scire*.

16. Wisdom of Solomon 13:5.

17. Cf. *Dionysiaca* 1:642 and *Letter Nine* 2:284 in *Pseudo-Dionysius: The Complete Works*. [English citations of Dionysius's work are hereafter given by page number from this volume.] For a discussion of this letter, see Ronald F. Hathaway, *Hierarchy and the Definition of Order in the Letters of Pseudo-Dionysius* (The Hague: Martinus Nijhoff, 1969), 104–25, and Rorem, *P–D*, 24–27.

18. Sarracenus: "exemplarium." Eriugena: "paradigmatum." Dionysius: "παραδειγμάτων." *Dionysiaca* 1:403.

19. *Divine Names*, 7.3., p. 108. *Dionysiaca* 1:402–3.

20. Javelet points out that in *Explanacio domini Thome super misticam theologiam* (*Explanations on the Mystical Theology*), Ms Vienne 695, f. 83 rb, Gallus also refers to knowledge by *intellectus* as enigmatic, in some sense "dark," and that "in its own gentleness and sweetness only *affectus* unites one to God" (Javelet, "Thomas Gallus ou les Ecritures dans une dialectique mystique," 109).

21. Romans 1:19.

22. That is, *per ignorantiam cognita*. Often translated as "unknowing," it is an ignorant knowledge, a dark knowledge, a knowledge through lack of knowledge.

23. Cf. *Dionysiaca* 1:406 and *Divine Names*, 7.3, p. 109. This passage should be read in the context of the negative theology of Dionysius's *Mystical Theology* 1–5 and *Celestial Hierarchy* 2. Cf. *Pseudo-Dionysius: The Complete Works*, 109 n.211. Much of this passage from Dionysius is cited as well in *The Cloud of Unknowing*, chap. 70.

24. James 3:17. Neither the major Greek texts nor the Vulgate contains "of the Christians." The term is used, however, in Sarracenus's Latin translations of Dionysius's *Mystical Theology* 1.1 describing the Trinity as

the wisdom and guide of the Christians (see *Dionysiaca* 1:565, *"sapientiae Christianorum"*). Gallus, of course, uses the Sarracenus translation and in fact quotes *The Mystical Theology* in *Prologue*, S. The wisdom, as James 3:17–18 describes it, is "pure, peaceable, gentle, open to reason, full of mercy and good fruits, without uncertainty or insincerity."

25. James 1:17. Dionysius's *Celestial Hierarchy* begins with this verse, as do all medieval commentaries on the *Celestial Hierarchy*.

26. Cf. 1 Corinthians 2:9.

27. Wisdom of Solomon 9:10. The primary method of *ascent*, as we shall see in Gallus beginning with *Prologue*, E, is the apophatic *intellectus*. Wisdom of the heart, or *affectus*, *descends* from the throne of God by grace alone *(sola gratia)*. Apophatic languages of denial provide a method of ascent to an ineffable *God* (not the ineffability of subjective experience). This is the method of Gallus's *scire*, which leads as high as the level of angelic Dominions and into the lower levels of the angelic Cherubim, but not beyond. At the level of the Cherubim and Seraphim (cf. *Prologue*, M, N), Gallus merges the method of anagogic and apophatic ascent with the affective tradition of divine attraction, desire, and love. At this point the doctrine of divine ineffability recedes, as the doctrine of divine grace comes to the fore.

28. 1 Corinthians 2:6–11. On Gallus's application of the Holy Spirit's work in uniting this superintellectual wisdom to the "mature" Christian, see Barbet's comments in Gallus, *Comm. Cant.*, 45. See also *Prologue*, V, where Gallus makes explicit the fact that the unifying work of *nosse* is the work of the Spirit.

29. Gallus is presumably referring to both the *Extract* and *Explanation*. On dates and nature of these works, see the introduction to the section of the *Extract* contained in this volume.

30. On Dionysius's theoretical and Solomon's practical interpretation of the wisdom of mystical theology as interpreted by Dionysius, see Barbet in Gallus, *Com. Cant.*, 45–46. As James Walsh points out, this practical/theoretical distinction, or active/contemplative distinction, as it was also referred to in the medieval period, is linked to the two ways to knowing God. That is, theoretical knowledge is linked to intellectual knowledge or *scire*, while practical knowledge is linked to superintellectual knowledge or *nosse* (Walsh, "Thomas Gallus et l'effort contemplatif," 19).

31. The *Celestial Hierarchy*, 10.3, p. 174. *Dionysiaca* 2:923–4. Gallus comments additionally on this important passage from Dionysius in his *Explanatio*: "After having treated of the three angelic hierarchies and on the

three orders within each of the hierarchies, Dionysius goes on to speak of a profound mystery, a mystery worthy of being examined very attentively by mortal men and women: that these distinct hierarchies and orders are all to be found in every spirit, angelic or human" (cited in Latin in Walsh, "Thomas Gallus et l'effort contemplatif," 22 n.17, from *Explanatio, CH* 10).

32. In the same manner, as Dionysius makes clear above, there are within the hierarchical soul three hierarchies, each with three orders arranged in kind according to the angelic distribution. Note that Gallus begins from the lowest order, moving from the Angels to the Seraphim, while Dionysius begins with the highest, moving from the Seraphim to the Angels.

33. On Gallus's *Commentary on Isaiah*, his earliest known writing, written in 1218, see *DS* 15:802–3; G. Théry, ed., "Commentaire sur Isaïe de Thomas de Saint-Victor," *La Vie spirituelle* 47 (1936): 151–62; Walsh, "Thomas Gallus et l'effort contemplatif," 23 n.20; Barbet, in Dionysius, *Com. Cant.*, 167, pp. 57, 66–67. Gallus first develops his idea of a correspondence between the hierarchies of the soul and the hierarchies of the angels in the *Commentary on Isaiah*. He also used the commentary to develop his notion of *scintilla synderesis* (see *Prologue*, Y) as the highest affective part of the soul by which and through which the soul is united to God. As such, the *scintilla* came to be associated with the Seraphim. Gallus also relates the hierarchies of the soul to the angelic hierarchies in his short work *The Mirror of Contemplation (Speculum contemplationis)*, in which he refers directly to Richard of St. Victor's teaching in *De arca mystica* on the first four objects of contemplation (see *DS* 15:804–5).

34. Isaiah 6:1. This same verse opens the first section of *On the Six Wings of the Cherubim* by Hugh of St. Victor. *On the Six Wings* is a tropological exegesis of the Isaiah passage, and as such presents a practical application of scripture, just as Gallus claims that Solomon's Song of Songs is a practical expression of mystical theology.

35. On possible reasons for Gallus's use of Dionysius and Isaiah in this portion of his commentary on the Song of Songs see Barbet in Dionysius, *Com. Cant.*, 47–48. Barbet suggests that the Song of Songs, being a dialogue between the soul and God, or the Lover and Beloved, can best be commented upon by a "commentary in dialogue." Thus, echoing the dialogue between the Lover and Beloved, Gallus is in dialogue with Dionysius. It is through such a dialogue between the Bride and Bridegroom (mirrored in a sense between Dionysius as the "word" and Gallus as the commentator) that the soul is made hierarchical. Gallus is explicit in what

follows that the "hierarchy of the soul" traces the hierarchy of the angels, just as he is implicit that the soul in dialogue with the angels is the "kiss" between the soul and Christ (see *Prologue*, U-Z).

36. This is the first of numerous uses by Gallus of the term *excessu mentis*. From ἐχστάσις, *excessus* is found in the Vulgate as *excessus mentis* at Psalms 30:23; 67:28; IV Esdras 5:33; and as *excessus* at Psalm 115:11; IV Esdras 11:5. It was used often from the time of Ambrose to denote rapture, stupor, or ecstasy of the senses, spirit, or mind. It also had the connotation of excess, immoderation, even transgression or sin. It carried as well the implication of a vision or appearance, even a trance. Finally, it indicated a departure from this life, a death. Gallus would have been aware of Richard of St. Victor's use of *excessu mentis*, by which he describes the sixth and final level of contemplation (see, for instance, *De arca mystica*, V). *Excessu mentis* carried the weight of most if not all of the meanings listed above, but the implication of a "higher state" encountered while "standing outside the mind" is particularly appropriate to Gallus. Gallus himself contrasts the *mens sobria* of the angelic Dominations to the *mentis excessum* of the angelic Thrones, thus highlighting a sense of sobriety *vs.* intoxication as well. In the silence of the *ek-static* intellect, the soul in *excessu mentis* is receptive to the descent of God through grace, whereby the affective orders of the soul are activated. *Excessus* is also a way of indicating the transcendence of God. But this transcendence must also be understood as fecundity. For Gallus, the affective element of the soul that participates most fully in the reality of both transcendence and divine fecundity will be encountered in the Seraphim, where the theoretical and practical aspects of his mystical theology come together in a kiss.

37. Thus first, *sola natura*, middle, *natura et gratia*, highest, *sola gratia*. Bonaventure, in *Itinerarium*, 4.4, likewise comments on the relation of nature and grace in the angelic hierarchy of the soul. Dionysius, Gallus, and Bonaventure also key one of the classic models of spiritual progression—purification, illumination, perfection—to the lower, middle, and higher hierarchies: Angels, Archangels, and Virtues participate in purification; Powers, Principalities, and Dominions in illumination; Thrones, Cherubim, and Seraphim in perfection. In Gallus's teaching the first two hierarchies extend and suspend the intellective powers, while the final hierarchy moves from this extension to the apex of the affective powers.

38. That is, that first hierarchy which in turn illuminates our nature. Gallus here assimilates and modifies the Latin tradition that sees the celestial hierarchy as representing various divine theophanies and human spiritual

paths. The same Latin tradition finds an analogue in the celestial hierarchy to the soul. The function of the angelic orders vary according to commentator, so that in each case a correlation is made on the basis of the angelic "name" rather than its place in the order. Thus, for instance, Dionysius in the *Celestial Hierarchy* says that the Angels give revelation to the world. Gregory the Great, *Homily 34*, says that the Angels' ministry is to give comfort to humanity and announce messages; their spiritual path is to give what little they have to others. Bonaventure, *Itinerarium*, 4.4, and Bernard of Clairvaux, *On Consideration*, V.5.12, say that in the soul marked by announcing, God assists in the Angels as piety. And Alan of Lille's, *Treatise on the Celestial Hierarchy* notes that the gifts of the "Angels," Archangels, and Virtues are knowledge of and participation in God, that the Angels announce minor messages, and that their spiritual path is to assist humanity in diverse hardships. On correlations made by various other writers between angelic orders and their respective ministries, see "Spiritual Paths" in the General Introduction.

39. The Latin for this important term is *affectus*. The relation between "intellect" and "affect" was written of and debated throughout the period covered by the writers in this volume on angels. In the majority of cases *affectus* will be translated as "affect," though an alternate translation preferred by some is "love." See note 4 above.

40. Corresponding to each of the nine orders of angels are nine degrees by which the soul might be made hierarchic. The first of these, corresponding to the angelic order, is the degree of announcing. Bonaventure, *Itinerarium*, 4.4, following Gallus, also gives nine degrees by which the soul might be purified, illuminated, and perfected. These are, moving from the degree corresponding to Angels to the degree corresponding to Seraphim, announcing, dictating, guiding, ordering, strengthening, commanding, receiving, revealing, anointing *(nuntiatio, dictatio, ductio, ordinatio, roboratio, imperatio, susceptio, revelatio, unctio)*. Attributing a degree within the soul to each angelic order, Gallus, in what follows, gives the same list in the same order, except for the last. For the Seraphim, Gallus uses the corresponding degree of "uniting" *(unitio)*. Walsh points out that this last differs in only one letter from Bonaventure's *unctio* ("Thomas Gallus et l'effort contemplatif," 24).

41. Although Gallus does not name them in the text, this is the order of the Archangels.

42. Thus Gallus, in these three orders, has extended the boundaries of our "nature" based on the attributes of the three angelic orders. Through the Angels the nature of the hierarchical mind simply receives

"messages" (illumination) from on high without valuation as to profit or loss. The second order messages, transmitted through the Archangels, are "closer to the source" *(principalior)* and so contain within them, besides the content of their message, an implicit value—that is, that they are "more important" than angelic messages, in that they also teach the art and skill of the message's evaluation. Thus, in a sense, the Archangels carry both the message and the code for interpreting the message. And finally in the third order, the message or illumination contains within it the added apprehension of good and evil, and the will to cling to the good and to flee from evil. Thus the Principalities carry both the message and a code of ethical conduct for practicing the message.

43. In Alan of Lille's *Treatise on the Celestial Hierarchy* it is the Thrones that exercise the power of discernment. Here, with Gallus, it is the function of the Powers to "order" *(ordinantes)* and "examine" *(examinantes)* the mind for discernment. See Barbet's comments on discernment in Dionysius, *Com. Cant.*, 50–51.

44. The "natural virtues" are the so-called cardinal, acquired, or moral virtues: prudence, justice, courage, and temperance. Having to do with human conduct, they make a person good with regard to natural fulfillment (as opposed to supernatural destiny). Knowing God through *scire* would, in the active life, conform roughly to the natural virtues; men and women without grace might be perfected within a particular sphere, but not perfected generally.

45. The "gratuitous virtues" are those theological or supernatural virtues bestowed by grace or infused by God: faith, hope, and charity. The pivotal position of the virtues here at the very center of the human and angelic hierarchy is no accident. At this level one finds the integration of the "active" life as indicated by the natural virtues, and the "contemplative" life as indicated by the theological virtues. In addition they ensure the continued ordering of the operations of the lower orders and begin to move the soul toward that simple divine ray which is first encountered in the Dominions. The Virtues strengthen the intellect to seek divine Truth and the affective faculties to desire the divine Good. Thus the role of the virtues in the center of the hierarchy is to join all the angelic orders in the movement of the soul into truth and the fervor of charity (expressed finally in the Seraphim). This is so especially with the theological virtues, which move the contemplative in the transcendent direction. Only the theological virtues, which perfect in regard to the goal (happiness) of human life,

belong to humanity as partakers in the divine life and guide one in the transcendent direction to union between soul and God.

46. In Gallus, the "authentic exercise of discipline," the *authentica imperia*, implies that in the true expression of the free will one decides, by reason of the full self-possession or understanding, to orient one's intellect and affect toward the divine ray. The *authentica imperia* therefore profoundly and directly engages the *intellectus* and *affectus* in contemplation. It is thus a decision—in the context of the infused virtues and grace—for the sovereign Good.

47. The immediate effect of the "authentic decision" described above is Gallus's important category of *suspendium*. The concept may be considered as a synonym of contemplative effort, not a cessation of contemplative activity, but rather the supreme concentration of all the faculties on Divinity. *Suspendo*, "to hang up," has the additional meaning of "to keep in suspense," and, in the best sense, to "leave undecided." As a participle it carries the added nuances of "ambiguity," "uncertainty," and "doubt." In contemplation, which is the highest form of thinking for both Gallus and his teacher, Richard of St. Victor, the mind hovers, suspended. The contemplative, kept in suspense, ambiguity, and even doubt as to the adequacy of his or her own groping toward God, is left free for the implosive gift of grace. It may strike us as odd that to "think" contemplatively is to enter into the ambiguity of doubt or indecision, but for Gallus the work of contemplation is the peace of paradox. For Richard of St. Victor, the Cherubim are *suspensa;* to touch them is to hover (see Chase, *Angelic Wisdom*, 61). Gallus, on the other hand, giving a definition of *suspendium* in *Prologue*, V, says *suspension* of the intellective and affective faculties is "the expansion of the soul *(extensio mentis)* all the way to the summit of the order of Dominions by means of superluminous contemplations *(theorias)*." Here the soul or mind is still "sober," but intellect and affect reach out with all their strength to the divine ray. Thus, in Gallus, at the order of Dominions, *suspendium* indicates having attained a very high degree, the most intense state of "sobriety," but not "intoxication" of the mind or senses (ecstatic, intoxicating, and unitive contemplation—*unitiva et excessiva contemplatio*—begins with the Thrones). But in the Dominions intellect and affect manifest their supreme activity; they represent the highest conjunction of nature, industry, and grace. Barbet argues that the *suspendium* of the Dominions represents a midpoint form of contemplation of the *incomprehensibilia et invisibilia Dei;* the light of the invisible

things of God are passed down from the hierarchy above, and passed on to the Powers and Virtues (Barbet, in Dionysius, *Com. Cant.*, 52–54).

48. That is, *mentis excessum*. Note that while at the level of the Dominions in *Prologue*, K, the mind is "sober" *(mens sobria)*, here the soul must pass beyond mind in "ecstasy." Thus the soul in *suspendium* can receive divine visitations in two ways: through the "expansion of the soul" to the limits of human nature discussed above in the context of the Dominions, and here through the "death of the soul" in "ecstasy" whereby the visitation is *sola gratia*. Though still in touch with the Dominions, the Thrones at this level truly, along with the Cherubim and Seraphim in a purer way, begin to be raised up into ecstatic light, into an unknowing union. Richard of St. Victor had described *mentis excessum* or contemplation "beyond reason" *(supra rationem)* in Book V of his *De arca mystica*. There he delineates three modes of contemplation according to ecstasy of mind as *dilatatio mentis*, *sublevatio mentis*, and *alienatio mentis* (see *De arca mystica* V.ii, and Chase, *Angelic Wisdom*, Appendix A, pp. 137–41).

49. The Cherubim represent the culmination of knowledge as *scire* outlined by Gallus in *Prologue*, A. The soul without grace is not able to proceed beyond the Cherubim of the soul; *scire* as intellect carries within it this self-limiting aspect. The Seraphim will represent the culmination of knowledge of God through *nosse*, outlined in *Prologue*, B, above, which will, on the basis of the grace of charity, proceed to deification.

50. Gallus begins his subtle shift to affect within this section, which at the same time depicts the fullness, summit, then ecstasy, and finally death of intellect. The shift is registered by divine attraction, divine drawing power. Here for the first time *God's* desire for the soul is introduced; at the limits of intellect, divine affectivity begins to draw the soul Godward. Here in *Prologue*, M, *attracti* is used three times, *attractionem* once, *attrahuntur* once, and *attractus* once. In each case the words indicate God's invisible power of attraction. This desiring and drawing power is typical in affective mystical writing, whether as erotic imagery depicting the drawing power of divine beauty, as in Bernard of Clairvaux, or in Dante's *Divine Comedy*, in which attractiveness and love of God first through Beatrice and then in themselves draw Dante through hell and purgatory into paradise, or in John of the Cross, "notable for his austerity, who nevertheless nearly trips over himself when it comes to describing the beauty and attraction of God" (see Grace Jantzen, *Power, Gender, and Christian Mysticism* [Cambridge: Cambridge University Press, 1995], 286–89).

51. Gallus is obviously referring to the tradition that describes the function and nature of the Cherubim as *plenitudo scientiae*, or fullness of knowledge. On the Latin and Greek attribution of the Cherubim as a symbol of the fullness of knowledge, see Chase, *Angelic Wisdom*, chap. 1. Gregory the Great too claims the ministry of the Cherubim is fullness of knowledge, and in exercising that ministry the Cherubim are in immediate proximity to God. Gregory, noting that "charity is the full [knowledge] of the law" (Rom 13:10), adds that the cherubic soul is filled with love of God and neighbor.

52. With this last order of the highest hierarchy, Gallus moves from the Thrones, representing the reception of grace through the divine attraction upon intellect and affect, to the Cherubim, representing the final attraction and perfection of intellectual knowledge by illumination of grace (the *apex intellectus*), to, in this section, the Seraphim, representing the perfection of union in love or affect (the *apex affectus*). For a discussion of this transitional and contemplative ascent, see Andrew Louth, "The Influence of Dionysius the Areopagite on Eastern and Western Spirituality in the Fourteenth Century," in *Sobernost* 4.2 (1982): 192ff., and Walsh, "Thomas Gallus et l'effort contemplatif," 24ff.

53. Intellect, having fainted away with the Cherubim, the principle of divine unification is finally, for Gallus, the affective principle *(affectio principalis Deo unibilis)*, the only power of the spirit capable of unification. Intellect can "touch" divinity (see *Prologue*, M), but not unite. Elsewhere Gallus calls this singular, unifying power of the spirit the *apex affectionis*, or simply the Seraphim of the spirit (cf. Gallus, *Com. Cant.*, 2, p. 148, and 5, p. 204).

54. *Divine Names*, 3.1; *Dionysiaca* 1:123. Gallus cites this section from *The Divine Names* no fewer than seventeen times in the *Commentary on the Song of Songs* (cf. Barbet, in Gallus, *Com. Cant.*, 59). In the chapter Dionysius discusses "God's most important name, Good," and the Trinity, which is the source of that Good. Dionysius then cites three disciplines by which we might become self-consciously present to that Trinity: "But if we invoke it (Trinity) with holy prayers, with a naked soul, and with an aptitude for union with God, then we are present to it." Gallus roughly parallels Dionysius's disciplines by means of three spiritual arts (first mentioned in *Prologue*, Q) by which one might be held in the presence of God: most holy or pure prayers *(orationes castissime)*, here in *Prologue*, N, and later in Q; a denuding of the soul *(revelatio mentis)*, *Prologue*, Q, and S, by which the soul is stripped of all exterior longings and assimilated to the divine

simplicity; and through this denuded spirit the practice of a contemplative aptitude for union *(aptitudo ad unitionem)*, in *Prologue*, T, by which the soul is made "fluid" for union with the Spouse *(anima mea liquafacta est)*, Cant. 5, 9. Gallus uses two other forms of spiritual discipline beyond those of Dionysius. One is the suspension of affective and intellective powers *(suspendium)* in *Prologue*, K, V, W, at the summit of the order of the Dominions marking the entry into the order of the Thrones. The second is the *excessus mentis*, *Prologue*, Q, X. This latter, by which Gallus moves completely beyond Dionysius's ascetic disciplines, makes use of the *scintilla* at the summit of the Seraphim to suggest union. This seraphic participation marks the supreme affective participation in divine Goodness; it moves beyond Dionysius's categories of mind altogether, even beyond Dionysius's category of "beyond" mind.

55. That is, this is not the form of knowing God based on *scire*, which uses the created world, the self, and even scripture as a mirror (though an enigmatic or darkened mirror, cf. 1 Corinthians 13:12) by which the soul mounts toward God. There is, however, a burning divine mirror into which the restructured soul gazes in deifying union (cf. *Prologue*, Z).

56. Luke 10:42.

57. Hugh of St. Victor uses the same word, *perspicax*, translated here as "penetrating," to define contemplation in a text Gallus cites in *Prologue*, A: "Contemplation is the free, *penetrating* gaze of the soul reflecting upon and looking deeply into things in every possible direction" *(Contemplatio est perspicax, et liber animi contuitus in res perspeciendas usquequaque diffusus) (In Eccl., Homilia Prima, PL* 175:117A).

58. *Divine Names*, 4.8–9; *Dionysiaca* 1:189–91. Dionysius goes on to distinguish other movements of the human soul and celestial intelligences. In addition to this circular movement, both move also in a straight line and in a spiral. Charles-André Bernard, S.J., identifies the straight, circular, and spiral movements of the soul with symbolical, mystical, and discursive theology, respectively (cited in Dionysius, *Complete Works*, 78 n.146). In his *De arca mystica*, Richard of St. Victor, using birds to foreshadow his work on angels in contemplation, noted three types of slightly variant motions in bird flight: linear, circular, and hovering. He then applied these three patterns of flight to the process of *ratio* in order to extend the boundaries of the human soul's awareness of the presence of the trinitarian God: linear flight represented the pattern of thinking *(cogitatio)*, circular flight represented

the skill of meditation *(meditatio)*, and hovering flight represented the art of contemplation *(contemplatio)* (cf. *De arca mystica*, 1, iv-vi, x, xii).

59. Gallus's word here, *theoriarum*, from *theoria*, denotes contemplative or meditative speculation with a normally visionary content. In addition, in contrast to *contemplatio*, *theoria* denotes the contemplative "life," whereas *contemplatio* more often indicates a practice of prayer. These categories were not set in Gallus's time—they are fluid and often interchangeable—but to distinguish Gallus's use of them I will translate *theoria* as "meditation," and *contemplatio* as "contemplation."

60. This is the same root word used in *Prologue*, A and B. In A, used to describe *scire*, it is *intellectualis;* in B, used to describe *nosse*, it is *superintellectualis*. The word represents the faculty of comprehension, understanding, discernment, which for Gallus may or may not contain an "intellectual" component.

61. *Ecclesial Hierarchy* 7.11, p. 259; *Dionysiaca* 2:1474–75. See also *Divine Names*, 1.2, 3.1; *Ecclesial Hierarchy* 4.3.1.

62. Gallus is here drawing upon Richard of St. Victor's discussion of the six grades of contemplation in his *De arca mystica*. There, Richard uses the ark of the covenant as a structuring and systematizing device for both his theology and teaching on contemplation. On Richard's schema for the six grades of contemplation, see Chase, *Angelic Wisdom*, Table 1, 147–49. Though Richard's and Gallus's orderings are parallel, they are not identical. Richard's sixth grade, corresponding to Gallus's sixth order of the Dominions, is indeed a form of contemplation *in excessus mentis*. But Gallus, beginning with the Thrones, moves into an affective form of contemplation that Richard does not employ. In fact, for Richard, the structuring symbol of his treatise on contemplation, the Cherubim, represents the fullness of intellectual knowing. However, Richard did write on affective modes of divine knowledge in *De quatuor gradibus violentae charitatis*, PL 196:1207–25.

63. The "meditative ecstacies" *(theoricos excessus)*, described here in connection with the Thrones, was initially introduced by Gallus in *Prologue*, L, also in connection with the Thrones. "Longing" here is another incident, the first arising in *Prologue*, M, of an affective characteristic, in this case *cupiens*, interpenetrating and "resting" in close proximity to an intellective "dying" of the mind in contemplation. Constantly seeking a metaphor that will adequately express the relation of intellect and affect, Gallus turns finally, as he does in seeking a metaphor for the relation of soul to God, to the "embrace" and "kiss" of the Song of Songs.

64. Cf. *Divine Names*, 3.1, p. 68; *Dionysiaca* 1:122.

65. In the context of what precedes, it is through these three arts that the "contemplative soul" is able to rest in ecstasy of mind.

66. Here in *Prologue*, R, Gallus moves progressively through the positive, comparative, and superlative adjectival forms of *casta*, translated here as "holy and chaste." James Walsh points out that "all authentic prayer is chaste, but the positive, *oratio casta*, petitions (for oneself or for others) for material goods; the comparative *castior*, for spiritual goods; the superlative *castissima*, for God himself" (see Walsh, *The Pursuit of Wisdom*, 174 n.31.

67. Cf. 1 Timothy 2:1; Jeremiah 29:12.

68. Psalm 51:9–11, Vulgate 50:11–13.

69. Song of Songs 1:2, Vulgate C. 1:1.

70. Song of Songs 1:4, Vulg. C. 1:3.

71. Song of Songs 1:13–14, Vulgate C. 1:12. See also Song of Songs 1:14, Vulgate C. 1:13, 2:16, "my beloved is mine;" 6:3, "I am my beloved's and my beloved is mine."

72. Song of Songs 8:1.

73. Literally "revelation" *(revelatio mentis)*, but may be taken in the sense of opening, emptying, uncovering, or even nakedness of the soul to the presence of God. It does imply revelation in the personal sense, but it would be misleading to emphasize personal revelation alone. For Gallus, the emphasis is on revelation or knowledge *of God's self by God*. In order for this to occur, as Richard of St. Victor notes, the soul itself must be completely emptied: *"animam seipsam extra semetipsam totam effundere"* (cf. *De arca mystica* IV.xvi). Illumination is an issue, but union of the perfected soul (to God) is the larger issue. For a discussion on "revelations" as the stripping and nakedness of the soul in the contemplative tradition, see *DS* III, "Dépouillemment," 455–502.

74. Sarracenus: *"et omnia non exsistentia et exsistentia."* Eriugena: *"et omne non ens et ens."* Dionysius: *"οὐχ ὄντα καὶ ὄντα."* *Dionysiaca* 1:568.

75. Sarracenus: *"super substantiam."* Eriugena: *"super essentiam."* Dionysius: *"ὑπέρ οὐσίαν."* *Dionysiaca* 1:568.

76. *The Mystical Theology* 1.1, p. 135; *Dionysiaca* 1:567–69.

77. Song of Songs 5:3.

78. *Celestial Hierarchy*, 15.3, p. 186. *Dionysiaca* 2:1010.

79. An aptitude for union *(aptitudo ad unitionem)* is, as Gallus explains, a devotion that renders the soul "fluid." *Aptitudo* itself contains within its meaning something of this flowing together. In his commentary

on this section of the Canticles (Gallus, *Com. Cant.*, 5–6, pp. 197–99), Gallus says that the "disposition" or "aptitude" to union whereby the soul is made totally "fluid" through devotion comes about through the in-breathing (inspiration) or spiration through the kiss of the Bridegroom, that is, Christ.

80. Song of Songs 5:6.

81. Ecclesiastes 7:25, Vulgate 7:26.

82. Sarracenus: *"sine voce."* Dionysius: *"ἄφωνος."*

83. *Mystical Theology*, 3, p. 139. *Dionysiaca* 1:590–91.

84. In this section Gallus brings together two modes of human learning, two modes of divine teaching, two opposite yet interpenetrating modes of union. The first is the discursive, speculative, intellective, and apophatic discourse of deification laid out symbolically throughout the angelic hierarchy of the soul, which finds its most compelling symbol in the full knowledge of the Cherubim. This is joined with the second mode, the imagistic, desiring, affective, and cataphatic discourse called into play to draw listeners and readers into love, also depicted symbolically throughout the angelic hierarchy of the soul, which finds its fullest symbol in the burning love of the Seraphim. Words can no longer be spoken, even the words of love, but a kiss remains. The speaking lips are silenced in the embrace of a greater passion, silent but touching, in-spiring and burning. It is a union in *coniunctio* beyond mind *(id est coniunctionem sive unitionem super mentem)*, a *coincidentia oppositorum*, a movement in rest, a touching silence, the kiss of the ineffable.

85. Cf. *Divine Names*, 3.1, pp. 68–70, which speaks of the power and suitability of prayer for union with God.

86. Cf. *Mystical Theology*, 1.1., p. 135.

87. Job 7:15. Here Gallus would take *ossa* as bones, certainly, but also "bones" as the innermost center of the person, especially regarded in the medieval period as the seat of the emotions. See, for instance, *Prologue*, W, where Gallus expands on this notion.

88. The term *suspendium*, translated here as "suspension," was first introduced in *Prologue*, K, in conjunction with Gallus's discussion of the Dominions of the soul. He reintroduces it here in reference to the "simplicity/nudity" of union in the context of the Seraphim. The Seraphim represent the union of apex of the soul with divinity; "suspension" is one part of the movement toward that union. "Rest" and "waiting" are indicated by *suspendium*. There is also a strong connotation of strangulation or death by hanging in *suspendium*, even self-inflicted hanging; the intention

then would be to indicate something of the death of self in union. Gallus returns to the term here in *Prologue*, V, in order to insist that union is the work of the Spirit alone.

89. *Divine Names*, 1.2, p. 50. *Dionysiaca* 1:16–17.

90. Gallus cites Romans 8 at this point (Rom 8:5–8, 14–17, 26–27).

91. Daniel 10:16–17.

92. *Divine Names*, 7.3, p. 108. *Dionysiaca* 1:406.

93. Hebrews 4:12.

94. Sarracenus: "substantiae." Eriugena: "essentiae." Dionysius: "οὐσίας."

95. *Ecclesial Hierarchy*, 2.3.7, pp. 207–8. *Dionysiaca* 2:1155.

96. This is Gallus's *scintilla siquidem apicis affectualis*, that highest spark of love which brings the soul beyond mere contact with God (contact or touch being the highest capacity of intellect) into direct and complete unitive participation.

97. *Ecclesial Hierarchy*, 1.3, p. 198. *Dionysiaca* 2:1088–90.

98. John 1:1. See *Commentary*, Book 1, 22, in *Origen: Commentary on the Gospel of John, Books 1–10*, trans. Ronald E. Heine (Washington, D.C.: The Catholic University of America Press, 1989), 37. See also *Commentary*, Book 1, 23, p. 38; Book 1, 38, p. 42.

99. See note 88 above on *suspendium*.

100. Song of Songs 1:2, Vulgate, C. 1:1.

A Note on Selected Texts
and Suggestions for
Further Reading

Once the eye is focused to the rhythm of angels, one finds them cropping up in places both unexpected and varied. In scripture and in doctrinal, mystical, and pastoral writings angelic traces are abundant, even overwhelming. Thus the task of selecting texts for this volume was not an easy one.

The first criterion for inclusion was, of course, that the texts contribute to developing a comprehensive understanding of angelic spirituality in the Christian tradition. Beyond that, they were selected to include a range of genre and periods. Of important consideration also was that as many of the various themes within angelic spirituality as possible be adequately represented. The texts are placed in chronological order within each of the two sections. This placement is not meant to imply any kind of "progression" in the theology or history of angelic spirituality. Rather, they are arranged in such a manner for the reader's convenience.

A second criterion, often as important as the first, was that none of the selections included in *Angelic Spirituality* be available in other volumes of Paulist Press's Classics of Western Spirituality series. Thus, a number of very important texts were passed over. However, since these texts are available in good English translation and in the same series as this volume, it was decided that *Angelic Spirituality* should focus on texts that were, in most cases, not previously available in English translation and not available at all in the Classics of Western Spirituality. It is therefore the intention of the editor that the appropriate Classics of Western Spirituality series volumes serve as auxiliary resources to the theme of angelic spirituality introduced in this volume. Three themes in particular that can be found in other series volumes and are underrepresented in this book are angels in Christian liturgical settings, the relation between Mary and the angels, and angels and the Trinity.

The following selective list of suggestions is provided for further reading. Except in a few instances the suggestions are limited to texts available in English. The reader will find a rich vein of angelic spirituality in the other volumes of the Paulist Press series and in the few authors listed from outside the series. The suggestions are intended to serve as stepping-stones to a more comprehensive study of the place of angels in Christian spirituality.

Texts Available in English Translation
(CWS = Paulist Press's Classics of Western Spirituality series)

Achard of St. Victor. *Works*. Kalamazoo, Mich., 2001.

Alighieri, Dante. *The Divine Comedy, Paradiso*.

Angela of Foligno, *The Book of Blessed Angela of Foligno* (CWS).

Anonymous. *The Cloud of Unknowing* (CWS).

Anselm of Canterbury. *Cur Deus Homo*. Albany, 1969.

Aquinas, Thomas. *Summa Theologia*, 1, q.50–64; 107–14.

———. "Active and Contemplative Life," *Summa Theologia* (CWS).

Augustine. *On the Trinity*. Translated by Edmund Hill. New York: New City Press, 1991.

Barth, Karl. *Church Dogmatics*, III.3.

Bellarmine, Robert. *The Mind's Ascent to God* (CWS).

Bernard of Clairvaux. *On Consideration* (CWS).

Blake, William. *The Marriage of Heaven and Hell*. Oxford, 1926.

Bonaventure. *Breviloquim*, II.6–8.

———. *Soul's Journey into God* (CWS).

Calvin, John. *Institutes of the Christian Religion*, I.II.14.

Catherine of Siena. *The Dialogue* (CWS).

Elisabeth of Schönau. *Visions* (CWS).

Eriugena, John Scotus. *Periphyseon*. Editions Bellarmine, 1987.

Gregory the Great. *Morals on the Book of Job*. Oxford, 1844–50.

Hadewijch of Antwerp. *Visions* (CWS).

Hildegard of Bingen. *Scivias* (CWS).

Hilton, Walter. *The Scale of Perfection* (CWS).

Hugh of St. Victor. *On the Sacraments of the Christian Faith*. Translated by R. J. Defarrari. Cambridge, 1951.

Ignatius of Loyola. *Spiritual Exercises* (CWS).

Jacopone da Todi. *The Lauds* (CWS).

Luther, Martin. *Table Talk*. In *Luther's Works*, V.54.

Milton, John. *Paradise Lost*. New York, 1983.

Newman, John Henry. *Selected Sermons:* "Sermon XXIX, The Powers of Nature, The Feast of St. Michael and All the Angels" (CWS).

Origen. *On First Principles (De principiis)*, II,9;III,5–6. New York, 1966.

Richard of St. Victor. *The Mystical Ark* (CWS).

Rolle, Richard. *Ego Dormio* (CWS).

Savonarola. *The Compendium of Revelations* (CWS, *Apocalyptic Spirituality*).

Suso, Henry. *Life of Henry Suso* (CWS).

Swedenborg, Emanuel. *Angelic Wisdom Concerning the Divine Love and the Divine Wisdom*. New York, 1880.

———. *Heaven and Its Wonders and Hell from Things Heard and Seen*. Philadelphia, 1875.

———. *The Universal Human* (CWS).

Teresa of Avila. *The Interior Castle* (CWS).

———. *Life of Teresa of Avila*. Translated by Allison Peers. New York: Doubleday, 1991.

Selected Texts Not Yet Available in English Translation

Alan of Lille. *Prose Commentary on the Angels (Expositio prosae de angelis)*. Edited by Marie-Thérèse d'Alverny. Paris, 1965.

Albert the Great. *On the Celestial Hierarchy of Dionysius (Super Diony-sium de Caelesti Hierarchia).* In *Alberti Magni, Opera Omnia,* V.36:1.

Birgitta of Sweden. *Angelic Sermon on the Blessed Virgin (Sermo angelicus).* In *Sancta Birgitta, Opera minora II, Sermo Angelicus.* Edited by Sten Eklund. Uppsala, 1972. *Prologue to Angelic Ser-mon.* Available in Middle English in *The Bridgettine Breviary of Syon Abby.* Edited by A. Jefferies Collins. Worcester, 1969; the "Days" of the Offices used by the Sisters of the Brigittine Monastery of Sion containing *Angelic Sermon.* Available in Middle English in *Myroure of Oure Ladye: A Devotional Treatise on the Divine Service.* Edited by John Henery Blunt. London, 1873.

Dionysius the Carthusian. *Commentary on the Celestial or Angelic Hierarchy (Commentaria in librum de coelesti seu angelica hierar-chia).* In *D. Dionysii Cartusiani, Opera Omnia,* V.15.

———. *On the Feast of the Archangel Michael and of All the Angels (In festo S. Michaelis Archangeli).* In *D. Dionysii Cartusiani, Opera Omnia,* V.32.

Gerson, Jean. *Collation on the Angels (Collatio de angelis).* In Gerson, *Opera,* pars IV. Paris, 1960– .

———. *Linguistic Notations on the Celestial Hierarchy of Dionysius (Notulae super quaedam verba Dionysii de coelesti hierarchia).* In Gerson, *Opera,* tome III. Paris, 1960– .

Lombard, Peter. *Sentences (Libre IV sententiarum).* Florentiam: Ex Typographia Collegii S. Boaventurae, 1916.

Peter of Poiters. *Sentences (Sententiae).* Edited by Philip S. Moore et al., 1961.

Richard of St. Victor. *On the Revelation of St. John (In Apocalypsim Joanis).* In *PL,* 196.

Suarez, Francisci. *On the Angels (Summa Theologiae de rerum omnium creatore, II. De Angelis).* Lyon, 1620.

William of Auxerre. *The Golden Summa (Summa aurea).* Edited by Jean Ribailler. Paris, 1980.

Selected Bibliography

Primary Sources
Editions and Translations

Abbas Vercellensis (Ps. Thomas Gallus). *Le Commentaire du Cantiques des Cantiques "Dieformis animae gemitus.* Etude d'authenticité et édition critique par Jeanne Barbet. Publications de la Sorbonne, Série "Documents," 21. Paris: Bétrice-Nauwelaerts, 1972.

Alan of Lille. *Alain de Lille: textes inédits avec un introduction sur sa vie et ses oeuvres.* Edited by Marie Thérèse d'Alverny. Études de philosophie médiévale, 52. Paris: J. Vrin, 1965.

Anonymous. *De sex alis cherubim.* [Attributed to Alan of Lille]. *PL*, 210:267A–280C.

Augustine of Hippo. *Augustine: The City of God Against the Pagans.* Translated by Henry Bettenson with an introduction by David Knowles. New York: Penguin Books, 1972.

———. *De civitate Dei contra paganos, Libre XXII.* In *PL*, 41.

———. [Augustine, Saint, Bishop of Hippo]. *De civitate Dei. Corpus Christianorum.* Series latina, vols 47–48. Turnholt: Brepols, 1955.

———. *Saint Augustine: The City of God.* Translated by Marcus Dodds with an introduction by Thomas Merton. New York: The Modern Library, 1950.

Bernard of Clairvaux. *S. Bernardi Opera*, Vol. IV, *Sermones, In Psalmum "Qui habitat."* Edited by J. Leclercq and H. Rochais. Rome: Editiones Cistercienses, 1966.

———. *Oeuvres.* Traduites et préfacées par M.-M. Davy, Tome II. Des maîtres de la spiritualité Chrétienne. Aubier: Éditions Montaigne, 1950.

———. *Sermons on Conversion: On Conversion, A Sermon to Clerics and Lenten Sermons on the Psalm "He Who Dwells."* Translated with an introduction by Marie-Bernard Saïd. Cistercian Fathers Series 25. Kalamazoo, Mich.: Cistercian Publications, 1981.

Denys the Areopagite. *Dionysiaca: Recueil donnant l'ensemble des traductions Latines des ouvrages attribués au Denys de L'aréopage*. Two volumes. Paris: Desclée de Brouwer and Cie., Éditeurs, 1937–50.

———. *Denys l'Aréopagite: La hiérarchie céleste*. Introduction René Roques. Critical text Günter Heil. Translation and notes by Maurice de Gandillac. Sources Chrétiennes, no. 58. Paris: Les éditions du cerf, 1958.

———. *On the Celestial Hierarchy*. In *Pseudo-Dionysius: The Complete Works*. Translated by Colm Luibheid. Foreword, notes, and translation collaboration by Paul Rorem. New York: Paulist Press, 1987.

Eriugena, John Scotus. *Iohannis Scoti Eriugenae: Expositiones in Ierarchiam coelestem*. Edited by Jean Barbet. Corpus Christianorum Continuatio Mediaualis XXXI. Turnholt: Brepols, 1975.

Gallus, Thomas. *Commentaires du Cantique des Cantiques*. Texte critique avec introduction, notes et tables par Jeanne Barbet. Textes philosophiques du moyen âge, XIV. Paris: J. Vrin, 1967.

———. *Extractio (Paraphrase de l'abbé de Verceil Thomas Gallus sur la Hiérarchie dans les cieux)*. In *Dionysiaca* 2:1040–66.

Gregory the Great. *XL homiliarum in Evangelia libri duo, Homilia XXXIV*. In *PL*, 76:1188–96.

———. *Gregory the Great: Forty Gospel Homilies*. Translated by Dom David Hurst. Kalamazoo, Mich.: Cistercian Publications, 1990.

Hugh of St. Victor. *Commentariorum hierarchiam coelestem S. Dionysii Areopagite secundum interpretationem Joannis Scoti*. PL, 175:923–1154.

———. *De arca Noe morali*. PL, 176:617–680.

———. *Hugh of St. Victor: Selected Spiritual Writings*. Translated by a religious of the Community of St. Mary the Virgin. London: Faber and Faber, 1962.

Umiltà of Faenza. *Acta Sanctorum*. Maii VII, vol. XX, Appendix ad Diem XXII Maii. "Sermo Sanctae Humilitatis Abbatissae," 815–26. Antverpiae, 1685.

———. *Acta Sanctorum*. Maii V, vol. XVIII. "Vita Sanctae Humilitatis Abbatissae, Analecta," 214–16. Antverpiae, 1685.

———. *I Sermoni de Umiltà da Faenza*. Edited by Adele Simonetti. Società Internazionale per lo Studio del Medioevo Latino, 14. Spoleto, 1995.

————. *Sanctae Humilitatis de Faventia. Sermones.* Edited by T. Sala. Florence, 1884.

Secondary Sources Studies

Adler, Mortimer J. *The Angels and Us.* New York: Macmillan, 1982.

Avans, Roberts. *The New Gnosis: Heidegger, Hillman, and Angels.* Dallas Tex.: Spring Publications, 1984.

Barbet, Jeanne. "Thomas Gallus." In *Dictionnaire de spiritualité: ascétique et mystique, doctrine et histoire,* Fondé par M. Villier et al., 800–816. Volume 15. Paris: Beauchesne, 1991.

Baron, Roger. "Le commentaire de la 'Hiérarchie Céleste' par Hugues de Saint-Victor." In *Études sur Hugues de Saint-Victor,* 133–218. Paris: Desclée de Brouwer, 1964.

————, ed. *Hugh of St. Victor: Six opuscules spirituelles.* Paris, Desclée de Brouwer, 1969.

Barth, Karl. "The Kingdom of Heaven, The Ambasssadors of God and Their Opponents." In *Church Dogmatics,* volume III.3, edited by G. W. Bromiley and T. F. Torrance, 369–531. Edinburgh: T. & T. Clark, 1960.

Beierwaltes, Werner. "Negati Affirmatio: Or the World as Metaphor, Foundation, for Medieval Aesthetics from the Writings of John Scotus Eriugena." *Dionysius* 1 (1977): 127–59.

Bemrose, Stephen. *Dante's Angelic Intelligences.* Rome: Edizioni de Storia e Letteratura, 1983.

Benoit, Pierre. "Pauline Angelology and Demonology." *Religious Studies Bulletin* 3.1 (1983): 1–19.

Blanco, Arturo. "The Influence of Faith in Angels on the Medieval Vision of Nature and Man." In *Mensch und Natur im Mittelalter,* 4546–67. Miscellanea Mediaevalia, band 21/1, heraus. Albert Zimmermann. Berlin: Walter de Gruyter, 1991.

la Bonnardiére, Anne-Marie. "Anima iusti sedes sapientiae dans l'oeuvre de saint Augustin." In *Epektasis: mélanges patristiques offerts au Cardinal Jean Daniélou,* 111–20. Paris: Beauchesne, 1972.

Bougerol, Jacques G., O.F.M. "Bonaventure et le Pseudo-Dionysius." *Etudes Franciscaines* 28, supplement (1968): 33–123.

Butler, Cuthbert. *Western Mysticism: The Teaching of SS. Augustine, Gregory, and Bernard on Contemplation and the Contemplative Life.* Second edition with afterthoughts. London: Constable, 1927.

Cacciari, Massimo. *The Necessary Angel.* Albany, N.Y.: State University of New York Press, 1994.

Callus, Daniel A. "An Unknown Commentary of Thomas Gallus on the Pseudo-Dionysian Letters." *Dominican Studies* 1 (1948): 58–67.

Cappuyns, Dom Maieul. *Jean Scot Érigène, sa vie, son oeuvre, sa pensée.* Reprint. Brussels: Culture et Civilization, 1969.

Carabine, Deirdre. "Eriugena's Use of the Symbolism of Light, Cloud, and Darkness in the *Periphyseon.*" In *Eriugena: East and West,* edited by Bernard McGinn and Willemien Otten. Notre Dame, Ind.: University of Notre Dame Press, 1994.

Carr, Wesley. *Angels and Principalities: The Background, Meaning and Development of the Pauline Phrase "hai archai kai hai exousiai."* Cambridge: Cambridge University Press, 1981.

Cavidini, John C. *Gregory the Great: A Symposium.* Notre Dame, Ind.: University of Notre Dame Press, 1995.

Charry, Ellen T. *By the Renewing of Your Minds: The Pastoral Function of Christian Doctrine.* New York: Oxford University Press, 1997.

Chase, Steven. *Angelic Wisdom: The Cherubim and the Grace of Contemplation in Richard of St. Victor.* Studies in Spirituality and Theology 2. Notre Dame, Ind.: University of Notre Dame Press, 1995.

———. "Angels: The Classical Christian Tradition and Contemporary Spiritual Direction." *Listening: Journal of Religion and Culture* 32.2 (1997): 91–103.

Châtillon, Jean. "Hugues de Saint-Victor critique de Jean Scot." In *Jean Scot Érigène et l'histoire de la philosophie,* 415–31. Colloques internationaux du Centre National de la recherche scientifique, no. 561. Paris: Éditions du Centre National de la Recherche scientifique, 1977.

———. "De Guillaume de Champeaux à Thomas Gallus: chronique d'histoire littéraire et doctrinale de l'Ecole de Saint-Victor." *Revue du moyen âge latin* 8 (1952): 139–62, 247–73.

Chenu, M.-D. *Nature, Man, and Society in the Twelfth Century.* Edited and translated by Jerome Taylor and Lester K. Little. Chicago: University of Chicago Press, 1968.

Clark, Mary T. *Augustine of Hippo: Selected Writings.* Translation and introductions by Mary T. Clark. The Classics of Western Spirituality. New York: Paulist Press, 1984.

Clark, Stephen, R. L. "Where Have All the Angels Gone?" *Religious Studies* 28 (1992): 221–34.

Cousins, Ewert, ed. and trans. *Bonaventure: The Soul's Journey into God, The Tree of Life, The Life of St. Francis.* New York: Paulist Press, 1978.

———. "Preface." In *Benard of Clairvaux: Selected Works,* translated by G. R. Evans, introduction by Jean Leclercq, 5–11. New York and Mahwah, N.J.: Paulist Press, 1987.

———. *Christ of the Twenty-first Century.* Rockport, Mass.: Element, 1992.

Daniélou, Jean. *The Angels and Their Mission: According to the Fathers of the Church.* Translation by David Heimann. Westminster, Md.: Christian Classics, 1976.

Davidson, A. B. "Angel." In *A Dictionary of the Bible* (New York: Charles Scribner's Sons, 1898), 1:93–97.

Davidson, Gustav. *A Dictionary of Angels: Including the Fallen Angels.* New York: The Free Press, Macmillan, 1967.

Duclow, Donald F. "Isaiah Meets the Seraph: Breaking Ranks in Dionysius and Eriugena?" In *Eriugena: East and West,* edited by Bernard McGinn and Willemien Otten. Notre Dame, Ind.: University of Notre Dame Press, 1994.

Dudden, F. H. *Gregory the Great: His Place in History and Thought.* Two volumes. New York: Russell and Russell, 1905.

Duhr, Joseph. "Anges." In *Dictionnaire de spiritualité: ascétique et mystique doctrine et histoire.* 1936 edition. 1:580–625.

Evans, G. R. *Alan of Lille: The Frontiers of Theology in the Later Twelfth Century.* Cambridge: Cambridge University Press, 1983.

———. *Bernard of Clairvaux: Selected Works.* Translation and foreword by G. R. Evans. Introduction by Jean Leclercq. Preface by Ewert H. Cousins. Classics of Western Spirituality. New York and Mahwah, N.J.: Paulist Press, 1987.

———. *The Mind of Bernard of Clairvaux.* Oxford: Oxford University Press, 1983.

———. *The Thought of Gregory the Great.* Cambridge: Cambridge University Press, 1986.

Fallon, T. L., J. Michl, A. A. Bialas, and S. Tsuji. "Angels." In *The New Catholic Encyclopedia.* 1966 edition. 1:507–19.

Fox, Matthew, and Rupert Sheldrake. *The Physics of Angels: Exploring the Realm Where Science and Spirit Meet.* San Francisco: HarperSanFrancisco, 1996.

de Gandillac, Maurice. "Anges et hommes dans le commentaire de Jean Scot sur la *Hiérarchie céleste.*" In *Jean Scot Érigène et l'histoire de la philosophie*. Colloques internationaux du Centre National de la recherche scientifique, no. 561. Paris: Éditions du centre national de la recherche scientifique, 1977.

Garrett, Duane A. *Angels and the New Spirituality*. Nashville, Tenn.: Broadman and Hollman, 1995.

Gaster, T. H. "Angel." In *The Interpreter's Dictionary of the Bible*. 1991 edition. 128–34.

Gersh, Stephen. *From Iambllichus to Eriugena: An Investigation of the Prehistory and Evolution of the Pseudo-Dionysian Tradition*. Leiden: E. J. Brill, 1978.

———. *Kinesis Akinetos: A Study of Spiritual Motion in the Philosophy of Proclus*. Philosophia Antiqua XXVI. Leiden: E. J. Brill, 1973.

Gilson, E. *The Mystical Theology of St. Bernard*. Translation by A. H. C. Downes. London, 1940.

Giovetti, Paola. *Angels: The Role of Celestial Guardians and Beings of Light*. Translation by Toby McCormick. York Beach, Maine: Samuel Weiser, 1993.

Godwin, Malcolm. *Angels: An Endangered Species*. New York: Simon and Schuster, 1993.

Hadot, Pierre. *Philosophy as a Way of Life: Spiritual Exercises from Socrates to Foucault*. Edited by Arnold I. Davidson. Translated by Michael Chase. Oxford: Blackwell, 1995.

Harding, D. E. *The Hierarchy of Heaven and Earth*. New York: Harper & Brothers, 1953.

Häring, Nikolaus M. "John Scottus in Twelfth Century Angelology." In *The Mind of Eriugena*, edited by J. O'Meara and Ludwig Bieler, 158–69. Dublin: Irish University Press, 1973.

Heidt, William George. *Angelology in the Old Testament: A Study in Biblical Theology*. Washington D.C.: Catholic University of America Press, 1949.

James, William. "A Pluralistic Mystic." In *Essays in Philosophy*, 172–90. Cambridge, Mass.: Harvard University Press, 1978.

Jantzen, Grace. *Power, Gender, and Christian Mysticism*. Cambridge and New York: Cambridge University Press, 1995.

Javelet, Robert. "Thomas Gallus ou les Ecritures dans une dialectique mystique." In *L'homme devant Dieu: mélanges offerts au Pére Henri de Lubac*, 99–110. Paris: Aubier, 1963.

———. "Thomas Gallus et Richard de Saint-Victor, mystiques." *Recherches de théologie ancienne et mediévale* 29/30 (1962/1963): 206–33/88–121.

Jeanueau, Édouard. *Etudes érigéniennes.* Paris: Etudes Augustiniennes, 1987.

Juncker, Günter. "Christ as Angel: The Reclamation of a Primitive Title." *Trinity Journal* 15 (1994): 221–50.

Kadel, Andrew. *Matrology: A Bibliography of Writings by Christian Women from the First to the Fifteenth Centuries.* New York: Continuum, 1994.

Keck, David. *Angels and Angelology in the Middle Ages.* New York and Oxford: Oxford University Press, 1998.

Koch, Josef. "Uber die Lichtsymbolik im Bereich der Philosophie und der Mystik des Mittelalters." *Studium Generale* 13 (1960): 653–70.

Lang, David P. "Aquinas' Proofs for the Existence and Nature of Angels." *Faith and Reason* 21/1–2 (1995): 3–16.

Lang, B. and C. McDannell. *Heaven: A History.* New Haven, Conn.: Yale University Press, 1988.

Louth, Andrew. *Denys the Areopagite.* Wilton, Conn.: Morehouse-Barlow, 1989.

———. "The Influence of Denys the Areopagite on Eastern and Western Spirituality in the Fourteenth Century." *Sobornost* 4/2 (1982): 185–200.

———. *The Origins of the Christian Mystical Tradition.* Oxford: Clarendon Press, 1981.

Luscombe, David. "Conceptions of Hierarchy Before the Thirteenth Century." In *Soziale Ordnungen im Selbstverstandnis des Mittelalters,* 1–19. Miscellanea Mediaevalia, band 12/1, heraus. Albert Zimmermann. Berlin: Walter de Gruyter, 1979.

———. "The Reception of the Writings of Denis the Pseudo-Areopagite into England." In *Tradition and Change,* edited by Diana Greenway, Christopher Holdsworth, and Jane Sayers, 115–43. Cambridge: Cambridge University Press, 1985.

———. "Thomas Aquinas and Conceptions of Hierarchy in the Thirteenth Century." In *Thomas von Aquin: Werk und Wirkung im Licht Neuerer Forschungen,* 261–77. Miscellanea Mediaevalia, band 19, heraus. Albert Zimmermann. Berlin: Walter de Gruyter, 1988.

MacGregor, Geddes. *Angels: Ministers of Grace.* New York: Paragon House, 1988.

Mareto, Felice da. "Humilità (sainte)." In *Dictionnaire de spiritualité: ascétique et mystique, doctrine et histoire* 7:1187–88. Paris: Beauchesne, 1988.

Margolies, Morris B. *A Gathering of Angels: Angels in Jewish Life and Literature.* New York: Ballantine Books, 1994.

McGinn, Bernard. *The Foundations of Mysticism.* Volume 1 of *The Presence of God: A History of Western Christian Mysticism.* New York: Crossroad, 1992.

———. *The Growth of Mysticism.* Volume 2 of *The Presence of God: A History of Western Christian Mysticism.* New York: Crossroad, 1994.

———. "Love, Knowledge, and *Unio Mystica* in the Western Christian Tradition." In *Mystical Union and Monotheistic Faith: An Ecumenical Dialogue*, edited by Moshe Idel and Bernard McGinn, 59–86. New York: Macmillan, 1989.

———. "The Negative Element in the Anthropology of John the Scot." In *Jean Scot Érigène et l'histoire de la philosophie.* 315–25. Colloques internationaux du Centre National de la recherche scientifique, no. 561. Paris: Éditions du centre national de la recherche scientifique, 1977.

———. "Was Francis of Assisi a Mystic?" In *Conversations in Global Spirituality in Honor of Ewert Cousins*, edited by Steven Chase, 145–74. Quincy, Ill.: Franciscan Press, 1997.

McGinn, Bernard, and Willemien Otten, eds. *Eriugena East and West.* Notre Dame Conferences in Medieval Studies V. Notre Dame, Ind.: University of Notre Dame Press, 1994.

McKenna, Megan. *Angels Unawares.* Maryknoll, N.Y.: Orbis Books, 1995.

McNamee, Maurice B., S.J. *Vested Angels: Eucharistic Allusions in Early Netherlandish Paintings.* Leuven: Peeters, 1998.

Moran, Dermot. *The Philosophy of John Scottus Eriugena: A Study of Idealism in the Middle Ages.* Cambridge: Cambridge University Press, 1989.

Murata, Sachiko. "The Angels." In *Islamic Spirituality I: Foundations.* Volume 19 of *World Spirituality: An Encyclopedic History of the Religious Quest*, edited by Seyyed Hossein Nasr. New York: Crossroad, 1987.

Newsom, Carol A., Duane F. Watson. "Angels." In *The Anchor Bible Dictionary*, 1992 edition. 248–55.

Noll, Stephen F. *Angels of Light, Powers of Darkness: Thinking Biblically About Angels, Satan and Principalities.* Downers Grove, Ill.: InterVarsity Press, 1998.

O'Meara, John J. *Eriugena.* Oxford: Clarendon Press, 1988.

O'Meara, John J., and Ludwig Bieler, eds. *The Mind of Eriugena*. Dublin: Irish University Press, 1973.

Otten, Willemien. *The Anthropology of Johannes Scottus Eriugena*. Leiden: E. J. Brill, 1991.

Petersen, Joan M. "Greek Influences upon Gregory the Great's Exegesis of Luke 15,1–10 in *Homelia in Evang. II*, 34." In *Grégoire le Grand*, edited by J. Fontaine et al., 521–29. Paris: CNRS, 1986.

———. "'*Homo omnino Latinus?*' The Theological and Cultural Background of Pope Gregory the Great." *Speculum* 62:3 (1987): 529–51.

Petroff, Elizabeth Alvilda. *Body and Soul: Essays on Medieval Women and Mysticism*. New York and Oxford: Oxford University Press, 1994.

———. *Consolation of the Blessed*. New York: Alta Gaia Society, 1979.

———. *Medieval Women's Visionary Literature*. New York and Oxford: Oxford University Press, 1986.

Quay, Paul M. "Angels and Demons: The Teaching of IV Lateran." *Theological Studies* 42.1 (1981): 20–45.

Roques, René. "Connaissance de Dieu et théologie symbolique d'aprés l' 'In hierarchiam coelestem Sancti Dionysii' du Hugues de Saint-Victor." In *Structures théologique: de la Gnose à Richard de Saint-Victor. Essais et analyses critiques*, 294–364. Bibliothéque de l'Ecole des Hautes Études: Section des sciences religieuses, 72. Paris: Presses Universitaires de France, 1962.

———. "Jean Scot Érigène." In *Dictionnaire de spiritualité: ascétique et mystique, doctrine et histoire*, 8:735–61. Paris: Beauchesne, 1974.

———. *L'univers Dionysien, structure hiérarchique du monde selon pseudo-Denys*. Paris: Aubier, 1954.

Rorem, Paul. *Pseudo-Dionysius: A Commentary on the Texts and an Introduction to Their Influence*. New York and Oxford: Oxford University Press, 1993.

Ross, George MacDonald. "Angels." *Philosophy: The Journal of the Royal Institute of Philosophy* 60 (1985): 495–511.

Russell, Jeffrey Burton. *A History of Heaven: The Singing Silence*. Princeton, N.J.: Princeton University Press, 1997.

Schneiderman, S. *An Angel Passes*. New York: New York University Press, 1988.

Sicard, Patrice. *Diagrammes médiévaux et exégèse visuelle: le Libellus de formation arche de Hugues de Saint-Victor*. Bibliotheca Victorina IV. Turnhout: Brepols, 1993.

Straw, C. *Gregory the Great: Perfection in Imperfection.* Berkeley and Los Angeles: University of California Press, 1988.

Théry, Gabriel. "Documents concernant Jean Sarrazin, reviseur de la traduction érigénienne du Corpus Dionysiacum." *Archives d'histoire doctrinale et littéraire du moyen âge* 18 (1951): 45–87.

———. *Hilduin, traducteur de Denys.* Études Dionysiennes I/II, Études de philosophie médiévale, XVI/XIX. Paris: J. Vrin, 1932.

———. "Thomas Gallus. Aperçu biographique." *Archives d'histoire doctrinale et littéraire du moyen âge* 12 (1939): 141–208.

Trigg, Joseph W. "The Angel of Great Counsel: Christ and the Angelic Hierarchy in Origen's Theology." *The Journal of Theological Studies* 42 (1991): 35–51.

Tucci, Giuseppe. *The Theory and Practice of the Mandala.* Translation by Alan Houghton Brodrick. London: Rider, 1967.

Turner, Denys. *The Darkness of God: Negativity in Christian Mysticism.* Cambridge: Cambridge University Press, 1995.

———. *Eros and Allegory: Medieval Exegesis of the Song of Songs.* Kalamazoo, Mich.: Cistercian Publications, 1995.

Verbraken, Patrick. "Le Commentaire de Saint Grégoire sur le premier livre des Rois." *Revue Bénédictine* 66 (1956): 159–217.

Walsh, James. "The 'Expositions' of Thomas Gallus on the Pseudo-Dionysian Letters." *Archives d'histoire doctrinale et littéraire du moyen âge* 38 (1963): 199–220.

———. "Thomas Gallus et l'effort contemplatif." *Revue d'histoire de la spiritualité* 51 (1975): 17–42.

Walsh, P. G. "Alan of Lille as a Renaissance Figure." In *Renaissance and Renewal in Christian History*, edited by Derek Baker, 117–35. Oxford: Basil Blackwell, 1977.

Weisweiler, H. "Die Ps.-Dionysiuskommentare 'In coelestem Hierarchiam' des Skotus Eriugena und Hugos von St. Viktor." *Recherches de théologie ancienne et médiévale* 19 (1952): 26–47.

Wilson, Peter Lamborn. *The Little Book of Angels.* Rockport, Mass.: Element, 1993.

———. *Messengers of the Gods.* London: Thames and Hudson, 1980.

Zinn, Grover. "Book and Word: The Victorine Background of Bonaventure's Use of Symbols." In *S. Bonaventura 1274–1974*, 2:143–69. Rome: Grottaferrata, 1973.

————. "Hugh of St. Victor, Isaiah's Vision, and *De arca Noe.*" In *The Church and the Arts,* edited by Diana Wood. New York: Blackwell Publishers, 1992.

————, ed. *Richard of St. Victor: The Twelve Patriarchs, The Mystical Ark, Book Three of the Trinity.* Translation and introduction by Grover Zinn. Classics of Western Spirituality. New York and Mahwah, N.J.: Paulist Press, 1979.

Index

References in **boldface** are to material in General Introduction.

Alan of Lille, **2, 67,** 197–202;
  angelic hierarchy, **29–30;**
  celestial hierarchy, **24;**
  Cherubim, **49–50, 52;**
  contemplation and action,
  64, 65; *exordo,* **30;**
  imitation of angels, **55;** *On
  the Six Wings of the
  Cherubim* attributed to,
  121, 122; selections from,
  202–16; Seraphim, **49–50,
  52, 57;** theophanies,
  39–40
Angelic Hierarchy. See *On the
  Celestial Hierarchy*
  (Dionysius)
Angelization, **61–62**
Angels, **1–8;** allegorical power
  of, **5;** anagogic power of,
  5, 20, 45, 46, 123, 189,
  219–20; apophatic
  (negative) model, **36,
  41–44, 45, 47;** cataphatic
  (positive) model, **35,
  41–44, 45, 47, 165;** and

Christ, **25–26, 66–71,**
  188–89; Christ as angel, **68;**
  community of, **71;** creation
  of, 80, 87–89; deiforming
  qualities, **59–61;** and divine
  presence, **56–59;** and faith,
  80, 86–87; functions of,
  14–16, 55–56, 107–20; as
  guides, **15, 34,** 108,
  189–90; hierarchical
  orders, **13, 18–35,** 97, 151,
  66, 166, 169, 197, 199,
  202–16, 222–34, 243; and
  humanity, **16–17, 18, 27,
  55–56,** 91, 93–106;
  imitation of, **55–62,** 108;
  invisible *vs.* visible nature
  of, **47–48;** knowledge of,
  80–81, 89–90; as light, **17,
  21, 22, 35–39,** 165,
  188–89; as mediators
  between God and
  humanity, 78, 81–82,
  162–63, 238; as
  messengers, **6, 9, 15,**

Other Volumes in This Series

Abraham Isaac Kook • THE LIGHTS OF PENITENCE, LIGHTS OF
HOLINESS, THE MORAL PRINCIPLES, ESSAYS, LETTERS, AND POEMS

Abraham Miguel Cardozo • SELECTED WRITINGS

Albert and Thomas • SELECTED WRITINGS

Alphonsus de Liguori • SELECTED WRITINGS

Anchoritic Spirituality • ANCRENE WISSE AND ASSOCIATED WORKS

Angela of Foligno • COMPLETE WORKS

Angelus Silesius • THE CHERUBINIC WANDERER

Anglo-Saxon Spirituality • SELECTED WRITINGS

Apocalyptic Spirituality • TREATISES AND LETTERS OF LACTANTIUS,
ADSO OF MONTIER-EN-DER, JOACHIM OF FIORE, THE FRANCISCAN
SPIRITUALS, SAVONAROLA

Athanasius • THE LIFE OF ANTONY, AND THE LETTER TO MARCELLINUS

Augustine of Hippo • SELECTED WRITINGS

Bernard of Clairvaux • SELECTED WORKS

Bérulle and the French School • SELECTED WRITINGS

Birgitta of Sweden • LIFE AND SELECTED REVELATIONS

Bonaventure • THE SOUL'S JOURNEY INTO GOD, THE TREE OF LIFE, THE
LIFE OF ST. FRANCIS

Carthusian Spirituality • THE WRITINGS OF HUGH OF BALMA AND GUIGO
DE PONTE

Catherine of Genoa • PURGATION AND PURGATORY, THE SPIRITUAL
DIALOGUE

Catherine of Siena • THE DIALOGUE

Classic Midrash, The • TANNAITIC COMMENTARIES ON THE BIBLE

Celtic Spirituality •

Cloud of Unknowing, The •

Devotio Moderna • BASIC WRITINGS

Early Anabaptist Spirituality • SELECTED WRITINGS

Early Dominicans • SELECTED WRITINGS

Early Islamic Mysticism • SUFI, QUR'AN, MI'RAJ, POETIC AND
THEOLOGICAL WRITINGS

Early Kabbalah, The •

Elijah Benamozegh • ISRAEL AND HUMANITY

Elisabeth of Schönau • THE COMPLETE WORKS

Emanuel Swedenborg • THE UNIVERSAL HUMAN AND SOUL-BODY
INTERACTION

Ephrem the Syrian • HYMNS

Fakhruddin 'Iraqi • DIVINE FLASHES

Other Volumes in This Series

Francis and Clare • THE COMPLETE WORKS
Francis de Sales, Jane de Chantal • LETTERS OF SPIRITUAL DIRECTION
Francisco de Osuna • THE THIRD SPIRITUAL ALPHABET
George Herbert • THE COUNTRY PARSON, THE TEMPLE
Gertrude of Helfta • THE HERALD OF DIVINE LOVE
Gregory of Nyssa • THE LIFE OF MOSES
Gregory Palamas • THE TRIADS
Hadewijch • THE COMPLETE WORKS
Henry Suso • THE EXEMPLAR, WITH TWO GERMAN SERMONS
Hildegard of Bingen • SCIVIAS
Ibn 'Abbād of Ronda • LETTERS ON THE ṢŪFĪ PATH
Ibn 'Ata' Illah • THE BOOK OF WISDOM AND KWAJA ABDULLAH ANSARI: INTIMATE CONVERSATIONS
Ibn Al'-Arabi • THE BEZELS OF WISDOM
Ignatius of Loyola • SPIRITUAL EXERCISES AND SELECTED WORKS
Isaiah Horowitz • THE GENERATIONS OF ADAM
Jacob Boehme • THE WAY TO CHRIST
Jacopone da Todi • THE LAUDS
Jean Gerson • EARLY WORKS
Jeremy Taylor • SELECTED WORKS
Jewish Mystical Autobiographies • BOOK OF VISIONS AND BOOK OF SECRETS
Johann Arndt • TRUE CHRISTIANITY
Johannes Tauler • SERMONS
John Calvin • WRITINGS ON PASTORAL PIETY
John Cassian • CONFERENCES
John and Charles Wesley • SELECTED WRITINGS AND HYMNS
John Climacus • THE LADDER OF DIVINE ASCENT
John Comenius • THE LABYRINTH OF THE WORLD AND THE PARADISE OF THE HEART
John of the Cross • SELECTED WRITINGS
John Donne • SELECTIONS FROM DIVINE POEMS, SERMONS, DEVOTIONS AND PRAYERS
John Henry Newman • SELECTED SERMONS
John Ruusbroec • THE SPIRITUAL ESPOUSALS AND OTHER WORKS
Julian of Norwich • SHOWINGS
Luis de León • THE NAMES OF CHRIST
Margaret Ebner • MAJOR WORKS
Marguerite Porete • THE MIRROR OF SIMPLE SOULS

Other Volumes in This Series

Maria Maddalena de' Pazzi • SELECTED REVELATIONS
Martin Luther • THEOLOGIA GERMANICA
Maximus Confessor • SELECTED WRITINGS
Mechthild of Magdeburg • THE FLOWING LIGHT OF THE GODHEAD
Meister Eckhart • THE ESSENTIAL SERMONS, COMMENTARIES, TREATISES AND DEFENSE
Meister Eckhart • TEACHER AND PREACHER
Menahem Nahum of Chernobyl • UPRIGHT PRACTICES, THE LIGHT OF THE EYES
Nahman of Bratslav • THE TALES
Native Mesoamerican Spirituality • ANCIENT MYTHS, DISCOURSES, STORIES, DOCTRINES, HYMNS, POEMS FROM THE AZTEC, YUCATEC, QUICHE-MAYA AND OTHER SACRED TRADITIONS
Native North American Spirituality of the Eastern Woodlands • SACRED MYTHS, DREAMS, VISIONS, SPEECHES, HEALING FORMULAS, RITUALS AND CEREMONIALS
Nicholas of Cusa • SELECTED SPIRITUAL WRITINGS
Nicodemos of the Holy Mountain • A HANDBOOK OF SPIRITUAL COUNSEL
Nizam ad-din Awliya • MORALS FOR THE HEART
Origen • AN EXHORTATION TO MARTYRDOM, PRAYER AND SELECTED WORKS
Philo of Alexandria • THE CONTEMPLATIVE LIFE, THE GIANTS, AND SELECTIONS
Pietists • SELECTED WRITINGS
Pilgrim's Tale, The •
Pseudo-Dionysius • THE COMPLETE WORKS
Pseudo-Macarius • THE FIFTY SPIRITUAL HOMILIES AND THE GREAT LETTER
Pursuit of Wisdom, The • AND OTHER WORKS BY THE AUTHOR OF THE CLOUD OF UNKNOWING
Quaker Spirituality • SELECTED WRITINGS
Rabbinic Stories •
Richard Rolle • THE ENGLISH WRITINGS
Richard of St. Victor • THE TWELVE PATRIARCHS, THE MYSTICAL ARK, BOOK THREE OF THE TRINITY
Robert Bellarmine • SPIRITUAL WRITINGS
Safed Spirituality • RULES OF MYSTICAL PIETY, THE BEGINNING OF WISDOM

Other Volumes in This Series

Shakers, The • TWO CENTURIES OF SPIRITUAL REFLECTION
Sharafuddin Maneri • THE HUNDRED LETTERS
Symeon the New Theologian • THE DISCOURSES
Talmud, The • SELECTED WRITINGS
Teresa of Avila • THE INTERIOR CASTLE
Theatine Spirituality • SELECTED WRITINGS
'Umar Ibn al-Fāriḍ • SUFI VERSE, SAINTLY LIFE
Vincent de Paul and Louise de Marillac • RULES, CONFERENCES, AND WRITINGS
Walter Hilton • THE SCALE OF PERFECTION
William Law • A SERIOUS CALL TO A DEVOUT AND HOLY LIFE, THE SPIRIT OF LOVE
Zohar • THE BOOK OF ENLIGHTENMENT

The Classics of Western Spirituality is a ground-breaking collection of the original writings of more than 100 universally acknowledged teachers within the Catholic, Protestant, Eastern Orthodox, Jewish, Islamic, and Native American Indian traditions.

To order any title, or to request a complete catalog, contact Paulist Press at 800-218-1903 or visit us on the Web at www.paulistpress.com